TWILIGHT
OF THE
MONEY GODS

TWILIGHT OF THE MONEY GODS

Economics as a Religion and
How it all Went Wrong

JOHN RAPLEY

SIMON &
SCHUSTER

London · New York · Sydney · Toronto · New Delhi

A CBS COMPANY

First published in Great Britain by Simon & Schuster UK Ltd, 2017
A CBS COMPANY

1 3 5 7 9 10 8 6 4 2

Simon & Schuster UK Ltd
1st Floor
222 Gray's Inn Road
London WC1X 8HB

www.simonandschuster.co.uk
www.simonandschuster.com.au
www.simonandschuster.co.in

Simon & Schuster Australia, Sydney
Simon & Schuster India, New Delhi

A CIP catalogue record for this book
is available from the British Library

ISBN: 978-1-4711-5274-0
Trade paperback ISBN: 978-1-4711-5275-7
Ebook ISBN: 978-1-4711-5277-1

Typeset in Sabon by M Rules
Printed and bound by CPI Group (UK) Ltd, Croydon, CR0 4YY

CONTENTS

CHAPTER 1

I Believe I Can Fly

Money or God: which is more real?

It seems like a no-brainer. Even if God exists, He or She (or It, or They) is intangible. You can't prove God's existence, you simply have to believe, or not. But money? Surely it's as real as that pound note or dollar bill you can pull from your wallet, rubbing it between your fingers to prove it's there.

That is to say, it's no more real than an amulet or a crucifix that you might place around your neck: tangible expressions of a belief that is as potent as the strength with which you hold it. The reality is that money exists in our imagination. If we don't believe in it, that banknote is a worthless scrap. If we do, we can use it to change the world.

Do we worship money the way some of us worship God? Consider the thought. Our ancestors prayed for wealth, health and happiness. We devote our lives to getting money, often doing work we don't like, so we can get more of it. Instead of embracing hardship to reach heaven, we do it to get money. We organise our lives around its pursuit and attainment, compose songs to its beauty, achieve lightness and serenity and ecstasy in its presence.

Does that make us religious? Well, think about it. Think of the conversations that arise when you get together with friends or have a family dinner. 'No politics or religion at the table' goes the old rule, but we think nothing of speaking of, say, our new jumper, a planned holiday in Tuscany, our kitchen-remodelling, or a possible promotion. In one way or another, the topic will keep returning to how you either make, spend or save money. Now, each time such topics arise, there's a good chance you're expressing your innermost religious beliefs. When you say something like 'you get what you pay for' you are usually making a declaration of faith much like someone who says 'God is merciful'. When you click 'send' or sign the chit to transfer money into your pension fund, you're actually engaging in a spiritual act similar to the person who lights a candle in the church or prays before bed.

You see, when you hear the word 'money', your mind will probably drift to notes and coins. If you have a bank account, you might picture it like a drawer in a large secure vault in the basement of the building. Make a withdrawal and the drawer empties a little. Make a deposit and it fills back up. Build up enough savings, like that pension fund, and it might even fill a room, like the cavernous hall where Scrooge McDuck goes swimming in his lake of coins, and which you'll only run down when you retire and start living off your accumulated riches. And the bank's job is to provide you with a safe space where burglars in black balaclavas can't reach your hard-earned stash.

In fact, all of that – and not just the bit about Scrooge McDuck – is little more than make-believe. Any cupboards that might exist at the bank are filled only with IOUs, which are about as good as we think they are. The same goes for any bonds, shares or annuities you hold: it's all ethereal. Instead of regarding money as something physical, think of that fiver in your pocket as a promise or claim. That slip of paper entitles you to someone else's resources, of which the most important is usually their labour: you're in credit when someone owes you work, and in debt when you owe them work. It's kind of ironic, when you think of it, because while we often believe that money frees us from others and makes us 'independent' it's really a written testament of our bond to them.[1]

It may come as news to you, but you help to create money all the time, with little more than an act of will and a show of faith. Say you ask your grocer if you can pay next week for today's shopping. To all intents and purposes you're promising to set aside some of your labour time for them over the next week. And suppose your grocer takes your IOU to their butcher and, in return for some meat, offers to transfer your debt to him. Voilà, you've created a rudimentary form of money.

Humans began doing this thousands of years ago, in the earliest civilisations.[2] Over time, as societies grew larger and more complex, village economies evolved into regional economies, and IOUs, which may have been written down or simply kept as a word, began circulating. Inevitably, some entrepreneurs came along who simplified the process by keeping accounts, disbursing some agreed medium of exchange – anything from shells to pieces of silver or bronze, as long as it was not easily forged. Once they'd chosen their unit of exchange, these entrepreneurs would then measure the value of each type of labour in that unit. Because these middlemen often sat on a bench in the market where they could keep everyone's accounts, they became known as benchers – or, using the Latin word for bench, bankers. And when their proposed unit of exchange gained widespread acceptance, and buyers and sellers began listing their prices and keeping their own accounts in that medium, its free-flowing character gave it the term we use for money: currency, like the current in a river or breeze.

Governments then realised that if they issued their own currency, and required their subjects to tender taxes in it, they could get a handle on trade and use it to raise revenue. So they devised 'legal tender'. Once again, traders and bankers overtook them. Rather than weigh themselves down with heavy coins or the knives that were used in ancient China, they began issuing paper or cloth certificates, which were backed by money. This made currency move even more freely – or, as economists like to say, it became more liquid.

And so it's gone on ever since. Today, while governments regulate banks and watch over them with their own bank – the so-called central bank – the vast majority of the money we use is little more than figures on ledgers or digits in cyberspace, and no government can say with certainty how much money is circulating in its economy. It's like aeroplane engineering. You don't really know how that 400-ton tube of steel you're sitting in can lift off the ground and get you across the ocean, but you trust that someone else does.

Because it gives us command over people we'll never even meet, money has assumed almost mystical properties. And for as long as we believe that power is real, money enables us to create stuff out of nothing. Want to see how? Go ask your banker for a loan. She won't actually take money from one account to place in yours. Instead, she'll effectively promise to find cash equal to that figure should anyone want to see it – which hardly anyone ever does, since they trust the bank and take payment in a cheque or an alteration to the figures on their own ledger. The banker, meanwhile, will assume you'll either buy a house or another asset equivalent to the value of the loan, or at least keep your job and pay back the loan from future work. It's like she's found a way for you to harvest the fruits of tomorrow's labours, today. Needless to say, this whole system depends on everyone having faith in one another: faith there will be a future, and faith in the bank's ability to convert this ethereal, almost spiritual entity – our faith and promises – into matter (or what we prefer to call 'assets'). This transformation of nothing into something drives our modern economy forward, and though we take it for granted, to ancient eyes it would have looked like a miracle.

In truth, it pretty much *is* a miracle. Try this experiment. Go and withdraw a wad of bills from your cash machine, then wave it around in public. Watch how people react. When you reflect on that experience, it won't come as a shock to you to hear that when Melanesian islanders first encountered Westerners on their shores and saw how they would cross the world and kill one another over little slips of worn paper, they assumed the parchments had magical powers. As a result, just as medieval European alchemists had once done, their own scientists began experimenting with paper to uncover its secret code.

Like Peter Pan telling children to simply believe they can fly in order to make it happen, we can literally will money into and out of existence. If you take your bank loan to buy a house, and everyone believes the house will rise in value, well, it does. Wild, isn't it? It is as if by getting everyone to believe that gravity no longer exists, we could float heavenwards.

However, the moment we all stop believing, everything comes crashing back down to earth. That, too, happens. It happened just a few years ago, and it could happen again. Because you have to believe in this god for it to have power, and we seem to be losing our faith.

Where there is widely shared belief, religion often follows. So yes, perhaps without realising it, you quite possibly have a religion. It's called economics.

Start with some of the beliefs you hold most dear. That you work for what you earn. That if you paid for it, it's yours. That it would be therefore wrong for someone else to take it from you. That rich is better than poor. That a growing economy is therefore good and a recession bad. These are a few of what can be called the commandments of economics. They may or not be noble convictions, but it's difficult to call them facts, or truths, of the sort on which we are meant to build our lives.

Take, for instance, that 'rich is better than poor' adage. As a rough rule, it's not a bad start: most of us do want to get more money. Yet when actually looking at how it plays out in the things that make us happy, it becomes terribly complex. Sometimes it's true, sometimes it isn't – or when it's true, it's only so under a bunch of conditions. That's what the science tells us. Despite that, many people live their lives by this rule, to the extent they make themselves miserable and even sick to acquire more money. That is not the science of economics but the religion – and more specifically, religious fundamentalism, of the stick-to-basics, don't-doubt, don't-question sort.

How about the belief that you work for what you earn? We use that one to justify being among the richest tenth of the planet's population. Compare what you are paid to what someone in a developing country gets. For instance, you take home ten times what the average Jamaican does, and sixty times what the average

African would, for doing the same job. We usually attribute this discrepancy to our superior skill and hard work, and it seems easy enough to confirm this belief. Suppose you've holidayed in the Caribbean, or in some other tropical destination. You might have observed that the workers in the hotel you stayed in moved more slowly or showed less initiative than you might have done during the summer jobs you did to work your way through university. You therefore could have concluded that's why you ended up the client, and they the servers.

However, while your observation would have been correct, in that Caribbean workers do produce less per hour than workers in Western countries, you'd also have been comparing apples and oranges. If instead you'd compared what one dollar of your wages got your employer in output, you'd have discovered you're much less productive than that Caribbean worker. In fact, economic research tells us that differences in productivity account for only part of our higher earnings. Moreover, at an individual level, our work and investment plays only a minor role in what we earn. Most of what we take home is determined not by anything we've done, but by dumb luck[3] – and sometimes, too, outright injustice.

It's no big news that we pick and choose among the facts, and then further tailor them to our interests, so as to craft a belief system which justifies our place in the world. Humans have always done this. Social historians distinguish between the official religion of clerical establishments and this 'popular religion' of common beliefs. All through history, theologians have dedicated their lives to studying arcane points of doctrine only to have the folk in the pews flatten out the nuances to adopt simple beliefs and practices that may even contradict the scholarship. But if economics is our religion, would that make economists our theologians, our priests?

By now, any economists reading this book might be spitting out their coffee. Or not: in recent years the number of economists who see the parallels between their discipline and religion has grown,[4] and even Nobel laureates have been known to use the term 'fundamentalism' to describe strands of economics overly wedded to a particular doctrine.[5] But a religion, and a priesthood?

Well, think of the role economics plays in our lives. It offers a comprehensive doctrine with a moral code promising adherents salvation in this world; an ideology so compelling that the faithful remake whole societies to conform to its demands; a road map to the promised land and riches there far beyond what any god could offer and moral teachings (albeit in a language often intelligible only to a Talmudic caste, complete with its numerology and symbolism). It has its gnostics, mystics and magicians who conjure money out of thin air, using spells like 'derivative' or 'structured investment vehicle'. And, like the old religions it has displaced, it has its prophets, reformists, moralists and above all, its high priests, who uphold orthodoxy in the face of heresy.

'But,' an economist might object, 'we alone among social scientists get a Nobel Prize for "economic science". Even mathematicians don't get that!' Well, yes, but so what? The Nobel Prize in economics exists only because the economists created it, and it's a science only because – no prizes for this one – the economists called it a science. To burnish the discipline's credentials, the Bank of Sweden asked the Nobel Foundation if they could use its name to endow a prize in what they called 'economic science'.[6] However, it is a Nobel in name only since it is awarded separately from the Foundation's prestigious prizes. In reality, economics is wholly unlike any other science that exists. In fact, when you look under the bonnet, you'll see that it hardly resembles science at all.

For starters, it rests on a set of premises about the world not as it is, but as we – or at least, the economists – would like it to be. Just as any religious service includes a profession of faith, membership in the priesthood of economics entails certain core convictions about human nature. Among other things, economists believe that we humans are self-interested, rational, essentially individualistic, and prefer more money to less. These articles of faith are taken as self-evident. Back in the 1930s, the great economist Lionel Robbins laid down a rule, in language reminiscent of a papal bull, and that has stood ever since as a cardinal rule for millions of economists. He said these basic premises were 'deduction from simple assumptions reflecting very elementary facts of general experience' and as such were 'as universal as the laws of mathematics or mechanics, and as little capable of "suspension"'.[7] Now, deducing laws from premises deemed eternal and beyond question is a time-honoured method. For thousands of years, monks in medieval monasteries built a vast corpus of scholarship doing just that, using a method perfected by Thomas Aquinas known as scholasticism. However, it was not the method used by scientists, and this conflict provided part of the backdrop to Galileo's famous run-in with the Vatican. Scientists since antiquity had elevated observation over deduction, and to this day they tend to require assumptions to be tested empirically before a theory can be built out of them.[8] Funnily enough, as was mentioned, when the articles of economic faith have been subjected to empirical examination (most often, not by economists), they have been found wanting, or at best terribly nuanced and complicated.

All the same, just as saying 'Jesus is the son of God' or 'Mohammad is God's prophet' can affect the way you lead your life, so too can believing in the articles of economics. For instance, research has found that people who study economics tend, over time, to become more self-oriented in their behaviour.[9] In other words, these beliefs can be used to create a society in the image of economics. That, by the way, is actually the whole purpose of economics. From its birth, it aimed to make the world a better place. Its early practitioners wanted to supplement and sometimes replace existing religious doctrines by helping to guide humans towards a better life not just in the next world, but in this one. We can't therefore fault economists for trying to make us behave in a way they think will improve our well-being. Believing we are selfish and want to grow richer, they recommend social and political changes to help us reach those goals. They are, in that respect, true idealists.

Still, that doesn't make what they do a science. Compare economics to physics, not only because physics is often considered the scientific ideal – the true science – but also because most economists have long modelled their own discipline on physics. Physicists strive only to understand nature. They can't, however, change it. Getting us to all stop believing in gravity won't stop gravity. On the other hand, if, say, we all stop believing house prices will rise, then lo and behold they will stop rising (since people will no longer see them as a good investment and will stop buying them). Economics thus differs from science in that it goes beyond merely trying to discover the laws of nature, to actually making them.

Economics also differs from science in the way it evolves over time. The progress of science is generally linear. As new research confirms or replaces existing theories, one generation builds upon the next. Newton moved beyond Aristotle's physics, Einstein improved on some of Newton's, and so on. The history of science is thus littered with old theorems that died out in the face of scientific advancement. Economics, however, moves in cycles. A given doctrine can rise, fall and then later rise again. That's because economists don't confirm their theories in quite the same way physicists do, by just looking at the evidence. Instead, much as happens with preachers who gather a congregation, a school rises by building a following – among both politicians and the wider public.[10]

For example, Milton Friedman was one of the most influential economists of the late twentieth century. Yet he'd been around for decades before he got much of a hearing. Outside the academy, he might well have remained a marginal figure had it not been that politicians like Margaret Thatcher and Ronald Reagan were sold on his belief in the virtue of a free market. They sold that idea to the public, got elected, then remade society according to those designs. An economist who gets a following, gets a pulpit. Although scientists, in contrast, might appeal to public opinion to boost their careers or attract research funds, outside of pseudo-sciences, they don't win support for their theories in this way.

However, if you think describing economics as a religion debunks it, you're wrong. We need economics. It can be – it has been – a force for tremendous good. But only if we keep its purpose in mind, and always remember what it can and can't do. It's a cliché, featured in every film where a hero has lost his way and is told to 'remember where you came from'. You see, few economists do remember where they came from, since the history of the discipline – or any history, for that matter – is rarely required learning in today's economic departments. It therefore shouldn't surprise us that some of them seem to have lost their way, and perhaps even led us astray.

This book will tell the story of economics and its history. While that tale is usually told with an Enlightenment narrative, in which science fights a heroic battle against ignorance and ultimately replaces religion in giving us codes to live by, this one will instead relate the history of economics as a modern act in an ancient play – our search for meaning and purpose, and our dream of a better world.

We humans have always looked for something to believe in, a faith to order our lives. In fact, from the birth of our species our ancestors always lived with one foot in the material realm and another in the spiritual one. They separated mind from matter, body from soul, what we could see with our eyes from what we could know only in our heart. Then one day, about 500 years ago, all this began to change. The first shoots of capitalism had been stirring in Europe from around the turn of the first millennium CE, when the chronic warfare of the 'Dark Ages' settled down and people went back to farming rather than fighting. Simultaneously, improvements in agricultural technology began to slowly – imperceptibly, at first – raise output; the humble plough doing much to change the course of human history. The subsequent invention of modern banking in the Italian maritime republics in the centuries following and the evolution of navigation then further lubricated the development of technology. But when in 1492 Christopher Columbus landed in the Americas, he unleashed something that would be so momentous, even he could not have foreseen its consequences.

For in the centuries that followed, wealth from the Americas, and later from other colonial possessions Europeans had taken, flooded into Europe. This new money transformed the continent's social structure, and provided fuel to the capitalist fire. In consequence, by the eighteenth century, the economies of western Europe began growing more steadily, and rapidly, than ever before. Amid this prosperity, life seemed less vulnerable to the fickleness of nature and its elements. Humans began to feel a greater sense of control over their destinies.

Europe's old religions, which had provided an explanation and justification for static, stratified societies, now found themselves faced with questions they couldn't always answer. In particular, some philosophers began wondering if we really did live in two worlds. They wondered if they were resolving the ancient spirit–matter dilemma once and for all, and squarely in favour of the latter. Perhaps, they said, the world of matter determined everything, and even the things we experienced without physical sensation – like love, belonging or happiness – actually had material causes. As new discoveries shed ever more light on the dark recesses we'd populated with gods and spirits, these thinkers reasoned that our need for immaterial explanations would retreat. Amid this 'enlightenment' they said, we'd take on the powers we'd once left to the gods.

All the while, rising incomes enabled people and their governments to do more, to build more, to engage in intellectual and cultural pursuits beyond mere survival. Inevitably, some philosophers turned their eyes away from the mysteries of the eternal so as to ponder the here and now. These 'political economists' applied the new Enlightenment thinking to the study of production. Creation, they said, didn't exist outside us, didn't bless us with its bounty. It was there for our use, and we could apply our growing knowledge to exploit it in such a way as to make ourselves richer than ever.

And so, the economists gave us advice for living that could eventually replace the religions of old. Over time, successive economists slid into the role we'd removed from the churchmen: giving us guidance on how to reach a promised land of material abundance and endless contentment. For a long time, they seemed to deliver on that promise, succeeding in a way few other religions had ever done, our incomes rising thousands of times over[11] and delivering a cornucopia bursting with new inventions, cures and delights. This was our heaven, and richly did we reward the economic priesthood, with status, riches and power to shape our societies according to their vision. At the end of the twentieth century, amid an economic boom that saw the Western economies become richer than humanity had ever known, economics seemed to have conquered the globe. With nearly every country on the planet adhering to the same, free-market playbook, and with university students flocking to do degrees in the subject, economics attained the goal that had eluded every other religious doctrine in history: converting the entire planet to its creed, and thereby ushering in a millennial 'end to history'.

Then one day it all ended. Although we survived the crash of 2008, most of us have watched our living standards decline. Meanwhile, the priesthood seemed to withdraw to the cloisters, bickering over who got it wrong. Not surprisingly, our faith in the 'experts' has dissipated. But without faith, our whole world risks collapse. So here we now stand, at the twilight of the money gods, seeking new creeds to light our paths to the future.

Beginning with the earliest economic thinkers, soon after Columbus's arrival in the Americas; continuing on through the founding fathers of economics, like Adam Smith and David Ricardo; through the radical prophets like Karl Marx and V. I. Lenin, as well as their neoclassical critics who rejected their worldly apocalypse to reaffirm a faith in Smith's creed; on into the crisis of that faith caused by the Great Depression, which yielded the new testament of John Maynard Keynes; and then to the neoclassical reawakening led by the likes of Milton Friedman and Friedrich Hayek, this book will chart the rise and fall of our economic churches, showing how all these scholars were united by a common quest: to give humans a doctrine that could deliver us prosperity and contentment in this life. Setting these thinkers against the backdrop of their times and the economic changes, it will show how each school built its following by answering the questions people then had – and lost their flocks whenever the answers no longer addressed people's needs. Today, as we go through another crisis of faith amid the 'Great Stagnation'[12], in which none of the economic schools seems able to answer the questions we now have – can we restore the growth rates of old? Will our future be poorer than our present? Why doesn't new technology seem to be making us richer, as it once did? – we are left to ask ourselves what a new faith for these times would look like.

It is, indeed, the best and worst of times.

CHAPTER 2

GOD OF GOLD

Five centuries ago, while looking for a sea passage to the Far East, Europeans stumbled upon a world they hadn't known existed. Vikings had reached the Americas earlier but since they kept their records orally it hadn't been recorded for posterity. Thus, since no European maps showed these lands, they called it the New World. To them, it was a *tabula rasa*, one they quickly secured a firm grip on. And as history's winners always do, they then credited their technological and moral superiority for this triumph.

Today, it's easy to imagine this was somehow all inevitable. In reality the triumph of Europe is a twist of fate that has puzzled scholars ever since. Imagine you'd lived six centuries ago and you'd found a seer who predicted a great civilisation was about to rise which would, within a few centuries, dominate the entire planet; but then added that it was not known where this civilisation would arise, leaving you to ruminate over a list of likely candidates. What might you have speculated? China would have seemed an obvious candidate – a vast, ancient and technologically advanced kingdom that saw itself as the centre of the world, its economy accounting for a third of global output. But so too would the Ottoman Empire, then at its peak, having just finished off the millennium-old Byzantine Empire before then advancing as far west as the gates of Vienna. Meanwhile, the Muslim Moors penetrated deep into Spain. But

Europe? The notion that it might rise up and surpass all these other empires would probably have struck you as risible. The continent was poor, disease-ridden – your memory would still be fresh that just a century before a third of its people had been lost to the plague – politically fragmented and so technologically backwards that it was reduced to pilfering its philosophy from Arab libraries.[1]

And yet if you'd lived a long life you would have seen Europe ruling the Americas. Three more centuries and the continent would control most of the planet. One more century after that and so complete would the West's dominance become that the planet's output would be organised to satisfy its wants. The population of western Europe and its settler outposts in the Americas and the Antipodes, together comprising less than one fifth of humanity, would end up consuming four-fifths of what the earth produced. If you wanted a rags-to-riches tale for a continent, this would be it. What explained the dramatic turnaround?

You could start with the old proverb that it's always darkest before the dawn. Europe's darkest hour may have come in 1453, when the Ottoman Turks took Constantinople, thereby lowering the curtain on the empire that Constantine had proclaimed a thousand years before. Necessity, though, is the mother of invention, and Europe then had a lot of need. Having lost control of the overland trade routes to the Far East, Europeans began searching for a new way to get the cloth and spices their aristocrats demanded.[2] Thus began a period of intense experimentation with long-distance navigation. By coincidence, for domestic political reasons and to concentrate its firepower on land-based foes like the Mongols, China's government abandoned its ambitious naval policy and turned inwards, restricting its navy to coastal waters and managing its trade through a series of government-run ports. In contrast, the need to defend themselves far from home prompted Europeans to mount cannons on ships. Just as the Chinese empire – then still the world's largest economy – was withdrawing from the world, Europeans landed in the Americas with ship-borne artillery.

They surprised themselves with the ease of their conquest. On one hand, Europe's long history of political fragmentation, which had made warfare and weapons-building a central feature of political life, gave the invaders a big military edge over the peoples they encountered.[3] On the other hand, Europe's history of endemic disease had made Europeans resistant to a host of illnesses. In effect, this made their bodies into delivery systems for what were, in the circumstances, weapons of mass destruction. Before it could decide what to make of these fair-skinned men, the indigenous population was decimated. Subduing, evicting and enslaving the locals was therefore done promptly, and the land fell into European hands.[4] That released a huge stock of mineral wealth and, since European labour had now found an outlet, brought new farmland into production. This new output pumped fresh money into the European economy.

Better yet, if unpaid labour could be found, that meant not only abundant farmland and mines, but no money lost to wages. And so, beginning within a few years of the European landings in the Americas, their ships began prowling the African coast. Since African states often settled their wars by enslaving some of the defeated population, there was a ready supply of slaves available to traders. A period of constant warfare in west and central Africa resulted, as nascent kingdoms built their wealth on capturing slaves to sell to Europeans.[5] Although the effect on Africa was dire, the bounteous supplies of cheap workers created more money for Europe.[6] Since Africans weren't getting paid for the work they did, traders and plantation owners split the difference: plantation owners, having already got free land, could afford to pay for slaves off the future profits they were going to make from unpaid labour. With only a small amount of the total value created by slavery making its way into the hands of Africans, most of this money therefore found its way back to Europe.

These vast surpluses built fortunes. Landowners sent to Europe for silks, linen, wool clothing and hats, the cordage and gunpowder and metalwares – from the nails to build their houses to the cutlery and jewellery that went into them – which launched Britain's

Industrial Revolution. Over the course of the eighteenth century the value of British manufactured exports doubled, but the share going to Europe halved, to be replaced by Africa and the Americas, where the slave colonies were booming.[7] Although his estimate was probably on the high side, not for nothing did William Pitt reckon in 1783 that four-fifths of Britain's overseas wealth came from the West Indian trade.[8] Nor was the wealth restricted to those European states that did the actual colonising. It fanned out widely, benefiting much of western Europe and its settler colonies. The ships used drove demand for trees from Scandinavia. Luxury goods from Switzerland flowed into Latin America. And the food produced on British North American farms, which generally couldn't bear the cost and time of transport all the way to England, was instead sent to the slave colonies, the revenues from their sale then being used to buy British manufactures.[9] Such prosperity built the port cities that plied the Atlantic trade. One late eighteenth-century visitor to Nantes recorded marvelling at the sumptuous new buildings and the merchants of the slave trade who, dressed in finest linens and always in the season's fashions, constituted 'a class apart' and were approached by others 'only with the signs of a profound respect'.[10]

Though it may have been an accident of history, Europeans were first out of the blocks in the race to conquer these distant lands. The dividend of their victory was a river of money that, since it was fed by free land[11] and labour, cost them practically nothing.

In opening new seams of wealth in distant lands and bringing home the loot, Europe followed the pattern of countless empires that had risen (and fallen) since the dawn of civilisation. But it also did something no previous empire had ever done, something that would alter humankind for ever.

If you draw two lines on top of an axis that plots history from the birth of civilisation, with one line for the total number of humans and the other for their total economic output, you end up with lines that tend to hug the axis the whole way. Humans lived almost entirely off the land, and what they could eke out of a seemingly

reluctant earth varied little from one year to the next. Some years
the rains were good, or occasionally a new type of plough would
allow farmers to till new land. But by and large these effects were
modest and short-lived, quickly offset by a drought or flood or some
other natural disaster which sent things backwards. Limited by what
nature could provide, the planet's population consequently hardly
budged. Outside of a small aristocracy, luxury was all but unknown.
For entertainment, there was sex, songs and stories.

However, around 1700, the curves suddenly start to move
upwards. If you'd been alive at the time, you wouldn't have noticed
it at first. But the new wealth flowing in from the colonies had added
fuel to an economic fire which, until then, had always burned low.
As a result, the economy of western Europe began to grow. And it
kept on growing. Not much, about 1 per cent a year on average,[12]
which today would be barely above recession levels. But coming
after centuries in which nothing had changed much at all, it was
revolutionary. If you had been born in 1700 and gone on to live
a long life, you would have died twice as rich as you'd been born.
Think about how that must have felt at the time: your ancestors had
lived for centuries in a world where life was a struggle just to get
by while they prepared for eternity, and then one day you realised
that at some point the chain had been broken and you were going
to finish ahead of the game. You'd have worked out that something
significant was happening.

Unlike previous empires, Europeans were doing more than
just living off the unpaid labour and free land they'd grabbed
in the colonies. They did that, but they also did more than that.
Especially in northern Europe, the new money was not just spent,
but invested in new business ventures and used to develop technologies. Developments in banking also made it possible to speed up
the growth of the money supply. Initially, banks took deposits of
precious metals in return for promissory notes, but it didn't take long
for them to notice that their clients didn't all redeem their deposits
at once, happy as they were to circulate their notes as currency.
Bankers realised that they could increase the supply of banknotes

by holding merely a fraction of the supply in their gold and silver vaults, enabling them to multiply the effect of the new coinage arriving from the colonies. This 'fractional reserve' banking was then supplemented by the creation of the world's first central banks in Sweden (1668) and England (1694). The Bank of England further lubricated the flow of money by assisting government borrowing and thereby marshalling large-scale public investment, further stoking demand in the economy. All this helped to change the organisation of society. The clear dividing line between nobles and commoners was now blurred by the rise of the merchants, planters and craftsmen who were managing this new economic activity and selling into the growing markets. Because these nascent capitalists tended to live in or near cities, where the principal markets were found, they came to be known as townsmen – or more commonly, from the Latin word 'burgus' for town, the bourgeoisie.

They were riding a tide of prosperity swollen by both the new money coming from the Americas, and a home-grown increase in agricultural productivity. In the eighteenth century, most noticeably in England, noble families had started enclosing common lands and turning them over to new crops or livestock, or experimenting with the new and more efficient farming techniques that large, consolidated farms made possible. In effect, what Europe had done in the Americas in seizing new lands, the old landed classes did at home. But this in turn created new market opportunities in urban business which, outside of England, the nobility were often reluctant to take, many nobles thinking it beneath them to sully their hands in the demeaning work of manufacturing or banking. In time, many capitalists would overtake the nobles as some of the richest people in Europe – even, sometimes, lending money to nobles eager to keep themselves in the style to which they'd grown accustomed.

However, the nobles weren't going to give up their sense of superiority easily. With variations, they continued to occupy top political offices into the nineteenth century. Assured of their places in the legislature, such as Britain's House of Lords, they also held many cabinet posts in royal governments. As for social status, being

addressed as 'Lord' or 'Seigneur' obviously gave you more cachet in
exalted social circles. In France, where title-bearing public offices
were often sold to the highest bidder, the bourgeoisie showed a particular fondness for slipping into the aristocratic party by the back
door and joining the *noblesse de robe* – the term setting the new
class apart from the old nobility of the sword, those noble families
whose long history had distant origins in medieval Europe's warrior
caste. Elsewhere, the bourgeoisie would often emulate the nobility
by hiring artists, musicians and writers to immortalise them. That's
why, when you wander through an art gallery organised chrono-
logically, centuries of religious art suddenly give way to portraits
and scenes of landscapes. A good amount of the money coming into
Europe ultimately found its way into patronage of the arts, music and
learning. With new sources of revenue, a slightly greater percentage
of the population was now able to put aside the daily struggle of
manual toil to devote themselves to matters of the mind.

Leisured classes devoted to intellectual and artistic pursuits had
been around a long time. Around 12,000 years ago, when our ancestors stopped their wandering and discovered farming, in a long period
we now call the Neolithic Revolution, they found ways to squeeze
enough output from the land to support a small class that didn't
need to produce its own food. This class, in time, had assembled in
the temples; later still in the academies, seminaries and universities.
What was novel about the leisure-class expansion of early modern
Europe, though, was both the scale and rapidity of its growth, and
the source of its patronage. Between the foundation of Europe's
first university in Bologna in 1088 and Columbus's arrival in the
Americas, the continent had produced some three dozen universities.
In the three centuries that followed, however, this number, including
those in the colonies, would nearly triple. Moreover, the source of
patronage changed the orientation of scholars. Medieval universities
had been created by religious orders to produce priests, or by princes
to supply their governments with lawyers and administrators. Many
of the new universities, on the other hand, were created to provide
education to the young men of the rising bourgeoisie – who forewent

theological studies and instead took a keen interest in more worldly subjects like science, the classics and literature.

Back in the Middle Ages, there hadn't been much money in writing novels or plays, and so stories and tunes typically became common property – 'folk' tales or music, from the German word *volk*, meaning people. In the age of Shakespeare and Molière, on the other hand, enough paying customers could be found to make a living by entertaining them.[13] And, as soon became apparent, the tastes of these audiences differed from those of the priests and philosophers of yesteryear.

'As soon as they became recognisably human,' wrote Karen Armstrong in *A History of God*, 'men and women started to worship gods.'[14] Just why they did so remains something of a mystery. Believers say that someone, or something, created us with a sense of a world beyond. Non-believers obviously opt for materialist explanations. Evolutionary biology, for instance, argues that since human life evolved as a series of random mutations and adaptations, the same can be said of the belief systems that grew up alongside us. Convictions that were functional to our survival and propagation reproduced themselves – spreading, in the words of Richard Dawkins,[15] virally as memes. Another popular explanation lies in anthropology, which shows how priestly castes grew up alongside ruling classes, justifying the privileges of both and socialising the masses into passive acceptance of their leaders' superiority. But whatever their motivations, what is undeniable is that from their earliest history our ancestors revealed themselves to be what Armstrong called *homo religiosus*.

At first those ancestors tended towards forms of animism in religious practice. Living at the mercy of nature, they looked to it for guidance and safety, treating the animals and plants they depended on for life as sacred.[16] That's why the earliest evidence of religious symbolism, like cave paintings, make animals and nature so central. But once civilisation began and a leisure class emerged, they turned their eyes heavenwards, to that part of nature they had not had time to ponder – the stars, imagining lands beyond the mountains, and who or what might live there or have created them.

Sometime around the first millennium BCE, there occurred one of those strange, seemingly inexplicable coincidences that history will sometimes yield. Over a long period that the philosopher Karl Jaspers would call the Axial Age, in different corners of the world, elaborate systems of belief arose largely independent of one another, yet with remarkably similar features. Confucianism in China; Hinduism, Buddhism and Jainism in India; Zoroastrianism in Persia; philosophy in Greece; and Judaism in Palestine. All were character-ised by a hunger for meaning and the emergence of priestly castes.[17]

Like any grand theory, the Jaspers thesis is much debated. Nevertheless, one can't help but notice how much the preoccupations of these different belief systems resembled one another. They debated or outlined the duties of the ruling classes, the rights and respon-sibilities of the individual, the meaning of existence, the search for justice and a vision of a better world – whether in this life or another. As if born with a sense that there was something beyond this world, and that humans were entitled to a life free of sorrow, hunger and violence, and moreover that there existed somewhere a garden of plenty or a promised land where they would find it, our ancestors began to ponder how to reconcile the gap between the world as it was and the world as it might yet be. Mindful of both human frailty and the scarcities that made life so fragile, these religions dreamed of abundance and looked to supernatural intervention to provide it. In modern economic parlance, we'd say they looked to some exogenous variable, something 'outside the model', to complete it. For the most part, ordinary people left it to the experts to manage relations with this other realm. Consumed as they were with the daily grind of coaxing a living from a reluctant earth or sea, they paid their temple-dues and followed the priesthood's guidance in the rituals required to help make the rains come or the herds return. For as long as they could deliver the goods, the priests retained their flock.

After the death of Jesus Christ, an itinerant Jewish preacher on the outer edges of the early Roman Empire, a new sect appeared which would eventually grow into one of the biggest and most enduring religions in history. Shaped by Jewish traditions and literature, as well as the Greek philosophy then current among its scholars, this faith would spread along the trade routes of the empire to eventually conquer western Europe. Called 'Roman' because its highest temple ended up being located in the imperial capital, it built upon an evolving Jewish tradition that had replaced the earlier belief that the Jews, like every nation, had their own tribal god – or in the case of other peoples, including the Romans, gods – with the new conviction that there was in fact only one god – theirs. The new faith, though, adopted more liberal membership rules and saw as its mission to eventually convert the world, so it took as its moniker the Greek word for 'universal': Catholic.

However, reasoned its founders, until the day the whole world converted to Roman Catholicism and Christ returned to Earth, humans would have to live with one foot in each of two worlds: the City of God and the City of Man. This belief, which had been developed by one of the early Church fathers, Saint Augustine, held that humans had to navigate a course through two overlapping realms, the material one and the spiritual one. Citing Christ's injunction to his followers to 'render unto Caesar that which belongs to Caesar and unto God that which belongs to God', Augustine argued that Christians had to respect the rules of both the king and the bishop – but that in the final reckoning, both answered to God. Meanwhile, we were all bound together to God in the act of communion, the commemoration of Christ's last meal before his execution for treason by the Romans. For centuries, therefore, Europe's academies and seminaries devoted themselves to working out the details of the laws that would govern daily behaviour. Was usury wrong? What was a just price? If the lord and serf were equal before God, but one ruled the other on Earth, what were their respective rights and duties? These were the sorts of questions that were debated for centuries in the monasteries and convent schools.

Ever since the fall of the Roman Empire, such Church institutions had incubated the culture of the Western world (which was sometimes called Christendom). The tradition of scholarship it engendered was passed down through the generations in the documents produced by scribes; monastic authors who transcribed religious and scholarly literature. Artists in their own right, they would reveal their genius not only by crafting beautiful lettering, but also by the illustrations that adorned their texts. But they took a long time to produce, and so the energy of the scribes had to be reserved for the writings of churchmen. Theirs was not the age of the bodice-ripper.

The change in the economic landscape that followed the advent of European imperialism in the fifteenth century would profoundly disrupt this order of Church, scholars and scribes. The rising bourgeoisie, and the nobles who chose to throw in their lot with capitalism, increasingly wanted to emancipate themselves from the rule of clerics. The rise of a literate bourgeoisie increased demand for literature, putting a strain on the traditional methods of reproduction. Moreover, the tastes of this new consuming class differed from those of the Church's intellectuals. Rather than scholastic religious commentaries written in Latin, the children of the bourgeoisie had tastes of a more profane sort than the monasteries could satisfy. They wanted light fiction, poetry or even bawdy, raucous tales like *The Canterbury Tales* or *The Decameron* – and moreover, they wanted them in their own languages, which could better convey the richness of puns and imagery in which those writers excelled. It was their age's equivalent of preferring reality television to nature documentaries.

Recent technological developments made possible this meeting of writers and readers. Johannes Gutenberg, a native of Mainz who later moved to Strasbourg, worked with what we would today call venture capitalists – investors who would lend him the money to develop various schemes. For a long time, his labours bore little fruit and his investors were growing restless when, around 1440, he suddenly worked out a way to speed up the printing of manuscripts.

Gutenberg's hadn't been the first printing press, but it was the first to appear in Europe, and this mattered. Unlike the presses invented in Asia, Gutenberg's press would find its principal customers in the private sector. The public's growing appetite for literature made printing a lucrative venture, and so the technology spread rapidly across the continent. With further improvements the press made reproduction of books vastly more efficient, raising the speed they could be printed at by over 2,000 per cent. In 1455, the number of new titles could have fit in a wagon, whereas fifty years later the number of new titles ran to tens of thousands.[18] The continent now witnessed a new phenomenon – the best-selling author. Writers like Erasmus, who would have once reached a small audience of scholars, sold hundreds of thousands of books. By the time Europeans were penetrating the interior of the Americas, there were hundreds of presses operating across Europe.

As often happens with inventors, Gutenberg struggled financially. No sooner did he attract new investors than the old ones wanted their money back. The Steve Jobs of his time, he proved to be a better visionary than manager, and his projects often ran over budget. But Europe would never be the same. Early in the 1500s an Augustinian monk became embroiled in what might otherwise have been a local-ised theological controversy. Martin Luther had written to his bishop to complain about a Vatican agent funding the construction of St Peter's Basilica by selling indulgences – financial contributions that supposedly bought a reduction in the time a soul had to spend in purgatory before gaining admission to heaven. Today, such an agent would probably land a high-paying job as a fundraiser or run an ex-politician's charity, but Luther's was a time that looked askance at such behaviour. However, beyond assailing the crassness of price lists for sins, Luther made an even more provocative criticism of the Church. He said it couldn't mediate between individuals and the life hereafter. Only if they had personal faith could individuals save themselves. He insisted that nothing the Church could do would alter that.

Luther was hardly the first rebel in Church history. Many had come and gone, many had been forgotten, many were mere footnotes in histories only scholars knew. If the Church didn't like what someone had to say, it could have the scribes strike him, or her, from the record. But this time, when Luther shared his letter with a few friends, they took it to the press. Before long, several hundred thousand people had read it.[19] Among Luther's fans were many of the new bourgeoisie, drawn to the idea that they alone determined their salvation, along with some princes who were only too happy to take some powers away from the Church.[20] This marriage of individualist ideas and capitalist business sense helped make the Reformation. It also legitimised the idea that men could chart their own path to heaven. Luther might not have intended the revolution to be so sweeping, but once the idea spread it was out of his hands.

By the time Martin Luther was stirring up a hornet's nest in Catholic Europe, the growth of prosperity was already weakening the sense of life's fragility. As wealth grew, it became possible to envisage new things that could be done with it, beyond building cathedrals or endowing religious foundations (the traditional good works of the nobility). The eyes of the intellectuals turned away from the heavens and once more looked at the world around them. But unlike their distant ancestors, who'd seen nature as the sovereign on which they depended, this time the relationship was reversed. Humans now started to see themselves as sovereign, and it was nature that would be bent to their will.

Beginning soon after the European arrival in the Americas, and taking firm hold amid the prosperity of the seventeenth century, a new movement looked to displace the role of the Church in intellectual creativity. Preferring empirical observation to the Catholic scholasticism of reasoned deduction from the a priori premises of faith, they looked at the world with eyes sceptical of old assumptions. Because this movement's chief proponents believed the new knowledge would shed light on areas of human existence that had been shrouded in ignorance, they called it the Age of Enlightenment.

The thinkers of the Enlightenment did not necessarily set out to upend religious thought. On the contrary, men like John Locke, René

Descartes, Francis Bacon and Isaac Newton were devout believers who maintained that the new mode of enquiry would more fully reveal the mind of God, so hidden during the centuries when daily life was a constant struggle. However, they departed from the traditional worldview in which God was revealed in the sacraments or the Bible or the wisdom of the Church, and looked to reason and scientific observation to unfold His presence and will. This scepticism, which defined Enlightenment thought, was then taken by subsequent thinkers to its logical extreme. In the eighteenth century, French intellectuals like Voltaire and Denis Diderot rocked the Catholic Church with their provocative doubt, which questioned everything the Church had taught. Diderot even landed himself briefly in prison in 1749 with a series of explosive publications like *Indiscreet Jewels*, a satire of the French monarchy that related the experiences of court women from the vantage point of their vaginas (suffice to say the book was action-packed).

By then, Paris had become a hotbed of Enlightenment thought. The daughters of the new bourgeoisie, along with some forward-thinking noblewomen, eagerly patronised the flourishing artists and intellectuals of the Enlightenment at dinner parties they called 'salons'. Originating in Italy in the 1500s, salons spread among the French bourgeoisie and nobility in the next century, reaching a zenith as a genre at the mid-eighteenth century. At these literary soirées where the most fashionable writers, artists, musicians and intellectuals mingled with the beautiful people of the time over sumptuous meals and rivers of wine, the women of both the old and new orders helped birth the new age's thought.

The evolution of the material and spiritual worlds thus reinforced one another, helping to create the new Europe being so debated in those stately homes. On one hand, capitalism, itself given a fillip by the spread of empire, helped sustain the Reformation and subsequent Enlightenment. On the other, the Enlightenment helped sustain capitalism, by challenging the old medieval aristocratic order and its veneration of land and dismissal of commerce and finance. Opening new vistas of thought, scholars were turning their attention away from the traditional pursuits of intellectuals, like questions of eternity, and focusing their energies on the here and now. Some devoted themselves to that most material of intellectual undertakings: trying to understand and channel the economic transformation then underway.

CHAPTER 3

PROPHETS FOR
A MATERIAL AGE

Today, we think of Paris as a city of grand boulevards, parks, fountains and squares, a haven for lovers with its romantic views of the
gentle River Seine and the elegant buildings with balconies lining it.
But that is a legacy of the reconstruction of Paris that took place in
the late nineteenth century, following generations of the sort of street
battles immortalised in *Les Miserables*. In the era of the salons, the
French capital was quite a different place – a congested, squalid
medieval city that groaned against its walls like a child who has out-
grown its crib. Houses crowded narrow lanes, and the lanes doubled
as sewers before draining into the river. So narrow and cramped were
the streets that there was scarcely room for a cart to pass through.
Most Parisians had to walk miles a day and wait in long lines to fill a
bucket of water at one of the few public fountains. Dark at night and
dangerous, its warren of alleys providing endless escape for those
who challenged authority, the city stewed with rebellion.

Amid this restless sea of humanity, though, stood quiet islands
where the nobility kept their city homes alongside the residences
of the new bourgeoisie. Attended by servants who kept the food
coming and the wine flowing, *salonnières* assembled their favoured
intellectuals in gatherings that stirred the pot of intellectual ferment.
Salon society turned its back on the nearby Sorbonne, the ancient

university whose dwindling priesthood had retreated into arcane
theological debates and provided a lively new stage for the people
who were building a revolution in thought: men like Voltaire, Jean-
Jacques Rousseau, Maximilien Robespierre, Benjamin Franklin and
Thomas Jefferson.

A timid, awkward Scotsman turned up there in the winter of
1765.[1] Adam Smith was a bookish academic, famous back in
Edinburgh for long absent-minded strolls when he burrowed so
deeply into his thoughts that, on one occasion, he managed to walk
fifteen miles before realising he was still in his bathrobe.[2] With
more than half of Britain's universities (despite having less than a
tenth of its population), Scotland was home to its own current of the
Enlightenment. Centred not on salons but on reading circles where
scholars eagerly consumed and debated the latest literature from the
continent, the Scottish Enlightenment retained a distinctly Scottish
flavour – practical, optimistic, aiming to use the new knowledge to
better the world. A friend of the philosopher David Hume, Smith had
made his name with a book on moral philosophy titled *The Theory
of Moral Sentiments*. If a little concerned by Hume's radical scepticism, Smith nonetheless shared his friend's wish to discern truth not
in deduction or reflection upon religious teaching, but in empirical
observation of the world around him. In his subtle and carefully reasoned book, Smith took a hopeful view of human nature. Although
he challenged centuries of Christian teaching on ethics by arguing
that human morality came not from transcendental sources like
stone tablets descended from a mountain, but from the mundane
experience of humans understanding others, he nonetheless agreed
that benevolence and love were the foundations of a harmonious
society. Moral sentiments, he said, came from the experiences of this
world, not knowledge of another one.

In a Parisian high society that placed as much value on style as
substance, Smith was a bit of a square peg. With none of the charm
that brought Hume success among women, equipped by nature with
bad teeth and looks that he himself acknowledged weren't exactly
spellbinding, and with so little French he could at first barely carry

a conversation, it was inevitable he would underwhelm. One woman he encountered at a party would later simply recount that 'he was as ugly as the devil'.[3] But the insouciant Smith soldiered on happily, immersing himself in Parisian life, delighting in frequent trips to the theatre and the opera, accepting any salon invitations he received. In time, his modest and companionable demeanour won over even those who used to avoid him.

Smith was impressed by the fact that France, like Britain, was going through a long and unprecedented era of economic growth, and was captivated by the ideas of philosophers who were trying to make sense of it. Just as political philosophers like Voltaire had turned away from questions of eternity, these 'political economists' were asking questions about what was happening, literally, in the ground beneath their feet. Had humans found the secret to transforming the environment in a way they had long assumed only God could do, making it release more wealth into their hands than they had previously imagined possible?

Paris was then the centre of this nascent economic thought. It had coalesced around a group of thinkers called the physiocrats, who were a big draw on the salon circuit. Encountering them one evening, Smith was smitten.

The physiocrats were not the first scholars to turn their attention to the economy. No sooner had Europeans opened America's seams of wealth than men of letters had begun pondering what all this new money might do to their homelands. The earliest of these intellectuals, who came to be known as the mercantilists, were more high-brow bureaucrats than scholars, trying to calculate what impact the gold and silver they were mining in the colonies would have on Europe.

Gold is a funny thing. A shiny rock that produces nothing, it nevertheless retains a hold on our imagination that has always defied reason. Warren Buffett once summed up the enigma of gold by saying we 'dig it out of the ground ... Then we melt it down, dig another hole, bury it again and pay people to stand around guarding it.'[4] Humans through history and in almost all lands have attributed almost mystical properties to the precious metal, using it as both a store of value and a symbol of wealth and power. This inexhaustible demand for what is a scarce mineral has always made it very valuable. The desire to acquire it, and the lengths to which humans will go to find it, is a recurrent theme in the human imagination and the folklore it has produced.

Never was this more so than in the age of mercantilism, when gold hoards were considered the measure of a state's power. Despite centuries of experimentation in the proto-science of alchemy, nobody ever found a way to make gold, leaving humans to make do with what the planet yielded them. And that wasn't much – in the 1700s, barely enough to fill a swimming pool. So if the gold supply was ordained by nature, it logically followed that the planet's stock of wealth was itself unalterable. And since for thousands of years humans had never known anything in the way of a significant and long-lasting rise in their productivity, this appeared a reasonable conclusion. The mercantilists were thus satisfied that Europe's post-Columbian wealth was simply the result of the transfer of wealth from the colonies to the heartland. Dream as they did of a hidden El Dorado, such a land of endless abundance could only exist at the margins of the earth, in an imagined golden age of the past or a utopian future. As a result, the mercantilist doctrine did not depart very far from the medieval mind in its acceptance of the sovereignty of God and the immutability of His creation.

Then along came the physiocrats who proposed something radical. They suggested a rational economic organisation could cause farmland to produce greater yields, and it was this, and not the influx of gold and silver, that was behind Europe's rising output. Significantly, the physiocrats departed from the normative rhetoric that had governed earlier, philosophical work on the economy, concerning themselves not with the world as it could be, but with the world as it was – or at least, as they understood it to be.

François Quesnay, the court physician to King Louis XV who became his trusted adviser, was the celebrity-scholar among the physiocrats. Surrounded by fawning admirers who took their cue from the king, Quesnay devised a model of the economy that (not surprisingly for a doctor) took it to be a living organism. In true Enlightenment fashion, Quesnay tried to replicate Newton's success in modelling the operation of the universe. The fact that the resulting chart was so bewildering that only he could decipher it, further burnished his reputation for brilliance (a lesson that wasn't lost on subsequent generations of economists). Quesnay thus assumed the aura of a seer among his followers.[5]

Nevertheless, if theirs was a supposed science of the economy, in one vital way the physiocrats still didn't break with the medieval mindset. As their name suggested – 'physio' being the Greek word for nature, 'kratein' for 'to rule' – they believed nature held the reins, conceiving a natural order in which creation, once freed from governmental restrictions on commerce, would realise its potential. Although they rejected feudalism's organic conception of society, preferring a *laissez-faire* model in which labour could be freely allocated to its most productive uses, their theory allowed less room for human ingenuity. They believed that land, not people, was the basis of production, and land could become more productive. As a result, they had little regard for industry or services, and least of all for banks, concluding that these sectors added nothing to the economy but merely circulated the wealth produced by the farms. The emergence of urban capitalism therefore testified not to progress, but to a decline into an unnatural and degraded state. Idealising the peasantry and rural life – Thomas Jefferson, whose vision for the young American republic was of a nation of independent farmers, was an admirer – the physiocrats saw corrupt government wedded to war and luxury as the chief hindrance to progress. That this bore more than a passing resemblance to Chinese Confucianism was not accidental. Thanks to the Jesuit mission in the Far East, the physiocrats had access to Confucian literature, and they consumed it avidly.[6]

In medieval Europe, children had been taught to bow their heads in prayer whenever a funeral procession passed by. 'No man is an island,' wrote the English poet John Donne, expressing a conception of an ordered society bound together by ties of reciprocal duty. You were born with a set of rights and obligations that secured your place in society. If your parents had been tenant farmers and you were prepared to keep the farm going, you'd probably have been entitled to the tenancy. If they'd been blacksmiths, you could probably have learnt the trade and kept the forge going. On the other hand, had your passion been carpentry rather than ironwork, you might have found it hard to enter the wood-working guild. What you gained from the old order in security, therefore, you lost in freedom. And that, said Adam Smith, had to go.

The times were changing. States were rising, the Church was declining, and a new order called for a new morality. Ever since the Reformation, when Martin Luther shook up the Church by saying it had no authority to stand between Christians and their Bible, the book he took to be the ultimate source of religious authority, northern Europe's kings had been weakening the secular power the Vatican had long enjoyed. They may have acted on principle, or they may have been simply seizing an opportunity. Some of them claimed the right to select bishops and rule over the Church, as happened in France. Some pushed the Pope aside and placed the Church directly under their authority, as happened in Britain and Scandinavia. With royal or, in the case of the republics, national governments improving their tax administration and bureaucracy, and with their right to tax overseas trade helping to swell their treasuries, power began to move towards the centre. Even when noble families still dominated the government, as was the case in England through the nineteenth century, power was shifting from their great country estates to the capital city.

By protecting sea lanes, regulating commerce and creating stand-ard measures, these governments became essential partners to the rising bourgeoisie.[7] With capital playing an ever-greater role, it was inevitable that over time people's loyalties would drift away from the pluralistic spheres of the Middle Ages, in which they had been defined by their religion and locale ('I'm so-and-so from this village, and my father is . . .'). A newly evolving concept, that of citizenship, which would take clear form during the 1789 French Revolution, called on everyone to see the ultimate arbiter of their lives in the nation state. Although the vast majority of Europeans still attended religious services, church courts were dissolved and religion was now made subject to the laws of the land. Not surprisingly, given they looked to create a new age, Enlightenment thinkers tended to swim in the swelling currents of this nationalism.

Political economists thus saw themselves as servants to their government, helping it to find ways to augment its revenues and boost national wealth. In effect, political economists assumed the role of royal advisers who had at one time been priests and cardinals. A tradition begun by the mercantilists, it was carried on by the physiocrats, who, while rejecting the mercantilist balance-sheet approach to empire, nonetheless wanted to raise the productivity of domestic agriculture. This political alignment of scholars, therefore, produced schools of political economy with distinctly national characters.

After finishing his French tour, Adam Smith would devote the next decade of his life to producing what would become the bible of British political economy. *An Inquiry into the Nature and Causes of the Wealth of Nations*, which appeared in 1776, would be one of the most influential books to ever appear in the English language. He provided a finely crafted argument to show why humans, if allowed to pursue their own desires, would invent new products and processes that would ultimately raise the output of society as a whole. Everyone would benefit, since workers would get jobs and manufacturers would thereby obtain richer customers. Smith said the old religious ethics should play no role in the economy. There would be no 'just prices' calculated to align need with ability to pay, no bans on usury, no fixed stations in life. Such rules and interventions, he held, messed with the economy's natural operation. Instead, prices should be set by traders in competitive markets according to the interaction of supply and demand. And so, for instance, if cloth became too expensive and customers had to cut their purchases, the attraction of high prices would lead textiles manufacturers to ramp up production, making cloth more abundant and affordable once more.

No doubt because he lived in what he called a nation of shop-keepers, but also because he came from a lowland Scotland then witnessing the birth of the Industrial Revolution, Adam Smith would reject the physiocratic veneration of farming. He agreed agriculture could be made more productive. But to him it wasn't a basket into which you could put too many eggs, not when other opportunities had just begun knocking. Smith thought all labour, and especially industrial labour, could be made productive. He suspected it was the productivity of labour itself, and not the land, which was pow-ering the country's rising prosperity. And what made labour more productive? The capital added to make it more efficient – which is to say, to enable it to produce more with less. Although the concept of the division of labour wasn't his invention, Smith developed it into a full-blown theory of how specialisation made workers more productive. He reasoned that industrialists who applied their capital to the creation of such integrated production units were key actors in the transformation of human potential, and no less important to the success of capitalism. Unlike the Confucian and physiocratic posi-tion, which saw commerce as essentially parasitic, Smith insisted that bankers and traders played essential roles organising and facilitating the division of labour. That, he argued, was the genius of capitalism.

And so Smith came to the ultimate preoccupation of all political economists, the role of government in this new order. He called for a state whose functions were clear but restrained. It was to maintain public order, defend against foreign invasion, and provide public consumption goods – those goods that markets and society needed in order to function properly, but that no private business would provide since there was no way to make money from them: policing, roads, courts and so on. He didn't advocate a complete hands-off approach to the economy. For instance, he thought it best if the government broke up organisations that limited competition, such as guilds, unions and cartels. Nevertheless, his ideal govern-ment would be one that acted in the name of economic efficiency and not in the pursuit of any other goal. Instead, he suggested that if the government maintained basic order and left individuals with

maximum freedom of movement, an 'invisible hand'[8] would guide
the society towards higher states of civility, revealing a natural order
within its inner workings.

The Wealth of Nations, which sold out its first printing in a matter
of months, became the cornerstone of a new doctrine. At its heart
lay a new commandment. Two thousand years after Christ told his
followers to 'Love your neighbour as yourself' Smith now instructed
his to simply 'Love yourself'. What appeared to be private vice would
actually yield public benefits.

How could this be? Smith resolved this paradox by saying that
if you made yourself rich, you would have more to spend, and so
you'd make someone else rich too. He hadn't invented this notion.
The thesis that the individual's pursuit of his or her own self-interest
would lead to social benefit, what was known as the doctrine of
unintended consequences, went back to at least the early eighteenth
century. Its first expression appears to have been a short book by
Bernard Mandeville called *The Fable of the Bees*. At the time,
Mandeville's idea was scandalous, since it turned centuries of religious teaching completely on its head.

Yet while Smith had written the doctrine of unintended consequences into his creed, he'd been no proto-Gordon Gekko declaring
that greed was good. On the contrary, Smith presumed that the
capitalist economy would operate in an environment much like
that in which he lived, with a shared moral universe that guided
and limited the behaviour of individuals.[9] Smith may not have been
a terribly religious man, but his was an age in which most people
still went to church and almost everyone believed in the God of
Christianity and the moral codes bequeathed by that religion. Far
from an atomist vision of society in which each person was self-
sufficient and engaged with other individuals only to maximise one's
interests, Smith offered detailed passages outlining the ways society
was comprised of a myriad of interdependent individuals, each playing a part essential to the whole. In effect, the invisible hand was
the individual's unwitting enactment of the human animal's social

nature, love of self inadvertently leading one to love the society one lived in. All the same, in producing a worldview in which the pursuit of self-interest was celebrated as good, a belief that generations of political economists would take as an article of faith, Smith had helped create a new moral code for a rapidly changing world. Later generations of libertarian thinkers, often paying little attention to what Smith actually wrote, would often elevate this commandment into a celebration of love of self *tout court*.

If Adam Smith had provided the gospel of this new doctrine, his disciples would soon add the Acts and Letters which fleshed it out fully. Among the first to do so was a young broker who in 1799 picked up *The Wealth of Nations* for the first time. David Ricardo had never been one to miss an opportunity to ruffle feathers. He had broken with his Jewish family when he eloped with a Quaker girl and would later go on to make a fortune speculating on government bonds using methods that would today land him in court on insider-trading charges. But when he read Smith's work, he would outdo even its author in upending received wisdom.

Although the physiocrats had called for free trade, what they'd really meant was free trade within France. In the eighteenth century, you could barely move from one French town to the next without paying some form of toll. But when it came to foreign trade, the physiocrats still wanted to maximise the nation's wealth by conventional means. They wanted to export lots and import little. Smith, therefore, had already overturned political economy's boat when he suggested that if a foreign country could produce something more cheaply than Britain, Britain would do well to import it. Yes, domestic producers would go out of business, but that would make them start producing the things Britain could produce more cheaply than its rivals, and then export the surplus. As he put it, Britain would do best to specialise in those products in which it enjoyed what he called an absolute advantage.

Ricardo now took this a step further. He said that even if a trading partner had an absolute advantage over Britain in the production of *all* goods, Britain should still open its borders. This sounded suicidal, but Ricardo explained why it made sense. He contrived an imaginary scenario based on trade between Britain and her oldest ally, Portugal. Suppose, he said, that Portugal could produce both wine and cloth more cheaply than Britain – which is to say that it needed fewer worker-hours to produce the same amount of output. The theory of absolute advantage suggested Portuguese goods would swamp Britain. Not necessarily, said Ricardo. Let us assume, in turn, that Portugal also had a *comparative* advantage in the production of wine – that while it could make both wine and cloth more cheaply than Britain, it could make wine cheapest of all. Under a regime of free trade with Britain, it would have an interest in putting all its resources into producing wine, import cloth back from Britain, and bank the difference it would make in its vastly increased wine sales. Portugal would thus specialise in wine, Britain in cloth.

In the early age of the nation state, when governments were determined to safeguard their national wealth, this was shocking advice: tear down all your walls and throw your country open to foreign goods. It was the economic equivalent of sending all your soldiers home and raising your border posts. Yet Ricardo insisted, using some simple mathematics to drive his point home, that this bold move would actually enrich the country.

Like many a prophet, Smith had his moments of doubt, when he wondered whether his new morality would actually work. Slavery, for instance, still existed in his day. While he criticised the institution, Smith also resigned himself to its existence. What slave owner, he gloomily said, was going to want to give up labour he didn't have to pay for?[10] Moreover, he had to admit that the colonies were providing Europe with a good deal of the wealth then driving its ascent.[11]

One of those colonies, Jamaica, had become the richest in the British Empire – although, since most of its inhabitants were unpaid slaves, the colony's wealth existed principally on paper, in the London bank accounts and great houses of the plantation owners. Nevertheless, given the sheer volume of the profits of Jamaica's sugar plantations, some of which stretched for miles and possessed hundreds of slaves, even the proportionately small amount of their income that the planters spent in the colony supported a large foreign trade. Each week, therefore, dozens of sailing ships laden with cargo would dock at the ports of Montego Bay, Lucea or Kingston, offloading furniture from London workshops, Portuguese wine and French brandy, clothing from Paris for the planters and Wiltshire cloths for the slaves, new supplies of slaves from Africa or precious hardwoods from the Far East to be used in the construction of the island's houses.

Like slave owners throughout the Americas, Jamaica's planter class comprised many men and women who'd risen up the social ladder by migrating to the colonies, where they were able to make themselves as rich as aristocrats back home. Thomas Thistlewood was rather typical.[12] The son of a tenant farmer from Lincolnshire, his various business initiatives had amounted to little, so at the age of twenty-nine he boarded a ship for the West Indies. After landing in Jamaica, he managed to get work as a plantation overseer, and gradually adapted to the sticky heat and isolation of life on the farm. Over the following years he worked his way up the social ladder until he owned his own property. And as so often happens with people who are catapulted upwards, he developed an appetite for refinement. Unusually for a man in his position, he was an avid reader, seeing himself as a vehicle by which the Enlightenment would reach Jamaica. Each year he'd order a steamer trunk full of books from his favourite London bookseller and then circulate them through reading groups of his fellow planters. He acquired a copy of *The Wealth of Nations* within months of its publication.[13] Although he was often invited to the dinners plantation houses put on to fill their social calendar, he was happy in his study, and could go months without the company of another white person.

This immersion in a transplanted African society shaped his mind and formed his fears, as it did all the slave owners. Unlike some of the other islands in the West Indies, where farms were smaller and a higher proportion of slaves were domestic servants, those in Jamaica worked overwhelmingly on the land. They had relatively limited contact with the master and, because the economy's appetite for labour demanded a constant supply of new slaves, they still spoke their own languages. Thistlewood grasped early on the precarious position of the planter class: a thin veneer of white painted over an oppressed black population which, on the plantations, outnumbered their owners twenty to one. He observed how slave owners used terror to control the population.

Thistlewood, who was admired by some other colonists for the botanical research he undertook on his own farm and who kept his mind sharp by conducting medical experiments on his slaves, took that same hunger for learning into his studies of torture. He perfected his flogging technique, opening ruts in his slaves' flesh sufficiently deep to maximise the burning of a mixture of pepper, lime and salt that he rubbed into their wounds, yielding a finely balanced agony that was not so debilitating as to prevent them returning to work. Inventive and imaginative, he devised one particularly grisly punishment called 'Derby's dose', whereby he'd force one slave to defecate into another's mouth, then gag the victim for four to five hours.

If you do this sort of thing long enough, your pangs of conscience will gradually weaken to the point where your actions can be rationalised. Just as today we can, say, wave off suicides by workers at the plants that make our mobile phones by saying 'They're still happier than if they'd stayed on the farm', Thistlewood was able to tell himself he was just doing his job. His diaries reveal that he thought Africans innately predisposed to savagery and thus responsive only to violence. There was nothing personal in his barbarity, it was just business. The numbers were stacked against him, he would have rebelled had he been in their place, and so he had to use brutality to keep them down. Beyond the job requirements, he had no principled objection to mingling with his slaves, to judge from the detailed record in his diaries of his sexual conquests (though conquest is admittedly easy when the target of your longing is registered as your property).

In his bizarre blend of barbaric behaviour and Enlightenment thought, Thomas Thistlewood appeared the embodiment of a paradox. But perhaps he understood one fundamental truth better than Adam Smith. Like the hero in J. M. Coetzee's *Waiting for the Barbarians*, he could see that great civilisations are built on top of no small amount of oppression, with much of their civility a function of the fact that the oppression has been pushed out of sight, to the frontiers of the empire. Like the ancient Romans, who built monuments and legal codes that lasted for millennia, then entertained themselves by feeding their captives to wild animals, Thistlewood saw no contradiction between destroying bodies by day, then cultivating his mind by night. He may have been less compassionate than Smith, or merely more aware that the very prosperity that supported the Enlightenment, which made it possible for people like him to build personal libraries, was being fuelled at its base by the kind of work he was doing.

In developing their theories later economic thinkers would confine their attention to what was happening in their own countries, regardless of how much those activities depended upon external events. Topics like slavery and imperialism would fade into the background. But this wasn't merely a function of ignorance or carelessness. In Smith's homeland the landscape was changing fundamentally, in ways that would make it possible for the country to exploit the bounty of their colonies more productively than the Spanish and Portuguese did.

CHAPTER 4

THE EARLY CONVERSIONS

We're all products of our environment. If you come from a Western country you'll probably dismiss, say, a Ugandan who opposes homosexuality for lacking enlightenment. But how many of us reached enlightenment by comparing the writings of John Locke and Robert Filmer before concluding in favour of individual liberty? More likely we came to our beliefs through a behaviourist process of repeating those statements that bring us positive affirmation from a peer-group we admire and avoiding those which yield negative feedback, until over time our beliefs coalesce into what we call 'our views'.

Adam Smith was no different. Unlike his European counterparts, he could take a sanguine view of industry because he'd been able to observe its inner workings first-hand. Whereas French or Spanish political economists still lived in overwhelmingly agricultural societies, Britain, if still rural, had nonetheless seen the first stirrings of an industrial economy. By the time Smith was putting pen to paper and developing his model of the economy, the country had developed a layer of industry that used something called the putting-out system.

Guilds, proto-unions that regulated the various trades and crafts and limited the number of new apprentices to maintain wages, had for centuries acted as a brake on European industry. However, in the late eighteenth century, English capitalists found a way to contract various parts of the production process to small family producers, who often worked from their homes. This 'cottage industry' would provide the embryo of the emergent industrial economy, since manufacturing allowed capitalists to exploit the division of labour in a way that wasn't possible in agriculture. However, it wasn't obvious that Britain should be the birthplace of the Industrial Revolution. After all, the country had been relatively late to the imperialist game, being nearly a century behind Portugal and Spain in the race to acquire overseas colonies. But a peculiar feature of the British political system allowed the country to capitalise on the new flow of money that Iberian ships were bringing to Europe.

Back in the Middle Ages there had been no such thing as estate agents, because there'd been no real estate in the way we know it today. You couldn't just decide one day to try hobby farming or country living and buy yourself a patch of farmland. That's because in the medieval European mind, and consequently its legal system as well, the earth belonged to God and its human occupants were its stewards. Of course, in any village most of the land was controlled by the nobleman: some descendant of a baron who had seized it in ancient times (like the warrior-nobles who helped carve up the Roman Empire when it fell and were paid for their service in land, or in Britain's case the knights who fought alongside William the Conqueror). But even these men did not enjoy absolute rights to land. On their sometimes vast estates, the peasants who were bound to them got small plots of their own, from which they would pay a form of rent to the nobleman. For as long as they farmed these plots, they had a right to stay. In addition, there were plots of land that belonged to nobody in particular. In England these were called commons, since everyone could use them for specific purposes, such as grazing their livestock. Over time what resulted was a rural landscape of fragmented holdings and scattered fields, alongside common lands. The medieval countryside looked something like an artist's studio: a jumble of chaotic disorder in which everything nonetheless had its place.

Some lords had long wanted to reorganise this landscape, to

consolidate their fields into contiguous units, while also bringing the common lands into their holdings. In England, a textiles sector had emerged in the late Middle Ages, raising demand for wool and thus making the raising of sheep more lucrative than the farming of food crops. But grazing sheep was no easy business if your shepherds had to move them constantly between a small number of plots. You could try to remove your tenants, but that required a change to the law.

And this is where England's aristocrats had an edge over their continental counterparts. After centuries of conflict between kings and noble families, in which the balance of power between the two tilted back and forth, the English Civil War firmly resolved the battle in favour of the latter. After the monarchy was restored in 1660, Parliament assumed its place as the ultimate law-giver. Derived from the French word *parler*, meaning 'to speak', Parliament was, strictly speaking, the king or queen in counsel with both their lords and the representatives of the common people, the two groups meeting in their own separate chambers. In practice, the upper house, to which noblemen and bishops belonged by birthright, enjoyed considerable power. Meanwhile the seats in the lower house were dominated by rural gentry, often with the conniv-ance of the local nobleman. Because the aristocracy had managed to retain its cohesion during the conflicts with the king, rather than carve England into a number of autonomous fiefdoms, it had banded together to counterbalance royal power – which ironically strengthened the cohesion of the central government. From this parliamentary perch, the nobility could now begin to change the laws,[1] with lords petitioning Parliament to bring the lands on their estates into their sole possession.

Enclosure, the process by which common lands were consolidated, then ringed off with the walls and hedgerows that criss-cross the English landscape, had begun back in the Middle Ages. Then, it had been a piecemeal process often stirred by local factors – perhaps a fall in population after a plague outbreak that left lands idle. But in the 1700s, parliamentary Enclosure proceeded on an industrial scale.[2] The dispossession of a large number of the rural population, who moved to the cities, created an army of landless labourers desperate for work. They, in turn, would provide the labour for the wool workshops then popping up in villages. Having abandoned the ancient way of doing things, Britain's nobility would reveal itself to be more pragmatic in its dealings with early capitalists than, say, the French or Russian aristocracies, who remained tied to the land and the rents it generated. Some British nobles would go so far as to turn themselves into urban capitalists, investing in new industry or in banking.

Finally, because Parliament was drawing more power to the centre, it was able to authorise expenditure on roads whilst eliminating the patchwork of tolls and barriers that limited commerce elsewhere.[3] Better roads helped to provide a necessary condition for the Industrial Revolution to take off. There was no use developing more efficient industrial operations if all the inputs had to be found, and the outputs sold, in a radius of just a few miles; the market would soon saturate. At the start of the eighteenth century, most goods were shipped on packhorses that travelled short distances, had to be frequently watered and rested, and required human overseers. As a result, any village more than a few miles from a navigable water-way was more or less confined to its surrounding area for trade. Later on in the eighteenth century, though, the initial growth of the road network and improvements to transportation technology like stronger wagons, reduced the cost and extended the range of shipping. Adding further impetus, as the century progressed, was the lengthening and deepening of Britain's canals: one horse pulling a barge from a towpath could now move ten times the volume of before. Therefore a national market evolved, giving British producers access to a much larger source of both suppliers and customers than any other European country. Budding entrepreneurs were now in an unprecedented position to do business.[4]

Enclosure and market integration in Britain had an effect a bit like lifting a divider from an ice-cube tray: once money from the Americas began entering Britain via its trade with Europe and its piracy of Spanish ships, rather than fill just one or two wells, it sloshed throughout the economy. That rising tide of revenue helped to then reinforce the rapid changes in the social environment, as the objects of human contemplation began to change. Although many of the intellectuals who rose to prominence at this time followed the course of Voltaire or Adam Smith and formed broad social visions of what the emerging society could look like, some of the age's most creative thinkers found, rather as Gutenberg had done, that there was money to be made in more practical matters: improving the production processes in the workshops of the early industrial period.

Tourists looking for a beach holiday might not enjoy Britain's climate, but sheep do. Although textile manufacturing in the Midlands and around London had grown steadily throughout the 1700s, providing cloth for local markets and selling finer woollens abroad, late in the century some fledgling manufacturers hit upon a lucrative new opportunity. In the generation before Smith wrote *The Wealth of Nations*, the British East India Company had established itself in India, giving traders access to cheap and abundant supplies of cotton. However, before they could exploit this cheap input, clothing manufacturers had to get past an obstacle. Turning cotton into cloth involves a laborious process of pulling out individual strands manually. That made cotton cloth expensive to produce. If anyone could work out a way to speed this up, fortunes beckoned. So in the course of the eighteenth century, machine-makers working at the edges of the textiles industry experimented with various techniques. As a result, at around the same time as Adam Smith was building his reputation in Paris's salons, inventors like Thomas Highs, a reed-maker from Lancashire who produced parts for looms, were busy inventing and improving cloth-making machines.

By the nineteenth century, previously sleepy villages like Manchester and Leeds grew to become major cities, and Britain's industrial centre of gravity migrated northwards. As it approached mid-century, Liverpool's population was nearly doubling each decade and several dozen ships were calling into its port each week.[5]

By then, having made peace with its erstwhile colonies in the United States, Britain began importing its cotton from plantations in the American south. It sold finished cloth throughout the world, and especially throughout its own, expanding empire.

The north-country industrialists were hence aggressive globalisers forging a new economy. They imported their raw materials, exported their products and built close ties to their suppliers and markets overseas. To them, the loss of a 'Merrye Englande' of age-old traditions and social bonds was scarcely worth losing sleep over. If their little island had ever been a rural idyll, it was nothing compared to what it might now become as the workshop of the world. The Romantic poets, appalled by the erosion of rural life and by the multiplication of the 'satanic mills' belching smoke and soot and creating a network of charmless brick factories, were then celebrating the arcadia of rural England, but Britain's bourgeois gentlemen spent little time with their books. Instead, they snapped up the literature of the political economists, convinced that those same charmless buildings were the crucibles that would mould a great nation.

All the same, the road to this bourgeoisie's promised land was strewn with obstacles; one in particular. Although royal power had been steadily ceding to Parliament, the seats in the House of Commons were still allocated along ancient lines. The result was that big rural interests, namely the nobility and the Church, still enjoyed more political power than the rising capitalist class. Even if they could be dynamic and inventive in the way they managed their estates, most lords still lived off the land. They maintained, as France's physiocrats had done, that the nation's strength was built on its farms, and that relying on foreign lands for one's food would leave Britain at their mercy. And since wheat was produced more cheaply overseas, they argued it was necessary to protect British farmers by maintaining an import duty on imported wheat so as to maintain its price.

Until 1815, the Napoleonic Wars had protected the British market from competition. When the wars ended in that year, continental grain threatened to swamp the market – this at a time when trade doctrine was still dominated by mercantilist thought, and dependence on food imports was seen as a strategic vulnerability. Although Britain was then still a primarily agrarian economy, the industrial sector had expanded rapidly over the previous few decades, and this boom-and-bust cycle in food prices added a new element of uncertainty to the country's affairs. Under the influence of Church teachings that regarded the new 'commercial spirit' of capitalism with some suspicion, and in a bid to restore some stability to the economy and to regain control over the country's food supply, the Conservative government imposed a tariff on imported grain.[6] The Corn Laws had the immediate effect of making imported grain so expensive that the foreign supply dried up (though in future years, as the population expanded and demand rose, the laws were tweaked to restore some imports).

Bread was then a staple food of the working-class diet, so the Corn Laws raised the cost of living for labourers. It didn't matter so much if you were a farm worker, since you could grow your own food and might even benefit from the higher wages that inflated prices brought. But if you'd moved to the city, as many people had done in the earlier years of Enclosure when they lost their farms, it made living more expensive. Employers felt the pressure to compensate with higher wages – even the least-enlightened industrialist still needed his workers to eat. So in 1839, a group of northern businessmen got together under the leadership of a successful calico-printer named Richard Cobden and formed the Anti-Corn Law League, which they then used to take the free-trade gospel of Adam Smith and David Ricardo to the nation.

Although you'd never divine their shared paternity from reading them these days, given their contrary opinions on just about every topic, both the *Manchester Guardian* and *Economist* newspapers were formed at this time to provide pulpits for Anti-Corn Law evangelists. In the pages of those publications, and in the public gatherings where they spoke, these men articulated a wholly different vision of England's future from that of the traditional ruling classes. In place of village, church and lord, they celebrated competition and the prosperity they said free trade would deliver to their land. If the old order found its hearth in the country homes and increasingly empty village churches, the emerging one took the pulpit in the independent chapels, coffee houses and trade associations then springing up in working-class neighbourhoods. There, even an atheist preacher could draw an audience of thousands.

It used to be said that the Church of England was the Conservative Party at prayer. However, Britain was changing rapidly, and so was its religious landscape. As the population moved to the cities, the old network of village churches dominated by aristocratic patrons went into decline. In the cities, the Church compensated with outreach to the working classes, building new churches and schools, but by their nature these tended to reinforce the country's rising evangelical movement.[7] Manual labourers initially drifted out of the Church and into non-conformist sects like the Methodists, or simply out of the Church altogether.[8] The old Church's leaders instead renewed their vows with the landowning classes and found their home in the ranks of the Tories (who later became known as the Conservative Party). By the 1840s, even though Britain had a Tory government, its supporters were praying that its members would keep the faith amid the Anti-Corn Law agitation. For, worryingly, as they confronted the growing dissatisfaction with the old order, the Tories then had a leader whose own faith seemed to be – as a later Tory prime minister used to say – wobbly. Though he wouldn't be drawn on what he made of them, Robert Peel confessed to having read Adam Smith and the other political economists.

'Vote your hopes, not your fears.' That slogan, used in a 1992 South African referendum campaign about the end of apartheid, is a recurrent theme in modern democracies. We all like to see ourselves as fearless, as the sort of people who will close our eyes and race into an unknown we can tame with optimism and force of will. Hope is young, hope is fresh, hope is Barack Obama to Hillary Clinton.

Nevertheless, fear exercises an equally powerful hold on our minds. It's a good thing it does. Over millions of years we've evolved refinements in our instinct for caution, giving us the trigger that has proved necessary for our survival: the ability to discern a threat, then respond by either fighting or fleeing. So essential is fear to our survival that when we live in an environment in which existential threats are reduced to a minimum, we seek out contrived threats, from amusement-park rides to horror films, just to keep our instincts sharpened.

The debate over the Corn Laws pitted hope against fear. At stake were the votes of a Parliament that leaned towards the latter. The Tories knew that behind the door of a Corn Law repeal lay lower prices on imported grain. But just what that would mean down the road was uncertain. Nothing is more frightening than what we don't know, since we are left to plug the gaps in our knowledge with what we can imagine. And Britain's landowners were able to imagine rivers of cheap grain that might destroy Britain's agrarian economy, creating an army of unemployed farm workers and ending a whole way of life.

On the other hand, imported grain would also bring cheaper food, which might improve living standards for those who kept their jobs. Yet while time seemed to favour the Anti-Corn Law League, scholarly opinion wasn't entirely on their side. Between the publication of Smith's *Wealth of Nations* and the league's founding in 1839 more than half a century had elapsed. The nascent discipline of political economy had taken form as several more scholars made contributions to the body of literature then coalescing. Although everybody took Smith as the starting point of their journey, not all of them reached his destination. Some, like Ricardo, agreed enthusiastically with Smith that free trade would be good for the economy.

However, others took a gloomier view. In particular, Thomas Robert Malthus rejected the Anti-Corn Law League's hopeful view of a changing world, convinced instead of the chronic fallibility of human nature, which he doubted any science or improved morality could ever ameliorate. A country vicar who rejected the doctrine of unintended consequences running through classical political economy, Malthus had made himself a minor celebrity with a 1798 essay on population growth, which argued that while food production increased arithmetically, population increased exponentially. That ensured the natural environment placed limits, painful if need be, on growth, and it was folly to try to resist this. In fact, his belief that a population unchecked by such things as natural disasters or famine would expand endlessly led Malthus to propose the 'iron law of wages' that Ricardo would later develop (though Malthus himself didn't use that term) – namely, that wages would always tend down towards subsistence levels as the pool of workers grew bigger and bigger. Significantly, Malthus rejected Smithian doctrine on self-interest in favour of traditional Christian tenets, arguing that individuals should be free to pursue their self-interest *only* on the condition they adhered to the 'rules of justice'.[9]

Others carried on in the same spirit of Ricardo. Men like Jean-Baptiste Say, one of Smith's French followers, added his Say's Law to the canon, namely that supply creates its own demand – if the supply suddenly increases, the price will drop, and buyers will snap up the extra supply. In effect, like Talmudic scholars once did with the Bible, political economists were providing commentaries on Smith or teasing out the full implications of his ideas. In that vein, the Malthus–Ricardo debate of the 1820s resembled the ancient debates among the early fathers of the Christian Church. None of the early Christian leaders had contested the authority of Christ, but because gaps in the record sometimes left the meaning of his statements or actions unclear – was he literally saying his followers would eat his flesh and drink his blood, or was he just using symbolic language? – they'd been left to argue and debate until gradually a shared position emerged, which became their orthodoxy. Malthus arguably represented one of the last attempts to restore the primacy of Christian ethics to political economy. Ricardo, who neither felt nor had reason to feel any loyalty to the old Church, fell squarely in line with those articulating a vision of a new world.

The debate over the Corn Laws came down to whether one wanted to stick with the world one knew or take a chance on the world that might yet be. Meanwhile, in the pages of *Blackwood's*

Edinburgh Review, which was the most widely read journal of the day, an alternative political philosophy began to form. Shaped by Tory and Anglican thought, it presented a vision of an aristocratic rather than industrial England – but added a nuance, saying that with great privilege went great responsibility: the duty to protect society's most vulnerable. As if anticipating the economic debates of the next century, the key thinkers in this school called for the use of government patronage and poor relief to maintain effective demand during downturns.[10]

Those who favoured repeal of the Corn Laws, on the other hand, resorted to visionary, almost utopian language to make their case. Scrapping the laws, they declared, would lower bread prices, create jobs, thereby boosting demand for manufacturers, who'd go on to hire yet more workers in a virtuous circle. One speaker, at the launch of the Manchester Anti-Corn Law Association, went further yet. Delighting that the Western visitor to the Holy Land now 'clambers up Mount Lebanon to find one of the ancient Druses clothed in garments with which our industrious countrymen provided him!', he went on to say that the spread of British manufactures would go so far as to produce peace on Earth: 'for be assured that while this country is diffusing blessings, she is creating an interest, she is erecting in the minds of those she serves an affection towards her, and that commerce is a communication of good and a dispensing of which were never enjoyed before.'[11] Thereby was planted an idea that would become a powerful belief in the power of the free market: that humanity could trade its way to a promised land of peace and abundance, and that attempts to rein in the market would only retard that progress.

In the three decades since the Corn Laws had taken effect, Britain had changed dramatically. The country was more industrialised, and more urban. As a result, fewer people could live off the land, depending instead on markets for their food; national security mattered less to them than reasonable prices. This concern intensified when a series of poor harvests across Europe threatened to reduce the grain supply, raising prices. But not only were there more industrialists and workers and fewer farmers in Britain, but many farmers had taken advantage of the young stock market to diversify their holdings beyond agriculture.[12] The old landowning class was declining, and less able to resist change. In 1846, Prime Minister Peel finally went over to the other side. Tabling a motion for repeal, he accepted the call of political economy. The motion passed, the Tories split and his government fell. Britain had just converted to the free-trade gospel.

The next quarter-century would transform Britain in ways that vindicated both the hopes and fears the Corn Law debate had raised. Cheap grain flooded the nation. Larger landowners with capital were sometimes able to reorientate their production towards new crops, but many smaller farmers couldn't adapt. Unable to sell what they produced, they lost their farms. Most ended up moving to the nearest town in the hopes of finding work, further swelling the rural exodus that Enclosure had begun. Over the next generation, the number of Britons living in cities or large towns would overtake those who lived in rural areas, a feat no other country would accomplish before the next century.[13] Often destitute landless workers filled the poorest neighbourhoods. Vast slums posed a challenge to city administrations, which had little in the way of planning or public services. With no proper water supply or sewage disposal, residents emptied their kitchen rubbish and chamber pots from windows, leaving it to the rain to do the rest. The streets were crowded, fetid and crawling with vermin, the air thick with the coal-smoke of the open fires on which everyone did their cooking. Those who were lucky enough to find jobs went to work in relatively unregulated industries. Their hours were long, their travails dangerous and the compensations for injuries none. Those less fortunate had to make do as pickpockets or thieves, or if they were women, as new recruits in the rapidly expanding army of prostitutes that filled Victorian cities. In a landmark 1857 study,[14] one writer estimated that one in twelve British women were working as prostitutes.

There was therefore no shortage of source material for a writer or poet who wanted to lament humanity's fallen state. Charles Dickens enjoyed huge success with his serialised novels depicting the daily battles and indignities of the urban working class, and the extreme contrast between them and the industrial owners who were thriving in this environment. Indeed, the abundance of unemployed workers that this migration fuelled kept wages low.

But that meant industrialists eager to expand their operations had plentiful cheap labour to hire. Moreover, the elimination of import tariffs on grain ensured an abundant supply of affordable bread.[15] For poor slum dwellers, this fall in their cost of living was an obvious boon. It also relieved pressure on factory owners to pay them better wages, since an employed worker felt an improvement in his or her living standard even without a wage rise. Happily for industrialists, too, the repeal of the Corn Laws coincided with a decision by the United States Congress to reduce tariffs on British manufactured goods. So, just as the Americans were opening up the West of the continent and planting more wheat, they were using their rising incomes to buy more goods from British factories.[16]

Back during the Corn Law debates, the leading Tory Benjamin Disraeli had ridiculed the predictions of the Manchester Liberals, and the political economy on which they had based their claims, saying they were deluded to think that Europe would 'suffer England to be the workshop for the world'. But in fact the continent, and the rest of the planet for that matter, did just that. With its vastly expanded transportation network, whose extent far exceeded those of its rivals,[17] Britain could ship cheaply and abundantly to foreign markets. Textiles from Manchester and Liverpool, brassware and guns from Birmingham, pottery from Stoke, steel, kitchenware and table settings from Sheffield, all were put on ships, themselves built in booming ports like Newcastle, then sent around the world. Over the next quarter-century, the country's industrial output doubled, and per capita income rose by nearly a half, a rate of increase that would have felt revolutionary to those who lived through it. Before 1700, it had taken about three centuries for Britain's per capita GDP to double. After 1700, it took about a century.[18] But in the middle of the nineteenth century, from the time you started your first job to

the time you retired and lived off your children, who often stepped
into the same job, your income would double.

To celebrate its triumph, in 1851 Britain staged the Great
Exhibition. Erecting an awe-inspiring pavilion out of steel and glass,
it filled this 'Crystal Palace' with samples of the products of its factories and workshops. A hundred thousand objects, spread over ten
miles of laneways, showcased such marvels as steam-hammers, a
printing press that could churn out 5,000 copies an hour of the then-
popular *Illustrated London News*, farm machines, folding pianos,
steam engines, textile looms and at the centre of the building, a
fountain made from four tons of glass. When Queen Victoria visited
the exhibition, she was moved to record in her journal:

> ... before we neared the Crystal Palace, the sun shone and
> gleamed upon the gigantic edifice, upon which the flags of every
> nation were flying ... The sight as we came to the centre where
> the steps and chair (on which I did not sit) was placed, facing the
> beautiful crystal fountain was magic and impressive. The tremen-
> dous cheering, the joy expressed in every face, the vastness of the
> building, with all its decoration and exhibits, the sound of the
> organ ... all this was indeed moving.[19]

If anyone wanted proof that the political economists had unlocked
the secrets of human productivity, this was surely it. Whereas the
Church had warned that the new doctrine would lead to the country's moral decay and economic ruin, instead Britain surged into
a position of global dominance. The country's merchant shipping
fleet raced to keep up with the demand for trade. Britain built better
ships faster than anyone else, and the advent of steamships, heavier
guns and iron hulls tipped the balance of military power away from
land to the sea, favouring Britain's rise.[20] Over the course of the
century, the country could plausibly lay claim to ruling the world's
waves, no other even approaching it for the scale of its force and
projection. This sense that they could go anywhere and do anything
fanned through society, prompting Britons to go out into the world.

Explorers penetrated deep into Africa (outside of a few coastal colonies the one continent not yet touched by European imperialism). Britain was restless for novelty and the country set about finding and retrieving exotic plants, animals and foods from every corner of the earth.

CHAPTER 5

FILLING THE PEWS

If you're like most Westerners, the odds are that you seldom set foot in a church, temple or mosque. The occasional baptism or funeral maybe, a wedding, but to actually go to church on a Sunday morning? In most European countries today, less than one in ten bother. The social functions churches once performed have been usurped. Need alms? Call the social worker. Need prayers for health or care for the sick? Go to a surgery. Want your children to read but can't afford tuition fees? Send them to state schools. Need spiritual guidance because you're worried about what will follow this life? Probably not: since 1800 we've doubled life-expectancy and beaten back innumerable illnesses, so death and disease no longer lurks among us as it once did for our ancestors. The truth is, most of us don't feel we need religion in our daily lives.

One popular explanation for religion's decline, which sociologists call the secularisation hypothesis, tells a tale of enlightenment that radiated out from the salons to wider society. Most of us who have moved beyond the religions of our ancestors embrace this narrative because, well, who doesn't like to be enlightened? And as it did for the original Enlightenment, empire played a central role in this drama.

In the nineteenth century overseas exploration opened European eyes to a wider world. New species and environments, different peoples and cultures, political and social practices wholly unlike anything they had experienced: all this made Europeans wonder if the basic truths they had always taken for granted were in fact so immutable. Some, unsettled by the threat to their ideas, reinforced their convictions. 'What should they know of England who only England know?' said Rudyard Kipling: you realised how great it was to be British only when you had encountered what it meant to not be British. The resulting sense of superiority diminished any guilt that Europeans might have felt at benefiting more from the empires than the people they encountered, satisfied that their greater wealth was owed to this superiority.

However, others left their homelands convinced of the rightness of the doctrines they had learned as children, but returned changed men, their foundations shaken. Charles Darwin, for instance, started his five-year voyage around the world believing that nature was God's design and arrived back in England filled with doubts. He and other scholars of his generation were absorbing the scientific discoveries that had emerged with exploration, such as the advances in geology revealing the earth to be much older than medieval cosmology had assumed, or evolutionary theories suggesting that humans were not created as the Bible said. Those who felt that the new science undermined the old faith withdrew into a defence of tradition at all costs. In a celebrated 1860 debate in Oxford, the Anglican Bishop Samuel Wilberforce ridiculed the self-described agnostic T. H. Huxley's defence of Darwin, asking him whether it was on his grandmother's or grandfather's side that he'd descended from an ape. Huxley retorted he'd sooner be related to an ape than to a highly intelligent man like Wilberforce, who used his rhetorical skills to obscure science.

Thereby did Huxley give history an early example of what we'd today call a sound bite. If he'd been living in our time, it would have become an Internet meme – practically the only thing remembered of the event, but which has entered popular lore as a turning point in our migration from religion to science. But in fact, the God-versus-science narrative appears to have been a later invention.

Wilberforce had actually taken Darwinism to task on scientific grounds that at the time remained contested, and which Darwin himself allowed were valid objections.[1] Moreover, a growing number of churchmen – some of them, like John Fiske, friends of Huxley's[2] – were already making a home for the science of evolution in their interpretations of the Bible. If anyone kept Wilberforce up at night, it was probably they more than Huxley who was responsible. No, what was really sending the Church into terminal decline wasn't so much scientific enlightenment: to this day, studies report that as little as a tenth of the population is 'scientifically literate' making it unlikely that scientific awareness played the dominant role in our drift away from the old faiths.[3] What drove religion's decline was the fact that most people felt less need for it in their daily lives.

The crowded, filthy, violent slums of Victorian Britain bred not just disease, but discontent. For some this took the form of crime and antisocial behaviour. New actors corralled some of this ferment and turned it to political ends. Social reformers with a conscience and radicals with an axe to grind started organising the working class in such a way that its anger and rebellion would not be dissipated in random acts on one another. Instead, just as a choked gun barrel compresses an explosion to increase its power, working-class anger was channelled into demands for voting rights, better wages, shorter working days, safer factories and clean streets. Political economy evolved to meet these demands, John Stuart Mill writing of the need for society to look after its members. This demand for change from below then dovetailed with an imperative from above – namely, the fact that the increasing technological sophistication of industry required literate, healthy workers. In the second half of the nineteenth century, governments, able to see that fitter workers meant better productivity, more growth and thus more taxes, got into the business of mass education and public health. Schools, previously the preserve of churches and charities, were built by the government and mandatory primary education became the norm. The increasingly filthy conditions of cities filled with rural migrants led to the construction of the first sewer systems, which greatly reduced the spread of diseases like typhoid and cholera (though the actual mechanics of how they did so weren't fully appreciated at the time). And governments began experimenting with some of the first forms of state welfare provision.[4] The combination of rising wages and lower prices enabled the public gradually to win access to a wider variety of goods. Meanwhile, improved agricultural productivity lowered food prices while the spread of the railways allowed produce to travel greater distances. British workers could afford to buy meat and milk, greatly improving their health and lengthening their lives.

As it watched its social functions taken over by the state, the old Church had less and less to do with the social transformations. In the first half of the century the Church of England built churches to reach all the new migrants who had left their village churches behind. Yet these chapels were often taken by pastors with the greatest interest in missionary work, the nonconformists whose politics tended towards the liberal and democratic, and who helped erode traditional hierarchy. By late in the century, as the nonconformists prospered, their politics became more conservative and their role in the lives of the working class was assumed by the new Labour Party. By then the schools were largely state-run, and the social functions these churches performed had diminished.[5]

The decline of the Church did not so much turn people towards science as to a new patron: the state. More specifically, loyalties were being transferred to the relatively new invention of the nation state, a merger of centralised political authority and a new identity, that of the nation. As cities grew and people migrated greater distances to work, their old loyalties to family, village and lord frayed, and they now had to look for basic services from those who would provide them: for security, the police; for education, the school; for better pay and work conditions, the union, health inspector and Member of Parliament (for whom, as the century progressed, more and more men could vote). With the nation state's agents increasingly present in the lives of citizens, their loyalties shifted away from the old religion.

People weren't necessarily less religious. If anything, their passionate commitment to their nation state, for which millions of them would later both kill and die, would provide them with a devotional icon so powerful it could lead to fanaticism. But the nation state was a wholly different god from that of the Bible. It was one that men themselves created and controlled.

But here was the funny thing: just as Christianity began declining in its heartland, in many of the colonies, notably those falling behind their mother countries, it was if anything growing more important. Enlightenment values may have reached no further than the verandahs of men like Thomas Thistlewood, but the Bible did. It was like two adjacent seesaws moving in opposite directions. On a seesaw of material abundance, the West was rising; in contrast, by the end of the nineteenth century, as imperialism widened to new places like Africa, a trend began to emerge in which the 'white dominions' – colonies where Europeans settled in large numbers – saw their incomes grow as fast as or even faster than the mother country, whereas the rest fell behind in relative and sometimes even absolute terms.

Meanwhile, on a parallel seesaw of religious practice, the exact opposite was happening. With the exception of the United States, where the 'Third Great Awakening' was underway, the religious revival of the 1800s had largely run its course by the end of the century. But in the colonies that were falling behind, a home-grown religious revival, which borrowed liberally from the missionaries, had begun. Black preachers in the West Indies, for instance, had got hold of the Bible, most often against the planter's wishes, and read their own history into that of the Jews' emancipation. In India, Hindu revivalists studied the theology of the missionaries and crafted an indigenous response to resist cultural assimilation.[6] The churches thus found new converts to replace the old. Over time, the passion of the new colonial converts often prompted a retreat back home: the marriage of black rebellion and Christian missionaries which had, early in the century, led to the abolition first of the slave trade then of slavery itself in the British Empire, gave way to an Anglican Church that would endorse repression of further colonial unrest.[7]

Besides, the material ambitions of empire could always find detours around any new moral restraints, like those imposed by emancipation. Freed slaves were left to fend for themselves as landless labourers, and it was the planters and not they who got compensation. Similarly, when Haiti's slaves rose up and overthrew French rule, their erstwhile masters returned with gunboats and extracted reparations for the dispossessed slave owners – a burden so onerous that it absorbed 15 per cent of the new country's national income over the next six decades, making Haiti as dependent as ever on its former mother country.[8] By then, new opportunities were beckoning elsewhere. Within a few years of emancipation, British warships were forcing China to open its ports to opium. By the 1830s, because Britain was importing ever-bigger volumes of tea, silk and porcelain from China, it was running a large trade-deficit since China, determinedly self-sufficient, wanted nothing in return. Rather than spend its own money, Britain wanted the Chinese to buy something back to even the accounts, and so the East India Company began pushing the sale of opium from its Indian colonies to China. When the Chinese government understandably tried to block its entry, Britain used its military superiority to force open the doors.

China's inability to withstand Britain militarily proved devastating to the Middle Kingdom. Its monarchy began a steady decline, which eventually, early the next century, led to its collapse, while its economy moved into a relentless slide that would continue, more or less unabated, for nearly two centuries.[9] A Second Opium War in the 1860s forced China to open its markets even wider to European imports, and the country's manufacturing sector was swamped by the cheaper goods of European factories (funny how times change). Back in 1700, Asia as a whole had accounted for two-thirds of the planet's economic output; two centuries later, it was a mere quarter. In the course of the nineteenth century alone, China's share of global industrial production dropped from 33 per cent to 6 per cent, India's from 20 per cent to 2 per cent.[10]

The decline of China, and Asia more generally, was part of a broader pattern of political decay in the major non-European centres of power. Using its military strength the West was able to colonise the world economy even when it didn't actually seize much land. India, fragmented among hundreds of different rulers, was finally taken from the East India Company and put under the direct control of the British government. The Ottoman Empire, which had once made Europeans quake, became a hollow shell of its former self. By the end of the century it was on its last legs, and the lands it once controlled across the Middle East and North Africa became fair game for European adventurers. And American gunboats forced Japan to open its ports to Western trade, bringing an end to Japanese isolation in much the same way the British had done in China.

What this meant back in the West was that politics no longer had to be a zero-sum game. As an increasingly militant working class demanded a better deal, its rulers were now in a position to act generously without having to dip into their own pockets. Colonial transfers could subsidise concessions made to the Western public. A similar dynamic played out in the United States and the British Empire's white dominions. When the swelling cities in the east of the United States churned with working-class ferment in the later 1800s, the government was able to release pressure through the valve of western settlement.[11] By force or negotiation, lands held by Native Americans were given to European settlers, and the challenge to 'go west young man' was taken up by generations of migrants. In effect, a good part of the bill for improving the well-being of Western populations was transferred to the people who had come under their dominance (the global equivalent of a pickpocket who buys drinks for the house).

Third World nationalist historians would in time contend that Europe's empires were little more than immense vacuum-cleaners sucking wealth from the colonies, and that it was this wealth transfer that enriched the West. We now know this oversimplifies what went on.

Although China did go into reverse, in many colonies incomes actually rose in absolute terms and new industries came into being.[12] In India, even as British textile imports were killing off older industries, early forms of subcontracting for British firms were getting started. This nuance matters more than radical historians allow, but less than liberal ones do: although imperialism didn't necessarily bring a vast sucking sound, where incomes did rise, they may have done so anyhow – and possibly done even better had the country not been colonised.

Disentangling cause and effect is difficult when studying the impact of the imperial countries and their colonies on one another, but it does seem safe to say that the two processes – of imperial rise and relative colonial decline – reinforced one another. Europe was able to impose itself on the rest of the world because it had begun a more rapid transformation of its economy and channelled the resources it thereby created into, among other things, superior navigational and military technology. Thus, while some of the rise in incomes in the West was due to what were in effect colonial subsidies, the increased incomes then translated into increased demand for industrial goods, which created a virtuous cycle. In the end, most of the investment and trade within Western capitalism was internally generated.[13] Nevertheless, to conclude that the West arose of its own speed is as misleading as saying that the West simply leeched off everyone else. Just because the spark and kindling for a fire come from your yard, it would still be a bigger fire when you add your neighbour's firewood.

As the second half of the nineteenth century wore on, the empires would become ever more central to Western interests. After taking India under its direct control, Britain began to leave behind its free-trading past to build a preferential trading system within its empire. Other European countries noted Britain's rise with concern, and began looking for their own colonies. Beyond that, though, Britain's rivals judged they would have to change the rules of the game if they were to catch up with the industrial powerhouse. What resulted were some novel forms of capitalism.

*

Think back to when you were a child. If you had an older brother or sister who liked to challenge you to races or some other such competition and you complained they had an unfair advantage, your parents may have resolved it in one of two ways. They might have said run the race, you'll lose, but accept it because running against bigger kids will one day make you the fastest child in school. Alternatively, if they were the kind of parents who thought repeated failure might make you give up trying altogether, they may well have told your sibling to give you a head start. If your parents preferred the first approach, they would have liked Adam Smith's classical political economy, or what was known by the late nineteenth century as the British School. If they preferred the second one, they would have gravitated towards just about any other of the schools of political economy that came into existence in the mid-nineteenth century.

In 1850, Britain dominated industry, accounting for nearly a fifth of global output.[14] Its manufacturing technology was years and in some cases decades ahead of its rivals. In the size of its factories, it had massive concentrations of capital. Nearly half of Britain lived in cities, providing its booming industries with an abundant supply of cheap labour. Barely a fifth of France lived in cities, Germany was less urbanised than that, and America was so rural it was still living Thomas Jefferson's dream of being a nation of farmers. New York could barely muster a fifth of London's population while Chicago, which had only just opened its first railway, was a glorified frontier-town of barely 30,000 hardy souls.[15] For every one of the prairie town's residents, London could turn out eighty.

Listening to present-day American conservatives, you'd think the United States had always been espousing an ultra-Smithian version of capitalism in which winner takes all and government is for losers. Surprisingly, it wasn't always that way. In the late eighteenth century, when Adam Smith's ideas were first gaining traction in England, Jefferson's vision of rural utopia competed with Alexander Hamilton's plan to build industry. Hamilton didn't think the market would develop America on its own. In a 1791 report to Congress, the young republic's first treasury secretary explicitly rejected Smith's call for a standoffish government, insisting that America needed a guiding hand, not an invisible one, if it was ever to catch up to its erstwhile master. Although Hamilton's ideas were not implemented in his lifetime, they would inform political debate through the next century. As an industrial economy began to emerge in the American north-east, leading businessmen increasingly called for protection against competition from British imports. They, however, found themselves staring down powerful southern planters, who then dominated both the economy and Congress. The planters wanted free access to the British market for their cotton, and the freedom to buy British manufactured goods. After all, for southern belles and gentlemen accustomed to the finer things in life, British goods were the finest on the planet.

Thus, northern industrialists struggled for decades to seize the American political agenda. But their calls for protection were unwavering and would make a strong impression on a visitor to America, Friedrich List. After a six-year sojourn during the 1820s, List abandoned his own earlier free-trade advocacy and returned home to a Germany which, while fragmented into some 400 different states – some no bigger than cities – was bubbling up with a movement for national integration.[16] As the physiocrats had done in the previous century for France, List advocated free trade within Germany but barriers against it outside. Instead, he called for the new country to use what he called industrial policy to build its own economy. In 1841 he published *The National System of Political Economy*, a book that would become the foundational scripture of many a non-Smithian economist, arguing that free trade would merely cement British dominance over everyone else.

Suggesting that the nation, not Smith's liberated individual, was the building block of society, List developed a comprehensive vision of state-led industrialisation. Individuals, he said, did not build societies; societies made individuals. Collectively, the nation had both a right and a duty to marshal its resources to develop itself. All nations, he said, would pass through the same stages of development, but some were further ahead than others. Therefore the appropriate policies to be adopted were those specific to that phase in which a nation found itself. While free trade was good for a country that had reached a higher level of industrialisation than Germany or America had in the early nineteenth century, it would allow more advanced countries to overwhelm those at an earlier stage of development. Accordingly, he advocated a period of state protection until the country caught up with Britain.[17]

Unfortunately for List, his ardent wish went unfulfilled in his own lifetime. In worsening health, suffering a series of financial setbacks, and finally in despair at having his vision largely rejected in his homeland, he took his life in 1846. Nevertheless, his ideas lived on and would, interestingly, work their way back across the ocean. For, during his American sojourn, List had befriended Matthew Carey, an Irish-nationalist refugee from British rule who wanted to free his adopted homeland from Britain's economic dominance.[18] Carey's son, Henry, took List's theory and developed it into what would become the American school of economics, which called for a Hamiltonian approach to building the country's industry.

Meanwhile, List's ideas would also later shape a distinctly German school of political economy. Retaining his focus on historical stages of evolution, the appropriately named Historical School (sometimes called the institutional school), explicitly repudiated the classical political economy of Smith and Ricardo. Generally suspicious that the pursuit of self-interest could ever be a good thing, its members argued that history rather than science was the best template for studying the economy. The Historical School maintained that economic development resulted not from a free market but rather from a strong state that unified a nation and gave its entrepreneurs space and guidance. It was therefore imperative that the government take the lead in industrialisation.

By an interesting path, the Historical School would then work its way back to America, where it reinforced the influence of Carey's American School. Germany's nineteenth-century educational reforms had, among other things, created the modern doctoral degree, leading other countries to eventually replicate it. In the late nineteenth century, Americans with academic ambitions would thus do an undergraduate degree at home, go to Germany for graduate studies, then return to create doctoral programmes of their own. Not only did they import the German approach to education, but they also brought much of the curriculum. As a result, German historicism loomed large over US campuses.[19] It, in turn, would finally find expression in American policy during and after the Civil War, when Henry Carey became President Lincoln's economic adviser. With the southern planters having seceded from the Union, and with the federal government anxious to raise funds for its war-machine, northern industrialists in Congress were now free to raise import taxes.

List's work didn't go unnoticed in Japan, either. After a US naval expedition sailed unmolested into the country's waters in 1854, the country had no choice but to open its ports to trade. As had happened in China when Western gunboats forced open its economy, the humiliation deprived Japan's government of much of its legitimacy. Ruled for centuries by shoguns, aristocratic generals who exercised power under the nominal authority of an emperor, Japan then erupted into turmoil as internal rifts tore the country's nobility apart. The last of the shogun rulers, the Tokugawa shogunate, fell in 1868, whereupon a revolution restored the emperor's dominance. A movement of modernisers then coalesced around him with a mission to put Japan on a level playing field with the West. Sending delegations abroad to study Western industry, importing teachers to instruct its citizens in the use and development of Western technology, the new government sought to withstand the West by mastering its game. They translated the works of Henry Carey and Friedrich List, and before long German economics had pushed aside classical political economy in most Japanese schools and virtually all state corridors.[20] Prevented by its treaties with the West from protecting its markets with import duties, Japan instead used tax revenues to fund the development of new industries in textiles and steel, and to build railways.

Japan's late-century shift to German economics would be mirrored in Russia, where a bureaucrat named Sergei Witte published
a paper in the 1880s titled 'National Savings and Friedrich List'. In
it, he called for Russia to adopt a similarly state-led programme of
industrialisation, focusing heavily on the construction of railways
and other infrastructure that would both facilitate economic activity and stoke demand for Russian industry. Subsequently becoming
finance minister, Witte put his plans into action, building railways
to new markets, limiting imports, attracting foreign investment
into industry, and taxing basic goods to raise revenue for industrial
subsidies.[21] As it happened, at the same time the French government was using a similar programme of railway construction and
industrial subsidies to spearhead the country's industrialisation,
sticking with its long tradition of industrial nurturing that went all
the way back to the *Ancien Régime*'s 'Colbertism'[22] (List, in fact,
had studied the works of French protectionists when developing
his own theory.[23])

Taken all together, these various national approaches to development provided the foundation of what would later be called the
infant industry model. That model would distinguish itself from
import substitution, which advocated essentially unlimited protection of local industries. Instead, exponents of industrial policy
recommended sheltering selected industries for a limited time while
they built themselves into export powerhouses. Those who followed
in the tradition of List didn't want their countries to quit the global
race. Like concerned parents, they just wanted to give them a bit of
a head start. Sold on political economy's promised land of material
wealth and industrial development, the new schools merely differed
on the path there, offering new routes to their followers – ethical
guidebooks that replaced the British School's individualism with a
collective path to the heavenly kingdom, with the aim of restoring
balance to their rivalry with Britain.

Although it remained true to its roots, even British political economy
was moving in a more statist direction. John Stuart Mill, the leading

political economist in mid-nineteenth-century Britain, swam in a current of liberal thought that was evolving away from its strictly individualistic roots towards a more utilitarian approach, justifying state interventions to bring about a greater good. Mill held that the laws of economics operated within institutional constraints – which presumably meant the institutions could be changed to alter the operation of the laws. Over time Mill migrated from a basic adherence to free-market principles to an acceptance, and even embrace, of socialism's possibilities. Nevertheless, throughout, he clung to the ethical goal he'd held since childhood, of creating a society in which the greatest number of individuals could realise the greatest possible gain.

That political economy should have aligned itself into national schools at this time is hardly surprising. Even if Britain led the way, most Western countries were growing rapidly by the late nineteenth century. The volume of trade rose, the distances that both goods and people moved lengthened, and the number of people leaving the farm for the town was increasing everywhere. Markets, which throughout the Middle Ages had been localised, with villages and towns serving as hubs for surrounding areas, now became increasingly national. Traders met in large cities and negotiated deals to move goods and investment across the country. Gradually, parochial identities waned as people identified less with their village of birth, and associated more in cities with people from across the surrounding region. Local dialects blended into regional ones as people adopted the lingua franca, typically the dialect of the dominant city. The advent of universal education late in the century accentuated this trend, as instruction in the national language was standardised. The state's schools used a common curriculum that inculcated loyalty to the nation and its leaders. So the decline of the Church did not leave people drifting. On the contrary, their new identity was if anything stronger than what they had left behind. Especially in places where their living standards were improving, people had every reason to feel a strong loyalty to the emergent community they now called home.

Having started out as worldly prophets advising their kings on how to augment the state's wealth, it was a natural evolution for political economists to now see their task as helping to fortify the evolving nations to which they belonged. Adam Smith had lived at a time when most people still operated largely outside the market economy, producing their own food and bartering with neighbours, while living in a realm of shared social norms. A century later, especially in Europe's booming cities, people were far more immersed in the capitalist economy, where the rules of the market increasingly governed their lives. Even if old habits would linger for generations, the decline of the Church meant that the foundation of their shared moral universe was weakening. Philosophers were starting to wrestle with the alternatives, and they weren't always pretty. The German Arthur Schopenhauer expressed misgivings about where liberation from ethical constraints might lead, suggesting that humans were governed by a malignant will, a thought that Friedrich Nietzsche would later push to a troubling conclusion: that a world without God would be one in which might was right and the powerful could do as they pleased (something which, admittedly, Nietzsche regarded with a certain glee). Mid-nineteenth-century political economists were polymaths, and very often, like Mill himself, philosophers in their own right. They spent a lot of time pondering the challenges that capitalism brought and saw it as their task to offer people a new moral foundation for their lives. It was a task that would soon, and suddenly, grow more difficult.

Despite the many divisions that separated national schools of economic thought, they were united in their belief that the middle decades of the nineteenth century vindicated their roles as moral guides. On average west Europeans were healthier, better fed, earned better wages and had more things to spend them on. British and French life expectancy rose from about forty at mid-century to forty-five in 1880,[24] while the average Westerner ate between 10 and 30 per cent more in 1880 than they had in 1850, the French and Americans already gobbling down an average of more than 3,000 calories a day.[25] The development of the railways, the shortening of the working day and the advent of holidays created a new industry in holidaymaking. Workers in Manchester and Liverpool could now get on trains on a Sunday and head to Blackpool, where they'd lounge by the seaside or make new friends (an experience that would be further improved with the invention of beer caps).

As other countries joined the race, incomes rose across much of the Western world. World trade would nearly triple in the period. The tonnage in British ships rose some five times over in the three decades after 1850.[26] Demand for steel and iron to build Europe's expanding railway network created employment for factory workers, which created demand for food, which raised incomes for farmers. Across the board, average per capita incomes rose, with the real per capita incomes in the United States leading the way and nearly doubling in the three decades after 1850.[27] The railway-building boom got a further swell when the American Civil War ended and the US government opened the West to European settlement. As the cavalry rushed ahead to evict Native Americans, railway companies followed, eventually laying over 6,000 miles of track a year.[28] Investors everywhere, foreseeing endless expansion, bought shares and bonds in railway companies. The optimism created a virtuous cycle as investors bid up share prices, which attracted yet further investors into the market, which made possible yet more construction. Entrepreneurs with dreams of creating their own businesses found ready supplies of capital from investors whose own wealth was expanding by the week. The telegraph lines running alongside the rails further transformed lives, as reports of new discoveries or inventions flashed around the world: a new mine discovery in Africa was the morning headline in New York. The political economists had said they could lead people to a promised land of the sort earlier generations had only dreamed could exist in an afterlife. Promise made, promise kept.

But then one Friday in May 1873, the telegraphs delivered alarming news. The Vienna stock exchange had crashed. Anxiety fanned through Western financial markets. In New York, investors comparing stories couldn't help but notice that Jay Cooke & Company,

one of the largest banks invested in the railway boom and the under-
writer of the Northern Pacific Railway, was having trouble selling its
bonds. Swapping *sotto voce* 'I didn't buy any did you?' tales in the
saloons around the exchange, nobody could find anyone who was
still buying the company's bonds. That raised the inevitable question:
'Who *is* buying them?' It soon emerged that the bank had been using
its own reserves to make up the resulting capital deficit, so much
so that it was almost fully invested in the one venture. Worse, the
railway wasn't yet generating enough revenue to pay its bondholders.
The news sent panic through the markets. The bank's clients raced
to withdraw their deposits before they got swallowed up. Soon, Jay
Cooke had a fully fledged run on its hands.

In the evening of 18 September, traders in London got news
that the company had closed the doors of its Manhattan office.
They heard that investors in New York were running about the
stock exchange trying to obtain as much cash as possible, and
that their rush to dump shares was driving prices down sharply.
When London's markets opened the next morning, the contagion
spread, moving onwards from there to the continent. As share prices
collapsed, railway companies couldn't get credit, so they laid off
workers to cut costs. Construction in the American West suddenly
stopped. Farm prices, anticipating the drop in demand, fell. Everyone
cut their spending to hoard their own cash and soon the economy
was in recession. It slowly dawned on everyone that the resulting
recession would stretch on for a while – for years, in fact, until it
would eventually come to be called the 'Long Depression'.

Like the promised god who doesn't materialise, the invisible hand,
in which classical political economy had placed its faith for a restoration of health to the economy, was nowhere to be seen. Meanwhile
tariffs, which had become more widespread as institutional and
historical schools of political economy spread their influence, might
have protected domestic industry from cheap imports, but could do
little to restore domestic demand. As if it were an omen of the dark
days ahead, the last of the men widely considered to be among the
founding fathers of classical political economy, John Stuart Mill,

had died the day before the Vienna market crashed. For his and all political economy's disciples, the Long Depression would test faith deeply. Many simply stopped believing its promises, and were lured by the siren calls of an entirely different prophet.

CHAPTER 6

HORSEMEN OF
THE APOCALYPSE

If you're like most people, you look for something outside yourself, something bigger and grander, to give your loyalty, even possibly your life, and which provides you with a sense of belonging and meaning. Your team, your school, your country, a cause, a religion – there is probably something that can get you misty-eyed, angry, depressed, or exhilarated, and which in moments of shared joy or sorrow makes you feel a common bond with complete strangers.

It's literally in our nature. We humans are social animals. Aside from the odd mountain man or desert recluse, we live in communities and have always done so. As Adam Smith observed in *The Wealth of Nations*, by doing so, we are able to produce and accomplish far more than if we lived solitary lives. Recognising how important community is, we seek to celebrate the things that tie us to others. Few things are more stressful than the feeling of being the only person in your group not to have got the invitation, and Internet trolls destroy lives by making their victims feel isolated and alone. Bullies of all ages thrive not on physical so much as emotional violence, singling out the different kid for the ridicule that ejects one from an in-group. From the earliest times, as recorded in ancient moral codes, exile from the community was considered a punishment almost as bad as a death sentence.

The philosopher Jean-Paul Sartre said hell was other people, but for most of us other people offer release from a life that would otherwise be nasty, brutish and short (as Thomas Hobbes said it would be for the solitary individual). As a species, with our well-being enhanced by others, we evolved emotional and cultural expressions of a desire to belong to a greater whole. In the modern period, these expressions yielded to ones with a more worldly basis, like nationalism or the ideologies that emerged in the Industrial Age. But even in these cases, the rational and material bases of these belief systems coexisted with a sense of spiritual belonging. Just watch the tears of people singing their national anthem when their team wins the trophy, or observe the passion of a human-rights lawyer condemning the violence done to someone in a far-off land, and you can see how strongly we can feel bonds even to people we may never meet.

Even if you have no religion, you probably have a pantheon of saints, prophets and martyrs who you admire and around whose teaching or example you organise your life. Whether it's trying to look like Kim Kardashian, live like Nelson Mandela or bend the ball like David Beckham, you are probably able to wax eloquent as you reflect on those idealised people. Some of us worship tribal gods, looking to our team or nation to provide us with hope and meaning. Some of us prefer universal gods, whether it be a one true god accessible to all humans or an ideal of solidarity that will unite people around the world in a common cause.

Humans worshipped gods for thousands of years before the idea began to emerge that all of them might share the same one. The evolution of economic thought in the nineteenth century reflected a similar sort of transition from the particular to the universal. On the whole, the political economists of the early nineteenth century generally aligned with the emergent nation states they served as advisers. That was the case even for the classical political economy of Adam Smith and his disciples which, despite its claims to universality, was seen by most political economists outside Britain as a veiled way for the UK to solidify its early industrial advantage over its rivals. That's why it was most commonly known as the British School. However, around mid-century, some new doctrines began to emerge. Claiming to offer a message common for all humankind, they aimed to fulfil Smith's mission, albeit in different ways.

One of them found its roots in the messianic figure of Napoleon Bonaparte. Early in the century, after overthrowing the French government, Napoleon launched a series of foreign military campaigns, overwhelming his opponents with his battlefield genius. Sweeping aside traditional dynasties and giving the world a new legal code, he appeared to many observers as the embodiment of a sort of divine emissary, sent by some greater force – God, fate, history – to remake a decadent Europe. In 1804 Ludwig van Beethoven was inspired to dedicate his *Eroica* symphony to Napoleon, portraying him as a heroic figure who would alter the course of history. Although the composer would later recoil at Napoleon's subsequent decision to crown himself emperor, the theme of the hero would continue to shape much of the Romantic canon of the decades following. Looking beyond the Enlightenment idea that reason and science would enable humans to better comprehend and shape reality, the Romantics restored the idea that great individuals, as if sent from heaven, would appear on Earth to shape its destiny.

In 1806, a struggling academic in the German university town of Jena was finishing his book on philosophy, *The Phenomenology of Spirit*, when Napoleon marched into the city. Georg Hegel, who in a short earlier work had conceived sin as the separation of the individual from the universal, recorded his thoughts on the occasion in a letter he wrote to a friend: 'I saw the Emperor – this world-soul – riding out of the city on reconnaissance. It is indeed a wonderful sensation to see such an individual, who, concentrated here at a single point, astride a horse, reaches out over the world and masters it ... this extraordinary man, whom it is impossible not to admire.'[1]

Moved by the occasion, Hegel would conclude that he was witnessing the unfolding of a spirit driving history forward. Like an expectant millenarian, he saw in the epochal changes Napoleon was bringing to Europe the approach of history's end point.

There is an old joke that a German dilemma on reaching heaven is to find two doors, one marked 'Eternal Bliss' and the other marked 'Lecture on Eternal Bliss'. Anyone who has read Hegel can only form a deep respect for the capacity of German university students to wade through heavy tomes of demanding theory expressed in prose that is the literary equivalent to juggling half a dozen balls. But in his day, Hegel was as close to being a celebrity scholar as one could be in the age before mass media and the Internet.

He came from a tradition that responded in an entirely different way to the phenomena that had preoccupied the physiocrats and classical political economists. Whereas they had set out to study the world as it was, the idealist tradition Hegel belonged to might have replied 'it's all in the mind': all in the mind in that, to Hegel and his ilk, it was difficult if not impossible to separate the world as it was from our conception of how it was. Moreover, when it came to deciding whether our environment shaped our thinking or our thinking the environment, the idealist philosophers gave the nod to the latter. Ideas, they said, shaped reality; or as Hegel put it, spirit shaped matter.

The world of early capitalism seemed to be riven with contradictions – between ancient traditions and modern practices, between individual freedom and social order, between the emerging cities and the countryside, between industry and farming, between the spirituality of the medieval legacy and the materialism of a world where there was suddenly a lot more stuff. Some, like the Romantics, seemingly overwhelmed by the tensions that resulted, retreated from the world of reason and back into the world of the spirit. Rejecting the materialism that shaped political economy, they dethroned science and refused to believe that humans could be reduced to their material drives. In place of logical argument, they trusted in the insights of inspired genius and the truths revealed by intense emotions. Refusing to celebrate the new, they abandoned the growing industrial cities and composed odes to ruined abbeys or painted dramatic tableaux of gothic foreboding, often with the aim of recapturing what they felt was the ineffable beauty of the medieval era. And above all, they celebrated the inspired genius of the hero, that individual who changed history.

Hegel saw something profoundly spiritual in Napoleon's conquering of much of the continent, as if it revealed a transcendent plan. However, his restoration of the spirit to the centre of human existence would eschew Romanticism. He saw the spiritual realm shaping the physical world in such a way as to drive the latter towards ever-higher levels of development. To him, there was not an impossible tension that required one to fall on one side of the material–spiritual divide or the other. At the heart of each, he said, lay a progressive force, a sort of narrative thread bringing humanity's spiritual and material sides into ever-closer harmony.

When you think of it, this idea that conflict and contradiction drive history forward, bringing it to a final resolution, is one we all get. Consider your favourite novel or movie. Running through it will be some sort of conflict – between the hero and villain, between competing urges within a hero, between lovers. Always driving the story forward, though, is some kind of struggle that finds its resolution in the climax, when the star sweeps up the co-star and they finally make peace and love all at once.

Hegel maintained that the contradictions running through history revealed a similar sort of plot. Driving it forward was what Hegel called a spirit. He said that humans differed from animals in that we lived not only in reality but in ideality. To animals, instinctual desires and their satisfaction were one and the same, but to us, the knowledge of an ideal world acts as a control on our impulses. The spirit which inhabited this ideal world was an independent force that impelled humans to advance closer and closer to its realm. 'The spirit is free,' he wrote, 'and the aim of the world spirit in world history is to realise its essence.'[2]

It did this through something of a process of trial, error and re-trial. It provoked a conflict between a thesis, which one could liken to the dominant idea of the age, and an antithesis, which opposed it. Like a prizefighter who spars with partners so as to perfect his technique, the dialectical struggle between a thesis and an antithesis would eventually yield a synthesis of the two, retaining the best aspects of both. This new synthesis then became the new thesis, and the cycle resumed. However, to Hegel, this was not an endless cycle, of the sort contained in some Eastern philosophies and in which some of his contemporaries were then dabbling. Instead, conflict in the realm of ideas was leading humanity to higher and higher states of existence as history worked its way towards its end point. Hegel saw the nation state, then emerging as the dominant model of political organisation across the West, as a culmination of this process – and he held that the Prussian state had reached the highest state of evolution ever attained.

In 1818, Hegel moved to the University of Berlin, where he would stay until the end of his career. Attracting an enthusiastic following of students, he would spawn new schools of thought. Some of his followers stuck quite closely to his thought but others, notably a group of radical intellectuals called the Young Hegelians, took issue with their mentor's political conservatism and regard for religion. Nevertheless, by and large Hegel's intellectual offspring stayed within the tradition of German idealism that had shaped his thought, maintaining that those dramatic changes occurring in the modern world were being driven by the spirit at the heart of the human story. So, given this idealism, most political economists, who tended to be practical men concerned with matters of this world and who took relatively little interest in questions of ultimate truth, did not pay much attention to Hegel. But that would change when, five years after Hegel's death, a young Romantic transferred to the University of Berlin.

Karl Marx, whose academic career had until then been less than stellar, had been sent by his family to Berlin precisely in the hope the university would whip him into shape. But soon after arriving, he fell in with the Young Hegelians, and his life would never be the same. During those years, and in his subsequent work as a journalist, Marx would follow a pattern of evolution not unlike Adam Smith's in the previous century: moving gradually from the study of ideas and morals to an interest in the world of production. Starting with Hegel's dialectical method, he reversed the order between spirit and matter. In place of Hegel's idealism, he offered dialectical materialism. He argued that the conflict at the heart of human existence, driving history towards its final destination, was the conflict between social classes. In any class-divided society, which is to say almost every society, Marx said there would be a contradiction between the dominant and subordinate classes that revolved around each one's relations to the means of production, and which would drive them towards an unavoidable conflict. The class that controlled the means of production, which in capitalism was the bourgeoisie, was the thesis; its antithesis lay in the labouring class, which in capitalism Marx said controlled nothing but its labour-power, being employed by the capitalist and paid a wage. The surplus that resulted when the goods were sold on the market went to the owner. Marx thus concluded the workers did not get the full value of their labour.

He defined this extraction and appropriation of surplus by the owner as exploitation, saying it created an inescapable clash of interests. No matter how enlightened they tried to become, capitalists would always have different objective interests from their workers. Marx therefore concluded that only a revolution, which resolved the contradiction by eliminating social classes altogether, could bring an end to this tension. So he agreed with Hegel that history was progressing towards an eventual end point. But as he moved ever further into Europe's emerging revolutionary movement, he came to disagree about what that end point would be. For him, unlike for Hegel, it certainly wasn't the Prussian nation state.

After Marx left Berlin, a young Bavarian named Friedrich Engels also came into contact with the Young Hegelians. Engels was the scion of a prosperous factory-owning family, who had grown anxious that his rebellious spirit would only mean trouble and so decided to send him to manage one of their mills in Manchester. However, their hopes that he might come to his senses and settle into a quiet bourgeois life were derailed as soon as he reached the booming city. Befriending a radical young woman from a poor Irish family who served as his guide, he began touring the city's worst slums and compiling copious notes on the conditions of the working class. During one of his trips back to Germany to see his family, Engels stopped in Paris. Marx, whose radicalism had by then drawn unwanted attention from the Prussian authorities, had gone there to work as a journalist, arriving in 1843 with his wife. The two men, who had met once before briefly, got together at one of Marx's neighbourhood cafes, and ended up spending the next ten days together. So began one of history's most momentous friendships.[3]

Engels would still do a fine job of managing his family's factories. But how he spent his evenings, and his earnings, would be his own business.

In the mid-nineteenth century, although Britain was able to use the fruits of its empire and the profits from overseas trade to buy off its restive working class, that luxury didn't yet exist in many other European countries. Without large surpluses in their external accounts, or the abundant land that America would use to mollify angry workers in its eastern cities, governments were forced to ignore the calls for better conditions. The demands of rising protest movements varied from place to place, but the language of liberalism and the rising radicalism of men like Marx and Engels provided much of the rhetoric. Protest movements coalesced to resist autocracies rooted in the dynastic principle – the idea that a family was appointed by God to rule over a country – insisting instead that political authority came from the people. Unable or unwilling to meet these demands, governments responded by suppressing protest, repeatedly harassing intellectuals like Marx or hounding them into exile. Pressure built up further, and sooner or later the pot of rebellion was bound to explode.

That finally happened in 1848. Just as Britain was entering its

long phase of economic growth, unrest erupted across much of continental Europe. Marx and Engels had been working to refine their
theories of revolution for years, expunging them of their idealist
elements to give them a material focus. In 1845, Marx had finally
declared his complete break with idealism and wrote 'philosophers
have only interpreted the world in various ways, the point is to
change it.' So amid the increasingly febrile atmosphere of the months
leading up to the 1848 revolutions, he and Engels sat down to write
what they hoped would become the manifesto of the imminent uprising. Although it was drafted in haste, and would later be dwarfed
in scale by their studies of the capitalist economy, *The Communist
Manifesto* would eventually become their best-known work. Early
drafts were written as a 'confession of faith',[4] but they decided in
revision to abandon the creation of a catechism to instead write a
historical essay that distilled the vast sweep of human history into
a simple, elegant model of change. The *Manifesto* used Marx's dialectical materialism to explain why history was inevitably advancing
towards an end point of world communism.

The two men presented history as a sort of Jacob's ladder on
which humanity, through a series of conflicts and overthrows, climbed
to ever-higher planes of existence. History began with primitive
communism, humanity's earliest years as hunter-gatherers, which
they said were more or less class-free. With the advent of agriculture,
however, societies began to polarise into dominant and subordinate
classes, with slaves being put to work on the land and states emerging to control them. Thus came the second stage of history – slavery.
The need to acquire slaves then prompted the state to expand into
neighbouring territories, creating empires which eventually got so
big they collapsed under their own weight. As they broke up, the
aristocracy that had administered them carved the territory into
autonomous fiefdoms, in which semi-free peasants were bonded
to lords in ties of reciprocal obligation – the third stage of history,
or feudalism. The rise of trade then led to the formation of a nascent bourgeoisie, which immediately came into conflict with the
aristocracy, since among other things the capitalists wanted to

free the serfs from their bonds of dependence so that they could work in their firms. That brought on the liberal revolution, and the penultimate phase of history, capitalism. Capitalists now owned the means of production, and workers nothing but their own labour, which they had to sell to the capitalist in order to live. At that point, the capitalist push to increase profits by squeezing wages created a conflict in which workers ultimately rose up to overthrow the capitalists.

Some German philosophers were then reviving the ancient notion that history consisted of an unending series of such cycles.[5] However, Marx followed Hegel in retaining the Christian tradition's vision of history as a relentless advance towards an eventual end point. The cycle was not eternal. Instead, he and Engels reasoned that communism would end the cycle. Unlike the outcome of previous revolutions, where the victors could take their share of the spoils and go home, workers were bound to one another. Even if you had wanted to, you couldn't just take your part of the assembly line and set yourself up on your own estate, as nobles and capitalists had been able to do after their respective revolutions. The only solution was to create a system of collective ownership. And since this meant there would no longer be a dominant and subordinate class, it meant society would return to a classless state – albeit at a much higher level of development than had been the case in primitive communism. But it also meant that since class contradiction no longer existed, the motive force of history would be gone. History would have then reached its end point. The state, no longer needed to keep a subordinate class down, would just wither away. And rather than enriching a few, the profits of industry would be divided among everyone. In the resulting prosperity, humans would no longer need to devote their lives to chasing money. They could do more activities: hunt in the morning, fish in the afternoon and talk philosophy in the evening.

The classical political economists had offered the world a vision of a harmonious society in which self-interested individuals, looking to advance their own well-being, would inadvertently produce benefits for all. Marx rejected this, insisting that in a class-divided society, the pursuit of self-interest by the dominant class would inevitably lead to misery for everyone else. But while he rejected the moral order of the Smithian universe, his was not a voice calling for a restoration of the old Christian morality. Far from it; Marx repudiated religion as an 'opiate' in which the oppressed found relief from their suffering – but not an end to their suffering, more like a pressure-release valve, and one which the working class had therefore to throw off before it could open its eyes fully to the reality of its oppression.

The old theology had said man's fallen state would be reversed in another life. Smith said a better world could be created in this life. Marx agreed, but he said it wouldn't come in the individual pursuit of self-interest. It would come in a secular apocalypse that washed humanity clean of the original sin that had burdened it for millennia: social class.

Cycles of repression, revolt and reaction occur throughout history. As Crane Brinton argued in his seminal *The Anatomy of Revolution*, they often follow a similar plot. Most recently, in a contagion reminiscent of 1848, the year 2011 saw revolts break out across the Arab world. It all started when an impoverished Tunisian fruit vendor, desperate after his handcart, which was his only means of making a living, was confiscated by the police for being unlicensed, set himself on fire outside his town's municipal offices. A small protest erupted and when the police responded in their usual manner, beating everyone up, the resulting outrage fanned demonstrations across the country. Within weeks the dictator fled and Arabs in neighbouring countries, following events eagerly on social media, took to their own streets. Within months, much of the Arab world was in open revolt.

But the wild enthusiasm of Tunisia soon ran aground, as it did back in 1848. Some governments collapsed, plunging their countries into civil war. Others shored up their defences and crushed the uprisings. And those that did so successfully seemed to have studied the history of 1848.

In 1848, after a period in which the spectre of revolt appeared to have rulers running scared, they fought back. Within months, the forces of order had moved in. Putting down the protests and locking up their leaders, Prussia's rulers told Marx never to return. The new French government allowed Marx to stay in France but, under pressure from the Prussians, told him he could do so only if he went to a marshy district of Brittany, where they reckoned he could do no harm.[6] Not exactly enticed to stay, Marx opted instead to move his young family to London, living in Camberwell until, in 1850, his landlord evicted him for non-payment of rent. Not for the first or last time, Engels came to his rescue, giving him a loan with which he was able to obtain a small, cramped, two-room flat above a shop in Soho.[7] Never the most touristy part of London, then it was an overcrowded place with no public sewage and a filthy water supply. It wasn't long after Marx moved in that a cholera outbreak sent panic through the quarter.

He managed to pick up a bit of work as a journalist, but it was not enough to live on. Engels's business was doing sufficiently well that he could sometimes offer his friend help with his expenses. But even then, Marx was indigent, begging for credit from local shopkeepers and sometimes hiding when landlords or bill-collectors knocked at his door. A man seemingly beset with as many contradictions as the societies he studied – a radical firebrand who dressed and behaved like a bourgeois scholar, a devoted husband who gave his housekeeper a child, a lover of bawdy humour who however reverted to a 'protective chivalry' in mixed company; one friend noting that 'in the presence of children and women his language was so gentle and refined that even an English governess could have no cause for complaint'[8] – whenever Marx came into a little money he would put on generous dinners for his friends. However, his irascible personality often drove them to keep their friendship at arm's length. He gradually grew distant from his relatives back in Germany, who looked askance at his repeated requests for financial assistance and his deepening involvement in radical politics. One sister, visiting him in London, reminded him that he was the son of a respectable Trier lawyer, and should act accordingly.[9] The constant poverty and poor conditions he lived in with his family brought them hardship and tragedy, with only three of his seven children making it out of childhood. Constantly on the brink of starvation, frequently depressed, withdrawn from political activity after he saw his beloved revolution crushed, he wrote despairingly to a friend in 1852, 'my wife is ill, little Jenny is ill, Lenchen has a sort of nervous fever. I could not and cannot call the doctor as I have no money for medicine. For 8–10 days I have fed the family on bread and potatoes and it is still questionable whether I can get any together today.'[10]

Yet even in his darkest period, like an early Christian dismayed Christ hadn't kept his promise to return but who still believed that he would nonetheless do so one day, Marx kept his faith and soldiered on. He decided that if he was to predict when and how capitalism would fall, if he was to be able to identify the signs announcing that the end was nigh, he needed to understand its inner workings better. So he began spending his days in the Reading Room of the recently opened British Museum, scribbling down notes at the wooden desks under the glass-domed roof which lit the hall. In the evenings, he would return to his flat and, under gas light, work well into the night trying to organise the thick files of papers accumulating on the table in the flat's small reception room. With a monastic dedication he burrowed deep into the heart of capitalism. For a man known primarily as an apostle of communism, he ended up spending little time in speculating what a future workers' paradise might look like. Saying that it wasn't his job to write 'recipes for the cookshops of the future'[11] he left the shape of a future communist society to be determined by the dynamic creativity of a proletariat in revolt. Instead, he confined his attention to the present, approaching the study of capitalism with forensic patience and looking everywhere for clues of the presence of the demiurge of class struggle he took to be the ghost in its machine, driving it relentlessly to its doom.

Over time Marx began to detect some recurrent features. He

noticed that as an industry developed, competition whittled down the number of firms, leaving capital and profits concentrated in fewer hands. However, the rising volume of profits obscured the fact that the rate of profit, which is to say the ratio of profits to the firm's revenues, was steadily declining. In other words, firms made more profits as they got bigger; but they had to get bigger or their profits would actually fall. So they got bigger. By adding ever-more machinery and building larger factories to house them, owners made their workers more productive, and so lowered the prices on the goods they sold. Along the way, they killed off their competitors and gobbled up their clients. Employment and wages rose within the firm, which made it look the model of health. But in the sector as a whole, unemployment would rise and firms go out of business.

Marx tied it all together into a theory of what he called the shift in the organic composition of capital.[12] Capitalists were in competition with one another and depended entirely on the market for their well-being. Unlike the feudal nobility, they didn't govern estates which, in a pinch, could provide all their household needs. That meant they had no choice but to keep undercutting their competitors on price. This meant they constantly had to find ways to reduce costs, which in turn required them to always add new technology to increase their workers' productivity. That, to Marx, was the genius of capitalism, something for which he both despised and admired it. Insisting it would one day collapse, he nonetheless considered capitalism so advanced that imperialism by necessity had to be progressive, since it hastened the spread of capitalism across the globe.[13] Gone for good was his youthful Romanticism. He now dismissed as utopians those who longed for a pre-industrial arcadia, saying it wasn't dreams of a better future that would bring about a revolution, but the material imperatives of the present day.[14]

Nevertheless, for all its virtues, Marx believed capitalism had one critical vice so intrinsic to its character it could never be expunged or reformed: its class contradiction. As a result, while the genius of capitalism benefited the few lucky workers who held on to their jobs, it would harm the working class as a whole. The proletariat, left to the cold mercy of the market, would sink deeper into misery. Capitalism was prone to recurrent crises, and as their succeeding intensity grew, so too would working-class anger. The relentless downward pressure on profit-rates would force owners to intensify work ever more, enriching a few but immiserating the many. Unable to resolve its internal contradictions, namely the class conflict which drove the plot forward by forcing capital to concentrate into fewer hands, capitalism would slowly dig its own grave. Eventually, most of the proletariat would be idle, and angry. Capitalism would then begin to look something like an inverted pyramid, with a huge concentration of capital resting on a proletarian base. It wouldn't take much to knock it over.

Marx, one must note, put labour at the base of all production. In so doing he adopted an insight from David Ricardo that would become central to his theory. Ricardo, in turn, had been trying to solve a conundrum raised by Adam Smith, but left unanswered. Smith had understood that the achievement of capitalism was to make workers more productive, and he saw capital playing a role in this. But just how much of the increase in productivity was due to labour, and how much to capital had not been clear to him. David Ricardo took the position that labour was the sole determinant of the value of a given unit of output, and that the more labour it took to produce something the more expensive it became.

Marx made this theory, about which economists differed, a cornerstone of his doctrine. To him capitalism without a working class was inconceivable. As the economy generated mass unemployment it would undermine its own basis. For its part, the working class would rise up not because it had been converted to a new gospel but because their conditions of existence made them liable to do so. A new vision wouldn't make them drive capitalism to its climax, capitalism's climax would give them a new vision. Only then would the recipes of the future get written. The workers were actors in a drama, but they were performing a plot that no individual could write or change.

*

There's a haunting 2004 German film called *Downfall*, which chronicles the final week in Hitler's bunker in April 1945. Amid political, social and physical collapse as Soviet troops encircle Berlin, scenes unfold showing the sort of desperation that breaks out any time people confront an existential threat that looks likely to overwhelm them. A few, perched on some kind of higher ground, see a way out and begin planning their escapes. Some resort to extreme fatalism, accept there is no hope and turn to tell the person they've always fancied but never dared to approach what they've always wanted to do. Others disappear behind a veil of denial and begin drinking and celebrating, aware that it's all over. And some, unable to accept the horrible fate that awaits them, cling to desperate hopes that some external force – in Hitler's case, an imagined German army column – would emerge from nowhere to rescue them.

Today, we look at Hitler's vain hope with disdain, just as we chuckle at people who walk around with signs that say 'the end is nigh'. But when the alternative is passive acceptance of a horrific fate, such millenarianism may not be all that irrational. At least it enables you to soldier on. In *The Pursuit of the Millennium*, the historian Norman Cohn looked at medieval millenarian movements for the common threads running through the eruptions of chiliastic fervour that occurred throughout the High Middle Ages. At times of mass disorder and anxiety – say, during a plague outbreak or famine – popular and often violent movements would rise up in the belief that the world would soon be purged by a returned messiah. Cohn found a number of features common to these movements. They were all collective, in that a community and not an individual would find salvation. The end was seen to be imminent. The millennium was terrestrial, with the rapture happening here and now rather than in an afterlife. And the final conflict was total, in that it would completely remake society and history.

With the innovation that revolution would be brought about by a demiurge internal to capitalism and not by a god descended to Earth, Marx's view of the future course of history remains squarely in that tradition. He joined that vast camp of end-times prophets that history has managed to outlast. Marx, who by now had cultivated his famously hirsute appearance without which, he once joked, 'no prophet can succeed',[15] seemed comfortable in his role as scholarly sage. But while we today might snicker at his misplaced faith in an imminent revolution, in the context of his time it wasn't so unlikely. Given how immersed Marx and Engels were in the struggles of the working class, Marx living in the poverty and disease that made him acutely aware of the inner-city's abysmal conditions, the persistent claim that capitalism just needed a bit more time to sort out its problems must have looked equally if not more irrational. Not surprisingly, Marx's doctrine would later receive a warm reception in the colonies, which would end up picking up a good part of the tab of the English working class's improved conditions. Besides, subsequent history would appear to repeatedly vindicate Marx's belief that capitalism was prone to boom-and-bust cycles.

An early omen of a coming apocalypse came in 1857, when a banking crisis in New York spread quickly to London. Though its impact proved brief, it revealed how capitalism was now developing on a global scale. With American railway stocks and bonds having become popular investments on European exchanges, contagion leapt across the ocean much faster than a steamer could move cargo. Having already concluded that the revolution to overthrow capitalism would have to be 'world-historical', which is to say that it would break out once capitalism had spread its tentacles right across the globe, Marx felt energised by the apparent onset of crisis, and redoubled his work in the British Museum. Finally, in 1867, after more than twenty years of research and constant revision, and assisted in the final push by Engels, he put out the first and most famous of what would be his three-volume work, *Capital*.[16] As soon as he corrected the final proofs in August, he wrote to Engels and said, 'It is you alone that I have to thank for making this possible! Without your sacrifice for me it would have been impossible to complete the enormous labour.'[17]

Capital captured the zeitgeist of a time of flux and uncertainty. Marx's prediction that the proletariat would sink into misery was already finding apparent confirmation. When the Long Depression hit in 1873, employers did what employers do whenever demand for their goods drops: they laid off workers. As workers lost their jobs, they had less money to spend, and so demand dropped even further. On both sides of the Atlantic, rising joblessness bred anger. In America, relief rolls in the cities exploded and the unemployment rate in New York shot up to 25 per cent. There were riots and demonstrations there, and in Boston and Chicago as well. In the Pennsylvania coalfields, a secret labour group called the Molly Maguires launched an armed assault on a private security force working for the state. In distant Russia and Ukraine, pogroms were targeting the Jewish community, who were scapegoated as the culprits behind the malaise.[18]

By now, governments had begun turning against the free-trade church. The United States had taken the lead when, after the Panic of 1857, the ideas of Henry Carey began to gain widespread circulation. When the southern states seceded from the Union to precipitate the Civil War, the bulwark against protectionism they had maintained in the Senate collapsed, and a tariff bill finally passed. Tariffs were raised two more times in the 1860s, helping to fund the war, in the process creating a protectionist American trade regime that would last for the next half century. British sentiment was predictably outraged at these steps, with one prominent political economist decrying the measure as 'the most retrograde piece of legislation that this century has witnessed'[19] – quite something in a century that also gave the world laws declaring American blacks subhuman or banning Jews from public office in European countries.

In 1864, Marx attended a meeting of a hodgepodge of various European radicals at St Martin's Hall in London and volunteered to help draft the constitution of an organisation that would unite communist activists across national boundaries. Soon after, meeting in Marx's flat, the organisation formed itself into the International Workingmen's Association, eventually coming to be known as the First International. Marx once again found himself in the throes of exhilarating times, combining thought and action as he had always longed to do. *Capital* provided the rationale and the International the means to smash capitalism and the classical political economy that ordered it.

But he, and his intellectual heirs, would soon find that not everyone was done with the doctrine of Adam Smith just yet.

CHAPTER 7

THE NEOCLASSICAL SCHISM

What do you believe? And why do you believe it?

The first question is easy enough for us to answer, but the second takes time. Karl Marx spent quite a lot of time on it, and he developed an interesting theory about belief. Among other things – he held that for the working class to become sufficiently radicalised to rise up in revolution, it had to shake off beliefs that bred inertia – like Christian patience and forbearance. His description of religion as the opiate of the masses is among his best-known phrases. Yet it is often misunderstood to mean that Marx was saying religion was something that had been deliberately crafted to brainwash the working class, like the narcotic soma fed to people in Aldous Huxley's novel *Brave New World* to keep them submissive. But Marx's view was a bit more nuanced than that.[1] To him, religion became an opiate in the way the oppressed consumed it. It served an immediate need, which was to provide them with consolation and a possible explanation for their suffering. Rather than being passive agents in their socialisation, therefore, believers were active if subordinate participants.

The history of religion is filled with this kind of give-and-take. Consider the evolution of early Christianity. Like any successful organism, it adapted to its environment. It began as a Jewish sect in Palestine, but expanded quickly in the Roman Empire by picking up ideas and practices common there, such as clerical robes modelled on the Roman nobility's vestments or ideas of physics derived from Greek philosophy. Christianity then altered itself further when it expanded north into Europe and moulded itself to suit the cultures of the forest tribes: turning local deities into saints, retaining a belief in the magical power of objects (the cult of relics), or adopting pagan festivals and rewriting them with Christian themes, as happened with Christmas. As one historian of Christianity put it, the Church, sometimes happily and sometimes reluctantly (to judge from the many theological controversies running through its history) picked up local practices, traditions and beliefs everywhere it went and Christianised them by sprinkling them with a little holy water.[2]

Hence, when using the bottom-up approach of social history to look at such things as the medieval witch hunts and millenarian preachers documented in Norman Cohn's *The Pursuit of the Millennium*, new features come to light. When observed from a distance, they are easily written off as the means by which the Church asserted its control, destroying anyone who brought its ideology into question. However, closer examination of such phenomena often reveals a more complicated picture in which Church authorities were racing to catch up with movements started on the ground, often by populist preachers. The record of contemporary witch-hunting in Africa for instance often confirms a picture in which self-appointed crusaders – what one might call religious entrepreneurs – tap into public anxiety, eliciting considerable unease in the Church hierarchy. It may be, therefore, that the tenacity of Christianity, Islam and other long-standing religions owes at least as much to their effective co-option of people's needs as to effective brainwashing. A successful product, after all, depends not just on clever advertising but on good market research.

When you ponder some of the more outlandish or miraculous claims religious doctrines make for themselves, it's easy to conclude that atheism, or agnosticism, is the only thing a rational mind can believe in. But consider the success of atheism itself. It's probably no accident that for the most part it's a significant phenomenon only in developed societies. We like to think this is due to the superior scientific and rational education of Western societies. But research on scientific literacy finds it to be relatively rare. For instance, a 1989 survey discovered that nearly 50 per cent of Britons thought that humans and dinosaurs had coexisted, apparently taking their palaeontology lessons from *The Flintstones*, while a third of Britons and Americans thought radioactive milk could be rendered safe with boiling.[3] However, if you ever query self-professed atheists on their reasons for non-belief, you'll find that few of them have actually given much thought to their convictions – often, little more than believers have done to theirs.

They don't have to. When you have grown up in a society where death will probably be a remote possibility until well on in your life, where you will never worry about starvation, where illness is cured with a visit to a doctor or hospital, and where nature will not destroy you, you are freed from the kinds of worry that have been the constant companion of humans throughout history. When, in contrast, you're sitting in a squalid refugee camp, watching helplessly as a hurricane washes your few personal possessions out to sea, or trying to find work to pay for a dying child's medicine, you might regard the slogan of an advertising campaign put out by British atheists a few years ago – 'There's probably no God, now stop worrying and enjoy your life' – as a tasteless joke. Atheism-lite is a belief suited to our environment, but it bears only a passing connection to the demanding, even disturbing, philosophy of atheistic thinkers like Friedrich Nietzsche.

Those who say that religion has the power to enslave people in false beliefs don't understand that the power of religion comes from those same people. Without believers, religions have no force. The same goes for schools of economics. Their strength comes from winning enough followers to shape the policy agenda of a society and remake it in its own image. Marx had caught the mood of the times once before, in 1848, only to see his radicalism dwindle out of sight amid the prosperity of the next quarter of a century. Having spent that time working to refine his doctrine, it was going to succeed to the extent it now met the needs of the working class to which his message was addressed. However, when the Long Depression tipped classical political economy into crisis, his would not be the only offering available to those looking for a solution to the daily woes the recession had brought on.

So let's go back to that question about what you believe, including what you believe is right or wrong. Professional footballers are paid up to four hundred times what a nurse is paid. Do you think that's good or bad?

The odds are you can answer that question without consulting an economics book – you probably have already answered it. While scarcely anyone who hasn't studied theoretical physics to an advanced level has an opinion on string theory, almost everyone has opinions on a wide range of economic issues. That sometimes irks professional economists, who complain that people should leave such matters to the specialists, just as they happily leave medicine or physics to the experts. But what few economists are prepared to admit is that they generally formed their own answers to questions like these the same way you did. Whereas scientists might reach their opinions in their field after looking at the evidence, on a wide variety of questions regarding public policy the direction in economics is reversed. Individuals know what they want to find, and tend to gravitate towards the school of economics that will help them confirm those answers. In one study comparing positions taken by economists, Anthony Randazzo and Jonathan Haidt found that economists most often began with moral narratives of the way the world ought to be, then reached substantive conclusions that accorded with those narratives.[4]

The premises on which we found our belief systems are very often ones we come to not through rational enquiry, but through sentiment and predisposition. In the social sciences, we tend to move towards those schools of thought that fit our pre-existing worldview – which is to say, those that conform to our personal narrative of life. Karl Marx showed his rebellious streak early in life. Although he started out thinking that the paramount goal was to change hearts – as he wrote to a friend in 1843, 'To obtain forgiveness for its sins, mankind needs only to declare them for what they are'[5] – his disputatious, brawling personality made him a natural fit with the Young Hegelians. For all his attempt to create a scientific socialism, Marx railed like an angry prophet, writing in *Capital* that capitalism came 'dripping from head to foot, from every pore, with blood and dirt'.

The Cambridge economist Alfred Marshall, on the other hand, widely considered the founder of modern economics, was a man cut from a different cloth. Like Marx, he shared the same desire to ameliorate the conditions of the poor, and also warmed to socialism. But his temperament was that of a placid scholar. Marx was a bohemian vagabond, Marshall a don who enjoyed long walks in the Scottish Highlands. Marx argued loudly in London's coffee houses whereas Marshall, a former seminarian 'anxious to do good',[6] drank port in his college. Where Marx looked for a worldly apocalypse to purify humanity and remake our nature, Marshall began his magnum opus by declaring 'Nature makes no sudden leaps.'[7] Therefore, while Marshall read Marx's work, it was to be expected that he would drift more naturally to the work of those who saw progress coming not in soaring bounds of revolution, but in the small steps of social reform. Where Marx saw irreconcilable contradictions that would produce a crisis, Marshall preferred to think of them as temporary imbalances that would find their way back to a new state of equilibrium. Marshall thus discovered the marginalists.

Think back to Adam Smith's axiom that the price of any product or service is determined by the interaction of supply and demand. If, for example, a bumper harvest boosts the supply of wheat, the price of wheat will fall to the point that people will snap up all the cheap bread that results. That's why shops offer discounts and sales – to clear their stock.

This seems straightforward. But when you take a moment to consider how you do your own shopping and make your spending decisions, you quickly see it's a bit more complicated than that. For instance, if you shop for food on an empty stomach, there's a good chance you'll load your basket fuller than if you shopped right after a big meal. That's because at that particular moment the added satisfaction you'd get from each mouthful of food would surpass that of someone who walked into the store moaning, in Mr Creosote-like fashion, 'I can't eat another bite.'

The same is true on the supply side of the equation. A shopkeeper with overdue bills or otherwise pressed to generate cash in a hurry might accept lower prices if it means things sell more quickly. In the mid-nineteenth century, to capture the effect on prices of such incremental changes in supply and demand, several scholars in Britain and Europe came up with the concept of 'marginal utility'. The fact that they did so more or less simultaneously, yet independently of one another, made the discovery seem to many political economists like a revelation of sorts.

Utility, to an economist, is simply what you find useful, or pleasurable. By leaving it to the individual to determine what he or she found pleasurable, the marginalists aimed to create a term devoid of normative content. In principle, that meant they could use the same logic to study the buying and spending of individuals with completely different tastes. They maintained that this use of a universal rule would therefore help to turn political economy into a science. Although they shared this ambition with Marx, the marginalists believed that his strongly ethical approach kept his doctrine in the realm of religion, whereas they had finally managed the shift to a value-free science. Breaking loose from the more philosophical and ethical approach of political economy, they gave birth to what we today call economics.

A practical challenge also helped prompt this adoption of scientific method. Since the margins analysed by these scholars were potentially infinite, calculating prices and behaviour relied on setting two sliding scales – supply and demand – against one another. Guesswork of the sort used by businesses and their customers, however, wasn't going to help the economists improve their precision very much. As it happened, at the same time the marginalists were developing their ideas, physicists were developing a better understanding of the atomic world, and applying the calculus pioneered by Isaac Newton to guide their work. Political economists had been watching with some interest, since calculus suggested itself as a possible means to measure marginal utility.

However, there was another reason that modelling their work on that of the physicists appealed to the economists: physics was then emerging as the most canonical of the sciences. Although some economists, Marshall included, borrowed metaphors from evolutionary biology, Darwin's work was not yet well understood (they were more likely to refer to the work of Herbert Spencer). Moreover, as Marshall noted, 'biological conceptions are more complex than those of mechanics'.[8] Whether it was the most appropriate model, physics offered the precise estimates the economists felt would make their predictions more scientific.

Theoretical physicists could calculate and plot the movement of the physical world with an exceptional degree of precision, and their mathematical models approached classical Greek ideals of human beauty – symmetrical, clean and with clear lines. This search for perfected form, similar to what had driven the sculptors of antiquity, wasn't accidental. Thousands of years before, Plato had speculated that beneath all reality was a set of hidden mathematical codes, which, once revealed, would uncover the ultimate truths of existence. If a way could be found to apply the new calculus to their work, the marginalists dreamed they might unlock the hidden codes underlying our behaviour.

Marshall himself, recognising the limitations of the static models of mechanics, warned his colleagues against imbibing too much of this heady brew. Widely credited with bringing these diverse strands of thought together into a new synthesis, he famously advised his peers to 'burn the maths'. What he meant was not that economists should chuck maths in the bin, but rather that they should restrict it to the early stages of their work, using it merely to help refine their models. Once they were satisfied they had a good one, he felt they would do well to express it in the traditional narrative methods that

had been used since Adam Smith's time. Writing to a colleague in
1906, he remarked:

> I had a growing feeling in the later years of my work at the subject
> that a good mathematical theorem dealing with economic hypoth-
> eses was very unlikely to be good economics: and I went more and
> more on the rules—(1) Use mathematics as a short-hand language,
> rather than as an engine of inquiry. (2) Keep to them till you have
> done. (3) Translate into English. (4) Then illustrate by examples
> that are important in real life. (5) Burn the mathematics. (6) If you
> can't succeed in 4, burn 3. This last I did often.[9]

Yet even as Marshall wrote these words, mathematics was gaining a
firm foothold in this new school. The tide overtook the great man.

When Adam Smith wrote *The Wealth of Nations*, most people saw
society as a living organism. Every person in it had a distinct function to perform that was necessary to the health of the whole, whilst
animating it was a kind of soul. Thus, the material well-being of a
society depended on its spiritual well-being. When this suffered,
so too did society – an approach that informed Edward Gibbon's
The History of the Decline and Fall of the Roman Empire, which
appeared in the same year as Smith's book. Hegel's theory of the
spirit retained this idea and would go on to influence philosophers
for generations, as when Oswald Spengler theorised in *The Decline
of the West* that every civilisation had a soul which defined it and
which, if it was lost, would lead to the civilisation's decay.

The economists, however, came up with an entirely new view of
society. They conceived it as a sort of inert galaxy driven by imper-
sonal physical forces, thereby removing the need for an animating
spirit. Think of what happens when you stick a piece of hot iron in
a bucket of cold water. It sizzles, steam rises, the rod cools and the
water warms until the two eventually reach the same temperature.
That's because the energy in the iron rushes into the water until it
is evenly distributed throughout the bucket. It's called equilibrium,

from the Latin word meaning 'equal balance'. Like a kitchen scales whose two sides are aligned, the rod and bucket have found the point at which they meet and reach a resting state.

Now, think of the hot iron as a shopkeeper and the bucket of water as a customer, and think of energy as money. Suppose you walk into a shop that is selling something pretty hot. Let's say it's Gucci instead of Primark. As far as customers go, however, you're a pretty cold bucket of water. With only a few banknotes in your pocket and a maxed-out credit card, the only way you could buy the handbag is if the shopkeeper dropped the price a lot. The shopkeeper will probably politely ignore you and wait for a hotter customer to walk in, one with a full wallet of cash. That way, the handbag will sell at an equilibrium-price far more pleasing to the shopkeeper.

That's sort of how the marginalists conceived market transactions. As with energy transfer in the physical world, the market would always find its equilibrium in the end as buyers and sellers went looking for one another. So amid the Long Depression, which Marx believed signalled a crisis in capitalism, the economists advised patience. If you couldn't buy the Gucci because there was a recession on and your pay had been frozen, the odds would be good that lots of other people were in the same boat. If you kept calling on the shopkeeper day after day, you might find her a bit less arrogant as time passed and the realisation dawned on her that she wasn't going to get her asking price. Once she resigned herself to the fact that she wasn't going to find a bucket of hot water in this economy, she would be willing to drop her price to a level you could afford. And presumably, at that price, other people would be able to enter the shop as well. Her stock would begin moving off the shelves. And as it did so, she could place more orders, which would cause the factory to employ more people, and so on in a virtuous cycle that would end the recession.

Physicists describe atoms with plenty of energy as excited, which means they are moving around a lot. That's not unlike how you feel on payday, when you have a lot of money and will similarly move around a lot – to the pub, club, shopping centre or betting shop. This kind of analogy isn't actually that far-fetched, because some of the early marginalists explicitly likened the energy in physics to pleasure in economics, taking both to be elemental forces at the heart of exist-ence.[10] And just as a physicist says all matter is nothing more than combinations of atoms, so the marginalists said the economy was the sum of all transactions. To understand it, therefore, you had to take a microscope to each of its transactions and predict how it would go. Hence, they called for a 'microeconomic' analysis. Economists set aside the traditional method in political economy, which looked at everything from philosophy to history, and adopted a precise method that zeroed in on individual decisions.

That microeconomic approach enabled the marginalists to focus laser-like on markets. As a result, they split off from the other social scientists and formed a new discipline. Nevertheless, the separation of economics from political economy occurred gradually. Many departments of political economy, in which students of politics and the economy worked alongside each other, survived well into the twentieth century, just as political economy journals continued to publish articles by historians or political scientists. Meanwhile, within the new economics departments, the marginalist method was taught alongside other schools of political economy, and it would be a long time before the uniformly mathematical approach we now associate with economics would establish its dominance. Equally, although we now associate economics with a market-based approach, early marginalism accommodated a wide variety of political orientations, from strongly free-market capitalist positions to Marshall's own social reformism. Nevertheless, all those who followed in Marshall's tradition were united by their common faith in the market's ability to eventually move towards its equilibrium point.

The marginalists saw their work as the fulfilment of Adam Smith's teaching. His *Wealth of Nations* had always been the foundational text, a sort of Bible of political economy. However, over time, as the world around them had changed and Smith's early capitalism gave way to the 'satanic mills' of the Industrial Revolution, they gradually departed from it on various points. John Stuart Mill, for instance, argued that for the market to work effectively, an institutional framework would be needed to guide it and rein in its excesses. Then when Marx came along, he aimed to transcend Smith altogether by arguing that Smith's model was doomed to eventual collapse.

As a result, the 'marginal revolution', as economists today call it, was a bit like Martin Luther's Reformation applied to political economy: a restoration of the foundational book's authority. Leaping back over the edifice that political economists had created in the century after Smith's death in 1790, the marginalists removed the non-Smithian elements in the canon and kept only those that built upon or elucidated his work. Marx therefore was expunged from the canon. What resulted was a purified, formalised, Smithian approach that, because it restored his classical political economy to its altar, eventually came to be known as the neoclassical school.[11]

Rather as Luther had said there need be no ritualistic adornment of the simple belief in Christ and his teaching, the marginalists reaffirmed their faith in the market's simple but sure self-restorative powers. However, the neoclassicals parted with Marx over some other points which today might appear like arcane doctrinal disputes, but which would have enormous social implications. In particular, their belief that the market would always find its way back to equilibrium dispensed with Marx's cyclical view of history, in which progress occurred through conflict, crisis and resolution. Beneath the surface of those waves of boom and bust, said the neoclassicals, was a gradual and evolutionary progress of small steps. In addition, whereas Marx had taken David Ricardo's labour theory of value as foundational, the neoclassicals removed it from their doctrine. In time, they would come to regard any mention of it in someone's work in the way the medieval Catholic Church regarded reference to an Apocryphal text: as sufficient proof of the author's error.

To a lay person, the debate over the labour theory of value might appear like the conflict between Catholics and Protestants over the physical properties of a communion wafer: the two sides of the debate practically indistinguishable to the outsider, but to the insider gravely important. To illustrate the difference in the two economic positions, let's go back to that Gucci bag and ask how it became so expensive. Marx and his followers said it was because a lot of people – some of them, like the designers and marketers, highly paid people – worked to make the bag, and so it cost a lot to produce. The neoclassicals would say no, the price was high because enough people attached a high-marginal utility to it, and the bag itself was sufficiently scarce, so the shopkeeper could afford to wait until one of those 'full-bucket' customers walked through her door.

Now to this you might well say, isn't it the same thing? The bag is expensive because people attach a high marginal-utility to it, and they attach a high marginal utility to it because all those expensive people produced a very good bag. Equally, it's scarce because it's so expensive to make. But when it comes to turning the premise into a policy proposal, the politics can get nasty.

The Marxists, and the left more generally, in seeing value determined in production, would see humans as being fundamentally producers: in making things, they found their full humanity and joy. This might seem hopelessly romantic to someone whose job feels like drudgery, but reflect upon the notion for a moment. Consider the satisfaction you might get from baking cakes for loved ones and having them sing your praises as they eat them, or the pleasure you might feel after subjecting yourself to the pain of a back-breaking workout to then admire your buff body in the mirror. Now think of doing the same thing, but for someone else: working in an industrial bakery, or moving blocks on someone else's construction site. Marx said alienation from the fruits of our labours is what turned our work into drudgery: it was alienated to someone else who owned it and got to sell it, compensating us with a wage for giving it up. So to the Marxists and their followers it was important to create a work environment in which people were well paid, had secure jobs, were happy with what they did and felt they had some ownership of what they were doing.

The neoclassicals disagreed. Believing value to be determined by supply and demand, and thus ultimately by individual purchasing decisions, they saw humans first and foremost as consumers. Thus, we don't get our satisfaction from making things so much as from *buying* them. You may like your job, you may even love your job, but think of the pleasure you get when you hit the shopping centres. Meddling in the workplace to improve workers' lives, many neoclassicals would say, added to the costs of running a business and made it hard for new firms to get off the ground. That meant there would end up being less stuff to buy, which would leave us all less happy.

You can see how this disagreement would work its way into the politics of our own societies today. Take any free-trade deal. The debate around it usually boils down to 'bad for workers, good for shoppers' and which side you take depends on which of those two identities matters more to you. And you know how nasty free-trade debates, whether NAFTA or Brexit, can become. In time, not only would the Marxists and neoclassicals stop reading one another, but for each school it practically became the mark of the devil to even be seen carrying around a text from the other school's canon. Other than possibly to demonstrate its errors and heresies, no neoclassical economist aiming for tenure would ever be seen with a copy of Marx's *Capital*, just as no ambitious Marxist political economist would deign to touch Marshall's *Principles of Economics*. And that was a war that would indeed become religious.

Today it is an article of faith among neoclassical economists that the marginal revolution turned their discipline into a science – precisely why they call it a revolution. It's easy to see why they might think this. Place a physics paper and an article by a neoclassical economist side by side, and you'll see a lot of resemblances in language and maths. However, on closer inspection, some important differences appear, differences that go right to the heart of the doctrine's foundation. In resting on premises that were little more than articles of faith, neoclassical economics retained a quasi-religious character that departed less from classical political economy than is often supposed. But to an extent these beliefs spread through society until they would ultimately shape our own views, and define how we live our lives.

First, while physicists could prove empirically that when an atom gains energy it gets excited and moves around more, the same couldn't be said of humans and pleasure. At the time, it seemed reasonable enough for neoclassical scholars to found their science on the assumption that, as they would later put it, humans were rational utility-maximisers – that the more we get, the happier we are. It seems obvious, doesn't it? After all, who turns down a pay rise? But, surprisingly, it would be another century before anyone would seriously test the premise to see if it was true. When they did so, the results would surprise them. It turned out that people weren't necessarily always happier with more.[12] But think of how many people today live their lives as if that premise must be true.

An obvious implication of that first assumption was that more was always better than less – which in practice meant that economic growth, since it raised incomes and output, was by definition a good thing. Again, in the late nineteenth century, hardly anyone could take issue with this. But once this assumption was enshrined, it would become very difficult to challenge, even when research later suggested that the statement probably at least needed substantial qualification. Take the climate-change debate, for example. Today there is a growing body of research showing the rising toll in political instability, health,[13] crime[14] and damage to the natural environment[15] that unrestrained growth has had. It's well established that recessions are good for the environment.[16] But the option of slowing growth to save the planet is practically ruled out from the get-go; not because it's unscientific, but because it runs contrary to the 'Thou shalt grow the economy' commandment. Who's the last politician to win election with a 'less is more' campaign?

Equally, physicists could prove that matter could be broken into its constituent parts, and that an atom could detach itself from the whole. Neoclassical scholars made much the same assumption of societies and their supposed constituents, people, tending towards a Hobbesian view in which humans in the state of nature were solitary creatures who led lives that were 'nasty, brutish and short' – the dog-eat-dog world of Victorian capitalism. It's not that the marginalists necessarily thought this a good thing. Indeed, Alfred Marshall wanted to understand how the economy operated in order to be able to tailor it to serve human needs while mitigating its harsh effects. Nevertheless, it wasn't going to be difficult for later economists and popularisers to turn this belief into a moral imperative. As the philosopher Ayn Rand revealed by her impact on influential economists in the twentieth century, 'the virtue of selfishness' which she celebrated[17] could easily morph into a 'Greed is good' mantra by which many could rationalise selfish and antisocial behaviour of a sort that Adam Smith would not have countenanced.

Following on from this atomistic conception, the economists assumed that just as physicists could do with atoms, what could be said about any one individual would go for any other. Others, like the Marxists or the German Historical School, differed. Seeing humans as social animals whose decisions were shaped by their environment, they argued that behaviour would depend on context. But the neoclassical school theory focused on the essential similarity among humans, and proposed that we are all guided by the same underlying laws. Although neoclassical doctrine took this as an article of faith, many sociologists would find reality more complicated.

Economists didn't ignore anomalies that arose in their work. Instead, they tried smoothing out the wrinkles by inventing a rule of thumb, the 'ceteris paribus' rule (from the Latin phrase meaning 'all other things being equal'). Assuming all other things remain equal, they said, humans would still make their decisions in an individualistic manner that maximised their utility. As innocuous as the rule might appear, in the wrong hands it could at times resemble Jesuitical casuistry, conveniently used to justify dispensing with those things that didn't fit the model – or which might have changed *everything*. Many political economists, notably Marx, saw that the world wasn't equal. The dynamism of industrial capitalism couldn't easily be separated from such things as the bounty of empire then stoking its furnace, or the capital resources that Enclosure had marshalled. However, the neoclassical model took these things out of the picture and focused on the market as it was then. It would have been a bit like putting Muhammad Ali into the ring with a lightweight and then simply comparing their footwork to determine why he won.

However, that is what we do today when we, for instance, compare our wealth to Third World poverty and conclude the gap must be due to something inherently superior in our model – our work ethic, our superior institutions, our higher productivity – without taking account of the way the different histories of imperial and colonial countries might have shaped all those variables. The connection between imperialism and development is not straightforward: some former empires, like Spain or Portugal, did not grow rich, while the performance of former colonies after they became independent varied greatly, some like Singapore and South Korea growing quite rich indeed. But as a rule, with the principal exceptions being the colonies of settlement (the 'white dominions'), the gap in incomes between mother countries and their colonies was greater at the time the latter had become independent than it was when they were first colonised. Thus, much as medieval religions offered an organic conception to justify a society stratified between aristocrats and the rest, so too did the new economic faith say our own stratification was natural – except that now *we* were the blessed few standing at the apex of the global class system. Marshall himself, on the rare occasions he did make reference to the poverty of what would later be called the Third World, attributed it to an inferior work ethic.[18]

Building a model on arbitrary premises, as the neoclassicals did, is not a problem. All social scientists do it. A half-century after Marshall published his *Principles of Economics*, the neoclassical scholar Milton Friedman would formalise the methodology of economics in such a way as to address this issue. In 'The Methodology of Positive Economics'[19] he said the economist didn't need to spend too much time trying to determine whether or not the premises of a model were correct, but rather should focus his energies on determining whether the model could provide reasonably accurate predictions. If your model seemed to superimpose well on reality, then you could take it as correct.

Ironically, though, many of Friedman's disciples revealed themselves to be less agnostic than this when it came to testing their models, instead finding the 'facts' that confirmed their beliefs. Criticising this wasn't always so easy, though. Mark Blaug would blame this in part on the popularity of Friedman's method among economists, arguing that in the hands of technicians less accomplished than Friedman, it amounted to 'playing tennis with the net down': rather than produce testable hypotheses through a rigorous theoretical approach, economists grabbed theories willy-nilly and then verified rather than test them empirically.[20] For in declaring itself a science, neoclassical economics had actually laid a foundation that would enable later followers to turn it into a religion. Just as no physicist would say atoms don't exist, it would prove tempting for many an economist to say their assumptions were beyond question since a century of research had established them, and thus their findings were beyond critique. After all, who wants to be accused of being anti-scientific?

Presumably, if the model was 'scientific' it could not be wrong; and if could not be wrong, then any appearances of being so had to be illusions, or based on incomplete evidence. There would be no need to debate, you simply had to assert the eternal truths. So, for 'You think Christ was just a man, you're a heretic' substitute 'You think too much growth is bad, you're a Luddite.' In place of 'Yes the marauders are despoiling our land but God will come to our rescue because God always does' substitute 'Yes, global warming is a problem but the free market will find a solution because the free market always finds a solution.' Each of these statements may well be correct. But believers don't subject them to empirical testing, and if someone else does and raises doubts, the believer falls back on faith: Yes, God hasn't come or the free market hasn't saved us, but it will, it just needs a bit more time.

*

Both Karl Marx and Alfred Marshall agreed that the promised land would be found in this life and in this world, and both envisaged a land of endless material abundance in which human contentment would flourish. They disagreed on the means of this salvation, though. Marx maintained it would come in a collective apocalypse and Marshall, as Martin Luther had done in his own Reformation, said it would come via individuals finding their own way to heaven.

In the decades that followed, England's experience would apparently vindicate Marshall's faith in small steps. Marx had committed a basic logical error in his theory of the falling rate of profit, one which economists call a fallacy of composition. He assumed that what held for one industry applied to the whole economy. As it happened, instead of just sinking a society into poverty and economic stagnation, the capital and workers released as firms went out of business became available to new entrepreneurs, who were eager to meet the rising demand of those still employed. New sectors and sub-sectors that Marx could not even have imagined came into being, new products were developed, and new services were invented. In the tradition of those political economists who respected the production of things and had little regard for the services that facilitated their creation, Marx privileged manufacturing and failed to foresee just how important the service sector would become in the economy. Indeed, employed workers with higher wages to spend didn't just buy things. Those holiday excursions to Blackpool required lodgings to be built and meals to be cooked, all of which created new jobs and economic activity. The prosperity of Europe and its settler colonies in the final decades of the nineteenth century apparently spoke well of the economists' mastery of society's inner workings.

Nevertheless, this testified less to the advance of science than to the triumph of a new faith. Steven B. Smith argues that the elevation of self-interest as an organisational principle for society reflected not scientific progress but more an Enlightenment effort to substitute a more democratic, egalitarian morality for the aristocratic ideal of old Europe. In place of the hero who stood above history and helped shape it, an idea revived by Hegel and the Romantics, the neoclassicals restored Smith's belief that we are all fundamentally similar, atom-like particles driven by the same forces. Because the pursuit of self-interest was deemed to have a tranquillising effect on human behaviour, it was expected that society would end up being more peaceful and prosperous.[21] That certainly seemed to be the case in the late nineteenth century, and it was that rather than any scientific discoveries that confirmed our faith in this new doctrine.

Nevertheless, this achievement depended in no small part on practices anything but peaceful and tranquillising, and which in fact pre-dated the scientific age by some distance. During the 1880s, the decade Alfred Marshall spent working on his magnum opus, Europe was entering the most intensive period of its imperial history, adding dozens of new colonies and using them to augment the overall output of the empires. Marshall paid little attention to any of this. The same couldn't be said of the residents of the colonies, millions of whom saw an entirely different side to the capitalism he wrote about.

CHAPTER 8

THE GOLDEN AGE

At some point in your life, the chances are that you or someone close to you has lost a loved one to a rival. It could have been a boyfriend or girlfriend leaving for someone else, a husband or wife walking out with a neighbour, or maybe it was you who did the walking. But it's likely that in the closing conversation, some variant of 'I wasn't happy' came up in explanation.

In the end, you probably accepted this justification for the simple reason that you could put yourself in his or her shoes. In the same position, you'd have done the same thing, or at least you'd have wanted to be able to. Ironically, therefore, even those of us who have abandoned our religious heritage have kept the golden rule: Do unto others as you would have them do unto you. All we've done is change our vantage point. Instead of seeing yourself as a loser, wishing your beloved cared for your feelings and stuck around to avoid hurting them, you prefer to see yourself as an eventual winner, and want that freedom to walk when your opportunity comes.

In *The Anti-Christ*, Friedrich Nietzsche pilloried Christianity for being a loser's ethic, or as he called it, a slave morality. He said it was crafted by history's losers to rein in its winners, and maintained that all of the creativity in human history was provided by those who had risen to the top in nature's struggle – what he called the *Ubermensch* (sometimes translated as supermen). As a result, he said that no limit should be placed on their freedom and power. In fact, everyone else should exist for their glory. It should be enough for the rest of us to bask in the warm glow we get from the *Ubermensch*, as we do when we line up for hours in the hopes of getting a glimpse of the Queen or a selfie with Kim Kardashian. 'What is more harmful than any vice?' he asked, rhetorically. 'Active sympathy for the ill-constituted and weak.'[1]

Call it the New Golden Rule, or the winner's code. Nietzsche hadn't been the first to float it. When Adam Smith began developing a new ethic for a new age, he was wading into a river of thought already raging. Some, including him, subscribed to the doctrine of unintended consequences, believing that the pursuit of self-interest would ultimately lead to social gain: the principle that private vice produces public virtue. But others took the matter much further, adopting a proto-Nietzschean position.

At the time Smith was writing *The Wealth of Nations*, the young Marquis de Sade was on the run from the French authorities, wanted for imprisoning and torturing young girls in his castle. When they finally caught up with him and locked him in prison, Sade used his enforced leisure to elaborate his thought. In *The 120 Days of Sodom* he imagined a scenario in which an aristocratic elite would be left free to pursue its every desire, no matter how barbaric those desires might have appeared to gentler eyes. In his subsequent novels *Justine* and *Juliette* he completely inverted the moral tales of Christian tradition: Justine, a paragon of virtue, ends up descending into a miserable life; Juliette, a self-interested and amoral woman, rises to a position of power and wealth. Sade was so far ahead of his time that he would die in disgrace and be practically wiped from the face of history, to be exhumed two centuries later as a sort of early sexual revolutionary and champion of individual liberty. But he espoused a principle which would have deeply troubled Smith: namely, that we should pursue our self-interest not for the good of society, but for our own good, regardless of the social consequences.

In *The Theory of Moral Sentiments*, Smith had instead tried to reconstruct traditional morality on a new basis. What made his task easier was that that he lived in a time when most people's pursuit of self-interest was reined in by traditional codes. In effect, his New Golden Rule retained the vestiges of the old, creating a morality that was good for everyone. Sade, however, essentially argued that you couldn't have it both ways. You could have either a winner's code of freedom, or a loser's code of restraint. Nobody loves a loser.

To some degree, how you compare the New Golden Rule to the old depends on where you stand. It's easy, if you're living amid the prosperity of developed countries, to point to the progress which the free market delivered to the countries that first adopted it. But if you're standing in one of the former colonies, you can just as easily point to imperialism and slavery as its fruits. And the dilemmas posed by the new morality arose at once with the early conversions to the faith.

When England repealed its Corn Laws and ushered in the age of free markets, there happened to occur a string of bad harvests across Europe. Whether due to pragmatism or because they lived by the code of *noblesse oblige* – the medieval moral code, with biblical roots, that required those blessed with power and wealth to care for the poor and indigent – the old autocracies of Europe staved off the worst effects of hunger with programmes of poor relief. So too did the Conservative government of Robert Peel in England which, having repealed the Corn Laws partly to ensure sufficient supply amid the fall in production, then imported American wheat to build a stockpile of emergency supplies to make up any possible shortfall. But after Peel lost office, the new Liberal government took a different view. Filled as it was with true believers in the new creed of political economy, it insisted that such government programmes would distort the market and therefore the potato famine then ravaging Ireland had to be left to run its course while supply and demand rebalanced. Having criticised the Tory approach to famine as an overreaction, it initially operated soup kitchens in the summer of 1847, but abandoned them in the autumn, at which time the greatest ravages of the famine began.[2] Wedded to Adam Smith's dictum that free trade 'is not only the best palliative of the inconveniences of a dearth, but the best preventative of that calamity' and backed by the editorialists in the fledgling *Economist*,[3] the government then stood and watched as a million Irish died. Some defenders of the new faith would go so far as to invoke Malthusian logic to suggest there were too many Irish in the first place, and that nature was merely restoring its balance.[4]

This new belief set a pattern for British policy in the free-market age. In *Late Victorian Holocausts*, the historian Mike Davis documents a series of famines throughout the British Empire in the late nineteenth century, when in the name of free-market principles officials refused to intervene.[5] Following the practice established in the Irish famine, food exports continued throughout the period even as people starved. It was said that diverting that output to famine relief would interfere with prices and thus hinder growth. In total, Davis estimates, some 30–60 million people died as traditional remedies to famine were set aside and colonies were converted to the free-market faith. Free markets did not cause these famines: there had always been famines, and the spread of trade was increasing overall output. However, a fundamentalist commitment to a minimalist state elevated the sanctity of the free market over that of human life, and governments turned a blind eye to suffering in their adherence to doctrine.

The Old Golden Rule had never guaranteed against abuses by the powerful. Indeed, the 'saving' of others was easily twisted into such atrocities as the Crusades, or the Spanish Inquisition, or forcible conversions. On the other hand, it did occasionally saddle the powerful with guilt, which could sometimes rein in their worst vices, as when England's King Henry II had himself whipped in Canterbury cathedral for the murder of a troublesome bishop. Empirically, it's hard to judge between the Old and New Golden Rules. By the rough estimates historians can make, medieval Crusades killed about 0.2 per cent of the world's then population; the Wars of Religion – which some historians say are misnamed, being really the first modern wars of nationalism – about 0.6 per cent; the free-market crusades of the late nineteenth century about 0.4 per cent.[6]

You wouldn't want to assess a religion by tallying up the numbers it was willing to deliver in sacrifice to its idols. All that can be said of economics was that in the pursuit of its ideals, it showed no less zeal than its predecessors, while giving the rich a reason for their success, and the poor a reason for their suffering.

In February 1884, the German Chancellor Otto von Bismarck stood in his office in Berlin's old Palais Schulenburg and stared through the tall windows overlooking the courtyard. Outside, wet snow fell on the Wilhelmstrasse as the dull grey sky darkened towards sunset. It had been thirteen years since Bismarck had manoeuvred the hundreds of German states into unification, and he could look back on his achievement with some satisfaction. After that feat, he'd used selective warfare and skilful diplomacy to craft a delicate balance of power on the continent, thereby securing his country a modicum of security. And yet, the very fragility of that balance had been brought home to him by a dispatch that afternoon from his London embassy. The Portuguese and British had just agreed a treaty splitting control of Africa's Congo river, thereby giving themselves access to the continent's interior. Since everyone else in Europe felt understandably excluded by their gesture, tension was rising in several capitals.

European explorers had already been penetrating into Africa and mapping its lands for years. Stanley and Livingstone had come up from the south while Richard Burton, John Speke and James Grant had done so from the north, sailing down to the source of the Nile in the great lakes. Meanwhile, both the Belgians and French were exploring the Congo, Cecil Rhodes had claimed Rhodesia for Britain and, with the Ottoman Empire crumbling and its North African provinces coming up for grabs, France swooped in on Tunisia and Britain on Egypt.

Bismarck hadn't wanted colonies for Germany. He reckoned the cost of administering them greater than the riches they'd yield. Besides, his country had been prospering by trading with its European partners, and if they wanted to sail around the world for the booty to buy German grain and steel, that was their business. However, the political landscape was now changing. As the Long

Depression advanced, faith in the liberal gospel was yielding to a more pragmatic approach that mixed a bit of mercantilist water in the free-trade wine. It's not that governments were losing faith in the free-market teachings of Adam Smith and David Ricardo, more that they wanted to corral them for their own benefit by encouraging free trade within their empires while limiting it outside. Also, some of the laggards in the race to industrialise – including France, Russia, the United States and Japan – were drawn to the teaching of Friedrich List and his advocacy of time-limited protection so that manufacturers could catch up with Britain. As one country after another raised tariffs to cut imports, Germany responded in kind. But unlike Britain or France, which were cultivating trade within their empires to compensate; or America, which had penetrated deep into its interior, Germany felt itself isolated. Meanwhile, a rising nationalist movement wanted to apply the lessons of the British Empire, seizing colonies to give Germany the wealth it needed to become a great power.

Bismarck didn't care for this chest-thumping. He worried that it might disrupt Europe's delicate balance. Nonetheless, the tide was turning against his previous vision, and the situation in Africa risked spinning out of control. It was one thing to get proxies to fight among themselves in distant forests. But European countries scrambling to get in on the continent's action might inadvertently trigger a war back home. Moreover, if Germany stood by as the scramble unfolded, she risked being frozen out of the last continent still largely untouched by European imperialism.

By the 1880s, Spain was more or less out of that game. Her mercantilist empire having enriched almost everyone in Europe but herself, the country had fallen back into a shadow of its former self, and had been scarcely able to resist the wars of independence in its American colonies. Portugal, similarly, had lost its hold on Brazil – though it still retained substantial African colonies, particularly those in Angola and Mozambique. But other than those possessions, a British toehold in South Africa and a French one in Algeria, Africa was still, despite all the skirmishing, largely independent of foreign rule. Few expected that to last. Not that the Africans would have any say in the matter. As a British historian would later explain in reference to a decisive weapon invented in London, 'Whatever happens we have got/ The Maxim Gun, and they have not.'[7]

As the year progressed and tensions over the Anglo-Portuguese treaty rose, Bismarck would seize the initiative, summoning Europe's leaders to Berlin for a conference on the partition of Africa. All European countries, save the ever-neutral Switzerland, attended, as did the United States. No African governments were invited. The conference laid down the ground rules. Assigning King Leopold of Belgium personal ownership of the vast swathe of the Congo interior, it reversed the Anglo-Portuguese treaty (already abandoned by its signatories) and established free trade along the Congo and Niger rivers. Most significantly, it established the principle of 'effective occupation'. This meant that a country could not merely plant a flag on the coast to claim territory, but had to actually occupy and administer the land it wanted to take. Finally, the treaty confirmed Germany's comparatively modest territorial claims in south-west Africa and east Africa.

With the starting gun fired, Europe's imperial powers leapt out of the blocks. King Leopold took over his Congo allocation at once. France advanced inland from its coastal outposts in West Africa and occupied much of the continent's west and centre to the north of Congo. Britain moved up from Rhodesia and South Africa, taking the wedge between the Portuguese colonies until British troops reached the Congolese border. They also descended from the east coast to occupy what is today Kenya and Uganda. Italy, not wanting to miss out on all the fun, grabbed Eritrea and Somaliland.

Meanwhile, European expansion elsewhere was proceeding. In the Americas, the United States did as Russia had done centuries before and built an internal empire. Having already battled Mexico for control of California, the southwest and Texas; and having bought Louisiana off France, and Alaska off Russia, the United States moved west all the way to the Pacific coast. Late in the century, it then ventured overseas and, in a war with Spain, took Cuba and the Philippines. In similar fashion, Canada took hold of the Great Plains and opened them to European settlement, just as Australian settlers pressed more deeply into that continent (equipped with the colonial administration's 'terra nullius' declaration, which held that any land they occupied with government approval became theirs). In their East Indies colonies, the Dutch expanded and solidified their control, prodding the local population to grow cash crops, and encouraging further settlement by Dutch plantation owners.

By the end of the nineteenth century, therefore, most of the planet was directly under European control in the form of colonies, or indirectly: Latin American countries, despite having attained independence, largely perpetuated the imperial trade pattern of exporting primary goods in return for finished goods, while many nominally independent states like China were increasingly unable to resist European economic dominance. The closing decades of the nineteenth century would thus see European might reach its highest extent ever.

In America it was called the Gilded Age. In France *La Belle Epoque*. The British simply remembered the era, as they always do, by the reigning monarch's name, and the popular memory of the late Victorian and Edwardian ages was a rosy one of peace and prosperity. And while storm clouds were gathering it was a time that united the West in a shared sense of prosperity, optimism and peace. There were conflicts in some of the colonies or countries trying to resist European domination. However, with the exception of a couple of Balkan skirmishes, the last two decades of the nineteenth century found Europe in the unusually happy position of being at peace with itself. Economic growth, which had bottomed during the Long Depression, resumed in the 1880s and gradually gained speed in the 1890s.

It's sometimes hard for us to appreciate the dizzying pace of change people alive then experienced. Looking back over just the last generation, you might wonder how on earth you spent your time before you had mobile phones and the Internet. How did you avoid getting lost without your GPS? But for all the disruption communications technology has brought to our way of life, the level of change pales compared with what our predecessors lived through. It's not just that the impact of each technology was greater than the smartphone or tablet – the telegraph alone affected business and daily life more profoundly than anything we've seen in the computer age. The sheer number of inventions was also mind-boggling.

The German engineer Karl Benz designed the first automobile in 1886, and within less than two decades the United States was mass-producing cars. Thomas Edison developed the light bulb, and before the century was out electrification was spreading rapidly. Fashion design became a major industry, with Paris its centre, and a new trend emerged of cycling new designs on an annual basis. Rubbish output exploded as products were built and marketed to last a season or two.[8] The cinema came into being, as did the aeroplane. Each year, months were added to average lifespans as diet continued improving,[9] the spread of public sanitation greatly augmented public health, and discoveries like pasteurisation helped to reduce the number of killer diseases.

At the same time, with cities swelling across the Western world, the continuing tide of human migration uprooted ever more people. In testament to their wealth and power, these cities kept the tradition of all empires and built monuments to their greatness. Paris erected the Eiffel Tower to host the World Fair in 1889 and Chicago raised its first skyscrapers. Flush with the patronage of wealthy industrialists, the arts flourished in newly created galleries and museums. New York became a major art centre for the first time; Carnegie Hall opened its doors in 1891 with a premiere performance conducted by Pyotr Ilyich Tchaikovsky. Edith Wharton chronicled the lives of the Manhattan elite in their endless cavalcade of opera-visits and soirées in the ornate mansions they had built for themselves. Paris nightlife was even livelier, the city thrumming with burlesque. In literature, philosophy and architecture, modernism emerged to put a final end to homages to the past. Celebrating the possibilities of the artist unencumbered by tradition, engineers designed works that took pride in the present, using steel structures and taking advantage of the possibilities unleashed by the newly invented electric lift to construct edifices that soared high into the sky, far above what any medieval cathedral builder could have dreamed of.

Mind you, not everyone experienced the Gilded Age as an era of wealth and optimism. As the cities grew, so did their slums, where underclasses that enjoyed much less of the fruit of this progress bubbled with discontent. Inequality became stark.[10] Artists, writers and scholars began pondering this new, troubling landscape. If perhaps then a minority, nonetheless some philosophers were starting to recognise the darker underside of their civilisation. Nietzsche offered a less than rosy view of modernity and Sigmund Freud was probing the dark inner recesses of the human mind, suggesting that beneath a veneer of civility lurked barbarous impulses.

He probably could have saved himself a lot of time and worked that out simply by visiting one of the colonies. In the Congo, after subduing local states and enforcing their control, Leopold's troops forced the population to collect ivory and rubber for his personal estate, killing or chopping off the hands of those who failed to meet quotas (reflecting a belief system that likened skiving to theft, punishing it as other religions do the latter crime). Some estimates place the final death toll from Leopold's plunder at 10 million.[11] Famines raged in India. China was stumbling towards collapse, as was the Ottoman Empire. Elsewhere, the impact of European colonialism was less vicious but maintained the pattern of elevating Europe's living standards further above those of its colonies. On balance, colonialism was probably felt least in the French and British colonies of West Africa, where settlement and trading were limited, and experienced more acutely in older colonies where the Europeans had sunk deep roots, like India and the Dutch East Indies. There, the extraction of primary resources was creating a positive balance of trade for the mother countries.

Interestingly, however, where those surpluses then went varied. Instead of enriching the mother countries, the fruits of empire fanned out towards the newly independent countries of the West.

For instance, amidst the protectionist wave of the Long Depression, Britain started building a system of imperial preference that encouraged trade within the empire. Among the biggest beneficiaries were her white dominions. Canada, for instance, having become a self-governing dominion in 1867, ran a surplus on its balance of payments with her former imperial master, which in effect meant that Britain was subsidising the development of her former British North American colonies. However, Britain was able to finance this growth at no net cost to herself since she was running a large surplus on her trade with India (which further transferred subsidies to Britain through a currency system that was ultimately managed in London[12]).

Moreover, though it belonged to no imperial preference system, the United States, by dint of its sheer dynamism, was outpacing all its European rivals. Apart from anything else, someone had to feed all those European city dwellers, whose numbers were growing faster than the continent's own suppliers could satisfy. The opening of the West to European settlement turned the American frontier into the breadbasket of Europe – especially Britain, whose imports from the United States grew year on year.[13] Meanwhile, the construction of the railways and steady improvements in shipping speed and efficiency greatly reduced the costs of long-distance transportation, making it possible to export wheat to Europe inexpensively.

In effect, the centre of humanity's economic universe steadily radiated outwards, away from northern Europe and towards the United States. By the end of the nineteenth century, America had overtaken Britain as the world's largest economy. But it was all relative, because right across the West, it was an era of plenty. And although the growing divisions within society posed serious challenges to stability, Western governments had one big thing going for them: the resources needed to siphon off discontent, should it ever become too great. Germany took the lead, where the ever-shrewd Bismarck knew that he needed to maintain peace not only with his neighbours, but with his own working classes, if he was to prevent them drifting towards the radical parties he so loathed. At the same time he was preparing for the Berlin Conference, Bismarck was approving legislation that created the world's first welfare state, offering pensions and accident and health insurance as a means to mollify restive workers. By the century's end, social reformers in Britain had also succeeded in prodding the Liberal Party to shed its previous attachment to the unbridled free market and to adopt a rudimentary welfare state in its own platform. Relatively small gestures, since by and large welfare provision remained limited, they were nonetheless a sign of what more affluent times could make possible.

When the American Civil War ended, Horace Greeley penned an editorial in the *New York Tribune* – a newspaper Karl Marx had contributed to – in which he implored 'Go West, young man, and grow up with the country.'[14] Millions ended up taking his advice and doing just that. With the railways reaching ever further inland, the country's farm population tripled over the second half of the century. The United States felt no need for a welfare state like Germany's since, as Greeley advised unemployed young men, they could always go to the frontier where abundant land and opportunity beckoned. And no sooner did they leave than new immigrants from Europe arrived to take their places in the factories of the east.

In 1892, the United States opened an immigration-processing centre on Ellis Island. A wave of European migration to the Americas, underway since the Napoleonic Wars, now reached its peak. European emigrants also went to the European empires and into Latin America in search of better lives, but roughly half of them headed west across the sea to the United States. After landing in New York, some continued on to the coastal cities in search of work, while others hopped on trains and headed west. The American labour force, which the country could easily feed and accommodate thanks to the lands it was taking in the west, therefore grew much faster than Europe's, driving economic growth rates higher. As the century came to a close, US economic growth doubled Britain's rate,[15] and its wages rose above those of its former colonial master.

As the United States overtook the British economy, others were catching up, most notably France, Germany and Japan. Even Russia, despite being a sluggish behemoth in which most people still lived in conditions barely above serfdom, was itself going through a rapid burst of industrialisation.

In hindsight, it might seem inevitable that economic rivalry and jostling would sooner or later get transferred to the battlefield. One by-product of the imperial-preference trade regimes that spread in the final decades of the nineteenth century was to accentuate inter-imperial rivalry: as ties strengthened within empires, they weakened somewhat outside. All the same, war didn't seem inevitable to those living at the time – certainly not to Bismarck, who remained confident that a carefully crafted balance of power could maintain peace. It was perhaps fitting that he was a lover of English literature and, as a young man, English women as well. As chancellor of Germany he had employed the same sort of brio that had enabled the English aristocracy to avoid the kind of revolution that had swept aside its French counterpart. As a Junker, he was a member of an aristocracy that dated its origins to the time of Charlemagne, and felt it had a right to forever rule Germany. With his fiery temper, intolerance of opposition and huge appetite for food and drink – until, finally, his doctor put him on a strict diet in the 1880s – Bismarck was no social reformer eager to ameliorate the lot of his poor countrymen. But he was a pragmatist. His work insurance scheme, for instance, was designed not only to appease working-class radicalism, but also to reduce labour costs in the growing chemicals industry, where work was dangerous and employees wanted job guarantees before they'd put their lives and health at risk.[16] Similarly, in his foreign policy, precisely because he loved his country, he could see little gain in making too many enemies for a country surrounded on almost all sides.

However, less temperate minds grew intoxicated with thoughts of what Germany's growing wealth might buy it. In 1888 a new emperor came to the throne with dreams of helping Germany take its 'place in the sun'. Kaiser Wilhelm II saw no reason why a country as great and prosperous as his should have a navy half the size of Britain's. Quarrelling constantly with Bismarck until he finally dismissed him in 1890, Wilhelm replaced him with chancellors more willing to do his bidding – and less willing to restrain Germany from foreign entanglements. Now that Germany had African colonies, her interests sometimes ran up against those of her rivals, most particularly when the British went to war with the independent Boer republics in South Africa (which Germany supported). Anxious that his country not be too vulnerable to any possible future British blockade of its ports, in 1897 Wilhelm appointed a new naval secretary and launched an aggressive shipbuilding programme.

Equally, Japan's economic rise made it possible for it to strengthen militarily. Stung by its forcible opening up to the world earlier in the century, its fiercely independent government wanted to ensure no foreign country could ever again impose its will on the nation. Rather than withdraw into a shell, Japan leapt into the race. Following the 1868 Meiji Restoration, the imperial government had done away with its decentralised armed forces officered by nobility and instituted a standing army, staffed by national conscription and commanded by a professional officer corps. It then abandoned its centuries-long isolationism and started building a navy. Employing British advisers, the government modelled its fleet on the Royal Navy, then the largest and most formidable naval fighting force in the world. This new Japanese military was then put to the test; first, in repressing a domestic Samurai rebellion; and second, with an expedition against Taiwan in 1874. Then in 1894, satisfied the country was once more ready for serious warfare, Japanese Imperial forces engaged in the country's first major conflict abroad, successfully battling China for control of Korea. As part of its prize, Japan got Taiwan and the Penghu Islands close to the Chinese mainland, as well as parts of Manchuria.

For China, whose armed forces were largely cannibalised by widespread corruption and thoroughly humiliated by its smaller, but clearly ascendant neighbour, it was a further blow to a tottering and now decadent regime. For everyone else, it was a warning of what might lie ahead. Being a mountainous country whose population had to crowd into plains covering less than a third of its land, Japan's growing economy had to look abroad for food and raw materials. Increasingly dependent on foreign supplies, the country's rulers knew that if the need arose they had to be prepared to use force to keep the imports flowing. The world might yet regret forcing Japan to open up.

But all this was of only limited concern to the country that forced Japan back into the world, the United States. Bordered to the east and west by oceans, to the north by relatively friendly (and comparatively small, in terms of output and population) Canada, and by a weak southern neighbour in Mexico, she could stand by as tensions rose in Europe and the Pacific and keep reinvesting most of her surpluses not in battleships, but factories. It was, quite simply, a happy time to be a spectator in world affairs.

CHAPTER 9

INTO THE VALLEY OF
THE SHADOW OF DEATH

Like most of us, you probably seldom go to church, save perhaps for the occasional wedding or funeral. And even when you do, when the moment comes for the congregation to say a prayer or recite a creed together, you might well opt to remain silent. Some of us find these moments a bit creepy, as if everyone has been indoctrinated. But think about it. When you attend, say, a football match, how likely are you to refuse to rise for the national anthem? If you're like many of us, it would scarcely occur to you.

Which says a lot. The nation has become for us what the church was for our ancestors: a community of believers which provides a door to a powerful patron. Whereas the parish community would once have provided access to the services and resources provided by the church, from poor relief to education to emotional succour, today belonging to the nation gives us those rights. We call them privileges of citizenship, and with those rights go responsibilities – to pay taxes to the state, to obey its laws, to revere its symbols and to stand to attention before its officers. All this is a legacy of the nineteenth century.

Seldom has humanity experienced a century as transformative as that one. It started with China still a great empire and the world's biggest economy. When it ended, the Middle Kingdom was sinking into civil disorder, its government losing control of much of its territory, its internal affairs a playground for foreign powers. In 1800, the Ottoman Empire wrapped itself around much of the Mediterranean. In 1900, it was beating a hasty retreat to its Turkish heartland, its provinces snapped up like scraps by ascending European rivals. In the course of the century, Germany came into being, as did Italy. Japan entered the modern world. The states of Latin America became independent. The United States, having started out a rural backwater, in the next hundred years built the biggest economy in the history of humanity. Canada gained self-rule, as shortly would Australia and South Africa. As for the rest of Africa, nearly all its independent states had been absorbed into new European colonies – some colonies throwing together many different and often mismatched entities – with only Ethiopia and Liberia clinging to a tenuous freedom.

The century had begun with most humans living on the farm and earning roughly the same income as one another. A hundred years later a handful of Western countries, whose cities teemed with landless labourers who went to work each day in bigger and bigger factories, had raced ahead of the rest. Their armies fanned out across the globe, their bankers managed much of the world's money and their citizens, who had for centuries filled churches every Sunday to pray to their god for prosperity and security, more and more expected their government to deliver those goods to them.

By 1900, the state provided many of the services people depended on for their livelihood and well-being: policing the streets, laying sewers, building roads, setting the gauges used by the railways that brought their food and clothes to town, standardising and enforcing weights and measures in the markets where they did their shopping, lighting the streets at night and monitoring their working conditions by day. Universal conscription of armies was becoming more common, as was public education, and in the barracks and schools the state exposed its captive audiences to a liturgy of praise and reverence to itself. Citizens memorised the newly drafted national anthems, saluted their young flags and learned that their lives now belonged to a new idol.

Economists fell in line with this gradual funnelling of people's loyalties towards their nation states. Seeing their task as serving the nation, economists drifted towards nationalism. Although neoclassical theory, with its universalist ambitions, kept its foothold in British universities and spread to France, elsewhere, German-style historicist and institutionalist approaches dominated, their exponents counselling an interventionist state to protect the market against imports and assist the development of local firms. By the end of its Civil War, the United States was following Germany's earlier moves and using tariffs to build its industrial sector while Japan – and soon Russia as well – was aggressively developing manufacturing, finance and transportation.

Furthermore, even where neoclassical theory ruled the academy, governments implemented their recommendations in a selective manner, if at all. In the final decades of the nineteenth century, French government policy bore more resemblance to that of latecomers like Japan and Germany than to Britain's – and even in Britain the free-market faith was wavering. Over the last third of the nineteenth century, Britain's share of global manufacturing dropped from 31.8 per cent to 19.5 per cent, while Germany's rose from 13.2 per cent to 16.6 per cent. Not only was this trend set to continue, but since Germany's steel industry was showing particular dynamism, Britain's dominance of the seas could now be challenged by German shipbuilding. Some reformist politicians, led by Joseph Chamberlain, noting that Germany was doing all this under a protectionist trade regime, began to question Britain's free-trading gospel.[1]

At the turn of the twentieth century, Chamberlain launched a political campaign for an 'imperial-preference' trading regime, whereby Britain would free up trade within its empire, but erect barriers to it outside. British economists remained largely united around the free-trade creed, some of them accusing those who questioned the gospel of 'blasphemy'.[2] Nevertheless, as industry and lobby groups arose to help push Chamberlain's agenda, it became clear that the influence of the neoclassical doctrine outside the halls of Westminster remained weak.[3] Within their cloisters, neoclassical economists enforced orthodoxy by excluding heretics from academic posts, in contrast to the economic priesthoods in countries like Germany, where it was neoclassical economists who couldn't obtain university positions.[4] However, their authority did not extend so far into the public square, and they did not yet enjoy the kind of priestly status that later generations would accord them.

In fact, the economists who exercised the greatest impact on public discourse at this time often came from outside the walls of the temple. Broadly speaking, British economic thought was pulling in two different directions, only one of which was shaped by the economists themselves. While they were taking their young discipline in a universalist direction and, like the Marxism they consciously rivalled, thereby crafting a doctrine that sought to unify all humanity around shared beliefs, others, not unlike their historicist and institutionalist counterparts in Germany, Japan or the United States, aimed to provide economic thought with context. One of the most influential scholars of the late nineteenth century was not an economist but the historian Arnold Toynbee, who made the term 'Industrial Revolution' famous and argued that the economic behaviour of a market economy couldn't be divorced from the industrial context that produced it.[5] Like his contemporary Beatrice Webb, who was working among the poor of east London at the same time he was delivering his lectures – and who also would conduct a celebrated courtship with Chamberlain, before going on to marry Sidney Webb – Toynbee was a social reformer who believed that justice did not originate within the economic model, but had to be imposed by political and social action.

Even so, despite their considerable impact on political discussions, the contributions of such scholars did not work their way into the canon. Alfred Marshall, for instance, toyed with history, but used it principally for the purposes of illustration. As historians and sociologists began inserting themselves more forcefully into economic debates, Marshall eventually joined the move towards walling off his field of enquiry. In 1908, when he was due to vacate his chair at Cambridge, he favoured Arthur Pigou as his successor. Pigou further raised the temple walls by expelling history from the canon altogether, saying, 'antiquarian researchers have no great attraction for one who finds it difficult enough to read what is now thought on economic problems, without spending time in studying confessedly inadequate solutions that were offered centuries ago.'[6] As far as Pigou was concerned, economic scholarship was now far more advanced than any insights that could be gleaned from the past.

Yet while free-traders ultimately won the battle with Chamberlain, Britain taking only small steps towards imperial preference, the new purity of economics would initially win a limited following. Both Toynbee and Webb would arguably have more impact on policy debates than any economic theorist within the emerging canon. And even when they could impose orthodoxy, the economics priesthood could not ensure this silenced the voices of dissent. The heterodox John A. Hobson noted that he had lost his job thanks to 'the intervention of an Economics Professor who read my book and considered it as an equivalent in rationality to an attempt to prove the flatness of the earth'.[7] However, because Hobson went on to inform the economic policy of the young Labour Party, his thinking arguably did more to shape subsequent British history for generations to come than the priesthood that had purged him.[8] For the time being, the claims of economists to a higher, universal truth were going to have to give way to the insistent demands of the nation for loyalty. The dream of their own Vatican, their own Qom, to which economists everywhere pled loyalty and where political leaders would flock to for guidance, would have to wait another day.

In the European Middle Ages, the typical regime had been a fluid alliance of the king, the Church and the nobility. Later, by altering the state's economic base, from which it derived revenue, capitalism was inevitably altering its politics as well. From the point of view of capitalists and kings – or increasingly, presidents, since the republican ideal was spreading – the Industrial Revolution had been a mutually rewarding experience. Rising prosperity enriched the government, and the government then had the resources to provide the public services required for the smooth functioning of the economy. In addition to everything it did to maintain domestic order, the government enforced contracts and private property, oversaw the money supply and standardised currency by setting legal tender. It also opened foreign markets by force or diplomacy, and policed the sea lanes and secured supplies of necessary imports. Then, as the century progressed and the cries for reform met the increasing need for a skilled, healthy workforce, governments got into the business of educating and protecting the workers from the worst abuses of capitalism, thereby lifting such costs off business people and transferring them to the Treasury. Subject to these provisos, the government then allowed business to conduct its affairs in a market it left largely free, stepping in to collect taxes on the surpluses that resulted and punishing those firms and individuals that tried to conceal their earnings.

Think of it like a marriage between capital and king (if by king you mean the executive power at the top of the state). However, it was, by the end of the century, a marriage threatened by a jealous rival. Despite the steady rise of Europe's capitalists, whose political ambitions were embodied in the likes of self-made men like Joseph Chamberlain, many of Europe's states were still staffed by aristocrats. More often than not, they clung to old ideals and resented the bureaucratisation of the state, and modern life more generally. Although some noblemen were amenable to business, most notably in Britain, by and large the aristocracy of nineteenth-century Europe frowned on capitalism. They resented the bourgeois upstarts who were infiltrating the political system, calling for church disestablishment, more democracy, and the substitution of expertise for inherited status in the staffing of the public service. And by the turn of the century, as industry continued its relentless rise, aristocrats began to reassert their authority. In Germany and Russia, pragmatists like Bismarck and Sergei Witte were being edged out by conservatives who all too frequently wanted to resist the rising tide of democracy and social reform. Pining to restore an order of obedience to a monarch and submission to hereditary privilege, they were about to complicate matters.

Nationalism was originally seen by its proponents as a way to emancipate people from foreign rulers, as was the case in the Balkans or Ireland; to build a great entity out of previous disparate peoples with a shared heritage, as was the case in Germany, France or Britain; or to do both at once, as was the case in Italy, where one nationalist leader famously crowned the birth of modern Italy by declaring, 'We have made Italy, now we must make Italians.'[9] Despite such seemingly progressive origins, though, nationalism could also be used to turn back the clock or reinforce the existing order, exploited by rulers to shore up their own support.

For example, the Austro-Hungarian Empire was a multinational one which, like the Ottoman Empire, had been harassed all through the nineteenth century by movements for national independence – in Italy, the Balkans and Hungary, which even managed to force the government to give it equal status at the helm of the old Austrian Empire. The Balkans were an especially troubling region. The Serbians were proving particularly obstreperous; some members of its government hoping to draw support from their traditional Russian ally for a growing assertion of their autonomy from Vienna. Back in the imperial capital, there were those who felt that if an excuse could be found for going to war in Serbia, the government could unite its peoples in a passion of national pride and stamp out the fires of rebellion.

By the second decade of the twentieth century, that passion was growing ardent. Across the continent, a chorus for war grew louder. Some practically longed for it. Futurism, a modernist movement in philosophy which celebrated industry, cities and pretty much anything which destroyed tradition, called for a great conflict to purify society of its corrupting influences. 'We will glorify war' wrote the poet F. T. Marinetti in the founding manifesto of Futurism, published in a Parisian newspaper in 1909, describing conflict as 'the world's only hygiene' – a sentiment echoed by the English poet Rupert Brooke, who likened young men marching into battle to 'swimmers into cleanness leaping'. Paradoxically, many of Europe's old aristocrats shared this sentiment, believing a conflagration would cleanse European society of its modernist filth.

The rising war party posed a dilemma for Europe's growing socialist movement. Marx had said that workers across the world were united by their common experience of oppression. If war broke out, were the socialist leaders prepared to refuse to join and thereby sanction a modern apostasy: rejection of one's nation? Marxist economics was about to confront the same dilemma then facing its neoclassical rival. Like competing faiths insisting theirs was the one true god, both schools made claims – mutually exclusive claims – to universal truth, each holding up its own doctrine as the sole path to enlightenment and prosperity. Yet while each presented itself as a saviour for all humanity, each now felt the same pressure to align with national need: either make themselves into state churches of sorts, or risk becoming exiled prophets in the desert.

Karl Marx and Friedrich Engels may have been firebrands eager to obliterate capitalism, and they delighted in ridiculing those they thought wrong. But at heart they remained scholars in the German radical tradition. Both were free-thinkers who disliked anything that smacked of orthodoxy; Marx famously responding to others appropriating his label by telling Engels, 'I am not a Marxist.' The same was true of one of their Polish followers, Rosa Luxemburg, whose independence of mind was so strong that at times she did not hesitate to take issue with their teachings.

Born in Russian-ruled Poland in 1871, 'Red Rosa' quickly moved to the left. She was barely in her teens when complaints about her rebellious behaviour began showing up in her teachers' registers. When at the age of sixteen she graduated at the top of her class, she was denied the gold medal on account of her 'oppositional attitude to the authorities'. She migrated to Zurich soon after to escape the heavy hand of the Tsar's police and continued to taunt her university lecturers – who were sometimes more willing than the Russian secret service to forgive her simply for being so obviously intelligent.

All radicals agreed that their ultimate goal was to replace capitalism with a socialist society. However, there was some disagreement as to how they would do it. Near the end of his life in 1883, Marx had entertained the possibility that the transition to socialism might be achieved by peaceful and democratic means. This evolutionary current of thought had subsequently made its way into the German Social Democratic Party. But Rosa Luxemburg, who moved from Switzerland to Germany in the 1890s, had no time for it. For her, campaigning for social reform within capitalism was akin to feeding the workers lotus flowers and thereby lessening their revolutionary passion. And the Russian Marxist Vladimir Ilyich Ulyanov, who went by the name Lenin, agreed.

He not only agreed, he did so with relish. A zealot by nature, Lenin had, like Luxemburg, come to the faith early, complaining when he was sixteen that his older brother Alexander, then at university, spent all his time peering through a microscope and thus would 'never be a revolutionist'. But in fact, rather suddenly, Alexander had become a revolutionist. Joining a radical organisation and then helping concoct a plot to kill the Tsar, his cover was blown and he was caught by the police. When Lenin read the subsequent report of his brother's execution, it's said he declared, 'I'll make them pay for this, I swear it.'[10]

Lenin saw that the war against capitalism couldn't be won simply with convincing arguments. Nationalism and the Orthodox Church had a powerful grip on Russian minds, and he judged that communism had to achieve a similar hold if it was to rival the old forces. Luxemburg parted with him on this point. She detested nationalism, believing it a ploy by the ruling classes to divide the workers against one another. After all, the same generals who rallied their troops to slaughter one another weren't averse to spending their winters at the same resorts as their peers from other countries. To her, substituting one catechism for another denied the very freedom that socialism was meant to bring.

In the summer of 1903, forced as it was to assemble in secret or abroad, the Russian Social Democratic Labour Party opened its Second Congress in Belgium. Assembling in a flea-ridden Brussels flour warehouse, the delegates later moved to London to escape the prying eyes of the Belgian police. Once there, they held their meeting in an angling club whose walls were lined with trophies, carrying on after-hours discussions in nearby pubs and cafes.[11] A meeting of a few dozen men, they made up for numbers with energy, assembling thirty-seven times over a three-week period while they hammered out the young party's programme. There came a point in the deliberations when a rift opened between Lenin and some of the other delegates, who felt party members should be free to express disagreement. Lenin insisted that to organise a revolution in a society like Russia, the party needed followers with a cult-like devotion and a willingness to give their entire lives to the cause. When it was put to the vote, Lenin lost. However, when a few of those who had voted against him subsequently left, Lenin claimed, with a bit of chutzpah, that his group was now in the majority – in Russian, the *Bolshevikii*, a name that would stick to the Communist Party he then took over.

Lenin, who called his doctrine of utter devotion to the party line 'democratic centralism' would brook no heresy. One of his political opponents later said that the Bolshevik leader considered his theory an 'irrefutable dogma', which therefore exempted its adepts from 'all scruples of conscience and all demands of logic' adding that 'from his youth his revolutionary work was characterised by the spirit of cold intrigue and by the cruel arrogance of a man convinced that he was the bearer of ultimate truth.'[12] Democratic centralism was as paradoxical as the medieval inquisitor's belief that you liberated a soul by torturing its body, or the insistence by British free-trade liberals that allowing the empire's workers to starve freed labour to be more productive. To Lenin, true democracy meant submerging your will into that of the class, submitting without reservation or doubt to the commands of the centre. So he'd run his party much as the Tsar ran his empire – with an absolute rule that demanded spiritual conformity from all his ministers. Opposed to any compromises with a government that might try to alleviate the working class's lot with Bismarckian measures that lessened its revolutionary fervour, Lenin's vision of the 'new communist man' recalled the Puritan ideal of a perfect, sinless life. To Lenin, workers who prospered under capitalism and were thus won over to its virtues were a 'labour aristocracy' who'd betrayed their own kind.

For Luxemburg, this was too much. If Lenin was mindful of his people's fierce Orthodoxy, Luxemburg bore the imprint of her middle-class Jewish upbringing. Tidy, fastidious, private, she shared the same tastes 'as any cultured *fin de siècle* citizen of Berlin': for music, Mozart; in art, Titian and Rembrandt.[13] She was too much an individualist to stomach Lenin's heavy-handed theology. 'Socialist democracy is not something which begins only in the promised land, after the foundations of political economy are created,' she wrote. 'It begins at the very moment of the seizure of power by the socialist party.'[14]

Lenin regarded that condition the way an early churchman would have treated Christ's call for his followers to turn the other cheek: ideal, but in an imperfect world, an obstacle to winning over the warrior-nobility that would export the faith into the barbarous forests. Like his ecclesiastical predecessors, Lenin had practical impediments to overcome if the working-class uprising Marx had envisioned was to come to pass. Greatest of all was that in Russia there wasn't that much of a working class to begin with. Despite the industrial boom of the late nineteenth century, Russia remained an agrarian society, nine-tenths of its people being peasant farmers who had only recently been emancipated from their feudal bonds. So Lenin, instead, said they would 'telescope' the revolution. A 'dictatorship of the proletariat' would seize the state, use it to take over the means of production, then leapfrog the capitalist stage to build an industrial economy. To do all this, the party needed to annihilate the boundaries between state and market and fuse politics and economics – not unlike what had been the practice in Russian feudalism.

Marx's primary objection to capitalism was not its free market, but the private property that went with it. But Lenin disliked the market itself, holding that surpluses were extracted in the process of exchange, not just in production. Therefore, not only did he want the state to own everything, he also wanted bureaucrats to determine how it distributed and invested everything. Arguably, his form of socialist economics owed as much to the Marxist classics as the sale of the indulgences against which Martin Luther had railed did to the Bible. Nevertheless, although they would often distort his positions, Lenin and his followers retained Marx as their prophet.

It was once said that communism could not conquer Russia, but Russia could conquer communism. To some of his critics, that is what Lenin wanted to do all along: take the ideals of Marxism and adapt them to an autocratic state, imposing it on every facet of people's lives – monitoring their behaviour, shaping their thoughts, determining their livelihood, assigning their role in the economy and getting them to bury their identity within that of the revolutionary struggle. Like some medieval millenarians who wanted to usher in the Second Coming with a holy war, the Bolsheviks aimed to purify society and rebuild it anew.

In June 1914, the Austro-Hungarian government got its wish. A Serbian nationalist assassinated the crown prince while he was on a visit to Sarajevo and gave Vienna a pretext for war. With Germany's Kaiser Wilhelm eager to back the empire in a conflict he thought would be short and advantageous to his country, the blocks were removed from the lumbering war machine. The time finally came for the socialists to decide which way to go.

Although he was appalled by the outburst of national pride, Lenin reckoned his Bolsheviks could exploit it to their gain. But Rosa Luxemburg believed in her heart that the international working class's shared interests would lift the scales from their eyes and make them refuse to fight. Abiding by the Marxist credo to unite the workers of the world, in late July her German Social Democratic Party declared that 'not a drop of any German soldier's blood must be sacrificed to the power hunger of the Austrian ruling clique'.[15]

However, that summer's patriotic fervour was proving contagious. Many Social Democratic deputies were starting to waver in their convictions. Their ultimate profession of faith would come at the height of the summer, when the German parliament voted on whether or not to approve the war effort. Luxemburg feverishly buttonholed deputies and implored them not to lose sight of the bigger struggle. But her mood darkened when, amid her lobbying, the French socialist leader, her ally in the effort to build an international alliance of workers, was shot dead by a French nationalist in a Paris cafe. Four days later, when the time came for the German vote, she discovered she had managed to win only two deputies to her side. She looked on distraught as one old friend after another joined the war party, leaving her like an abandoned bride at an empty altar. On the verge of suicide,[16] she wrote to a friend that the international alliance of the working class had been 'broken to pieces' the workers 'scattered to the various battlefields'.[17] She then quit the party and formed a new communist group of her own, calling it the Spartacus League after the ancient Roman gladiator who led a slave revolt.

As the union of state and market enabled governments to eventually make themselves the principal and even sole target of citizen loyalty, nationalism evolved into a full-blown love of country. Used in Martin Luther's time to help north European princes emancipate themselves from the papacy as they converted to the new Protestant faiths and took control of their kingdoms' churches, nationalism would once more be used to liberate Europe's rulers – this time, from the threat posed by a working-class militancy that aimed to transcend national boundaries. The generals, old-school aristocrats, now had Europe's workers lining up in their serried ranks. The willingness of the continent's rulers to make their citizens pawns in a massive chess game, and more strikingly, the readiness and even eagerness of those citizens to march off to war when called to do so, recalled the fervour that in a distant age had motivated religious crusades. 'If I should die, think only this of me', wrote Rupert Brooke in 'The Soldier', 'That there's some corner of a foreign field/ That is for ever England.'

It's been said that generals always fight the last war. Of no conflict was that more true than the First World War. And the problem for the generals was that the last major European war had taken place in 1871 – way back in the days of cavalry charges and aristocratic codes of honour; the days before the invention of the machine gun, the aeroplane and mustard gas. The same entrepreneurial genius that had transformed the West's industrial production had been applied to the invention of weaponry and the mechanisation of warfare. The generals went in as romantics, believing the cavalry charge and the heroism of men would overwhelm the trenches into which each side had dug themselves. But they, or more properly their soldiers, came up against the cold, hard steel of science, which blew them to pieces and left millions of bodies mutilated, broken and destroyed, piling up in enormous anonymous heaps on the battlefields of Europe.

Meanwhile, the death of Rosa Luxemburg's ideals on Europe's battlefields meant that the torch of communist revolution had now passed to Russia. Luxemburg may have inspired her followers, but Lenin put the fear of god into his – and in the end, that proved more effective at turning them out for a fight. Out of loyalty to Serbia, the Tsar had joined the alliance against Germany and the Austro-Hungarian Empire. However, Russia's enthusiasm for war quickly dissolved amid the carnage wrought by the superior German army. Departing then for the front to take personal command of the armed forces, Tsar Nicholas left his wife in control back in the capital.

At that point the imperial court descended into intrigue and back-stabbing. As the Tsarina fell under the sway of a charismatic monk, Rasputin, whose bizarre behaviour seemed to herald some sort of impending apocalypse, Russia slid into chaos. Nicholas's authority collapsed and he abdicated in 1917, whereupon Lenin pounced. As a provisional government tried to re-establish order, Bolshevik workers seized factories and workspaces and formed workers' councils – in Russian, *Soviets*. Late that year, after organising the Soviets into a series of fighting cells, Lenin launched his assault and toppled the young government. Factional fighting then broke out and soon a full-blown civil war began. Lenin's foreign minister, Leon Trotsky, then hastily assembled a Red Army composed of defecting soldiers and units from the imperial army, along with peasant volunteers, marshalling them to defend the new regime against those loyal to the old order.

By the following autumn, Rosa Luxemburg was openly warning against Lenin's autocratic tendencies. Troubled by his willingness to crush a free press and eliminate political opponents, she denounced a socialism 'decreed from behind a few official desks'.[18] And she was briefly heartened when, after the German government fell in 1918, worker uprisings spread across Germany as well. For that meant she would now get to put her own, more democratic socialism to the test – an opportunity that came when a commune in Berlin allied itself to her Spartacist party.

But within days of the Spartacist rebellion, the shock troops of Germany's own provisional government moved in and crushed the uprising. Taking control of Berlin and terrorising all those who had backed the Spartacists, soldiers scoured the city for the little Polish woman who had inspired the revolution. Finding her one night hiding in a flat, with 'sunken cheeks and the dark rings under her eyes from so many sleepless nights'[19] they took her to Berlin's Eden Hotel. Expecting to be thrown in prison, Luxemburg packed a small case of her books, but her captors had other plans. One of the hotel's maids recounted how they 'knocked the poor woman and dragged her around'.[20] After a brief interrogation, they put her back in the car and, as it drove off, shot her dead, dumping her body in the Landwehr Canal.[21]

Henceforth, the battle between communism and capitalism would be fought between Russia and the West, a fault line that would prove as deep and potent as the prior religious division of Europe. Economists would now labour to propagate one of two faiths – either preserving the body of capitalism, or labouring to build a communist new Jerusalem.

As horrifying as the First World War had been, it did nothing to diminish the appeal of nationalism. A rising generation of political leaders in Europe's overseas empires, eager to free themselves from European rule, studied the continent's tragedy for insights. Nationalism, they could plainly see, able to move millions to give their lives to a greater cause, could be corralled to serve their own campaigns. Equally, the Bolshevik triumph over Russia left a lasting impression.

Resistance to colonial rule wasn't new, but earlier movements had looked backwards. Aiming to return colonial societies to their independent past, they had usually coalesced around traditional leaders or religious identities. But in the late nineteenth century, the first stirrings of a new type of movement had begun to appear – one which looked to the future. Among the first to arise was in India, where in 1885 a group of Western-educated Indians formed the Indian National Congress. One of its founders, Dadabhai Naoroji, would go on to publish a book titled *Poverty and Un-British Rule in India*, in which he attempted to calculate India's net national profit under British colonial rule. Britain, he suggested, was draining money from her colonies and enriching herself at their expense.

By and large, Western intellectuals at that time saw imperialism as a progressive, civilising force. Even Marx, while noting its violence, maintained it pulled India into the capitalist age. But Naoroji's claim, which would become a recurrent theme in the nationalist movements in the colonies, was that imperialism was in fact a game being played to the mother country's advantage. If both India and Britain derived benefits from empire, Britain derived far more, and was therefore leaving India further behind. Nevertheless, though he repudiated imperialism, Naoroji, like many nationalists, did not reject the West. On the contrary, like many in the new generation of colonial nationalists, he wanted to get what the West had: the money that would enable their people to free themselves from poverty, as well as the nation state to generate and distribute these resources. Although traditional leaders might have wanted to return their societies to a simpler agrarian past shorn of Western contamination, the nationalists wanted to go in the opposite direction. Naoroji himself opened his book by enumerating the benefits Western civilisation had brought India – English education, law and order, the railways. To him, the fundamental problem with British rule in India was that it wasn't true to its doctrine: it wasn't civilising India enough. 'A truly

British course', he said, 'can and certainly will be vastly beneficent both to Britain and India.'[22]

By the time Naoroji's book was published in 1901, radical opinion about imperialism had begun to veer away from Marx's relatively sanguine view. Luxemburg[23] and Lenin,[24] influenced in part by John A. Hobson's then recent book on the topic,[25] both took a dim view of imperialism, seeing it as a means by which capitalist countries exploited pre-capitalist ones. Moreover, as nationalist sentiment grew in the colonies, it tended to gravitate towards the Leninist view of the state. With colonial markets often dominated by foreigners, the nationalists regarded the state as a means by which colonised peoples could reclaim control of their economic destinies. However, most nationalists stopped short of Lenin's socialism. If alien, the market to them wasn't actually bad. More typically, Third World nationalists called for the state to engineer growth, but not to actually eliminate private property and the free market. And soon after the war ended, they got an illustration of how this sort of thing might be done.

In one of its last victorious battles in the First World War, the Ottoman Empire had withstood an allied invasion on the beaches of Gallipoli. One of the commanders on the Turkish side had been a young officer named Mustafa Kemal, whose successes there helped burnish credentials already marked by earlier achievements. When the tottering empire withdrew from the war in the autumn of 1918, leaving her German and Austrian allies to their fate, the British and French, reinforced by Armenians and Greeks, began carving up most of what remained of it. If it was a happy time for the Ottoman Empire's many ethnic minorities, it was a sad time for the Turkish majority.[26] Kemal decided to do something about it.

In 1919, he resigned his commission, set up a rival government with some like-minded officers, and organised remnants of the Ottoman Army into a force that could withstand the foreign allies. In vicious fighting over the next three years, he managed to carve a Turkish homeland out of the rump of the Ottoman Empire.

Burying the empire once and for all testified to Kemal's desire to break with the past. As a boy, he had resisted his mother's attempts to give him a religious education.[27] In fact, he had never shown much interest in the Islam of his forefathers. And as he grew older, he came to believe that the Ottoman Empire had been burdened with a religious tradition so heavy it could scarcely resist the Western challenge. Visiting a provincial village shortly after proclaiming the republic, he eschewed the customary fez and turned up wearing a panama, then proceeded to tell his audience, 'We will become civilized ... We will march forward ... Civilization is a fearful fire which consumes those who ignore it.'[28] In a region where Muslim brotherhoods were still strong and most people devout, this was as heretical as Jesus declaring himself a messiah before temple priests. Still, Kemal persisted. 'The Turkish republic cannot be a country of sheikhs,' he said, before going on to dismiss the shrines to Muslim saints that were ubiquitous: 'It is a disgrace for a civilized society to appeal for help to the dead.'[29]

Kemal closed dervish lodges, restricted the wearing of turbans and robes to Muslim officials, banned headscarves in government buildings (including schools) and required civil servants to wear Western hats. He then turned his attention to the economy. Having observed how industry and the state had supplanted the role of clerics in the West, he decided to move Turkey onto a similar course. However, he faced a peculiar challenge. Like Russia, Turkey was still largely a peasant society. What bourgeoisie existed was dominated by foreigners or ethnic minorities, like Greeks or Armenians. His prime minister, like him an aggressive Westerniser, had recently been to Russia, where he'd observed the dynamism of the Bolshevik state-led model. Returning to Ankara, he proposed a halfway house for Turkey – a unique experiment with a mixed economy, with the state dominating heavy industry, while allowing a private sector to flourish alongside it.

The nationalism that had ushered in the Turkish republic had been scarcely less violent than that which had run through the First World War. Whether massacres of Greeks and Armenians who resisted their subordination or repression of rebellions against the anti-clerical measures, violence was embraced in defence of the higher goal: a battle for a nation's soul. Nevertheless, Kemal, who would take the surname 'Atatürk' (father of the Turks) after legislating that all Turks had to assume family names, produced a model of national independence that would serve as a blueprint for anti-colonial leaders for the next two generations.

Back in the heartland of the world economy, though, nobody gave much thought to the possible economic retardation of the colonies. When they did, they were more likely to blame it on their initial backwardness. Winston Churchill went so far as to suggest Europeans were actually doing colonised peoples a favour. Complaining that empire was a 'lot of bother' he added that it was done 'for the good of the subject races'.[30] For their part, neoclassical economists, given their tendency to abstract theorising, paid little attention to the colonies other than perhaps to apply their theory to a particular issue that had arisen there – as when Alfred Marshall wrote that the imperial preference regime, which went against free-trade principles, would produce sub-optimal outcomes.[31] Exploration of the topic was left to heterodox economists like John A. Hobson, whose thinking influenced public policy but had little impact in the academy, finding its way into the work of only radical economists (by way of Luxemburg, Lenin and Nikolai Bukharin).

Besides, in the decade that followed the Treaty of Versailles, there hardly seemed any need for liberal economists to doubt the Western economic model. All you had to do was look around to see how well the free market was working. In the United States in the 1920s, a string of Republican presidents adopted a *laissez-faire* approach to the economy, boasting they had led Americans into a new age of prosperity. Following a brief post-war recession, the Western economy resumed growing, and by 1924 it was booming. This led President Calvin Coolidge to declare that 'the chief business of the American people is business'.[32] His expression of faith in the paradise that capitalism was building would then be echoed by his Commerce Secretary, Herbert Hoover, when he accepted the Republican Party's presidential nomination in 1928. 'We in America today are nearer to the final triumph over poverty than ever before in the history of any land. The poor-house is vanishing from among us,' he said in his acceptance speech at the 1928 Convention, adding, in a customary polite nod to divinity, 'we shall soon with the help of God be in sight of the day when poverty will be banished from this nation.'

The decade would be known as the Roaring Twenties. Admittedly, the roar wasn't heard everywhere – or at least it was heard in different ways. Germany, in particular, blamed for the recently concluded war and thus punished by the victorious Allies, stumbled into the decade. Crippled by a harsh reparations regime and the seizure of its industrial regions, the government had no option but to pay its bills by printing money – and doing it non-stop. Needless to say, as fast as the German mark came off the press, so did its value drop. The mark, which bought an American dime in 1920, was all but worthless three years later, when it took a billion of them to obtain a single dollar. The Spanish correspondent Eugeni Xammar reported on the bizarre scenes that resulted. One family, deciding it had had enough, sold their house to leave for America and start new lives, only to find that when they reached the port the proceeds from the sale could no longer cover even the cost of passage. Millions were plunged into poverty, diseases like rickets became widespread and tuberculosis reached epidemic proportions.[33] The writer Klaus Mann noted Germany was now witnessing 'the complete depreciation of the only truly credible value in this godforsaken era: that of money'.[34]

But elsewhere, money's power was if anything strengthening. After Henry Ford pioneered the assembly line, he turned the automobile into a mass-market item. Movies became widespread, as did the radio and the electricity that made it possible. Flappers filled the dancehalls, and F. Scott Fitzgerald chronicled the lives of the ultra-rich and their playgrounds in books like *The Great Gatsby*. By 1924, even Germany was recovering, the government having managed to stabilise the hyperinflation (though scars remained, since not all Germans felt the renewed prosperity).

The gurus of economics gave their blessing to government policy.

The most important economist of the day in America was Irving Fisher, who was also the first great neoclassical theorist to break the orthodoxy of German historicism in American economics departments. Working independently of the European marginalists as he wrote what would be Yale's first doctoral dissertation in economics, Fisher – whose initial training had been in mathematics – was the first major American scholar to apply mathematical techniques to the study of the economy. He broke away from the then dominant American tradition of narrative, historical approaches, and his work soon brought him into the British canon. A successful entrepreneur, having invented a card-filing system, which he then sold to an office-equipment maker, subsequently putting the proceeds to work in the stock market, Fisher had also given economics the quantity theory of money, reasoning that price stability was the holy grail of modern economics.

A simple commandment for the government followed from this: seek ye first stable prices, and all other things shall be added unto you. He further argued that the best way to guarantee price stability was for the state to manage the growth of money supply, but do little more. So the hands-off approach to the economy, embodied in the American government of the decade and whose fruits were manifest in the surging stock market, gave Fisher enough confidence that in late 1929 he declared high stock prices to be here for ever. His optimism was seconded by most university economics departments[35] and underscored when a prominent Wall Street speculator said any future falls in share prices would be offset by 'organised buying support' – a statement greeted on Wall Street 'as though the words had come from some financial Moses as holy writ'.[36] The West seemed to have truly entered its promised land.

Two days later, stock markets across the Western world crashed. In a day of pandemonium, as some brokers fell to their knees and began praying on the floor of the New York Stock Exchange, millionaires were wiped out and the life savings of millions evaporated. After the markets closed that 'Black Tuesday' the centuries-old church in the financial district, Trinity Wall Street, filled with people of all denominations.[37] President Hoover counselled patience, predicting that a rebound was around the corner. And he kept on doing it, as winter descended and the new year began.

But on Main Street, and on farms across the land, everyone could see that the Great Depression had begun. Meanwhile, in the temples of economic thought, the neoclassical doctrine that had established its orthodoxy across the English-speaking world, now faced a threatening new challenge. It came from a radical upstart sect it had hitherto mostly ignored.

CHAPTER 10

THE PEOPLE IN DARKNESS

Picture yourself having been born around 1905 in, say, a small English village. After finishing your education, you are taken by the urge to emigrate to America – perhaps a hunger for adventure, a need to escape, the lure of prosperity, who knows – and take all your savings, catch a train to Southampton and hop on a steamer with one trunk and a few Thomas Cook cheques. On the journey you make new friends, hear some of the jazz tunes that are popular in America when the orchestra comes to play in the dining saloon, and spend your days on deck reading a guidebook to your new homeland.

You arrive at Ellis Island, clear immigration, and then you and your friends go into the city to find lodgings. Though forewarned of Manhattan's dangers, you can also feel its energy. After the post-war recession the economy is clearly on the move again. And on your third day, armed with your school certificate, you find work in a bank for six dollars a week. That evening you do the maths and calculate that after living expenses, you'll save about a dollar a week – a princely sum. Although you'll allow yourself to soak up the Big Apple's excitement, with its speakeasies and flappers, you will restrict your own entertainment to pursuits that won't burn through your nest-egg, like going to the movies or catching the Sunday train to Coney Island.

You fall in love. After a couple of years, you decide to settle down. With enough saved between you to make a down payment on a small patch of land near the new railway in Long Island, you order a lovely home, a Gladstone, from the Sears Roebuck catalogue. You have it installed with that new marvel, electrical lighting, and even manage to equip it with an electric iron and laundry-machine. These extravagances clear your accounts. But coming after four years of periodic pay-rises, you now earn enough to resume saving. You celebrate your first Christmas in your new home.

After a couple of years, as the economy picks up speed, you start hearing your co-workers swapping tales about their stock-market trades. They seem to have lots of money to splash around. So one day you go to see your manager to ask him how it works. He sends you to his broker, who sells you on the idea at once. You take the money you have in your savings account and he invests it for you. At the end of the month you have made more than if you'd left it in the bank a whole year. So you keep investing small amounts, and you keep coming out ahead. By year's end, you have doubled your savings pool. You celebrate by taking the train into the city one evening to catch the latest Hollywood film at the picture palace, *The Jazz Singer*, wondering aloud how on earth they caught Al Jolson's voice on film. The next day, you work out that your income is now sufficient to afford a car. So you buy a sleek Pontiac on credit arranged by the dealer.

You visit your broker more often, and on one occasion he mentions something called a margin loan. It sounds too good to be true, but when he shows you the numbers, they all add up. For each dollar you put into the market he'll lend you three. That way, you can buy four dollars in shares. When the stock price rises, you can then sell the shares, pay back your loan and pocket the difference. Your spouse is too prudent to ever approve such a thing, but when you run it by colleagues several report doing it with success.

So you take a punt. It works. Your broker persuades you that since the market's going up, instead of cashing your profits you can use them as collateral for a bigger loan, and you can repeat the experience. You take his advice, and you make even more money. You start spending lunch breaks in the customers' room of your brokerage, where you enjoy the good humour and camaraderie as everyone watches the clerks erasing prices and chalking up the day's new, higher ones. You all agree this is the greatest time ever. You contemplate the possibility of a winter vacation in Florida, travelling in a luxurious Pullman on the newly launched Orange Blossom Special. You buy a Radiola for the house, and start listening to the live broadcasts of classical concerts ('to cultivate yourself,' you tell your spouse, befitting your rising social status). By the autumn of 1929, your holdings are worth so much you start to imagine buying a new home.

Then one day in October, the market does something it has not done before: it plunges. A messenger from your broker comes to see you at work to tell you either to sell your shares and pay your debts – with a loss, since your shares are suddenly worth less than your accumulated debt – or to send him enough cash to make up the difference. You go home anxious that evening. But in the morning the *New York Times* reports that the country's leading bankers and economists have rallied to support the market, saying it was just a flash. So you take a deep breath, empty your savings and clear your margins. The market does resume rising, and you go home for the weekend feeling a bit less nervous. But, unsure how it would be taken, you don't mention your brief brush with fate to your spouse.

The following Tuesday the market plunges once more. Again you get the same message from your broker. This time you have no more cash on hand. On your lunch break you race to the customers' room. The mood has darkened, people are angry, one woman is sobbing. The clerks can't keep up with the constant calls to revise prices, which only go down more. Your broker is nowhere to be found and an overwhelmed messenger tells you he has been trying to sell the shares of all the clients who didn't come in with cash that morning. You know that must mean he sold yours. On the train ride home you reassure yourself that perhaps he got a good enough price by selling early in the day.

The next day, you go to the brokerage first thing and hear that nobody is buying. Your, and everyone's, shares collapsed, and your broker extracted a fraction of their value. After using the sale's proceeds to pay your loan, you are still left with a large debt. You stay at your desk after the bank closes to do the maths. You work out that if from now on you put all your savings towards repaying your debt, you can wait for the market to bounce back and still keep your house.

Just before Christmas, your manager assembles the staff to announce that the bank has lost so many clients in the crash, it will have to cut everyone's pay by a fifth. You start skipping lunches to make your debt payments. You try to make Christmas as cheerful as usual, but you are in a sullen silence with your secret.

Six weeks later, your manager tells you he will have to let you go. He wishes you well. You dare not go home early, for fear of revealing what has happened. You buy coffee and a newspaper, and add up the sums in the margin. You will not make your payments on any of your loans – car, home and land. You know the banks, themselves desperate for cash, are seizing properties and auctioning them off. In the middle of winter you will lose everything.

Stuffing the newspaper into your coat pocket, you race around all afternoon looking for work. Nobody is hiring. Evening comes and you must now head home. Pulling the newspaper out from your pocket again, you notice a headline saying that things are as good as ever. 'Trade recovery now complete President told.'[1]

What would you do? What would you say?

At the south-western corner of the city of Cambridge there is a footpath that meanders by the River Cam. If you wander alongside the sleepy river, past the college playing fields and beside meadows, you eventually arrive at a small village called Grantchester. Walk beyond the village's thatched roofs and old church, and eventually you come to a teahouse. There you will find the best tea and scones in Cambridge.

It hasn't changed much in a hundred years. Long popular with writers, artists and Cambridge lecturers eager for a day's retreat in a setting even more bucolic than the city, its walls are adorned with photographs of some of the famous visitors. Outside, in the gardens, you can walk down a sloping path to the river, where punts are moored on the riverbank.

At the turn of the twentieth century, the young Cambridge economist John Maynard Keynes used to come here with friends, including the writers Lytton Strachey and E. M. Forster. This group of young men formed the nucleus of what would later, with the addition of female members like Virginia Woolf, be called the Bloomsbury Group (after the London neighbourhood where several of them lived). Despite having all been born in the Victorian age, they celebrated the pursuit of pleasure. They dipped into and out of relationships with one another, Keynes for a time taking the painter Duncan Grant as his lover. Despite being happily homosexual, Keynes would later marry a Russian ballerina with whom, to judge by his own accounts, he was just as enthusiastically heterosexual – Keynes had an appetite for carnal pleasures surpassed only by his curiosity for new ideas.[2]

He was one of those rare individuals who seemed to have it all – cultural refinement, brilliance, practical genius, eloquence. A gifted mathematician, in Cambridge he came to the attention of the great economist Alfred Marshall, who urged his charge to enter his field. But Keynes kept his wide range of interests, dabbling in art, studying philosophy and being in one respect like the great American neoclassical economist Irving Fisher (prior to his unanticipated 1929 wipe-out): a canny investor, both for himself and for his college. Keynes was charming and urbane, someone who could win debates by his persuasive speech and the force of his personality. Optimistic by nature, he shared with his mentor Marshall a strong faith in the human capacity to remake the world.

To this long list of qualities he could now add, by the 1920s, a reputation for foresight. As an adviser to the British government at the Versailles Conference that ended the First World War, he'd strongly counselled against harsh reparations, warning that vengeance would be penny-wise but pound-foolish. In *The Economic Consequences of the Peace*, he wrote, 'The policy of reducing Germany to servitude for a generation, of degrading the lives of millions of human beings, and of depriving a whole nation of happiness should be abhorrent and detestable ... If we aim deliberately at the impoverishment of Central Europe, vengeance, I dare predict, will not limp.'[3] Four years later, just as the hyperinflation caused by those reparations was peaking in Germany, an obscure politician named Adolf Hitler staged an abortive but ominous 'beer-hall putsch' to try to overthrow the government. It was an omen of a coming vengeance that would certainly not limp.

The hyperinflation that ravaged the German economy in the 1920s would not have broken out had Germany still been on the gold standard (which it had lifted during the war), since it wouldn't have been able to print money to pay all its bills. A gold standard, like the one then in use in the UK, pins a currency's exchange rate to a fixed amount of the precious metal. A government can therefore only increase the money supply if it obtains more gold to back it up. That requires increasing exports, taking payments in gold, which it can then store in the central bank's vaults. However, while a gold standard prevents inflation, it can also cause problems of its own – for instance at a time when you actually want a little inflation.

Such a time came to the UK a few years later. After the 1929 crash, Keynes, like Marshall and Fisher, called for an increase in the money supply, so that people could start spending and investing more. Since foreigners were buying fewer goods, Britain's gold reserves were declining. That forced the government to adjust the money supply downwards, which worsened the downturn. Keynes thus recommended dropping the gold standard.

In 1931 Britain did just that. Nevertheless, the Depression lingered. Keynes soon began to lose faith that monetary measures alone would restore growth. He began to consider a heretical notion: if private citizens weren't spending the extra money, was it the task of the government to do so? For its part, the British government was actually moving in the opposite direction. Amid the economic contraction, state revenues were declining and the government, eager to safeguard its reputation for prudence, cut expenditure. That, in turn, aggravated the downturn. So in 1933 Keynes published a series of articles in *The Times*, which were subsequently turned into a pamphlet called *The Means to Prosperity*, and which called on the government to reverse direction and stimulate the economy with counter-cyclical spending.[4]

The cloister erupted. One prominent economist published an essay decrying such 'dangerous agitation directed against the whole principle of economy in government expenditure.'[5] The temperature of the ensuing debate grew heated. In one celebrated exchange with the Austrian economist Friedrich von Hayek, who fiercely repudiated Keynes's advice, the Cambridge man dismissed his colleague's work as 'an extraordinary example of how, starting with a mistake, a remorseless logician can end up in Bedlam.'[6] Hayek shot back that Keynes was descending to *ad hominem* arguments to draw attention away from the fact that he didn't have a leg to stand on.[7]

In discarding the neoclassical faith in monetary policy and substituting a focus on fiscal policy, Keynes opened a huge rift among economists. Non-specialists looking at the debate might wonder what all the fuss was about, since both sides were aiming for the same outcome: getting money flowing through the economy, where it could do its magic. But like the ancient Christian debate about transubstantiation – whether Christ is physically or merely symbolically present at communion – or the great Muslim disagreement on the correct lineage of the Prophet, this was a case in which a seemingly minor point led to a permanent and fierce divide. Fiscal policy (from the Latin *fiscus*, or purse) concerned itself with the government's taxing, spending and borrowing, and to many economists the dangers of governments trying to spend their way out of recession were obvious. There was no guarantee it would work. It created too many temptations for governments to give jobs to the boys or build bridges to nowhere. And worst of all, government spending distorted markets. At a time when memories of the ravages

of German hyperinflation were still fresh, some economists warned
that spending which rose faster than production would stoke inflation. Moreover, they added, if the government went into debt, the
added demand for borrowing from a fixed pool of savings would
drive up interest rates, discouraging the private investment needed
to restore growth. To shift from monetary policy to fiscal policy
would be to step into a big unknown, breaking decisively with the
free-market doctrine that had seemed, at least until 1929, to be
working miracles.

The philosopher Bertrand Russell had begun his student days in
Cambridge barely a decade before Keynes. However, as he would
later remark, they might as well have been born in different epochs.
'We were still Victorian; they were Edwardian,' he said of the
Bloomsbury Group. 'The more self-confident among us may have
hoped to be leaders of the multitude, but none of us wished to be
divorced from it.' In stark contrast, said Russell, 'The generation
of Keynes and Lytton did not seek to preserve any kinship with
the Philistine. They aimed rather at a life of retirement among fine
shades and nice feelings, and conceived of the good as consisting
in the passionate mutual admirations of a clique of the elite.' He
didn't question his junior colleague's intellect. Indeed, he noted
admiringly that when he made the mistake of taking him on in a
debate, he 'seldom emerged without feeling something of a fool'.
But Russell maintained that when Keynes ventured into the public
sphere, he resembled a bishop among unbelievers, able to find 'true
salvation' only once he was safely back in Cambridge. With the
exception of *The Economic Consequences of the Peace*, he found
Keynes's writing soulless, marked by a 'hard, glittering, inhuman
quality'.[8]

Russell, an atheist, seemed to be looking for some place to plant
his own flag of conviction. In 1920, he had been part of a British
delegation sent to Russia to investigate the effects of the communist
revolution. Although famine gripped the Russian countryside and
civil war raged, pitting those who resisted the revolution against the

Red Army, Russell found Moscow orderly and peaceful, its theatres and opera full once more. During his stay he had dropped in on Lenin. He found his office surprisingly bare, equipped only with a desk, some maps, two bookcases and one comfortable chair reserved for visitors, into which Russell settled himself. His host was friendly, with good English and a penetrating stare. But though Lenin laughed frequently, Russell detected a certain grimness to it. He sensed in Lenin a cold, dictatorial tendency – 'incapable of fear', he described him, 'an embodied theory' for whom the materialist conception of history was 'life-blood'. Disarmed as Russell was by the austerity and simplicity of a man who was, after all, the head of one of Europe's great powers, he concluded that his host's strength must have come 'from his honesty, courage, and unwavering faith – religious faith in the Marxian gospel, which takes the place of the Christian martyr's hopes of Paradise.'[9]

Russell had gone to Russia willing to be sold on that version of paradise, saying that even 'if Bolshevism falls, it will have contributed a legend and a heroic attempt' – namely, that there was an alternative path to worldly salvation to capitalism's. But instead, he came away struck by the first signs of what he feared might become a worldly hell. He was troubled by the way Lenin cited Marx in defence of his arguments as if he were quoting sacred scripture, noting his dogmatic belief in premises, which, if plausible, were nonetheless impossible to prove.[10]

However, the other members of Russell's party did not share his anxiety. And by the 1930s, when Keynes was trying to work out how to end the Depression, the Soviet Union seemed to shine as a bright star in a dark economic universe – one that looked to a hope-filled future. After a brief compromise with private enterprise during the 1920s, when the demands of the war forced the government to allow peasants and small businesses to sell produce on private markets, the Bolsheviks had clamped their vice back on the economy. After Lenin died in 1924, Joseph Stalin had orchestrated the removal of his major political foes, starting with Leon Trotsky, thereby bringing all political power into his hands. At that point, Marxist–Leninist economics completed its divorce from the internationalism Marx had preached. Maintaining that Soviet Russia was encircled by hostile capitalist nations, Stalin instructed Russia's economists to devote themselves to building 'socialism in one country'. Only after a mature communist society was built at home, he said, could Russia return to the task of spreading the gospel abroad. This marriage of economics and the state meant that communism would ever after be a nationalist, statist creed – and thus, a complete antithesis to the neoclassical free-market faith of the West.

Stalin took complete control of the economy, nationalising all industry and forcing the peasantry into large collective or state farms. In place of the market, the state took over all allocation of resources. A vast planning commission, called *Gosplan*, set production targets for industry, apportioning the resources each firm would be given to fulfil its quotas. Five year plans spelled out who would produce what, in what quantity, and at what price. Pay was set by the government and all prices were fixed. The new doctrine held that human need, not demand and supply, would determine the value of goods. On the face of it, the experiment appeared to be a dramatic success. During the 1930s, at the very time capitalism seemed to be sputtering so badly in the West, the Soviet industrial sector was, as far as Western observers could tell, doubling every five or six years and developing new products on an almost annual basis.[11] Any visitor to Russia at the time could not help but be impressed at the rapid expansion in the number of factories and the spread of electricity.

The price in human suffering, though, was high. Beneath the surface of bureaucratic rationality, Soviet success owed less to scientific planning than to the same sort of primitive accumulation that the Enclosure movement had orchestrated in Britain centuries before. Farmers were given production quotas, which had to be filled before they could eat. If they couldn't meet them, they couldn't eat. Millions died of hunger while the country was exporting grain, whose revenues were used to build the new factories. Meanwhile, workers were made to put in long days to meet their own output quotas. The resources generated by this forced appropriation effectively raised the Soviet Union's saving rate and drove investment to the levels that made rapid industrialisation possible.

However, despite being such a harsh experiment, it still transfixed many Western intellectuals, some of whom recalled the violence that had, after all, attended the spread of the market gospel in previous centuries. Not even a century had passed since Britain had let its colonial farmers starve while it exported grain to build its economy. Arthur Koestler, like Russell a lapsed communist (in his case, losing his faith later, amid Stalin's tyranny), assigned a character in his novel *Darkness at Noon* the voice of Soviet logic, remarking coldly, 'Every year several million people are killed quite pointlessly by epidemics and other natural catastrophes. And we should shrink from sacrificing a few hundred thousand for the most promising experiment in history?'

Despite Russell's efforts to evangelise against the Soviet experiment, enthusiasm for communism found its way back to Cambridge. Keynes was just then developing a theory that unemployment could persist in a depression, contrary to the neoclassical belief that falling wages would cause hiring to resume. One of his friends and junior colleagues, Joan Robinson, further gave this idea a Marxist twist, arguing that unemployment was functional to capitalism because a 'reserve army' of unemployed workers, by preventing employed workers from striking for better pay for fear they'd be sacked and replaced, kept wages low and profits high.[12] Robinson thus looked kindly on the Soviet experiment,[13] and as she did so Soviet spies were secretly recruiting Cambridge fellows and students to become agents in their overseas network. Cambridge, that bastion of the English elite, seemed to be going Red.

If you've ever driven through Germany, you will have had the experience of travelling on the country's celebrated highway system, the *autobahnen*. A network of roads that in many places are congested and under repair, their legendary freedom from speed limits perhaps seems less impressive today. But when they were built in the 1930s,

the *autobahnen* were marvels of modernity. Prior to their construction, road networks everywhere had been comprised largely of dirt
tracks connecting one town or village to the next. Any long-distance
journey thus involved a meandering detour along a variety of country
lanes.

But it wasn't just Germany's infrastructure that was then changing
rapidly. Early in 1933, just as Keynes's acolyte Joan Robinson was
publishing her first book (establishing her reputation and making
her the first great female economist), Germany's President Paul
von Hindenburg was wrestling with a dilemma. In the previous
autumn's elections, Adolf Hitler's Nazi Party had won the most
seats, albeit falling short of a parliamentary majority. Hindenburg
despised Hitler, dismissing him as 'that corporal' and wanting above
all to keep him out of power. A war hero who had stood alongside
Bismarck back in 1871 when the new German state had been proclaimed, the now-ailing Hindenburg was hoping to cobble together
a government comprised of the traditional conservative parties.
Unfortunately, he couldn't get them to agree among themselves so
had to accept the assurance some of his aristocratic allies gave him
that Hitler would be easy for them to control. Appointing Hitler as
Chancellor, Hindenburg provided one of history's lessons in how
thick-headed aristocrats can be.[14]

Within a few months Hitler's Nazis had outmanoeuvred his
rivals and taken control of the country. First using the pretext of
a Reichstag fire to get the president to give him the authority to
crush his socialist rivals, Hitler then got the Reichstag to give his
government power to legislate without parliamentary approval.
Having eliminated the left, he turned to his right flank. Bullying
other parties to disband themselves while threading the Nazi Party
throughout the state and purging all those who might stand in its
way, the Nazis were the only party left standing by the time the
summer winds began blowing. Finally, Hitler turned on his own
ranks. In the Night of the Long Knives, he flushed out Nazi leaders
whose loyalty he doubted.

At any point during this consolidation Hindenburg could have stepped in and removed Hitler. But frail and increasingly senile, he simply lost control. When Hindenburg died the following year Hitler declared the position of President vacant, and added the headship of the state to his control, declaring himself simply the *Führer*, or leader.

Unlike the communists, for whom the economy was everything, the Nazis had taken power with no coherent economic programme. Hitler took little interest in economic affairs, obsessed as he was with his peculiar vision of a restored and purified Germany. More than anything else the Nazi Party's popularity owed more to its ability to stamp out apparent anarchy while crushing the communism that frightened well-to-do Germans.[15] Having eliminated that threat, Hitler's political *raison d'être* was gone. With the Depression still raging, Germans were now going to expect their government to restore their material well-being. Hitler quickly grasped the need to legitimise Nazi rule with an economic platform.

So he took over a tentative public works programme that had been started by the previous government, the *autobahnen*. Although the Nazis had originally been sceptical of the highway-building campaign, Hitler now claimed it as his own. Posing in films and photographs shovelling dirt while surrounded by grateful-looking workers, and repeatedly announcing the start of construction of another new road, Hitler set out to convey the impression of personally giving jobless men work. The construction of a highway system would eventually provide a flagship for the Nazi love of public monuments (Italy's fascist leader Benito Mussolini, who Hitler admired, having demonstrated the majesty of motorways by building the first in the world). Nazi propaganda greatly overstated the employment effects of the public works programme. More jobs were in fact created by Germany's aggressive rearmament – which *was* the war-starved Hitler's brainchild – than by the road building. Nonetheless, the image that came out of Germany, skilfully manipulated by its propagandists, was of an economy back on the march. Fritz Todt, Hitler's chief architect for the *autobahnen*, summarised the data succinctly: 6 million unemployed in 1933, a dearth of skilled labour in 1936.[16]

When it came to propagation of the faith – not just at home, but beyond its borders, where Nazism was winning converts – hardly anyone could rival Germany. Hardly anyone, that is, but Russia. There, with new factories filling the cities and the countryside transformed by the arrival of electricity, the Soviet model shone like a beacon to the future. Stalin capitalised on Russia's new aura of dynamism to seize the reins of world communism. After creating the Third International to coordinate the activities of communist parties worldwide, he imposed his particular vision on them. Having renounced Marx's idea of a world-historical revolution, which Trotsky had tried to keep alive before Stalin expelled him from the country in 1929, to then have him hunted down and murdered in Mexico, Stalin turned to his construction of socialism in one country. When the time came to begin exporting communism, he said it would do so through a ring of subordinate national communist parties, which would take their marching orders from Moscow. Lenin's highly concentrated democratic centralism was thus extended throughout the communist world.

However, being turned into lackeys of Moscow didn't necessarily dampen the appeal of communist parties. Bertrand Russell had perhaps been correct when he'd lamented that dogmatic belief was, after all, a great tool for organising a revolutionary army. Although crushed in Germany and Italy for being the principal rivals to fascism, elsewhere communism was winning believers. Increasingly popular in France in the 1930s, fighting with Oswald Mosley's Nazi-sympathising blackshirts in London's streets, burning churches in Spain, they were even organising American workers into unions and managed to pack Canada's biggest hockey arena at a rally.

It seemed that where democracy and individual freedom prevailed, people were going hungry, whereas dictators were guiding their peoples towards lands of milk and honey. For the unemployed, who in some countries amounted to as much as a fourth of the population, or for the millions more in insecure jobs who felt they were always one meal away from hunger, the trade-off stood in a new light. Like the person who'd like to believe in medical science but can't afford a life-saving medicine, even a false prophet can appear better than no prophet.

Let's now return to the United States in the winter of 1933. Europe's per capita incomes have fallen by a tenth and America's by a third.[17] Having lost your Long Island home – and who knows, perhaps your spouse as well – you're putting in twelve-hour days on Manhattan street corners peddling apples. You heard President Hoover's radio broadcast, in which he said the Depression was beyond anyone's control.[18] You hear that people are getting put to work in Germany. You hear everyone in Russia has a job. You hear that those are anti-democratic countries that give individuals no freedom of choice, but so what, how much freedom to choose do you now have anyway? You are cold, hungry and broke. What are you going to do?

Neoclassical theory had enshrined Adam Smith's belief in minimal government and the invisible hand. But in the Depression, that hand seemed more than invisible. It seemed non-existent. Trading freedom and rights for a job was a painful option, but variants of authoritarianism were clearly growing more appealing to millions in the West.

Meanwhile, some liberals were suggesting that maybe the trade-off didn't need to be so stark. Perhaps, they reasoned, a government that took a greater hand in the economy wouldn't have to sacrifice democracy to do it – or at least, it might be possible to keep the sacrifice within reasonable bounds. John Steinbeck's *The Grapes of Wrath* depicted a benevolent government that meddled in the market, but only to prevent abuses from those whose buying power had risen too far. 'Got nice toilets an' baths, an' you kin wash clothes in a tub, an' they's water right handy, good drinkin' water; an' nights the folks play music an' Sat'dy night they give a dance,' says one character, describing a federal work camp. 'Oh, you never seen anything so nice.'

This was not a socialism that cleansed humanity of its original sin, but a capitalism saved by an inner conscience from its worst vices. To John Maynard Keynes, that kind of vision seemed the answer to the desperate prayers of those who, like him, worried for Western civilisation. For in the doctrinal clash between capitalist democracy and its foes – communism, and now fascism too – the latter's prophets offered an accumulating list of miracles. Capitalism's apostles, on the other hand, could do little more than counsel patience and forbearance.

CHAPTER 11

THE KEYNESIAN REVELATION

In ancient Greece were two men who founded rival schools of thought. Although one of them, Zeno, was born in Cyprus and the other, Epicurus, came from the Aegean island of Samos, both ended up in Athens. Zeno did his teaching there, in the *Stoa Poikile* or 'Painted Porch' of the market, so his followers were called Stoics. Epicurus set his school up just down the road in a little garden, and his followers took his name, calling themselves Epicureans.

The Epicureans believed the highest goal in life was to pursue pleasure; the Stoics said it was to avoid pain and extreme emotions. Because Epicurus found the highest pleasure in friendship, and Zeno the avoidance of pain in serenity, in their early days the two schools didn't differ that much. But over time they evolved in different directions. Ultimately, by the time the Roman Epicurean Lucretius wrote *On the Nature of Things* in the final century BCE, Epicureanism had become known for the almost-orgiastic pursuit of pleasure. Celebrating lust without the encumbrances of commitment, Lucretius advised, 'Keep off imagination and frighten away whatever encourages love; turn your mind elsewhere. Get rid of the fluid in any body you can instead of keeping it for a single person.'[1] While the Stoics called for humans to live in accord with the divine will, the Epicureans insisted there was no divinity, leaving us free to decide according to our own wishes.

Most of us would probably fit into one or other school, perhaps having a bit of each, but more of one than the other – not because we have studied philosophy, but because that's the way we tend to line up. Contemporary research in psychology reveals that risk-seekers and risk-avoiders differ in the way they approach opportunities, with the former seeing potential returns and the latter potential pitfalls.[2] Those who are more Epicurean in their nature see the joy in a prospective gain, those who are more Stoic see the pain of a possible loss. Epicureans will seek the thrill of falling in love, Stoics will want to avoid the sorrow that would come if it ends badly.

So it goes for economists. Some assume humans are inherently conservative and want to avoid risk or loss, and build their models accordingly. Others believe humans seek out risks both for the returns they bring and for the satisfaction they give, and build a different set of models. The first focus on the costs inherent in any departure from conventional practice, and the latter on the potential gains of taking a new leap into the unknown.

John Maynard Keynes wore his Epicureanism on his sleeve, chasing after pleasures and reflecting on the virtues of their attainment. Despite openly questioning his neoclassical faith, going so far as to contemplate the government taking a hand in the economy, Keynes was no socialist. He might have read Marx but he didn't follow him. On the contrary, confronted with the Soviet model then bewitching so many of his colleagues, he once sneered, 'How can I accept a creed which, preferring the mud to the fish, exalts the boorish proletariat above the bourgeois and the intelligentsia who, with whatever faults, are the quality in life and surely carry the seeds of all human achievement.'[3] Blaming the popularity of communism in Cambridge on 'a recrudescence of the ancient strain of Puritanism in our blood',[4] a strain which preferred the painful solution to a problem precisely because it was painful, he clung to the essentially aristocratic worldview of the Bloomsbury Group, holding that everything good in life was attained through cultural enjoyment – and was thus implicitly beyond the proletariat. As his Bloomsbury colleague Clive Bell put it, civilisation needed someone to do the dirty work, a sentiment typical of an elitist group who took no interest in mass culture.[5]

Yet while he clung to the liberal tradition, suggesting individualism was not only more efficient than the collectivism propounded by Marx but, above all, a superior ethical option since it 'greatly widens the field for the exercise of personal choice',[6] Keynes could also see that individualism was under threat. And so while enlarging the role of government might have seemed a 'terrific encroachment on individualism' it was to him 'the only practicable means of avoiding the destruction of existing economic forms in their entirety and as the condition of the successful functioning of individual initiative.'[7] In that respect, he harked back to an old Tory strain, typified in the *Blackwood's* magazine school of the Corn Law era, which wanted to make England safe for its most privileged inhabitants by looking after its less privileged ones.

Like an iconoclast smashing ancient truths, he confronted the received wisdom head on. Out with the Victorian celebration of thrift and prudence, in with shopping like there's no tomorrow – so as to make for a better tomorrow. 'The growth of wealth, so far from being dependent on the abstinence of the rich, as is commonly supposed, is more likely to be impeded by it,' Keynes now counselled.[8] Not surprisingly, more stoical economists, for whom thrift underpinned prosperity, responded as a believer would to seeing ancient icons destroyed. One of the first American converts to the Keynesian gospel, for instance, found himself the target of a campaign to get him fired and to block alumni from donating to any school that used his book.[9] Nevertheless, Keynes was not to be deterred.

On New Year's Day 1935, John Maynard Keynes, never one to skimp on self-belief, wrote a letter to his friend, the playwright George Bernard Shaw, telling him that he was about to revolutionise the way humans thought about economics.[10] Having just put the finishing touches to *The General Theory of Employment, Interest and Money*, his magnum opus was about to hit the bookshops. And sure enough, when the tome appeared early in the new year, his self-confidence was vindicated. '[The] *General Theory* caught most economists under the age of thirty-five with the unexpected virulence of a disease first attacking and decimating an isolated tribe of South Sea islanders,'[11] wrote one famous economist of the epiphany Keynes gave him and all younger colleagues. Their older mentors simply couldn't understand what was happening, watching bewildered as the youth left their church to hear this new prophet.

In Keynes's day, economics students essentially learned micro-economics. The interaction of supply and demand, which Smith had used to explain the working of the market economy, had been turned by the marginalists into the microscopic study of individual buying, selling and investment decisions. As if zooming out the microscope, economists would generalise the rules of behaviour they discerned to the economy as a whole, on the premise that economies were just big collections of individuals. Accordingly, they held that the decisions that would lead an economy out of recession – a lengthy period in which output was contracting – would be taken, millions of times over, by millions of individuals. In *The General Theory*, however, Keynes now said that faith was misplaced. For even if the neoclassical nirvana of equilibrium was restored and the recession bottomed out, there was no reason to believe that growth would return.

You'll remember that analogy in chapter 7 of the heated iron rod and the bucket of water, which was used to illustrate the neoclassical notion of how prices are determined in a free market. Well, imagine the water in the bucket was frozen. Keynes said an economy could reach a point where demand was so low it just wouldn't get moving again. But if prices were dropping to low, low levels, why wouldn't buyers step up and snap goods off the shelves, as neoclassical theory presumed? Well, think about it. Would you? If prices today are lower than they were yesterday, it's only reasonable to assume that they'll go even lower tomorrow. So if you have a bit of money in your bucket, you'll do well to hang on to it, since it will buy you more stuff down the road. Keynes called this proclivity a liquidity preference, which is a fancy way of saying you hang on to your cash.

Assuming you hang on to your cash, you help to create a

self-fulfilling prophecy. If we all do it at once, sellers are forced to drop their prices further to try to clear their shelves. And since they're dropping their prices yet further, everyone keeps hanging on to their cash. The only things selling in this sort of environment will be items with low demand elasticities – which is to say, goods for which demand is little affected by price. You need to eat, for instance, so you'll keep buying food. But cars and movies? Wait a few more weeks and you'll get a bargain.

So Keynes said we had to stop thinking of the bucket as an individual, and think of it as the entire economy. Because everyone had the same liquidity preference, everyone would be limiting their buying, and all the buckets would remain frozen. Therefore aggregate demand, the sum of the millions of individual purchasing decisions in the economy, wouldn't budge. The standard neoclassical remedy, of making credit cheap and thereby enabling consumers and businesses to borrow for less, would do no good because everyone would keep hoarding their cash. With a recession on, individuals concerned they might lose their jobs would want to build a rainy-day fund, and businesses worried that they might lose yet more sales would want to set aside cash reserves to keep paying their bills if their income ever diminished.

Someone, therefore, had to thaw the ice. Keynes made that the government's job. It had to start doing what individuals weren't, and buy more stuff. The government needed to take unemployed workers and put them to work, stuffing money in their pockets so that they could go out and start shopping. It had to start paving roads and building dams, filling the order books of manufacturers. If it did all that, economic activity would resume and prices would stop falling. Once prices stopped falling, everyone with cash would stop waiting to spend it. Ideally, the job-creating programmes the government put together would also create infrastructure, which would in turn help improve the long-term supply conditions in the economy and thereby reduce the cost of business. But even if they were just make-work schemes, they would still give money to consumers who had none, and thereby give confidence to consumers who had some. As Keynes wrote, 'If the Treasury were to fill old bottles with banknotes, bury them at suitable depths in disused coalmines which they then filled up to the surface with town rubbish, and leave it to private enterprise on well-tried principles of *laissez-faire* to dig up the notes again . . . there need be no more unemployment.'[12]

Lifting an economy out of recession by putting people to work wasn't unheard of. Even the Hoover administration in the United States, widely condemned for idling amid the Depression, was building the Hoover Dam for that very purpose. What was so bold in Keynes's advice, though, was that he called on governments to *borrow* money to boost their spending.[13] He reasoned that once the economy was restored to health, the government would be able to step back, cut its spending and pay off its debts – which the increasing tax revenues of a now-humming economy would enable it to do.

Keynes's older peers were beside themselves. They warned that a sudden increase in demand would jolt inflation, dissuading people from buying as prices rose too high. Besides, they said, all the government would be doing was to boost demand by an amount equivalent to its debt. What it spent now, it would have to cut back later, making the effects short-lived. However, anticipating this objection, Keynes used a sort of contemporary fish-and-loaves trick, which he called the multiplier. Yes, he allowed, if you put an extra pound in someone's pocket, all you have done is increase demand by a pound. But if that person then runs off to the local grocer to spend the pound, and the grocer then calls the baker to restock his shelves, and the miller calls the farmer to ask for more wheat, a long series of transactions would recirculate that pound note many times over. One pound of government spending would thus reach many wallets.

The trick, said Keynes, lay in the timing. Pumping money into a healthy economy would do little good because, with their needs satisfied, people would start putting their money aside for a rainy day.[14] But amid recession, when human need is more acute, the first thing people do is spend their added cash. Once the economy started moving again, the government could ease up on the accelerator and start tightening its own belt so that inflation didn't pick up. If it seemed miraculous, well, that's how many of the old priesthood then saw it.

Keynes effectively created a new creed. Implicit in his model was a high degree of faith in human nature: he was willing to believe, as others did not, that politicians and bureaucrats *could* get the timing right, while also resisting the temptation to abuse government spending programmes for their own personal or political ends. He also reversed the relationship between supply and demand. Whereas the neoclassical model maintained the government's levers over the economy lay on the supply side, which is to say in managing money supply in the way Irving Fisher had advocated, Keynes suggested that demand preceded supply and it was there that the government should target its interventions. In the old catechism, pleasure was the reward for sacrifice, and you could spend only after you had earned: by increasing aggregate supply with your hard work, you'd earned the money you needed to go and spend. In the Keynesian revelation, it was pleasure that made people sacrifice, and they could be motivated to work with the lure of the delights that lay ahead – increasing demand so that supply would catch up. Keynes thus repudiated Say's Law, which said that supply created its own demand. It was demand, he said, which created supply. Importantly, his demand-side economics substituted macroeconomics for the conventional microeconomics. Rather than seeing the economy as an aggregation of individuals and their innumerable small decisions regarding spending and saving, he studied the parts of the economy in relation to the whole. And for him the whole, not the parts, set the entire thing in motion. His new doctrine was effectively to neoclassical economics a bit what Catholicism was to Protestantism: against the neoclassical belief in the need for individuals to find their own way to heaven, Keynes called for the community to be lifted as one.

Nevertheless, for all the revolt he inspired in the pews, Keynes was no lonely voice from the desert. Just as many a great prophet comes from a community that nurtures and sustains him, Keynes swam in intellectual currents that were widening and deepening.

In fact, the analogy of Keynesian economics to a powerful virus probably revealed less about *The General Theory* than it did about the state of economics in the English-speaking world in the 1930s, where neoclassical orthodoxy was so entrenched that Keynes rocked the temple. But elsewhere in Europe, neoclassicism had never won as large a following, and ideas very similar to his had been bubbling up for decades. In fact, the 'Stockholm School' could plausibly lay claim to having got to the mountaintop and seen the new world before Keynes, since Keynes was reading the work of economists like Knut Wicksell well before writing his new testament. Wicksell, who had developed a model of fiscal management very similar to Keynes's prior to his death in 1926, had mentored many young scholars who then went on to form the Stockholm School.

One of the most prominent scions of this school would be Gunnar Myrdal. Reflecting the broad training economists still got then, particularly on the continent, Myrdal had worked as a sociologist, lawyer and politician, and so remained distrustful of the drift towards purely mathematical methods that had cropped up in the English-speaking world. When Keynes himself had taken up his first lectureship back in 1908, he'd had no formal training in economics, and most of what he knew was learned on the job in the civil service. Nevertheless, he did not resist the mathematical drift of economics, and indeed wasn't averse to wielding his skill with mathematics as a weapon to club some of his continental critics.[15]

Similar to the eclectic approach of the Stockholm School, Germany's 'Freiburg School' blended legal studies with economics to show how the market could not operate efficiently without the state overseeing it. As one of its proponents put it, the government had to ensure the freedom of contract couldn't be 'used for the purpose of entering into contracts which restrict or eliminate the freedom of contract'.[16] This 'ordoliberalism' then provided a foundation upon which scholars would subsequently build a set of ideas for what would be called the social market. The French also had a long tradition of state economic management that dated back to the period before the 1789 Revolution, rooted less in theory than in practical experimentation, and which had made its intellectual home in the *grandes écoles* founded by Napoleon to build the French nation and economy. Not only did French bureaucrats, with some justification, see themselves as up to the task of overseeing the economy in an interventionist manner, but the practice of '*pantouflage*',[17] where civil servants would move into the private sector later in their careers, created close links between the corporate and administrative elites that made for effective planning.

All such scholars who called for the state to manage capitalism so as to ensure the market's survival could well have been reading from the playbook of Otto von Bismarck, who used welfare legislation to buy off the German working class and stabilise the economy. It's no coincidence that strategies to expand the state's economic role and provide basic welfare were often undertaken by conservative parties. Where they weren't, they would be continued by them. That flexibility in government reflected ancient statecraft. From the dawn of time, effective rulers have abided by a simple adage: If you can't beat 'em, join 'em. It was the insight which, seventeen centuries earlier, had led the Roman Emperor Constantine to end the persecution of Christians; though they refused to worship the emperor and threatened the Roman order, he recognised they had become so numerous that it was better to work with them. The rulers of the twentieth-century West, whatever they thought of the threat state economic management might pose to individual freedom, could see the new doctrines were popular, and therefore could be used to beat back the threat of communism. They were, as Constantine had no doubt been, sufficiently pragmatic to see their way of life had found its saviour. And when a church wins both a mass following and powerful patrons, it is set to become orthodoxy.

In the summer of 1932, after a hard-fought political convention that finally saw him emerge as the Democratic nominee for President, Franklin Delano Roosevelt rose to give his acceptance speech. Inside the cavernous hockey arena, stewing in a Chicago heatwave and packed with sweating delegates, Roosevelt said:

I pledge you, I pledge myself, to a new deal for the American people. Let us all here assembled constitute ourselves prophets of a new order of competence and of courage. This is more than a political campaign; it is a call to arms. Give me your help, not to win votes alone, but to win in this crusade to restore America to its own people.[18]

Roosevelt coasted through a fairly easy autumn campaign against President Hoover. Despite Hoover's warnings against the radicalism of Roosevelt's proposed New Deal, four years of Depression had left Americans eager for change. Roosevelt won a landslide big enough to carry Congress as well.

In those days, presidents-elect didn't take office until the March after the November election. So even though everyone was keen to know what Roosevelt would do once he took office, they had to wait another four months to find out, during which reporters peppering him with questions were simply treated to his engaging grin, the tilt upwards of his cigarette holder and the reply that they'd hear the answer on Inauguration Day.[19] He finally swore his oath on a raw, cold, cloudy day, resting his hand on his family Bible in front of the East Portico of the US Capitol.[20] Then, as millions across the land leaned in to their wireless sets, Roosevelt began his inaugural address. Declaring that the crisis upon them was not ordained by nature, but happened because 'the rulers of the exchange of mankind's goods have failed', he said they could no longer offer the nation healing with their pursuit of profit. He went on: 'Faced by failure of credit, they have proposed only the lending of more money.' Railing against their moral failure, he said, 'They only know the rules of a generation of self-seekers. They have no vision, and when there is no vision the people perish.'

But, he then said, there was still hope: 'The money changers have fled from their high seats in the temple of our civilization. We may now restore that temple to the ancient truths. The measure of that restoration lies in the extent to which we apply social values more noble than mere monetary profit.' He warned there were dark days ahead, but added they would be 'worth all they cost us if they teach us that our true destiny is not to be ministered unto but to minister to ourselves, to our fellow men.' Americans demanded action, he said, 'and action now'. Going on to detail his ambitious programme, he highlighted the single greatest task facing his government: 'to put people to work'.[21]

Keynes, no doubt seeing a kindred spirit, wrote an open letter to the New York Times in late 1933 in which he told President Roosevelt:

> You have made yourself the trustee for those in every country who seek to mend the evils of our condition by reasoned experiment within the framework of the existing social system. If you fail, rational change will be gravely prejudiced throughout the world, leaving orthodoxy and revolution to fight it out. But, if you succeed, new and bolder methods will be tried everywhere, and we may date the first chapter of a new economic era from your accession to office.[22]

But if Roosevelt seemed an obvious target for Keynesian evangelisation, he still retained his Episcopalian prudence. Like almost everyone of the day except Keynes, he was old-fashioned when it came to budgeting. He believed that any funding for job creation needed to be found from internal savings. His predecessor, Herbert Hoover, had left a big deficit on the books and Roosevelt had promised to balance them. Subsequently meeting with Keynes in 1934, Roosevelt wrote to a friend afterwards to say he 'had a grand talk with K and liked him immensely'[23] though he also told his labour secretary: 'I saw your friend Keynes. He left a whole rigmarole of figures. He must be a mathematician rather than a political economist.'[24] Such ambivalence coloured Roosevelt's reception of Keynes, and for the time being he chose to ignore the economist's advice on the virtues of debt-financed stimulus.

All the same, Roosevelt's programme was hugely ambitious. Right after the inauguration Congress got to work, and a week later Roosevelt gave the first of what would be his defining 'fireside chats'. Speaking to the nation by radio, he explained the banking crisis in simple language and outlined his proposed solutions. The next hundred days then saw a frenzy of activity on Capitol Hill as the Democratic Congress, working with their President, legislated his New Deal into being. Reorganising the financial sector to reopen banks, suspending the gold standard, regulating securities trading so as to prevent another crash, repealing Prohibition, strengthening the unions, reversing trade protection, introducing public pensions – thereby creating what would be the much-loved Social Security programme – giving the unemployed relief assistance, spending generously on public works so as to give people jobs, investing heavily in the depressed farm sector, and managing farm supply to raise prices, the federal government plunged into the economy in a way never seen before. And although the debt rose Roosevelt still committed himself to eventually bringing it back down, something he actually managed to do in 1937.

But that year would be fateful. For in 1937, the economy fell back into recession. Some of Roosevelt's advisers then gathered round and persuaded him it was time to try Keynes's advice.[25] Roosevelt agreed that the circumstances demanded a leap of faith. In his annual speech to Congress in January 1938, he declared that he would fund public projects without any further taxes. Conservatives on both sides of the partisan aisle erupted, but he got his way. Then, four years later, remaining doubts about the prudence of deficits were purged by an event outside America's control. Shortly after dawn on 7 December 1941, Japanese aircraft bombed Pearl Harbor, the US Navy's Pacific base. The next day, the United States was at war with Japan, with the conflict widening to include Nazi Germany and Mussolini's Italy after they declared war on America. Roosevelt, who until then had been covertly backing the British in the war, could now openly join the fray.

Deficit financing can be a bit like a game of chicken. If a government borrows to restore growth but everyone doubts its resolve, they might assume that future cutbacks will return the economy to recession, and so stash any extra money they get under the mattress as they prepare for the rainy day. They would therefore maintain their liquidity preference, and create the self-fulfilling prophecy that would keep the economy in recession.[26] Critics, not to mention his own doubts, initially kept FDR's ambitions on a tight leash. But once Hitler and Emperor Hirohito came into the picture, borrowing went from being a vice to a patriotic duty as Americans rushed out to buy war bonds. America's national debt, equivalent to about a fifth of the country's output at the start of Roosevelt's presidency and two-fifths on the eve of the war, mushroomed to be bigger in 1945 than the economy itself. However, with millions of young men getting called to service – young men who needed to be clothed, fed and armed – not only did the public payroll surge, but factories everywhere started ramping up production to feed the ravenous appetite of America's war machine. Almost overnight, the economy went from idling to overdrive.

And, like a racing car that keeps hurtling forward after it has crossed the finish line, momentum would carry the economy forward after the war, through a brief pit stop of a recession as wartime spending was slashed, and back into sustained growth. A humming economy then generated the tax receipts the government needed to pay back its debts.[27] All things told, wartime deficits had provided a laboratory for Keynes's thesis, which most dispassionate observers judged to have been validated. The Keynesian era then began in earnest.

In May of 1945, three weeks after Hitler's death and the subsequent German surrender, Winston Churchill, the British prime minister, got a phone call that would bring down his government.

Clement Attlee, the leader of the Labour Party and deputy prime minister, had helped carry Britain through the war with a coalition government that joined his party to Churchill's Conservatives. In many ways Attlee was the flip side of the Churchillian coin. The prime minister, charismatic and often inspirational, delivered rous-ing speeches laced with spontaneous wit, once famously responding to a female MP who criticised him for being drunk by saying 'my dear, you are ugly, but tomorrow I shall be sober'.[28] His deputy on the other hand was modest and soft-spoken, with little of Churchill's ability to win over a room. Churchill could bully and bluster his way through most challenges. Attlee worked the back channels, so quietly that even relatively friendly observers referred to him as 'a little mouse' or 'a little nonentity'. Churchill was a soldier who longed for the battlefield, and as a young man had sought to be posted to foreign conflicts. Attlee was a pacifist by nature, who throughout the early years of Hitler's rise had supported appeasement and opposed British rearmament.

But once it had become clear in the late 1930s that Hitler was not going to confine his ambitions to Germany, Attlee abandoned this stance. When war broke out and the government of Neville Chamberlain fell, Attlee joined Churchill in an effective partnership that would see the nation through six years of fighting. In their division of labour, Churchill led the war effort and Attlee managed the home front. Loyal, patriotic, an opponent of class warfare who loved causes that united all Britons, Attlee saw victory on the battlefield as the necessary prelude to a victory at home – bringing Britain together under a universal welfare state. Now, with the European battle won, Attlee was ready to start the next phase. And while he was personally willing to keep the coalition going until the war in the Pacific was also wrapped up, once he reached Labour's annual conference in Blackpool, he realised the mood of the delegates wasn't so sympathetic. His peers were eager to get hold of power to begin the transformation of Britain right away. So Attlee called Churchill to inform him that he would have to withdraw his party from the government, leaving the prime minister no choice but to call an election.

During the campaign, Winston Churchill delivered an infamous radio speech in which – apparently under the influence of John Maynard Keynes's perpetual sparring partner Friedrich Hayek, who had just written a book called *The Road to Serfdom* – he said that the Labour government would create some form of Gestapo to run the economy.[29] Despite being the hero of Britain's war, Churchill failed to see how ready his countrymen were for change. Labour won a sweeping mandate and proceeded to implement its platform: creating the National Health Service, expanding public pensions, providing sickness benefits, help with funeral expenses, welfare payments and a huge expansion in public housing.

In the century since Britain converted to the free-trade gospel in 1846, through the boom years of the mid-Victorian era when it was the biggest commercial power in history, across the decades of high imperialism, the Great Depression and the two World Wars, poverty in Britain remained stubbornly tenacious. Although incomes and living standards rose steadily, with the years of prosperity outpacing the periods of recession and depression, as a share of national income wages actually fell.[30] Workers did well, but nowhere near as well as the upper classes.[31] On the ground, this meant that while employed and particularly skilled workers enjoyed major improvements to their material conditions of existence, those who couldn't find good work suffered terribly. In 1901, just as the Edwardian age was beginning, one in three Londoners, despite living in the world's richest city, lived in poverty;[32] and one in five could expect to finish their lives with a solitary burial from the workhouse, poor-law hospital or lunatic asylum.[33] And so it continued, right up until the Second World War. Then, from the late 1930s until the late 1940s, poverty in Britain plunged, due first to the impact of wartime rationing (which ensured everyone received a minimal level of nutrition), and subsequently to the advent of the welfare state. In the end, the progress in small steps that Alfred Marshall's neoclassical economics promised, and the inevitable working of Adam Smith's invisible hand, had never come to pass. It took politics, not economics, to finally bring an end to the scourge of poverty.[34]

The collective memory of Britain in the 1950s is often of a dreary decade. Shop windows were filled with an enticing array of consumer products all labelled 'for export only' as the government tried to generate the foreign currency needed to pay its wartime debts. Clothes were recycled, food was bland and there was little of the ostentation

of the previous era of economic growth, the 1920s. But it was also a
time when a vast array of goods and services became available to many
people for the first time, from dental care to television. To some extent,
the drabness of 'austerity Britain'[35] reflected the fact that, as had been
the case in the war, Britons were in this together; the luxury which
once rose to the top was now being flattened into basic goods and
distributed to all. Unemployment, including seasonal unemployment,
which had been the problem for workers all through the Industrial
Revolution, largely disappeared as almost everyone could now find
good, stable work. That kind of shared interest, further reinforced by
the spread of national institutions like the BBC and NHS, helped forge
a political consensus around the welfare state, as all parties united in
its defence. So it would have hardly surprised the crowd that packed
Wembley stadium one spring day in 1951 to watch the FA Cup final
that the band of the Coldstream Guards who escorted the teams onto
the pitch earned wages similar to the players.[36]

Britain did not march alone in building a welfare state. In the two
decades that followed the war, governments across the West engaged
in equally ambitious schemes to provide housing, health care, jobs
and income support, all while widening the role of the state in the
economy. And even though this model often came to be known as the
Keynesian welfare state, as was the case with economic theory, each
country's model actually drew upon distinctive national traditions.

The German 'social market' was particularly telling, because its
origins lay not on the left but the right of German politics. Ever since
the dawn of the Industrial Age and the emergence of the democratic
movements, the Catholic Church had had an ambivalent reaction to
modernity. Long wedded to the organic conception of society of the
medieval era, the Church had resisted the rise of individualism. But
in the late nineteenth century, under the impact of the reforming
Pope Leo XIII (1878–1903), the Catholic Church began to embrace
democracy. Moreover, in a revived version of the *noblesse oblige* of
the *Blackwood's* variety, it took a keen interest in the well-being
of workers, to the point that during the Second World War the

worker-priest movement sent priests to become factory workers to bring the church closer to the labouring classes. Immediately after the war the Christian Democratic Party came into being and began implementing its vision of a society in which all citizens had a duty to look after everyone else. Informed by Catholic social thought and drawing upon German ordoliberalism, the model was refined by some scholars at the University of Cologne, who conceived of the market as something to be tinkered with to serve human well-being.[37] Similar models emerged in other countries where Christian democracy played a significant role, including Scandinavia and Italy, while in France too it was a conservative government that initially implemented a welfare state.

Japan's model likewise drew upon local tradition, thereby giving its form of the Keynesian welfare state a unique shape. After the war, the country continued the statist tradition of economic management it had developed in the late nineteenth century when it first studied the work of Friedrich List. The Ministry of International Trade and Industry became a capitalist *Gosplan*. Establishing close links between government officials and captains of private industry, similar to what had been done in France (and would later be done by its neighbour South Korea), MITI helped to coordinate industrial policy so as to nurture the industries that would fuel the country's revival. MITI helped Japanese business to flourish, negotiating trade policy to favour select industries, showering them with cheap credit, tax breaks and foreign exchange, helping them develop new technology.[38] In return, the businesses were expected to look after employees, giving them lifetime employment – the ubiquitous 'salary-men' who are expected to give their lives to their employers, working by day and socialising with their colleagues by night. Firms also looked after the health of their employees and families by enrolling them in pension and insurance schemes.

All these countries were, in fact, latecomers to the construction of welfare states. Sweden, after all, had been building one since the late nineteenth century.[39] But by the 1960s, all Western countries had put variants of the Keynesian welfare state into practice, the process finally climaxing in the 1960s with US President Lyndon Johnson's Great Society Programme. The new welfare states, far surpassing in ambition anything Otto von Bismarck could have imagined, all had four common elements: some kind of basic health coverage (though it would await the twenty-first century before the United States finally joined the rest of the West in providing something that approached universal coverage), income support, pensions and housing assistance. Workplace regulations were tightened and laws bolstered labour unions. Many countries joined Britain in nationalising industries, or creating new ones – like airlines – owned by the state. There was also a massive expansion of public education, particularly at the tertiary level, and over the following generation new universities cropped up to meet the demand for higher education from a middle class whose numbers were greatly increased by all these programmes.

By then, the Keynesian high priests had satisfied themselves they had mastered the tools of demand management and would be able to forestall there ever being another recession.[40] The welfare state itself was not necessarily essential to Keynesian demand management.[41] But by guaranteeing a minimum level of demand, it did initially appear to smooth out the business cycle, ensuring that consumption would never drop below a floor provided by income support, and offering 'automatic stabilisers' like unemployment relief during times of recession.

The age of free markets and the minimalist state in the West was now well and truly over.

Among economists, there's a chicken-and-egg debate about money. For the chicken, read transactions – buying and selling. For the egg, read money. Which came first? If you think this is a minor point, you'd be surprised to discover how it can rile experts.

Money had existed for as long as humans could remember. So when it came to describing its origins prior to recorded history, Adam Smith had been left to speculation. He imagined an ancient society in which specialisation and the division of labour first emerged. Now that they had stuff to trade, humans bartered with one another. But this created a problem. As Smith wrote in *The Wealth of Nations*, 'The butcher has more meat in his shop than he himself can consume, and the brewer and the baker would each of them be willing to purchase a part of it. But they have nothing to offer in exchange, except the different productions of their respective trades, and the butcher is already provided with all the bread and beer which he has immediate occasion for.'[42] So, he suggested, at some point they must have all got together, agreed a universal medium of exchange that could be used to buy all goods, and transacted their business in that currency.

Taking Smith as canonical, neoclassical doctrine pretty much enshrined this, building its edifice accordingly. But Keynes took a different view. Influenced by the German economist G. F. Knapp, who had said, 'Money is a creature of law,' Keynes reckoned the state played a central role in the creation of money.[43] Economists refer to the neoclassical position and that which Keynes took as, respectively, the exogenous and endogenous theories of money. This might appear like yet another angels-on-a-pinhead debate, one that couldn't possibly interest anyone other than a wonk. What do I care who made my money, as long as I can spend it? But when you work each position through to its logical conclusion, you hit upon an age-old dispute over which humans have been known to go to war.

Neoclassical theory took money to be something humans created to facilitate their economic activities: the market acted, and the government responded. The endogenous theory of money, however, said the state created it. So Keynes was essentially grafting Knapp's vision onto a doctrine that was already looking, to his older critics, dangerously collectivist. The debate which followed bore more than a passing resemblance to the centuries-old theological dispute about how one achieved salvation.

The Catholic Church always maintained that by partaking of the sacrament of communion, a prerequisite for which was a good Christian lifestyle, an individual won passage to heaven. Although Luther said that communion without faith was meaningless, and that a good lifestyle alone didn't make you a good Christian, he didn't fundamentally alter the principle that salvation was something the individual strove for. Since anybody could choose salvation and thereby swell the ranks of those destined for heaven, salvation was, in effect, endogenous to humanity.

Then along came John Calvin. He said that individuals didn't get to choose salvation, it was something that God granted them. Salvation, in effect, was exogenous to humanity and individual will couldn't change this. The most a person could do was to testify to his or her salvation by leading a life that was as unblemished by sin as possible. As Calvin put it, 'the end of regeneration is, that the life of the faithful may exhibit a symmetry and agreement between the righteousness of God and their obedience.'[44]

Now let's apply those distinct views to something closer to home, namely, earthly salvation. Rather as Catholic doctrine said the Church had it within its authority to expand the community of the saved by bringing more people to the altar, Keynes said the state could use its control of money to swell wealth in society. Using the simple rule that when investment exceeds saving the economy is overheating, and when saving exceeds investment it's in recession, he argued that by both discouraging saving and increasing investment and spending, the creation of money would generate new economic activity.

To some, this was pretty shocking stuff. Just as Calvin had, in effect, argued that the sum of salvation in the universe was fixed externally, and that nothing the Church did could change that, neo-classical doctrine insisted that the supply of money in the economy had to be in symmetry with the economy's production. Neoclassical scholars thus inferred that if, in the absence of a proportionate increase in economic output, the state raised the money supply, money would simply lose its value. It's not unlike the disapproval some Calvinistic Christians express of churches or individuals too ready to forgive, since to them opening the doors wide to sinners trivialises the virtuous life. So whereas the conventional wisdom of the Victorian age, in which neoclassical economics had been born, was that thrift was a good thing since it created the pool of savings that would fund future investment, Keynes concluded the opposite. Reproving his erstwhile mentor Alfred Marshall for being too much of a Victorian moralist,[45] Keynes wrote 'the engine which drives enterprise is not thrift but profit'.[46] The pursuit of pleasure, and not its containment, was thus what drove progress forward.

A latter-day Epicurean, Keynes rejected the orthodox position that the wages of debt would need to get paid in time. He reasoned that a clever government could take on debt more or less without cost. Just as Catholics in Luther's day reckoned that salvation was just one confession and act of penance away, Keynes adjudged that pleasure didn't have to have a price, at least not a permanent one. If not to the same extent as Marx had done, he restored a bit of collectivism to economic doctrine. To his claim that he was trying to save capitalism, his critics would end up taking a more Puritan view, saying that whoever wasn't for neoclassical doctrine was against it. Just as the devil comes in disguise, Keynesianism would come to be seen by them as communism in market-friendly clothing.

As with the endogenous theory of money, the doctrine of salvation is one that is inherently unprovable. You either believe in it or you don't. So it goes for the principle of equilibrium, another neoclassical article of faith that Keynes would reject. In arguing that a free market always finds its way back to equilibrium, neoclassical scholars thought they had buried both the notion of the business cycle upon which Marx had built his theory – the idea that there is an ebb and flow to capitalism which produces periods of intense crisis – and the need for the government to step in to restore equilibrium. Keynes revived the business cycle, but with a new twist: he believed the free market could find equilibrium even when unemployment remained high, and that it would take an external jolt to overcome this unemployment. Whereas Marx tended towards a fatalism that crises would grow successively more intense, Keynes had faith that clever government actions could overcome any crisis. Humans, he believed, had the power to take control of history's plot, making themselves the architects of their own fate.

*

While Keynes was alive, some of the converts to his creed, who didn't want to completely renounce their neoclassical faith, tried to heal the rift between him and the high priests. Blending the microeconomics of neoclassical orthodoxy with the Keynesian theory of the business cycle, they surmised that good economic management could actually eliminate cycles altogether. This new school of young economists suggested that regular fine-tuning by government could smooth out the cycle and confine booms and busts to the past. Although Keynes initially had doubts about this new synthesis, he ultimately gave the new doctrine his blessing. In 1948 the American economist Paul Samuelson – the economist who'd had a sort of Damascene conversion, likening the impact of Keynes's *General Theory* to a virus on a Pacific island – published an introductory textbook which enshrined this new orthodoxy. Thereby did the discipline get what one scholar called the 'closest thing to a bible'.[47] Generations of budding economists across the world now got their induction into this new faith as soon as they started college. Samuelson's new book, wrote Robert Nelson, 'was meant to instil, and to a considerable extent succeeded in instilling, a religious commitment to the market – now depicted as the "market mechanism" – and a commitment to the priestly authority of economists to manage this marvellously productive instrument for the general social benefit.'[48]

A small faction of Keynesian purists would in time break away from the new church, going back to the Keynesian classics after the master's death. Just as the early Church soft-pedalled Christ's pacifism to make the doctrine palatable to the warrior-nobility that took over the Roman Empire, but thereby risked removing one of its core elements, 'post-Keynesians' like Hyman Minsky would say the Samuelson synthesis stripped Keynesianism of its key innovation – the inevitability of the business cycle. But, like breakaway sects that soon wither, to retain but a few isolated adepts, post-Keynesianism would nearly disappear amid the triumph of the new faith. For, whatever its fateful compromises, the Samuelson synthesis managed to secure the triumph of the new doctrine. Just as the early Church adapted to the culture of the north European tribes that toppled Rome, so did the Samuelson synthesis make Keynesianism palatable right across the West, to say nothing of the new countries that would emerge from Europe's colonial empires. If in Keynes capitalism had found a saviour, in the post-war generation of economists it would find its rabbinical sages, trained to guide the faithful towards their earthly salvation: jobs, rising wages, cheaper and more abundant goods, low inflation and affordable mortgages.

And yet, if Keynesianism became the de facto state religion in much of the post-war world, it did so for reasons that lay beyond events in any one state. Keynesianism became a sort of intellectual veneer for programmes to expand the state's political and social roles, but which had (as we have seen) various domestic causes. But none of it may have been possible had it not been for the post-war triumph of the Keynesian vision on an international level. Because, just as medieval Christendom united diverse European states under a common religious identity, so too did Keynesianism create an international order geared to make the world safe for capitalism. And it did so with the same motive that had driven Keynes's own epiphany. After the war, capitalism's great rival, communism, was on the march again and looking stronger than ever. Thus, even as the new peacetime governments of Europe announced their conversions to the new statist gospel, the battle for souls remained far from won.

CHAPTER 12

THE NEW JERUSALEM

Man cannot live on bread alone, says the Bible. But just try living without it.

Like it or not, economics lies at the base of our existence. Even if, like John Maynard Keynes, we believe we were born to do more than just get rich or buy more stuff, whether that higher purpose is art, love, self-actualisation, or Nietzschean overcoming, we can't do any of it if we can't eat. If you've ever been stuck on a long journey growing hungry and tired, you know how quickly higher purposes can disappear from your thoughts. And if you're starving, you seldom ask the person offering you a meal if the food was ethically sourced.

During the 1930s, so many people had been hungry and tired for so long their attachment to democracy and liberal values wavered. Keynes knew that his own pursuit of aesthetic pleasures would be threatened in the sort of totalitarian society that appealed to many of those suffering the ravages of the Great Depression. Defeating Nazi Germany alone wouldn't suffice to prevent this threat ever recurring. To him it was imperative that Western countries created a global order that prevented another depression. If economics was to free people to nourish their minds and souls, it first had to fill their stomachs. If it failed to do that, people would once more look for other doctrines. Because amid drought, a pastor who tells his flock he can't make the rains come will quickly lose his congregation to the newest miracle worker to turn up in the village square.

For Adolf Hitler, the winter of 1941–2 changed his destiny from his beloved racial paradise to a frigid hell. The war had initially gone to plan for him. A non-aggression pact with the Soviet Union had freed him to fight on one front at a time, and he'd made lightning advances all the way to the Atlantic Ocean and across North Africa. Europe had seemed to lie supine before him. But then he decided to break the pact and invade Russia, mere months before Japan bombed Pearl Harbor and drew the Americans into the war. Once the combined industrial might of the Soviet Union and the United States bore down on Germany, the balance changed abruptly.

Only weeks after the US Congress unanimously heeded President Roosevelt's call to declare war, while German columns were bogged down in the ice and snow of the savage Russian winter, Hitler's armaments minister, Fritz Todt, flew to his East Prussian bunker for his regular briefing. Showing him detailed figures and estimates, he made it clear that in the coming years Russian and American factories would spew out more tanks, bombers and guns than Germany could ever hope to match. Hitler looked glum when his friend and chief architect, Albert Speer, showed up for his late-night appointment with the Führer, though Speer managed to cheer him up somewhat by showing him his plans to rebuild Berlin in a grandiose style befitting what was to be the Thousand Year Reich[1] (a project that would, in the end, never see the light of day).

Todt died when his plane crashed on the flight back to Berlin that night. But the message never changed. In their own capitals, allied intelligence officers were making similar reports of their assured superiority. What that meant to the governments in London and Washington, DC was that they'd eventually share the big prize – the right to determine the shape of the post-war world. For Winston Churchill, who in 1942 declared, 'I have not become the King's First Minister in order to preside at the liquidation of the British Empire,' that would entail some restoration of the old order, with

Britain's Empire as intact as possible. And he wasn't going to repeat the disastrous mistake of 1919. He'd make sure that this time John Maynard Keynes got a hearing.

Shortly after the United States entered the war, the Cambridge don was summoned to London and tasked with the job of devising a blueprint for the post-war world economy. Whatever he made of Churchill's imperialism, Keynes would have preferred that Britain retain her empire for as long as possible, using its resources to help rebuild the country's finances, so badly depleted by the war.[2] However, the Americans took a different view of empire. In place of vertical empires with command centres in European capitals, they envisioned a more confederal world order of nominally equal states, organised around a common set of rules and institutions, albeit dominated by Western countries. Preoccupied as they were by the communist threat emanating from Russia, they had no particular wish to help the Europeans revive their empires in their existing form, making allowances only in specific cases – like Algeria or Vietnam – where there was a risk that communists would take power at independence.[3] So, to come up with their own plans for the post-war world, they assigned an employee of the Treasury Department to draft their own blueprint, a man named Harry Dexter White.

It was an odd and, on the face of it, uneven match. White was the night-school version of Keynes. Late to do a PhD, with few scholarly publications and limited academic experience, he was a civil servant's civil servant, buried deep in the US Treasury Department. A Keynesian apostle, he faced the distinctly uneasy task of debating with a master whose gospel he had swallowed, but on which he disagreed on a couple of nice but important points. More significantly, his mandate was to subtly enable the United States to replace Britain at the heart of the global financial system – which he however wanted to do with the great man's blessing. With no renown to speak of and little of Keynes's charisma, he knew that in a showdown with Keynes he'd get crushed. But he had one very big ace up his sleeve. Britain, having been deprived by the war of both European trade and its imperial finances, had been forced to obtain food and arms

on credit from the United States. As the war wound on, Britain thus
ran up a big tab in Washington until it was ultimately the world's
largest debtor and America its largest creditor.[4] White therefore
knew he could, if he had to, call the piper's tune.

Keynes wanted to work one-on-one with White. In 1944, he
suggested the two men get together with their respective blueprints,
hammer out a deal, then present it for approval. White, however,
wanted to do just the opposite – gather all the Allies in a conference room and hash it out, something Keynes complained would
degenerate into 'a most monstrous monkey house'.[5] But that, in fact,
appeared to be just what White wanted. Amid the din of numerous
sessions and working groups, and no doubt mindful that Keynes's
then-failing health would make it difficult to keep up, he reckoned
his aides could keep slipping the American positions onto the agenda
before Keynes had a chance to even notice, let alone organise a coalition against them.[6]

White prevailed. In July 1944 the United States hosted a conference in a small New England town named Bretton Woods. By
then, Allied troops had successfully landed in France and secured
the beachhead from which they would launch their advance on
Germany. Hitler's war now became a desperate effort to resist the
inexorable fall. Meanwhile back in New Hampshire the Allied delegates, holed up in a hotel for three weeks of working groups amid a
constant stream of policy documents and proposals, negotiated the
framework of what would come to be known as the Bretton Woods
System. At its core would lie three institutions: the International
Monetary Fund (IMF), the International Bank for Reconstruction
and Development (World Bank) and the General Agreement on
Tariffs and Trade (GATT).

Bretton Woods aimed to create a world economy that was, in the
American design, as open and free flowing as possible. With fresh
memories of the protectionist spiral that had worsened the Great
Depression, when countries tried to protect jobs and conserve their
dwindling gold reserves by blocking imports, Keynes and White
wanted to ensure no country would ever again feel the need to pull

up its drawbridge. GATT thus bound all the member countries to reducing their import duties and tariffs over time, making it easier for everyone to export to each other. The IMF, meanwhile, was to be something of a global rainy-day fund into which member governments each made a deposit. If their foreign reserves ever ran low because they had imported more than they exported, they could just take an advance to cover their bills. The World Bank would work in a similar fashion, but its mission would be to provide loans to first rebuild war-torn Europe, and then second to help develop the newly independent states that were about to emerge from Europe's eroding empires (a last-minute adjustment to its mission which the Mexican delegate managed to slip onto the table[7]).

But while the IMF would ensure countries always had 'cash flow' to fund their trading, Keynes and White knew that it was possible a country might start living beyond its means, always import more than it exported and thus run-down its rainy-day fund. Previously, countries faced with dwindling reserves were tempted to tax imports, both to raise revenue and to reduce the drain of foreign reserves to imports. But that was the very sort of protectionism that had aggravated the Great Depression, as countries whose overseas markets were cut off engaged in tit-for-tat retaliation. Solving this temptation to 'beggar-thy-neighbour' lay at the heart of Bretton Woods.

When it came to finding a solution, Keynes regarded the problem rather like a coin with two sides. If a country was a chronic importer, that meant another was a chronic exporter. And while the chronic importer was a shopaholic living beyond its means, the chronic exporter was a skinflint that wasn't doing its bit for global trade. In a radio broadcast during the Great Depression, Keynes had famously advised people with jobs to go out and spend, so as to restart the economy. That's what he wanted the IMF to do for the world economy: badger everyone into doing their bit to restore growth, forcing the penny-pincher to loosen up – an epicurean global order that encouraged the prudent to splurge from time to time. White, though, was more of a Stoic, who like many of his compatriots believed in the old-fashioned virtue of thrift. Ultimately, he prevailed in the argument – not because he persuaded Keynes, but because he simply wouldn't budge on the issue. The final agreement would only give the IMF the power to discipline deficit countries: it could give them credit beyond their own allocation, but only on condition the recipient then tightened its belt to lower its spending (what today we call austerity).

Most significantly, Bretton Woods established a common currency for global trade. Keynes wanted to create a new currency to be used only for trade among countries. White instead suggested they use the dollar, on the understanding it would be backed by the substantial gold reserves the United States held in Fort Knox. Keynes, aware this would give the United States what the French President Charles de Gaulle would later complain was an 'exorbitant privilege', hadn't been too keen on this idea. Since virtually all governments would conduct their international business in dollars, that meant they would store their reserves in the American banking system. That, in turn, meant the United States would be able to pay for its imports simply by 'printing' dollars – which is to say, by just lodging an IOU in its trading partner's American account. It would probably also mean that New York would edge London aside as the world's financial capital. In effect, America would wrest the privilege Britain had long derived from its own empire; as the world's savings entered the American banking system, the country would get a credit subsidy within a new, confederal, US-dominated empire.

With White once again standing his ground, Bretton Woods set the gold exchange rate of the dollar at thirty-five – which is to say that for every thirty-five dollars a country held in its American reserves, it was entitled to an ounce of gold. In principle, any government could at any time take its dollar reserves, head to the gold window at the New York Federal Reserve and swap them for bullion. In practice, since dollars were easier to move than gold, and were anyway now literally as good as gold, hardly anyone ever bothered to do so. Bretton Woods thereby completed the transfer of the world economy's political centre of gravity from Europe to America. Keynes may have felt like an impotent prophet, watching as a skilled proselyte altered his message. But these are the compromises any creed makes on its way to becoming established, for Keynesianism became the state-church of the new global order.[8]

For all its self-assurance, Keynesianism proved to be a surprisingly tolerant church when it came to other doctrines. As has been said of the Catholic willingness to incorporate pre-Christian traditions to create Christmas and transform saints' relics just by sprinkling them with holy water, so too did the Keynesian priests always make room at the altar for those willing to permit the market a place. Thus, Harry Dexter White, loyal acolyte that he was,[9] saw no contradiction between his Keynesian economics and his strongly pro-Soviet leanings. Like Franklin Roosevelt, he fully expected the partnership the United States and Russia had forged to fight Hitler to endure into the post-war age.

But Stalin was having none of it. There was no way he was going to play second fiddle in an American-dominated global order. The traditional Russian paranoia that came with a long history of being surrounded by countries that didn't always have friendly intentions, overlaid with the legacy of Lenin's Bolshevik puritanism, led Stalin to see the world in Manichean terms: nobody shall come to the Workers' Paradise except through us; hence anybody who is not with us is against us.

Although the Soviets attended the Bretton Woods Conference, they left without signing. Stalin then turned his attention to an old Russian practice of creating a zone of buffer states between the Soviet Union and potential future enemies. In the six European countries it had liberated from Nazi rule, elections were manipulated or coups plotted so as to install puppet regimes. Winston Churchill, always more sceptical of Stalin than Roosevelt, noted in a 1946 speech that: 'From Stettin in the Baltic to Trieste in the Adriatic an "Iron Curtain" has descended across the continent', with the six Soviet satellite states of Poland, East Germany, Czechoslovakia, Hungary, Bulgaria and Romania lying behind it, cut off from the West.

Nor did Western concerns about the spread of communism stop with Russian intrigues. Communism was equally on the march outside the Soviet military orbit. Yugoslavia and Albania had fallen to domestic insurgencies and communist rebels were fighting the British-backed government in Greece. In the former Pacific war-theatre, having previously buried their differences with the Nationalist government to expel the Japanese, Mao Zedong's communist army now turned its sights on finishing its revolution. And even in some Western countries, in the first post-war elections communist parties surged to the top of the ticket. Notably in France and Italy, there was a real prospect the communist revolution would come via the ballot box.

It was no mystery why. Economic and social conditions in Europe remained bleak. Millions were homeless. Hunger was rife and famine threatened. Coal was scarce and a bitterly cold winter left even Britons at death's doorstep in 1946–7. With factories, electrical plants, roads, railways and houses reduced to rubble by six years of fighting, economies struggled to restart their engines. The 1948 Italian film *Bicycle Thieves*, in which the life of a poor worker in post-war Rome hinges on whether he can find the stolen bicycle he needs to get to work, captured the febrile atmosphere of the time. As far removed as it was from such desperate shores, Washington could see how precarious its European position was. The United States knew that even though the war was won, it might yet lose the peace to a rival doctrine. And just when the battle to make the world safe for capitalism needed an inspirational commander, Roosevelt died, throwing the task into the hands of a green new president just as the Second World War was ending.

Harry S. Truman was a simple man with modest expectations of life. A small-town shopkeeper who, after his presidency, would eventually return to a quiet life in his hometown, he had risen to the apex of power mostly by staying off the radar. He'd been Roosevelt's vice president for only eighty-two days when his boss died, and found himself with a dizzying task at the very moment American might was peaking. After he was sworn in, a stunned Truman – who didn't even know that the United States had been developing the atomic bomb that would end the Pacific War – had told reporters, 'Boys, if you ever pray, pray for me now. I don't know if you fellas ever had a load of hay fall on you, but when they told me what happened yesterday, I felt like the moon, the stars, and all the planets had fallen on me.'[10]

Europe's devastation had left the United States in an overwhelming position. At the war's conclusion, America accounted for a third of the world economy and more than half its industrial output.[11] Only it had the resources to station millions of soldiers overseas, and even Britain depended on American subsidies to maintain its troop deployments. The country Harry Truman became commander-in-chief of that day in April 1945 thus truly strode the planet like a colossus. In effect, therefore, at least for the time being, the White House Truman inherited was in a position to dictate world affairs to an extraordinary degree, and his decisions would shape world affairs for generations to come.

In 1947, two years after Truman had stepped into office, Europe was still struggling to emerge from its devastation and the Cold War was shaping into a struggle between two rival faiths. Truman recognised that simply continuing to play the strong hand that Bretton Woods had bequeathed him might serve America in the short term, but at the risk of turning many against the Western order. He decided that America's future now depended on a bit of liberal imperialism – enlightened despotism on a global scale.

Truman's Secretary of State, George Marshall, was scheduled to speak at Harvard University's graduation ceremony. Truman instructed him to use the occasion to outline a plan to employ American economic might to lift its allies from the morass. On 5 June 1947, Marshall took the podium before the graduating class and told them the world into which they were graduating was a dangerous one. The market economy faced imminent threat. In addition to 'the demoralizing effect on the world at large and the possibilities of disturbances arising as a result of the desperation of the people concerned,' he said a weak European economy would mean low demand for American exports. What America needed to do was dip into its pockets and launch an aid programme whose 'purpose should be the revival of a working economy in the world so as to permit the emergence of political and social conditions in which free institutions can exist.'

Soon afterwards 'Marshall Plan' aid money poured into Western Europe. This restored the confidence of the European banking sector. They resumed lending, which enabled firms to ramp up operations. The Truman administration also decided it was time to try a bit of Keynesian Epicureanism after all. It started spending lavishly on the goods its allies' factories began producing. Importing more than it sold back to Europe and Japan, the United States ran up trade deficits with its partners, thereby subsidising their recoveries. To cover its bills, Washington gave them what were IOUs, crediting their reserves by effectively printing US dollars. When it came time to using its exorbitant privilege, the United States opted to assist its allies rather than enrich itself at their expense. Nobody complained.

That's because what was good for Europe and Japan, was equally good for America. With the United States' new partners growing stronger by the day, demand for American goods resumed rising. Moreover, the investment opportunities a newly resurgent European economy offered to American firms promised good returns. Although the British and French might grumble quietly about how they'd been eclipsed by the American upstart, the fact was everyone was happy to sing to the tune of the new leader. Why wouldn't they? It was a party on someone else's tab.

Well, not everyone was happy. Socialists and communists derided the 'gifts from Uncle Harry' that were helping to wean the workers away from rebellion. Although they continued to support left-wing parties and still talked of revolution, with each material step forward, Europe's workers gained more and more purchase in the Keynesian Eden. As Uncle Harry's paradise began to rival anything Stalin could promise, Europe stepped away from the brink of communism, renewing its vows with the market economy. Under Truman's guidance, the United States had used its moment of power to create a Western system that both enshrined Harry Dexter White's version of Keynesianism at an international level and also created a supportive environment for national governments to use Keynesian management to rebuild their economies. To the Keynesian gospel, Truman had played the role of St Paul – taking the doctrine of a beleaguered community and ensuring it spread to the furthest reaches of the Western empire.

A few weeks after Marshall delivered his commencement address outside Boston, Jawaharlal Nehru, the leader of India's Congress, sat in Delhi's Constituent Assembly and prepared to give a historic speech of his own. After centuries of British colonialism, India was about to proclaim its birth as an independent nation. On 14 August 1947, as midnight approached, he rose before his parliamentary colleagues and, in the clipped English he had refined in his years at Harrow, Cambridge and the Inner Temple, said: 'Long years ago we made a tryst with destiny and now the time comes when we shall redeem our pledge.' Under the whirring fans, as the Assembly broke into applause, he declared, 'At the stroke of midnight, the hour when the world sleeps, India will wake to life and freedom.' Then, as the clock began ringing in the chamber and a trumpeting conch shell signalled that India was now independent, celebrations erupted across the capital.[12] Mosques and temples remained open throughout the night for those who wanted to pray, guns fired, temple bells rang, crowds filled the streets and fireworks the sky.[13]

In the face of rhetorical (if not always actual)[14] American support for decolonisation the European powers had struggled to restore their empires. As the Dutch discovered in Indonesia, and as the French would do in Vietnam and later Algeria, the locals weren't necessarily of a mind to welcome them back. For men like Nehru, the new American order presented them with a timely opportunity. Signing onto it gave them instant membership in the club of nations. They'd get *their* own seats at the newly formed United Nations, *their* presidents would be addressed as 'Your Excellency', *their* ambassadors would be received in the world's capitals – including, of course, those of the old mother countries – and *their* ministers would represent them at future trade and treaty negotiations.

True, most of the leaders of the new nation states hadn't sat at the table that had designed the new order, and the Bretton Woods system would not operate to their relative advantage. In loosening restrictions on trade, GATT privileged industrial over agricultural producers and exempted those industries, like textiles, in which the newly independent countries were most likely to be able to compete with the West.[15] As a result, regardless of their political independence, poor countries would struggle to reverse the flow of economic surpluses to the rich countries. Meanwhile, banking in dollars would require the newly independent countries to always set aside a portion of what they earned in trade and leave it in their American accounts.

These shortcomings weren't all apparent at first. Besides, once the Marshall Plan gave Europe's and Japan's recoveries the fillip they needed, the rebounding Western economy provided the new countries with expanding markets to sell their products. With the extra money these sales generated, national leaders would then be able to develop their economies and build modern states. In consequence, decolonisation didn't so much end empire as give it a new shape. In place of the administrative, centralised, territorial empires of Europe, what emerged was a global political-economic order similar to the late Roman Empire: an 'inside-out empire'[16] in which a collection of nominally independent states administered their own territories according to a set of rules and within a set of institutions designed and overseen by the Western powers, under the hegemony of a 'capital' that managed the financial system, all in such a way that maintained the economic advantage of the dominant region.

Once the external obstacles to independence had been lifted, there was little left to stop the nationalist movements that had been building in the colonies. Churchill understood that the independence of India would open a floodgate, confounding any efforts to, say, resettle Kenya with colonists (as the British tried) or tie Algeria ever closer to the mother country (as the French tried). Within a generation of

Nehru's speech, most of the world's former colonies were sovereign states. Only the Portuguese Empire, which had stayed outside the war and thus managed to hold on to its African colonies, withstood this tide – for now.

Formally, most of the new governments chose not to ally them-selves with one or other of the superpowers. Informally, while playing the Russians and Americans off against each other in aid and diplomatic negotiations, most of them ended up gravitating into the orbit of the American-led Western empire for one simple reason: it had the money and the richest markets. With the battle-fronts of the Cold War now firmly drawn, what resulted was a world conventionally described as split into three camps: the First World, which is to say the developed countries grouped around the United States in the Bretton Woods System; the Second World, the Soviet Union and its small network of allies; and the Third World, which is to say all the developing states, whose foreign trade was conducted disproportionately with the West.

No sooner did India's independence celebrations die down than Jawaharlal Nehru awoke to a daunting new task. Responsible now for the lives of his compatriots, he needed to do something, and do it fast. In 1947, Indians, like hundreds of millions of people in the Third World, lived at the margins of existence. The risk of famine hovered constantly. Most people spent their entire lives in the vil-lage where they'd been born, eking out a bare subsistence on small plots of land. Almost none had access to basic medicine. Most were illiterate and couldn't afford school, and millions were still locked into feudal relations with powerful lords, the *zamindars*, who main-tained large estates and seldom displayed much if any regard for their peasants.[17]

And the desperate economic need wasn't even the worst of it. Nehru knew only too well the independence celebrations had been largely confined to the cities, where only a small share of the coun-try's population lived. The urban middle and working classes were generally keen on independence, since control of the state provided them with new opportunities in employment, contracts and better working conditions. But the rural poor were harder to reach, and the national leaders meant little to them.

That's because, by and large, the leaders of the newly independent states didn't come from the landed classes or rural elites. The latter, in fact, very often regarded the new nation with some ambivalence since it was run by upstarts looking to dethrone them. More typically, like Nehru, the new independence leaders were colonially educated men who had made their names in law, politics, colonial administration – which is to say, in urban professions. Many of the people who had suddenly become citizens of Nehru's new country, however, living in their isolated villages, weren't even aware that such a thing called India existed,[18] let alone recognised its anthem or saluted its flag. Nationalism, the new worldly faith of which Nehru had been so eloquent an exponent, would scarcely win their love if it couldn't feed them. If the new masters of the Third World failed to build ties to their citizens strong enough to lure them away from the old ways and the men who controlled them, their attempt to create countries on a par with those of the West would flounder. Just as nineteenth-century national movements had done in Europe, the new governments needed to fill not just heads and hearts, but stomachs.

For Nehru's generation, the state shone as the saviour that could banish this darkness of poverty and oppression. 'Seek ye first the political kingdom,' the African nationalist leader Kwame Nkrumah counselled, 'and all things shall be added unto you.' Not only could the state be used to harness resources and engineer development, it could be used to bond governing elites to those they needed to reach. Expanding the state's powers – and with that public employment – building state firms, controlling the licensing of imports or foreign-exchange allocations in such a way that politicians could use their leverage over business to get them to take on more workers or improve their wages, controlling the trade of certain exports and thereby building pools of capital that could be used for patronage: such mechanisms offered a means by which the state could make itself the new patron.

Not surprisingly, therefore, independence leaders welcomed the Keynesian doctrine with the same enthusiasm early British industrialists had received the free-trade gospel. By the late 1940s, economics departments everywhere were teaching Keynesian macroeconomics and the Samuelson synthesis. Any students sent abroad to study the new techniques of economic management returned home versed in the new scholarship. In addition, now that scholars were finally starting to turn their attention to the economics of the newly independent states, what they discovered didn't always square with the old neoclassical canon. Some economists had uncovered evidence of what appeared to be a bias against Third World exporters. They found that prices on the goods produced in the former colonies, like crops and minerals, had been rising more slowly than those of the industrial products of the developed world. That meant that over time it was going to take ever more primary exports to import the same volume of manufactured goods.[20] Building industry to catch up to the West thus became something of an imperative in the Third World.

There was no shortage of apparently successful statist models, starting with the obvious case of Soviet Russia. But while Nehru held the Russians in high esteem, like many independence leaders he was more impressed with the way Turkey had mixed the state and market. There, much as Nehru wanted to do with India, Atatürk had used economic development to lure his people away from their old religions and clerical leaders to a new worldly faith directed by the state he was creating. Nehru also took note of Latin America's experience in the Great Depression. After a century of perpetuating the colonial model of exporting raw materials to Europe in return for finished goods, national governments suddenly found in the 1930s that they could no longer generate enough foreign exchange to continue importing. So instead they'd pioneered a technique that came to be known as import substitution industrialisation (ISI). With foreign exchange unavailable to buy imports, they left the local market to entrepreneurs, who eagerly established new firms. So quickly did the continent's industrial sectors grow that after the war Latin America's governments opted to enshrine the model. Placing tariffs and quotas on imported goods, they continued to shelter the nascent industrial sector from foreign competition. As a result, industry continued expanding.[20]

ISI became the model for much of the Third World. The Japanese method, of using an infant-industry model to build a few exporting sectors while relying on imports for everything else, shone brightly in East Asia, where a few countries ended up adopting it. But by and large the new states of the Third World found ISI a low-cost method to build their new states, something to which the World Bank had given its blessing.[21] And as the reconstruction of Europe gathered pace, the Bank was able to turn its attention, and its resources, to building the economies of the Third World.

Their colonial experiences had instilled in them a sense that the market was free for others but discriminated against them. Whatever the merit of that proposition, what the new leaders knew for certain was that the state was now theirs. In principle, they could use it to reclaim control of the market. Whether or not it occurred to them that this implicitly accepted the Leninist notion that the state was a moral sphere and the market a garden of selfishness, it was a view then widely shared. The free market was at that time a bereft, fallen idol, abandoned by all but its most loyal apostles.

Most importantly, all these variants of Keynesianism appeared to work. Beginning in 1948, and continuing for a full quarter-century afterwards, the world economy grew by an average of 4 to 6 per cent each year. There were years some Western countries did even better than that. They were in the driving seat, and the Western economy's steady post-war expansion kept demand for primary commodities from the Third World strong. Thus, almost everyone who wanted to join the ride could do so.

Now think about that for a moment. Think what it would have been like to be born in a Western country just after the war. If you had been a typical person and got a job on leaving school, and did nothing but what the job required, never getting a promotion or a bonus or a new job offer, your pay would still have doubled every decade. Add a modicum of ambition or good fortune, promotions or possibly the odd new job, and your pay might have gone up by a tenth or more each year. Think what successive Christmases would have been like.

Plus, there was more stuff to buy with all this money. The gradual expansion of global commerce as countries implemented the new trading regime meant that the choices available in the local markets multiplied. Improved road and rail networks, cheaper shipping and the increasing use of containers to move goods meant that more stuff could travel longer distances at less cost. Everyone could now get oranges at Christmas. Open-shelf supermarkets spread, enabling shoppers to wander long aisles scanning a selection of food that grew more varied by the year. Most families got to buy cars, and the system of roads and highways expanded to accommodate them. People could travel greater distances to go shopping, giving themselves an even bigger range of choices.

In the United States the first indoor shopping mall was opened. Soon plazas where shoppers could wander through a diverse selection of stores began popping up. Shopping became a pastime. Fuel remained cheap, so the cars got bigger and better. Increasingly mobile, people could now move further out of town, where they'd have their own garden and fresh air. Prices remained tame and homes were affordable. Suburbs mushroomed across the West. With more space to build, houses became larger, which meant you could fill them with more stuff. Televisions joined radios and stereos as the entertainment of choice. Housework became less burdensome, as vacuum cleaners, washing machines, dishwashers, blenders and electric mixers became commonplace. Vacations became more exciting. In place of the traditional local fare, like a week at the seaside or a mountain retreat, holidaymakers could now contemplate trips abroad. With airfares falling, flying went from being a luxury to a mass-market product, and the number of overseas holidaymakers doubled each decade.[22] Mediterranean resorts, where one could escape the cold dark winter and eat good inexpensive food, became popular across western Europe. Britons discovered Ibiza.

People were healthier and lived longer. Newly enlarged welfare states provided access to medical care, often for free. Indoor plumbing became the norm, as did refrigerators, and the resulting improvements in hygiene and food quality added a decade to lifespans. Retirement stopped being a necessity for people who simply couldn't work any longer and had to live off their children, and became a time of leisure when, freed from their children by state pensions, they could try new things. There were more opportunities. The massive expansion of higher education turned university from being a playground of the rich to being open to many more people. Generous subsidies made tuition either cheap or free.

Of course, nothing is perfect, and just as any idyll has its dark recesses, this model had its less attractive side. Immigration controls tightened and the new Third World states were told to look after their own. Thus, the ratio of First World to Third World wages, which stood around 30:1 in 1950, would widen further as a sort of global apartheid steered many of the gains from global trade to the 'white suburbs' of the north.[23] There were forms of internal apartheid, the United States in particular excluding African Americans from the festivities as persistent segregation confined them to lower-paying jobs. Similar patterns recurred in many of the newly independent states of the Third World as well, where dominant castes, or racial or ethnic groups, sometimes captured state power and used it to their advantage. Equally, the professional and middle classes who staffed the offices of the new states usually did much better than the labourers who swept the hallways or the farmers who grew the food.

And even within Western societies, there were worries. Like a nuclear holocaust, or the Russians turning up on the beaches. With the Cold War raging, the superpowers were building nuclear bombs and missiles until the stockpile of weaponry grew so large it could destroy humanity many times over. Families built backyard bomb shelters. When in 1962 the Russians and Americans confronted one another over Moscow's attempt to place missiles in Cuba, the world teetered on the brink of nuclear war. Many feared that communism was still spreading inch by inch across the globe, and wondered if

the Soviet leader Nikolai Khrushchev had been right when he had
told Western ambassadors in 1956, 'We will bury you!' After all, in
the decade that followed, the Russians had beaten the West in first
putting a satellite, then an animal, then a man, into space.

But the funny thing was, even this superpower stand-off gave the
world a certain orderliness, which allowed people to go about their
lives. In a world carved into spheres of influence, when most people
answered to one superpower or the other, there weren't many loose
cannons, renegades or lone-wolf terrorists. You worked for one guy
or the other. That meant the big bosses could always do a deal if you
threatened to get out of hand. Europe remained at peace, and after
the Americans went all out to finally beat the Russians at putting a
man on the moon, the West could enter the seventies feeling it had
reasserted its primacy once more. It was that sort of time, when
presidents could wave their hand and authorise spending countless
billions of dollars just to make a point. Since it seemed that the
money would never stop flowing, the only question was what to
spend it on. Moreover, since money was flowing across much of the
world economy, absolute increases often obscured relative declines.
In any event, if you lived in a Western country and were employed,
you were all but certainly better off than your parents had been, and
could dream bigger dreams than they had done. There appeared to
be room for everyone at the Keynesian feast.

Franklin Roosevelt had promised Americans a New Deal. Lyndon
Johnson went one better and gave them a Great Society, expanding
the public services available to Americans. In Britain, Labour had
come to office in 1945 saying it would create the New Jerusalem,
and it delivered. So popular was the new society that when the
Conservatives returned to power in 1951, they left the welfare state
they inherited intact. People who had lived through the Depression
still remembered its horrors, but by the 1970s their numbers were
declining. Those born after the war had never known a recession
worth mentioning. The wisdom of the sages assured everyone that
recessions had been relegated to historical footnotes. Economists
wrote textbooks confidently declaring they had now mastered the

economy's inner workings, and that there need never be another downturn. So complete was the consensus around the statist doctrine that even a conservative president like Richard Nixon, though sentimentally attached to the idea of free markets, could eventually admit: 'I am now a Keynesian.'[24]

Then one day in 1973, a Bedouin nomad in Egypt's Sinai Desert heard a loud roar and looked up into the sky, where he saw fighter jets heading to the eastern horizon. The Keynesian Garden of Eden was about to lose its innocence.

CHAPTER 13

THE END OF EDEN

'I believe in one, holy, catholic, and apostolic church' goes the Nicene Creed, a profession of faith recited by many Catholics whenever they gather in worship. Dismissed by some as a bit of papist triumphalism, 'catholic' refers to the Greek word for 'universal', and in keeping alive the dream of Christian unity the Catholic Church has tolerated a fair bit of diversity.

The same could be said of the Keynesian church in its heyday. Far from being a puritanical faith, it was from the outset pragmatic in doctrine. 'When the facts change, I change my mind,' said Keynes. Provided a market economy lay at the base of the society and that individuals enjoyed some freedom to transact their own business, his creed allowed for all manner of experimentation with state ownership and management, differing forms of welfare, varieties of taxation and redistribution, and even talk of eventually building socialism (particularly if it remained just talk). And by apparently delivering a golden age of prosperity from the late 1940s through the 1960s, Keynesianism seemed to do just that, winning converts from right across the political spectrum.

But if the miracles stopped flowing, the church would lose believers. And crisis came to Keynesianism in the 1970s. It all started in the birthplace of an ancient civilisation.

*

When nationalism became a powerful movement at the end of the nineteenth century, some European Jews felt they should also get a country they could call their own. The growing assertiveness of nationalism in Europe, which often isolated Jews as being somehow outside or even opposed to the nation, gave further impetus to this drive, especially when anti-Jewish pogroms broke out in Russia. As a people with a history that went back millennia, the Jews had as good a claim as anyone to being a nation. Their problem was they hadn't had a homeland for 2,000 years, when the Roman Empire had destroyed the last Jewish kingdom. Reclaiming a Palestine that had since been occupied by others was always going to be contentious. The retreat of the Ottoman Empire created a fortuitous political vacuum into which the early Zionists, as they called their movement, could settle, though the European empires that rushed in to snap up the former Ottoman provinces initially regarded Zionism with some ambivalence. For their part European Jews were divided in their attitude, some opposing the retaking of their Promised Land on religious grounds, others simply because their Jewish identity played a secondary role to their national loyalties. German Jews felt particularly attached to the new state created by Bismarck, since it was a land of culture and learning in which they could thrive.

However, everything changed after the horrors of the Second World War. When the United Nations approved a plan to divide Palestine into separate Jewish and Arab states, Zionist settlers in Palestine took the initiative and in 1948 declared Israel independent. Despite getting the blessing of the Americans and Russians, Israel's new founders encountered hostility. Neighbouring Arab countries, some of which were states only just emerging from the Ottoman Empire, wanted to destroy the Jewish upstart.

And so it continued ever since, with long uneasy truces punctuated by periodic outbursts of violence. Of these conflicts, the most significant was the 1967 Six Day War, during which the Israelis occupied Jerusalem while seizing the Sinai Peninsula from Egypt. Then Egypt looked for an opportunity to avenge its crushing defeat. And in 1973, it obtained a new, secret weapon.

The quarter-century of global growth that followed the Second World War had created a massive expansion not just in industrial output, but in planes, trains and motor cars. Car production alone increased almost tenfold over the period.[1] As a result, both fuel and electrical consumption exploded. Most of that electricity came from power stations with oil-fired turbines. Thus at the base of the expanding world economy lay oil. Although some of the world's biggest oil producers were industrial countries – Russia being the biggest, though the United States wasn't far behind – the United States and other Western countries still needed to import large amounts of oil. And a small number of countries with large oil fields had cornered most of the supply. Most of them were Arab states in the Persian Gulf.

The biggest of them all was Saudi Arabia, the family run kingdom that still operated like a tribal sheikhdom. Although notionally a friend of the United States the Saudis played their own game in world politics. For a generation, the Arab world had been polarised into two camps: traditionalists and modernisers. In the vanguard of the latter group were quasi-socialist states friendly with the Soviet Union – Iraq, Syria and Egypt – and in the 1960s they seemed to enjoy the upper hand in the battle for loyalties. The monarchies and sheikhdoms, which appeared wedded to the past, had by then reduced themselves to anachronisms that tolerated slavery or, as in the case of the old sultan of Oman's quixotic attempt to keep modernity at bay, banned medicine and spectacles. In a Middle East bubbling with revolt, one republican revolution followed another, and the traditionalists had withdrawn to a bastion of states ringing the Persian Gulf.[2]

But like a one-sided fight that suddenly changes course with one devastating punch, the autumn of 1973 turned things around. Late that summer, the Saudi king received a visit from the Egyptian president, Anwar Sadat. Sadat told him he was planning a surprise attack on Israel and asked for the king's backing – not military support, but something even more potent. He wanted the Saudis to organise Arab oil-producing states to create an embargo on oil to anyone who backed Israel.

In the Egyptian president, the Saudi king reckoned he saw a moderate who might be induced to dismantle the more radical legacy of his predecessor, the hero of Arab nationalism Gamal Abdel Nasser. As if to curry favour Sadat had already begun sending Soviet military advisers back home. So the king, eager to turn the tables on the radical Arab states, agreed. Sadat returned to Cairo, ready to pounce.[3]

Six weeks later, Egyptian jets started bombing Israel from the west. Egypt's Syrian ally, meanwhile, was flying sorties from the east. Artillery began raining down on Israeli positions, putting the Jewish state on the back foot and enabling Egyptian rafts to ferry troops across the Suez Canal and into the Sinai Peninsula. Within days, Israel's position looked desperate. Prime Minister Golda Meir wrote to the American president and begged him to come to her country's aid. With the Soviets airlifting planeloads of weapons and ammunition to Egypt and Syria, her country had only days left before it would be extinguished by Arab armies.[4]

President Richard Nixon, already embroiled in an unpopular war in Vietnam as well as a Congressional investigation into a 1972 break-in by Republican operatives at the Democratic Party's Watergate Hotel offices, ordered a resupply. No sooner did he do so, though, than he received a letter from the Saudi king, warning an embargo would be launched if he did not reverse his decision.[5] The United States, which awkwardly balanced friendship with both the Saudis and Israel, now faced an awful dilemma: them, or us.

The United States could survive a blockade. The problem was that Saudi Arabia was the world's biggest 'swing' producer. So much of what was traded on the world's oil exchanges came from the kingdom that it could alter oil prices. That then affected all prices on the world markets. Since Western demand for oil was inelastic – a power station burning oil had no choice but to keep buying it – the sharp drop in supply caused the world price of oil to skyrocket.

Even so, Nixon felt he had no choice but to stand his ground, and the embargo began. Within weeks, the cost of a barrel of oil had risen four times over. The Western economy, built on cheap energy, consumed lots of it. Once oil prices shot up, so did energy bills. And since energy was used to make almost everything else – factories couldn't operate without it – firms had to claw back their rising power bills by raising the price of the goods they manufactured. Inflation, which had been benign during the quarter-century world boom, now surged. And with everything now more expensive, people had to decide what to trim from their budget to pay their bills. Demand dropped throughout the Western economy and a deep recession began.

It wasn't just oil that had been cheap during the world economy's 'golden summer'. So had virtually all primary commodities, from food to minerals. With so many Third World countries exporting primary goods to fund their industrial development, world markets were always well supplied. Furthermore, the Bretton Woods trading regime tended to favour industrial countries over primary export-ers – almost all Third World countries. Free-trade principles were applied more aggressively to trade in manufactured goods than to trade in primary goods, and especially trade in food. First World countries wanted to keep their farmers on their farms, in no small measure because in many ways they were important political constit-uencies. And because wages were so much lower in the Third World, Western farmers could not always compete on price with their Third World peers. So Western farmers demanded, and got, protection from imports. Demand for manufactured goods remained strong, though, especially for the technology and machinery Third World countries were buying. And since there were as yet few new joiners to the club of industrialised nations, the world supply of manufactured goods remained dominated by Western countries.

Therefore, despite their independence, most Third World coun-tries saw their incomes fall even further behind those of the West: even when Third World incomes increased in absolute terms, those in the West raced further ahead. Exponents of the Keynesian welfare state, who cited the quarter-century economic expansion and broad consensus around their doctrine as proof of its success, seldom acknowledged this component of the model. Western living standards and the generous welfare state continued to be, at least in part, subsidised by a net wealth transfer from the former colonies to the heartland of the world economy. The great post-war 'social compact' did not include everyone. Rather than using their political freedom to gain their economic freedom, Third World governments had if anything grown more dependent on their patrons at the centre of the world economy.

But then, rather suddenly, the oil shock raised a new possibility. If exporters of other primary goods could do as the oil-producing states had done and form cartels among themselves, they could control supply to the world market and drive up their prices. What made the oil shock so effective is that when Saudi Arabia cut its production, other exporting countries didn't step in to pick up the slack. Because they all wanted higher prices, they all agreed to cooperate rather than compete with one another. OPEC, the Organisation of Petroleum Exporting Countries, formed back in 1960 to wrest control of the world's oil supply from the handful of multinational companies then dominating the industry, was now telling the First World there was a new boss in town.

Other countries that depended on mining or farming primary goods, from bauxite to coffee, now got starry-eyed. They began organising their own cartels or pressuring the multinational companies that traded in their commodities to agree new, more favourable pricing schemes. At the United Nations, Third World countries lobbied for a 'New International Economic Order' (NIEO) to replace Bretton Woods with a trading regime that raised prices on primary exports, widening access to First World markets for Third World exports, and increasing aid transfers to the developing countries.

And that wasn't all. Oil-exporting countries, now awash with cash, had more money than they could spend. Since the global oil trade was conducted in US dollars, they just banked their surpluses in Western accounts. The banks then had to pay interest on these deposits, which meant they had to find new borrowers. Under pressure to find new clients in a hurry, the banks did what banks always do in this sort of situation: they offered competitive terms. Dropping the interest rates on their loans, until real rates approached zero, they looked for large borrowers who could take up the excess deposits. And who was eager to borrow? Third World governments. Ultra-cheap loans meant they could build highways, dams and factories inexpensively, hasten their ascent up the industrial ladder, and (they hoped) pay back the money with the increased revenues the resulting growth would entail. It was a heady time in the Third World.

The following spring, the United Nations met in special session to take up the proposed NIEO. The delegate from China was a man who had only just resurfaced, having spent several years in exile when Mao Zedong's Cultural Revolution targeted him in its purge of 'bourgeois contaminants'. When he rose to take the podium in the General Assembly, what he delivered was a rousing Maoist speech. 'The old order based on colonialism, imperialism and hegemonism is being undermined and shaken to its foundations,' he thundered, 'the Western imperialist bloc is disintegrating.'[6]

However, when he spoke of how the world order was going to be shaken up, it's possible that Deng Xiaoping was already thinking of something entirely different from what the other Third World delegates had in mind.

The call for a new order was timely, because Bretton Woods had just broken down. Its institutions still operated but its anchor, the gold standard, had snapped. After years of printing dollars to cover its deficits, the United States had created a 'dollar overhang'. There were now considerably more dollars circulating in the world economy than gold to back them. In principle, a country with enough dollars stashed could have organised a run on the United States' gold reserves. So in 1971 President Nixon dropped the gold standard. Unmoored, world currency markets began veering sharply, as currencies traded freely against one another.

The old way of doing things was running into difficulties. When the oil shocks made the going get tough, the tough got Keynesian. Western leaders showered their economies with the balm that would make them whole again: stimulus. Taking advantage of the same cheap credit that Third World governments were doing, they ran up their budget deficits to build airports or boost civil-service wages, thereby topping up the economy's spending power to compensate for the higher prices. During the mid-1970s, the United States doubled its deficit, as did the United Kingdom, but with the desired effect. Following two years of recession, the economies of the West were back on the move.

The statist gospel had been proclaimed and the economy had said 'amen'. Except that this time there was something a little odd. While growth had resumed, inflation remained high. It wasn't really a problem – at least not yet – but it was a bit of a mystery. In the standard Keynesian catechism that most students of economics learned in their classes, one of the eternal truths was that inflation and unemployment were like the opposite ends of a seesaw. If one went up, the other went down: unemployed workers weren't shopping, so shopkeepers couldn't raise prices. But during the 1970s recession, inflation and unemployment rose together. Inflation, which had seldom moved above 3 per cent during the golden summer, now never dropped below 6 per cent, recession or not. This unusual, and unexpected, mix of stagnation with inflation came to be known, not surprisingly, as stagflation.

On the face of it, stagflation was just the effect of high oil prices. But closer examination revealed deeper currents. By the late 1960s, inflation had begun a slow, steady upward trend. Following decades of rapid growth, increases in labour productivity had started slowing.[7] However, after decades of regular pay rises, few employees were willing to adjust their expectations accordingly. Moreover, throughout the years of full employment, unions had got used to flexing their muscles by threatening employers with work stoppages if they tried to cut costs. Unlike, say, Sweden, where unions centralised their negotiations nationally and therefore looked at the big picture in wage negotiations, British and American labour relations had long been combative, usually revolving around getting the best deal possible at specific work places. The oil shock then exacerbated this, because when prices rose in the 1970s the unions demanded further

pay increases to compensate. By and large, they got them. And since
pay rises outstripped prices, there was always extra demand to keep
boosting prices further.

The West thus seemed to have arrived at an impasse. And to add
insult to injury, it appeared it might even be losing the Cold War.
America's attempt to stop the spread of communism in Vietnam had
failed, and in 1975 it was forced to evacuate its embassy in Saigon
by helicopter as North Vietnamese tanks rolled into the city. In the
same year, neighbouring Cambodia fell to a Maoist insurgency.
Meanwhile, the 1974 collapse of the Portuguese government, and
of the empire it had fought to retain, liberated its colonial possessions, notably in Africa. At once, Angola and Mozambique joined
the communist fold. The same year Ethiopian rebels overthrew the
monarchy and aligned themselves with Moscow. Closer to home, the
United States had watched communist uprisings in Central America,
Chile go socialist in the 1970 election and even Jamaica announce
it was now with Moscow (though unfortunately for the Jamaican
government it hadn't checked first to see if Moscow was interested
in having another Caribbean ally to subsidise alongside Cuba). The
brash confidence of the post-war period, in which the West felt it
had discovered the fountain of eternal prosperity, gave way to a new
mood of doubt. It didn't help the sense of general decay that the rot
seemed to have spread through the body politic as well. Once the
Congressional noose had tightened around President Nixon to the
point that impeachment was unavoidable, he had resigned, but the
bitter taste that Watergate left in American mouths wasn't going to
get washed out so easily.

As if it wanted to feel whole again, in 1976 the United States
elected a new president whose principal virtue was that he was not
Richard Nixon. Trustworthy and humble, Jimmy Carter had the
simple religious faith of a Sunday school teacher. The charisma too.
In his approach to the world he was like a good listener who wanted
to overcome conflicts by getting to know and understand America's
enemies. At home, he called for 'compassionate government' and
'shared sacrifice' in the face of new challenges: conservation to fight

the energy crisis and deficits to fund expanded federal programmes. It wasn't that different from what the new Labour government was doing at the same time in the United Kingdom, where it was raising social spending, improving workers' and union rights and boosting public-sector pensions.

And equally, like the Labour government, Jimmy Carter muddled through the first half of his term of office, scoring some victories, suffering some setbacks and facing criticism on the right for molly-coddling the country's enemies. Five years after the Yom Kippur War that had triggered the oil shock, Carter successively brokered a peace deal between Egypt and Israel, but when he generously announced that any Cubans wishing to flee to America would be welcomed, the Cuban leader Fidel Castro happily obliged, emptying his prisons and putting people on boats to Miami. As for the economy, if not roaring like the good old days, it was at least back to moving in the right direction: unemployment was falling and inflation, if still high, was coming back down. Overall, it seemed it would be enough to win him, like UK's Labour, re-election in the upcoming polls. It was perhaps not the best of times in the West, but certainly not the worst.

But then at the end of 1978, an unexpected event on the other side of the world changed everything. The Keynesian church, its columns creaking from the wear of stagflation, was about to collapse.

There was one big oil-exporting country in the Persian Gulf that was not Arab. Like Saudi Arabia, Iran was a friend to the United States. But unlike Saudi Arabia, whose royal family resisted modernity and preferred to run the country like a feudal family business, Iran felt a little more familiar to Americans. Its monarch, Shah Mohammad Reza Pahlavi, was a modernising ruler in the Turkish Kemalist mould, and he created a welcoming environment for the thousands of foreign engineers and businessmen who came to profit from the boom. Unlike the Saudi kingdom, where foreigners lived in com-pounds and women couldn't drive, Western oil-workers in Iran could delight in all the pleasures their generous paycheques could conjure.

Mohammad Reza Pahlavi wanted to make Tehran a world city,

one with modern architecture and sprinkled liberally with the sort of ornate palaces that inspired awe in visitors. The finest of these was the Saadabad, remodelled by his architect wife, who equipped its bathrooms with tubs fitted with gold-leaf dolphin taps (jade eyes in his, amethyst in hers). Each morning he oversaw the business of his kingdom from a desk in a vast reception room. Following lunch, he would go by helicopter to his stable in the mountains, where his horses were ready for his afternoon ride. While ascending he could look at the city that had changed beyond recognition from the rustic days of his childhood.[8]

On the face of it, things had never looked better. The country's treasury had been overflowing with petro-dollars throughout the 1970s. Back in 1971 he'd staged a lavish celebration to coincide with the 2,500th anniversary of the Persian Empire of antiquity. Building a 160-acre tent city in the middle of the desert, where Cyrus the Great had built a palace, later destroyed by Alexander the Great, he fed his guests quail eggs stuffed with caviar, lobster mousse with Nantua sauce, flaming lambs with arak, peacock stuffed with foie gras, platters of cheese, a salad of figs and raspberries, champagne sherbet and a 70-pound cake to mark the empress's birthday. Maxim's of Paris had catered, providing 165 chefs and an army of wine stewards and waiters who emptied some 25,000 bottles of wine into the guest's glasses.[9]

However, by 1978, all was not well. Such opulence was not evident on the streets of Tehran. Driven by the collapse of farming as oil took over the economy and, lured to the city by empty promises of employment – the oil industry required few workers, with many of those being so specialised they had to be recruited abroad – Iran's peasants flooded into Tehran. Their numbers grew faster than the houses, streets and sewers needed to serve them and crime became rampant. Excessive demands on the electricity supply caused blackouts, hurting industrial output and thus worsening the economic situation.

No sooner had 1978 begun than strikes broke out. Students took to the streets and angry mobs spilled out of the mosques after fiery sermons. Early in the year, rioting shut down the city of Qom. By spring the protests had spread to other cities, reaching Tehran in May. As the violence spiralled through the summer, the government imposed martial law in one city after another.

In November, the wave of strikes finally reached the oil sector, virtually shutting down supply. The Shah dismissed his government and instituted military rule. By now, foreign employees of the oil sector were leaving, while rich Iranians traded their rials for any foreign currencies available. As they prepared to depart, others got ready to return. In France, the religious leader Ayatollah Khomeini called for his supporters to overthrow the government and create an Islamic republic.

After briefly restoring order, the military government lost control of the situation. In December it collapsed. By then the first cracks in the military's once-united facade started to show as soldiers in Tabriz refused to follow orders. An old foe of the Shah's, Shahpur Bakhtiar, agreed to form a government, but only if the Shah left on a long holiday.

On 16 January, shortly after finishing his lunch, the Shah was ferried by helicopter to the airport in Tehran where his royal 707 awaited him and his empress. In a curious gesture to a lost time, a member of the Imperial Guard tried to kiss his feet, but the frail monarch bent over and pulled him up, as if acknowledging that his gilded autocracy was now finished.

That evening, as word spread through Tehran that the Shah had fled, people filled the streets and celebrated. Holding aloft pictures of the Ayatollah Khomeini, crowds tore down statues of the departed monarch and his father. In France the Ayatollah announced the creation of a provisional government. The revolution, he said, had only just begun.[10]

With the Shah's departure, not only did the United States lose a vital ally in the Middle East, but the massive oil-sector strike that toppled the Iranian monarch cut supplies to world markets. Traders bid prices up sharply and a second oil shock began. Inflation in the West once again leapt to double digits. With everyone having to spend more on their fuel bills, spending dropped and recession returned. Stagflation had come back.

Hours before the Shah had left, President Carter had delivered his State of the Union address. In the cinemas, Americans queued to see *The Deer Hunter*, the latest in a string of Vietnam-themed films, which mirrored the country's new sense of anxiety. Carter's speech that night seemed to embody his nation's chastened mood. Speaking with the halting diction that gave late-night comedians endless fodder, stumbling occasionally over a word, repeatedly moistening his lips, he forewent the common bold declaration of America's robust health. Instead Carter simply said there was 'every sign' the state of the union was strong. Since no one country could dominate the world any more, he added, America had to choose between finding a way to cooperate with its enemies, or anarchy. And so, faced with another energy crisis, he called on Americans to band together to find ways 'to conserve energy, to increase production and to speed development of solar power'. To lead that charge, he installed panels on the White House roof.

Carter's lack of bravado, and his apparent grasping at ad hoc solutions, spoke to a deeper problem: a fundamental crisis of faith. This 'stagflation' thing left the Keynesian priesthood around him bewildered. However, it vindicated the warnings of a hitherto little-noticed prophet, Milton Friedman. Though he'd been around since the 1940s, Friedman, having rejected the Keynesian church, had been a voice in the wilderness, known mostly to academics. However, his neoclassical epiphany, in which he'd rediscovered Irving Fisher's quantity theory of money, led him to predict stagflation back in the 1960s. Now that his soothsaying was proved right, he began to draw an audience in the public square. Friedman dismissed the Keynesian multiplier as less a miracle than hocus-pocus. Rather than go into investment and create new jobs, he said, government stimulus money would simply go straight to the shops. Shopkeepers would soon cotton on that once the government's binge wore off, they'd be stuck with a lot of unsold stock. So they wouldn't boost their orders, and the factories wouldn't ramp up their output and hire workers, they'd just jack up the prices on what they already had.

That seemed to be the very scenario facing Britain as well. The unions were the choir in the Keynesian church. To them, pay rises in a recession were as natural as roast on Sunday. They had taken pay freezes earlier in the decade to help wrestle inflation back to earth, and now they felt it was payback time. And with Britain headed for an election in the spring of 1979, the time to strike would never be better, since the government would need to win their favour. But what the union leaders didn't appreciate was that their own pastors were going through a crisis of faith, whereas 'monetarists' like Friedman had the back pews abuzz.

Besides, everyone was wondering who would foot the bill for spending increases. The government would either have to hike taxes or take loans. Tax increases were never vote-getters. And if it borrowed, the government would lure funds away from the banks and so drive up interest rates. Neither was an attractive option to households trying to stretch their budgets. Regardless, the unions were undeterred, starting a showdown not only with the government but with millions of Britons coping with hard times.

The weather that winter, as the Shah was bouncing around the world looking for a new home, only stretched tempers further. On the second day of the new year, a heavy snow buried Britain under fifteen-foot snowdrifts and sent the country into a deep freeze. Storms whipped up stones and threw them onto houses along the Devonshire coast. Hospitals were evacuated after plummeting temperatures burst their water pipes. With exquisite timing, the nation's lorry drivers then went on strike. Supplies of food and milk dwindled. Children were sent home from school. Businesses, unable to get supplies and forced to cut production due to the energy shortage, started laying off workers. Then dockworkers joined the strike, preventing the government from using imports to relieve the pressure. Soldiers had to occupy the ports to keep them open. When the government capitulated to the lorry drivers in a desperate effort to ease the pain, it only emboldened other unions to follow the truckers' lead.

On it went, through the cold, dark 'winter of discontent'. The very unions that, a generation earlier, had helped the Labour government to build the British welfare state, were now unwittingly undermining it. Britons grew impatient. The Labour Party, which had begun the campaign with a comfortable poll-lead, watched helplessly as its margin dwindled. Its leaders did not then know that the party was about to die a death from which there could be no quick resurrection.

CHAPTER 14

THE GREAT NEOCLASSICAL AWAKENING

When you imagined yourself having lived in the 1930s, losing your job and your house, it wasn't so hard to appreciate how irresistible a president who offered you work would be. But think how you might have reacted had you been, instead, living in the 1970s recession rather than the 1930s. Suppose you had been born after the war, or maybe just before it, and were too young to have memories of the Depression.

Instead, you came of age in a time when you didn't have to look for work, it came looking for you. You got a career in something like finance or advertising or insurance – one of the big growth-industries of the post-war period. It was a mid-level position, nothing too grand but just right for you, since you didn't care for the hassle and weekends at work that came with the corner office. On your salary you could afford a detached house in the suburbs, two cars, a week-long getaway with your family every year somewhere warm and every once in a while a summer trip further afield, overseas. You used liberally that great post-war invention, the credit card, but you always kept your debts within reasonable bounds. You cleared your balances at the end of each month and if you happened to go over budget you transferred the remaining balance onto your overdraft, which carried low interest since it was secured by your home equity.

Then the 1973 recession hit. There was talk of lay-offs of some support staff or part-time workers, but neither you nor anyone in your office was let go. However, you didn't get your annual Christmas bonus. After a while you noticed pay hikes were less frequent. The rising cost of living put a crimp in your style. Filling up the car put a big dent in your wallet. But cutting back wasn't an option because you commuted to work. So you had to cut elsewhere – which wasn't easy, because the cost of dining out, clothing, heating fuel, electricity and even going to the movies were all going up as well. Worse, interest rates followed inflation upwards, so the monthly payments on your overdraft started eating into your budget. You had to scrap plans to build the extension you had planned for the back of the house. You kept your winter trip, but stayed home for your summer vacation.

The evening news reported strike threats by teachers and carworkers, who wanted their pay indexed to inflation. 'Wouldn't we all,' you muttered. Although your salary rose slower than inflation, your tax write-offs hadn't changed, so you were actually paying more in taxes now. And the government was talking of raising taxes even more, to meet its own rising expenses. Around 1977, you noticed inflation starting to come back down, though prices remained high. When you finally got a pay increase it only brought you back to where you had been before. You still couldn't go ahead with renovating the house, but at least you could foresee a return to better days.

The next year, though, another recession hit and inflation surged once more. You had to start queuing to fill your car, which added time to your commute. It became so expensive to heat your home you began turning down the thermostat. You got used to wearing jumpers all winter. On very cold nights you sometimes went to bed early to get under the blankets. The unions kept asking for more pay rises, and when the government refused they went on strike. The trains stopped running so more people had to drive to work, which doubled your commuting time – not to mention your fuel bill. The union leaders talked about solidarity, but seemed to be looking out only for their own members. Meanwhile your company had another bad year, so you had to forgo a Christmas bonus again. There were no pay rises in the new year, at which time an office manager began coming around and looking for ways to cut costs. Prices in the canteen rose, they ditched the coffee machine and got a private company to come in and sell you coffee. So you started bringing your own flask.

An election was brewing. You read the papers more often and you heard there were two choices. The incumbent said it was time for everyone to tighten their belts. The challenger said it was time to tame the unions, cut taxes, reduce inflation and lower interest rates.

How, then, might you have voted?

Throughout the high age of Keynesianism, the Austrian economist Friedrich Hayek had been a Cassandra-like figure warning of the doom the statist model would bring the West. As a student in Vienna, he had started with socialist sympathies, but came under the influence of Ludwig von Mises, an early opponent of the Soviet experiment. Like his mentor, Hayek would come to distrust any doctrine that relied on the state or placed too much stress on the human capacity to plan society rationally.

When he first landed in Britain in 1928, he sought out John Maynard Keynes, not to commend his work, as a growing number of pilgrims were doing, but to inform him how great his error was. Keynes, not surprisingly, waved him off. Undeterred, Hayek decided to make himself a thorn in Keynes's side. The younger man would dog the master for the rest of his life, though in the course of their sparring they developed a sort of mutual respect and friendship – which was more than could be said of many of their followers.

The Austrian School didn't repudiate only Keynes. Given their belief in the limits of human rationality, they also rejected the neoclassical attempt to make economics resemble physics, insisting that it had to retain its philosophical core. Hayek himself would thus write not only on economics, but on law and politics as well, seeing them as all interrelated. The Austrians also rejected the neoclassical school's homogenising tendencies, and its assumption that all individuals could be reduced to fundamentally similar units that could be plugged into an economic model. Instead they leaned towards what might be called a heroic or great-man interpretation. To them, souls were not quite equal before the marketplace god. Steering history, and the economy, were entrepreneurs: courageous individuals who, with no promise of success, took risks and repeatedly failed yet kept trying all the same, applying the insights they got from each setback to developing new products, new technologies, new ways of doing things. As an Austrian economist might say, you can't model Steve Jobs.

So while others saw capitalism's inequality as one of its vices, Hayek saw it as a virtue. High returns on innovation were the reward that led entrepreneurs to take the risks needed to find new ways of doing things. Since many entrepreneurs whose experiments failed would be left penniless, only the lure of riches would encourage them to keep innovating rather than sticking to what was safe. Moreover, Hayek maintained that it was the ultra-rich who provided the original demand for luxury products, which, after they were invented, would then fan outward and become mass-consumption items. Watch a 1990s film like *Wall Street* and you'll see clunky mobiles that bear no obvious resemblance to the smartphones of today. Mobile phones then were luxury status symbols. But once the technology had been invented, it was then adapted for a large market.

Entrepreneurship did not depend only on inequality, though. It also required individuals to be free. To the Austrians, individual liberty was not merely an end in itself. Unlike most of their neoclassical peers, who deliberately eschewed philosophy, the Austrians argued what was essentially a moral and political case – that freedom was a necessary prerequisite for entrepreneurship to flourish. Moreover, while they believed the free market was the most advanced economic system, they didn't take for granted that capitalism was here to stay. In contrast to neoclassical scholars, who largely ignored Marx on the grounds that the labour theory of value had been rendered obsolete by the early marginalists, the Austrians took him very seriously.

One of them, Joseph Schumpeter, an academic who had served as Austria's finance minister, even maintained a grudging admiration for Marx. Schumpeter agreed that capitalism was doomed to collapse, but as a conservative he saw that as an eventuality to be regretted rather than welcomed. In his reckoning, the concentration of capital into ever larger firms would lead to a sort of regime of bureaucrats, who would stifle entrepreneurship and aim to defend their market share and the established way of doing things.[1] The existential threat to capitalism was to Schumpeter not the victory of the proletariat over the bourgeoisie, but the triumph of CEOs over entrepreneurs.

Thus, the Austrians regarded anything that weeded out bureaucratic inertia as a good thing. Unlike most, they welcomed market crashes as positive. In the same way the laws of nature cull the gene pool and improve the species, the laws of the market ensure that every once in a while reckless speculators are weeded out. Left standing are those who actually used their resources wisely. Hayek was clear: there are no short cuts out of a depression. The only thing that works is to bite the bullet and work through the pain, allowing equilibrium to restore itself in the course of time.

The analogy of the market with nature was not accidental. If there was a science the Austrians preferred to the physics that so impressed their neoclassical colleagues, it was evolutionary biology. The Austrians didn't believe human reason had the ability to design something as brilliant as the market, let alone come up with anything better. They thought that, like living organisms, the market had emerged through an unguided process of trial and adaptation, as humans invented new ways of organising exchange. The end result was a mechanism that collated a vast amount of information and synthesised it all into one simple symbol: a price.

Think of when you go shopping. When you look at the price of something, you can glean all sorts of knowledge about it. If, for example, someone offers you a branded handbag at a knock-down price you won't necessarily leap at it. You might ask why it's so cheap: was it stolen, damaged, counterfeit? That price tells you something. For the Austrians, each transaction embodies a volume of data more completely than a ream of bureaucratic spreadsheets could ever hope to manage. They reckoned that any state organisation designed to gather and update all that information, like the Soviet Union's *Gosplan*, would have to be immense.

Soviet economics presumed that science and technology could replace the often-irrational impulses that drive economic decision-making, modelling them mathematically and making resource allocation more rational. Hayek thought this was an impossible goal – in part because he considered irrational impulses to be essential bits of information.[2] Sure enough, at the same time that Hayek was buttonholing Keynes, Russia's planning bureaucracy was evolving from a few dozen employees to being one of Russia's biggest employers. Even the Russians themselves couldn't suppress their concern at bureaucracy's inflationary tendency, though they hid it from the West. One Soviet mathematician, asked to work out how long it would take the world's most advanced computer to process all the information pertinent to the economy, reported back: 100 million years.[3] In the absence of this computer, Hayek concluded the state would have no choice but to expand continually until it crushed all human autonomy in pursuit of the 'plan'. To him the debate with Keynes was a war for the survival of a free humanity.

Amid the Depression, Hayek's unshaken faith in the market, and his conviction that you had to let things work their own way through, made it hard for him to get an audience. However, in 1931 the London School of Economics, which was making itself into the free-market counterweight to Cambridge's emerging statism, offered Hayek a post. While many of his students would go on to become significant names in the Keynesian pantheon, a small number joined his dissident sect, making up for their modest numbers with a cult-like devotion. As one of his charges remarked, Hayek 'was our god'.[4]

Having failed to persuade Keynes of his errors, Hayek decided to move the debate to the public square. When Keynes found he could no longer ignore him, what resulted was one of the great debates of the twentieth century, arguably on a par with the Wilberforce–Huxley show of the previous century. It began when Hayek wrote a critical review of Keynes's *Treatise on Money*.[5] After Keynes published a scathing reply in the pages of the same journal,[6] the battle was joined. And on it went, in journals and in public, for the next fifteen years.

If the two men regarded one another as sparring partners, their acolytes saw the struggle in more titanic terms. One of Keynes's students said their mentor 'played the role of God in a morality play' dominating but only occasionally appearing, sending instructions from heaven through a 'messenger angel' chosen from his students.[7] One of his followers went down to the LSE as a 'missionary among heathens' hoping to convert a few lost souls.[8] While a handful of those he encountered there gave him an audience, the more committed of Hayek's followers might as well have brandished crucifixes, regarding the goings-on at Cambridge as 'very dangerous nonsense'.[9] The disappointed disciple could only take the ancient advice to proselytes – shake the dust off his feet, and return to Cambridge's more welcoming environment.

If bold and full of self-belief, Hayek was nonetheless handicapped in the debates not only by his unfashionable argument, but because he was essentially on enemy turf. With his aristocratic demeanour and Germanic formality, he spoke in heavily accented English. He also had a habit of turning to the blackboard behind him and, with his speech muffled, drawing diagrams incomprehensible to English audiences: most of the Austrian theory they needed to make sense of them had not yet been translated from German.[10] Hayek was simply no match for the charming manner and rhetorical flourishes Keynes deployed to overwhelm any opponent.[11]

In fact, Hayek felt that Keynes's ease at winning over audiences was itself a dangerous thing. If the Great Master could make everyone into true believers, would he be able to reach them once he saw the error of his ways and was prepared to recant? Hayek had little of the regard that Keynes held for himself, likening his conviction that he could always bend public opinion to a 'vestige of a belief in the efficacy of prayer'.[12] Judging that what was needed to lure people away from this false prophet was a coherent doctrine, Hayek joined with like-minded individuals to give form to this new faith. Meeting for the first time in Switzerland just after the war, the group took the name of the village in which they had gathered. The Mont-Pèlerin Society began by drafting the articles of faith that would define their 'neoliberal' creed, stressing individual liberty, limited government and the free market.[13] One of those present that April was a young American economist who would go on to become a friend of Hayek's, a refugee from Keynesianism named Milton Friedman.

Unlike Hayek, Friedman was a neoclassical theorist and a thoroughly mathematical economist. But unusually among neoclassical theorists, he shared Hayek's belief in the urgent need to defend individual liberty and free markets in non-economic treatises. If he lacked the philosophical sophistication of his Austrian colleague in his writing on politics, he made up for it with the one thing that Hayek lacked: first-rate oratory. To Hayek's bookish scholar, Friedman was the charismatic preacher. Although different in style to John Maynard Keynes's patrician refinement, Friedman was as good a homilist and as accessible a writer, taking the recondite literature of economics and distilling it into simple instructions for better living. Keeping a regular column in *Newsweek* magazine, producing a popular television series called *Free to Choose*, writing books for the lay person to which he gave pithy titles like *Capitalism and Freedom*, Friedman was always a big draw on the lecture circuit, where he won a following as devoted as Hayek's.

After moving back and forth between government and the academic world, in the 1940s Friedman found a home in the University of Chicago's Department of Economics. He would stay there for the rest of his life, during which time the department would become a centre of resistance to Keynesian economics and the home of a neoclassical revival. Friedman himself would later list the 'Chicago School's defining tenets as a belief in the superiority of the free market, scepticism of government action, and the vital role of money supply'[14] – as vital for economic prosperity as God was for a believer's salvation (with the difference that humans controlled this god).

Yet to some extent, this catechism reflected Friedman's own legacy. Before he joined the University of Chicago it had been somewhat eclectic in its orientation, even making a place for someone like Oskar Lange who was then devising the principles of market socialism. Lange, who left the Economics Department after the Second World War to head newly communist Poland's planning agency, had reasoned that since neoclassical theory supposedly enabled one to model the economy scientifically, that model could be operated just as effectively by bureaucrats. Unlike Hayek, he saw no reason to believe that state planners couldn't arrive at correct prices by way of trial and error.[15] But over the following decades, as the Economics Department's grandees created a more purely mathematical stream, the Chicago School became associated not only with free-market economics, but with the neoclassical school – so much so that when Hayek was offered a job there, Friedman successfully resisted the appointment on the grounds that his friend was not really an economist[16] (Hayek instead received a philosophy appointment).

There may have been something of the convert's passion in Friedman's devotion to free markets. Like many who had studied economics during the mass-conversions to Keynesianism in the 1930s, he had begun as a fairly conventional theoretician. Starting his career in Roosevelt's New Deal administration, he worked on programmes that would use fiscal policy to overcome the Depression. But then he had an epiphany. When in the late 1940s the head of the National Bureau of Economic Research asked him to look into the effect that the money supply had on the economy, Friedman began a collaboration with Anna Schwartz that would ultimately produce their book, *A Monetary History of the United States*. In the course of their investigations, they moved to a conclusion about the causes of the Depression that led them further away from Keynesian orthodoxy.

Keynes, one recalls, had said that the fundamental cause of the Depression was a lack of aggregate demand, which the government could rectify with fiscal policy: putting money back into the hands of consumers and businesses. Friedman and Schwartz went back to the classic work of Irving Fisher, who himself had refined the quantity theory of money. In contrast to Keynes, who said inflation and deflation were caused by a surplus or deficit of demand respectively, Friedman and Schwartz said each were due to a surplus or deficit respectively in the supply of money.

When there was too much money flowing through the economy buyers started bidding up prices. This then messed with the market by sending misleading signals to producers and consumers. Consumers would rush out to buy goods before they got too expensive. Meanwhile, as the resulting inflation eroded the value of their savings, people would empty their bank accounts. To keep savers, banks would then have to raise interest rates, which made them charge more for the loans they offered. And as interest rates rose and loans got more expensive, producers would stop investing. Production would thus grow more slowly, which only worsened inflation, since the supply of output couldn't keep up with demand. So unlike in the Keynesian model, when inflation and recession could not coexist, Friedman foresaw a situation in which inflation could actually cause a recession, and persist throughout it.

As for deflation, which is what happened when prices actually fell, Keynes had reasoned that during the Depression, the economy got into a vicious spiral in which falling prices made people sit on their nest eggs: why buy that new armchair when it'll be even cheaper in a month? But if everyone was sitting on their nest eggs, demand would drop further, which would make prices drop even more. The solution was to start buying, and if consumers wouldn't do it, it was the government's job to kick-start the process. Friedman disagreed. He and Schwartz claimed that during the Depression, the US Federal Reserve (the American central bank) failed to increase the money supply. They argued that had the Federal Reserve instead made money cheaper and increased the amount flowing through the economy, the Depression might never have happened.

This might seem to a lay person like an arcane debate – it's all about getting people to spend or save, after all, so does it really matter whether you do it by giving them a job or giving them cheap credit? But the policy and political implications of Friedman and Schwartz's conclusion would in time drive a deep wedge into the politics of Western societies. In 1967, Friedman was to deliver the presidential address to the American Economics Association – the economic equivalent of the Pope addressing the College of Cardinals. Friedman used the occasion to deliver an important paper that suggested it was more or less impossible for government to effectively manage the economy, arguing that discretionary interventions would always backfire in the end. Instead, the money supply should be programmed to expand at a stable, moderate level, and then left alone. The government's job was to get out of the way and let those 'basic forces of enterprise, ingenuity, invention, hard work, and thrift that are the true springs of economic growth' do their work.[17] Keynes had trusted in the wisdom of government; Friedman had lost that faith.

Friedman also rejected the standard presumption of a trade-off between inflation and unemployment, saying things only worked that way in the short run.[18] The coming years would see inflation begin rising in the West. When after 1973 unemployment rose as well, Friedman's prediction of 'stagflation' looked prophetic. By then, other scholars in the Chicago School had produced work that further solidified the doctrine that not just monetary policy but free markets were the best way to deliver prosperity. Ronald Coase developed the Coase theorem, suggesting that the problem of externalities – the costs of an activity in which you engage but which are not borne by you, such as when you run a nightclub that keeps the neighbours up at night – was best addressed not by the traditional method of government regulation, but by well-defined property rights. If, for example, the law specifies that your property grants you a right to quiet nights, the neighbours can just sue the nightclub owner. Eugene Fama produced the efficient markets hypothesis, which maintained that since a free market collated all available information to traders, the prices it yielded could never be wrong. And Gary Becker began applying neoclassical theory to the analysis of a wide range of phenomena beyond the traditional purview of microeconomics, such as crime, dating, marriage and childbearing, arguing that in everything they did, humans were out to better their lot with an unconscious economic calculus.

In fact, Friedman identified this belief in the applicability of economic method to all sorts of social phenomena as another defining element of the Chicago School. From Alfred Marshall's initial call for economics to restrict its focus to the world of monetary transactions, economics had evolved to become a science of everything – or at least, everything human. Needless to say, some of Friedman's critics would complain of the neoclassical school's 'economic imperialism' as it set out to impose its doctrine and method on all the other social sciences.[19] Beyond the original neoclassical goal of improving material well-being, which carried into the Keynesian conviction that the purpose of economics was to free humans to pursue higher goals, like the contemplation of art, scholars like Friedman maintained that in all they did humans were motivated above all by the desire to maximise their utility. Accordingly, even their most intimate activities could be modelled and measured economically. Economics would no longer restrict itself to the saving of bodies, it would save souls as well. To Karen Armstrong's claim that we are all *homo religiosus*, Friedman would have confidently replied: no, we are all *homo economicus*.

Milton Friedman had a low opinion of politicians. Like so many other economists in the neoclassical revival, he believed the temptations of using the spoils of power to buy votes – creating jobs for one's followers, steering contracts to one's donors, loosening regulations on the sector in which a friend had interests – were temptations that would prove irresistible to all but the most principled of individuals. The lure of greater wealth was simply too hard to resist. His vision of society, which would in time become orthodox, was one in which a technocratic elite, expertly trained in economics and insulated from politics, would control most of the policy decisions affecting the economy.

As Thomas More had said of his utopia, Friedman allowed that his ideal world would probably never exist in pure form. Nevertheless, he offered it as dream to aspire to, a better world in which elected officials had limited power to engage in discretionary spending or fiscal stimulus. Instead, economic management would be done through regulation of the money supply, which would be the purview of the central bank. Ideally, the central bank's officers would be selected purely on the basis of their technical expertise and be independent of the government or legislature. That way they'd be in a position to discipline wayward politicians. If, for instance, a populist government wanted to run up its debt to boost social programmes, the central bank could raise interest rates and thus take the extra money back out of the economy, limiting its inflationary impact (while also making it more expensive for the government to maintain its largesse). Democracy, to Friedman, was not the power of the community to make decisions for the individual, it was the individual's freedom to run his or her own affairs.

Some of Friedman's colleagues in the economics discipline would later complain that when he left the academic cloisters and entered the public square, he made more of his conclusions than they really justified. His monetarism, said his critics, didn't actually necessitate the minimalist government he insisted on.[20] But whether or not he made too much of his scholarship, Friedman's public sermons, like Hayek's, were never just about economics. His thinking flowed into a current that, if always present at a subterranean level in the West, was now resurfacing as a major torrent, particularly in America, a country whose culture had always preserved a strong individualist streak. In Britain the Conservative Party had converted to Keynesianism, but there had always been a significant component on the right wing of the American Republican Party that disliked the statist drift begun by Roosevelt's New Deal. In the 1964 presidential election, after President Lyndon Johnson had announced his plan to expand the welfare state with his Great Society programme, the Republican candidate Barry Goldwater announced he would do just the opposite. Campaigning against 'the ever increasing concentrations of authority in Washington', he declared, 'I believe we must now make a choice in this land and not continue drifting endlessly down and down to a time when all of us, our lives, our property, our hopes, and even our prayers will become just cogs in a vast government machine.'[21]

Back in 1964, this rhetoric failed to exercise most Americans. Yes, a third of their income went in taxes; yes, the public sector was expanding; yes, the federal government was running up its debt; and yes, maybe the economic sages advising Goldwater, among whom was numbered Milton Friedman, might well be geniuses. But, most Americans could then reasonably ask themselves, could the Chicago School set really be smarter than the Keynesians, who had delivered nearly twenty years of prosperity and were still going strong? After all, extra taxes were barely noticeable when your income rose every year. Nothing had sufficiently churned America's intellectual soil to make it receptive to these seeds of conservative discontent. Goldwater got buried in an electoral landslide.[22]

Undeterred though they were, the apostles of the free market would nonetheless have to spend the next decade in the wilderness – the lesson the Republican establishment drew from the Goldwater debacle was that the American electorate would not support a candidate as right wing as him. Their next presidential nominee, Richard Nixon, made his confession and drank from the Keynesian chalice. Thus spurned, the dissidents now turned their attention to evangelisation. Over the next decade, various strands of anti-statist thought, only one of which was economic, began to coalesce into a synthesis that provided a fairly complete doctrine, with positions on politics, economics, society, religion and the family.

A conservative renaissance was then bubbling which rejected the secular drift of American politics, the civil rights movement, and the expansion of the federal government. William Buckley's *National Review*, founded in 1955, provided a venue in which an emerging conservative critique could find a voice, much of it conflating liberalism, Keynesianism and secularism into one great Gomorrah. This found an echo in Britain, if less loud, where Mary Whitehouse was campaigning against what she considered the declining standards of British public life and media.

Simultaneously, philosophers were reviving classical liberalism. As the neoclassical economists had done in restoring the centrality of Adam Smith, neoclassical liberal philosophers wanted to leap past the developments in liberal thought over the previous hundred years to restore the centrality of the founders, and in particular John Locke. Ever since the mid-nineteenth century, liberal thought had moved from its original focus on individual liberty towards the position that poverty limited the real freedoms of many people, making it necessary for the state to redistribute wealth so as to make liberty real. However, in the 1960s and 1970s, liberal philosophers like Robert Nozick and Kenneth Minogue argued that this principle created a slippery slope of government expansion, which ultimately deprived individuals of the fruits of their labour in the name of some vague social justice. The novelist Ayn Rand, whose overworked prose elicited snickers in the literary community, nonetheless built a devoted following with a radical libertarian philosophy embodied in heroic characters. One of her loyal acolytes, a young Alan Greenspan, would later go on to run the US Federal Reserve, from which throne he would practise his doctrine of non-intervention in markets (opposing, for example, regulation of the financial sector, which during his tenure at the turn of the millennium was experimenting with the new financial products then driving the stock market and housing booms). Finally, Christian conservatives showed a new energy and political engagement. Traditionally an apolitical lot, in the 1960s a new generation of southern Baptist preachers emerged who felt it was incumbent upon them to try to reverse what they saw as the rising godlessness of society amid both the sexual revolution and the civil rights movement.

In Britain, the counter-revolution was initially fought less in the public square, and more in the academy. It started a bit later, when in 1974 a group of right-wing Conservatives got together to form the Centre for Policy Studies, a think tank committed to limiting the scope of government, which would enshrine the thinking of both Milton Friedman and Friedrich Hayek. If the desire to restore religion to public life was less widely shared than in America, it was nonetheless a strongly motivating force for many of the members of this new political movement. Of nobody was this more true than the devoutly religious Margaret Thatcher, who felt the government should not be usurping the functions traditionally performed by the churches, including looking after the poor. As for unemployment, she deemed this a matter of personal responsibility, and invoked the Protestant work ethic to justify the government relinquishing its post-war commitment to full employment.[23]

Because it merged neoclassical economics with neoclassical liberalism, the new synthesis came to be known variously, and confusingly, as both neoliberalism and neoconservatism. However, neoconservatism eventually came to be identified with a particular position on American foreign policy – namely, muscular interventions abroad to promote American ideals – whereas neoliberalism concerned itself primarily with domestic policy. Given the varied and sometimes contradictory strands of thought that were coalescing into this new synthesis, it could often appear somewhat incoherent or jumbled. Hence, when the avowedly atheist Ayn Rand first met William Buckley, who was a devout Catholic, she greeted him by saying, 'You are much too intelligent to believe in *Gott*.'[24]

However, popularisers managed to distil the evolving synthesis into catchy slogans, conveying a broad philosophy with sufficient ambiguity that they could mean different things to different people. Ronald Reagan's 'Get government off the backs of the people', Margaret Thatcher's 'There's no such thing as society', Milton Friedman's 'There's no free lunch' were like doorways into a new worldview for many people who, for various personal reasons, felt the government was becoming too big, intrusive and expensive, and felt themselves at the mercy of forces they couldn't control – whether it was Britain's unions or America's civil rights leaders.

For their part, however much critics on the left disliked the new creed, they often couldn't help but note that its exponents were generating new ideas. Still, if there was little new under the Keynesian sun, no one other than the neoliberal heretics feel there needed to be. All the evidence still witnessed to the success of the Keynesian faith, whereby a state-priesthood managed the economy's way to greater prosperity and distributed the resources the citizenry needed to fulfil their potential. All that was required was a little tinkering with the machine or periodic adjustments to its levers and dials; an esoteric task best left to the experts. Goldwater's trouncing in 1964 and the subsequent Republican reconciliation with Keynesianism had, like the British Conservative Party's earlier acceptance of the Keynesian chalice, revealed the basic truth: the public were satisfied with the work of their leaders.

But then the 1970s oil shocks happened, and everything changed. New pharaohs arose who were determined to finally bring their favourite prophets back from the wilderness.

CHAPTER 15

MISSIONARIES IN
HEATHEN LANDS

During the European Reformation of the sixteenth century, when the Vatican lost northern Europe to the new Protestant doctrines, it didn't retreat into the Catholic bastion of southern Europe. It took the long view (no doubt something that fifteen centuries of institutional memory made easier). To fight a rearguard defence of Catholicism, the Vatican formed the Jesuit order and sent its missionaries across the globe, into the then newly acquired colonies of the Americas and East Asia. Today those parts of the world produce most of the world's Catholics, send missionaries back to the West and account for most of the church's clergy. Spurned at home, prophets must often travel to distant lands to find receptive soil for their message. If in greatly compressed fashion – it happened over decades rather than centuries – the neoclassical revival followed a similar model. Although it originated in First World academies, the new doctrine would win its first converts in the developing world.

Some Third World countries had begun experimenting with neo-liberal policies as early as the 1960s, but only in a piecemeal fashion, like Christmas-and-Easter church visitors. But the 1970s would see the first major conversion to the neoliberal faith, and it would happen in Latin America.

*

Despite having won their political independence, throughout the post-war period most developing countries were falling further behind the West. Incomes rose during the world economy's boom years in the 1950s and 1960s, but not as quickly as those in the West. It wasn't merely the external environment, nor the continued dominance of the West, which was pushing them backwards – though these things mattered.[1] By the late 1960s, when the earliest shoots of inflation had first emerged in the West, there were signs that the state-led import substitution model most former colonies were using to develop their economies was itself part of the problem. When explaining their halting success in building the rich, free future that independence had promised, Third World leaders kept closely to the narrative Deng Xiaoping had used in his 1974 United Nations speech, railing against the lingering effects of Western imperialism. But in their more reflective moments, they acknowledged that many of their problems might actually have begun closer to home. In its early years, the import-substitution industrialisation (ISI) model adopted by many developing countries – whereby import restrictions sheltered the market from foreign competition and assisted local manufacturers to get off the ground – seemed to have worked miracles. Turkey's Kemalist economy kept growing strongly right through the 1930s Depression, Latin American countries developed so quickly after the war that analysts started speaking of things like the 'Brazilian miracle' and India multiplied its steel production six-fold in less than twenty years.[2] But in the deeper currents of the Third World, turbulence was brewing.

In particular, although ISI was good at building factories, it was much less effective at ensuring that what went on in them was actually innovative or efficient. Countries that used the model – and by the 1960s, that was most of the Third World – essentially mimicked the production of First World economies by taking replicas of their plants and plunking them on their own soil. Sometimes, with what were called turnkey projects, they did this quite literally. Paying a foreign company to build them a plant, they'd take possession of the factory keys upon its completion. Other times a government might issue investors with a licence that gave them permission to operate, sometimes further sweetening the pot by promising to bar other companies from competing with them. A few countries tried to reinvent the wheel, developing the technology themselves. However, given the cost of research and development, this approach usually made the venture too expensive to compete with existing firms, thus wasting scarce resources. Instead, importing capital goods, then using them to produce consumer goods for the domestic market, became the norm.

That ensured Third World countries would always be a step behind their former masters. Some First World companies would go so far as to write this into the contracts they signed to sell their machines – stipulating, for example, that whatever was produced in the Third World factory could only be sold locally. Other times, they withheld their most advanced technology and transferred only their older machinery, something which often suited the buying country since it was cheaper. Or, if they set up branch plants, foreign companies instructed their managers not to re-export to the home country. The end result was that Third World cities were filled with factories that exported very little of what they made.

But developing countries still imported a great deal. To pay for all the foreign-made machinery their plants used, not to mention the foreign engineers they often had to recruit to help them operate what was relatively advanced technology, Third World countries had to keep exporting the one thing they could sell in large volumes to the First World: primary goods. As a result, while they had planned to rise beyond being hewers of wood and drawers of water, those countries often became, in the profile of their exports, even more Third World than they'd started out at independence. Nowhere was this trend more acute than in Africa, whose share of global manufactured exports declined through the 1950s and 1960s.[3]

Moreover, the technology used to build their factories had been developed in rich countries with large markets. As a result, plants tended to be sufficiently large to exploit economies of scale – the rule of thumb that the more a plant produces, the less it costs to produce each unit of output (since, up to a point, as the workforce and plant get bigger, you can specialise ever more, giving each worker a specified task on the assembly line and thus enabling the assembly line to move faster). Such modern factories usually used labour-saving technology to reduce the need for expensive, skilled workers. Transplanted to the small markets of the Third World, however, these factories were often under-utilised, a lot of their impressive machinery lying idle or operating at less than full speed. And the steep bill for building the factory had to be covered by its limited local sales. This wasn't troubling to the owner, who could just jack up prices to cover losses: the market, after all, was protected and the consumers captive. But that meant local consumers paid inflated prices, which left them with less money to buy other things, limiting the growth of the economy. In any event, there weren't enough consumers to begin with. Since labour-saving technology created few jobs, and those employed needed a relatively high level of skill, ISI generated a small number of relatively high-paying positions, while putting more labour-intensive traditional producers out of work.[4]

Since, as a rule, governments were raising the money needed to keep importing capital goods by taxing the one sector that was export-competitive – the primary sector, and especially farming – they often ended up squeezing it to the point where they retarded its long-term growth. They did so indirectly, by controlling the purchase and sale of primary products through marketing boards, which often skimmed off large surpluses for the government by paying farmers low prices. Faced with low prices, farmers (or more often, their children) looked with envy at the wages they could earn if they found work in the city, and so many just left the farm. As a result, while primary output often stagnated or grew slowly, an immense wave of human migration swelled as people all over the Third World moved to the towns and cities, in numbers that far exceeded the work available.[5] Governments then struggled to satisfy the enormous added demand on public services. With many Third World cities doubling in size every six or seven years, the extra need for resources and infrastructure often overwhelmed even the richest governments, as the Shah of Iran had found to his dismay.

Idle hands do the radical devil's work, and governments eager to allay restiveness tried to give people jobs by creating positions for them in the state, from teachers and civil servants all the way down to street sweepers. By and large, in the early decades of the post-colonial period, the share of the working population employed by the government grew throughout the Third World.[6] However, this method of letting off steam could work for only so long. The more the public sector grew, the more the government had to tax the rest of the economy to cover its expenses. And the more it raised taxes, the more it discouraged private investment. In fact, since governments often controlled the allocation of resources, ambitious individuals often found it more attractive to skip entrepreneurship altogether and go into government, in the hopes of using a political or bureaucratic position to skim off resources through corruption. Over a twenty-year period, the economy of the Philippines lost nearly $50 billion this way.[7] Given that much of that money then found its way either into Swiss banks or German luxury car showrooms, it further inflated the flow of resources from the poor countries to the rich.

By the late 1960s, after an initial burst of constructing factories and road-building, growth in much of the Third World began slowing. Governments tried to keep it going through the seventies by borrowing petrodollars, but the effect of pumping more money into stagnant economies mainly raised prices. So the problem of stagflation started hitting Third World countries too.

The final stage of a failed ISI experiment often followed a textbook pattern. It began with a burst of populist largesse, as a government tried to shore up support by showering its supporters with money, and instead unleashed an inflationary spiral that sent prices leaping skyward. The urban poor these programmes were designed to benefit would then be reduced to queuing for food just as the shelves in shops went bare – since governments, to try to rein in prices, usually imposed price controls, making it unprofitable for merchants to keep ordering stock. As prices rose, shortages developed and employers laid off workers, there would come the moment when the populist revolution ended up devouring its own children.

That's where, in the weeks leading up to the 1973 Yom Kippur War, Chile entered the narrative.

When it came to hope and change, few had promised more than the socialist President Salvador Allende – and few had ended up delivering less, until all that remained for his supporters was a desperate hope. After his 1970 election, he'd launched into a programme of what might be called ultra-Keynesianism: wage increases, welfare spending and public employment, with an admixture of nationalisation and land reform thrown in for good measure. Initially, he'd managed to jump-start the moribund Chilean economy.[8] However, his burst of stimulus turned out to be what financial analysts like to call a sugar-high. Wage rises that outstripped productivity ended up juicing inflation, which led restive unions to demand yet higher wages. Meanwhile a fall in the world price of copper, Chile's main export, hurt the economy. In 1971, with prices doubling on an almost monthly basis,[9] output contracted, and by the middle of 1973, in the Chilean winter, Santiago's residents were lining up outside the shops while strikes and protests brought the country to a crawl. Then, amid increasing lawlessness, in late July the lorry-drivers' union went on strike to protest over the government's effort to nationalise the industry, bringing a nation dependent on road transport to a standstill.

In Washington, the administration of Richard Nixon decided that Allende had to go. A law and order president with little love for socialism, Nixon worried that a red tide was sweeping the planet and that Chile might be the domino that set Latin America tumbling. As American corporations in Chile began scaling back their activities, Washington sold off its copper reserves to depress the world price on Chile's principal export, then used its leverage over international lending agencies to prevent Chile obtaining financial relief.[10] As Chile's misery deepened, radicals in the Allende government began pushing for a violent revolution. Determined not to let this happen, right-wing terrorists arose to take the fight to them.

In early September, while he was at home celebrating his daughter's birthday, the commander of the army, General Augusto Pinochet, received some callers. His counterparts in the country's other military services asked to meet him in private, whereupon they retreated to a back room. There they presented him with a plan to overthrow the president. Although Latin American armies often meddled in politics, Chile's had a history of non-interference, and Pinochet was reluctant to break it. But he faced a united front from his colleagues, and agreed to go along with them.[11]

And so in the early hours of 11 September, Pinochet answered his phone before dawn to hear an anxious Allende relaying news of a mutiny in the port city of Valparaiso. Feigning sleepiness, Pinochet replied that he'd investigate at once and call back.[12] Then he threw on his coat and headed out the door, racing to the command centre, where he found his colleagues pacing the floor. By then, soldiers had already left their bases and were marching towards the presidential palace.

After an hour passed and Pinochet had still not called back, Allende worked out what was happening and leapt into a motorcade to rush to the palace, just as police barricades were beginning to crop up in the city centre. He arrived in the office to the news that Concepción, the country's third largest city, was in the army's hands. One after another, pro-government radio stations went silent as they were taken off the air. As soldiers converged on the palace, pro-government snipers hidden on rooftops took aim at them. However, as time passed and the reinforcements they had expected to swell their ranks failed to materialise, and as the army began to turn the tide of the battle, their mood of defiance gradually turned to despair. Government loyalists, trying furiously to organise resistance, kept finding their phone lines dead. Most of the country's radicals, who might have arisen to defend the revolution, had gone on sleeping, drinking their coffee or reading their morning papers, unaware their dreams of a worker's paradise were about to die.[13]

By 9.30 am, Allende judged his situation hopeless. He delivered a short radio message to the Chilean people in which he spoke in defence of his revolution, at which point he received an ultimatum from the air force: surrender peacefully, or face bombardment. He refused to give in. Minutes before noon, bombs began falling into the Palace compound. Tanks took up positions around the presidential palace and fired tear gas into the building. Allende hastily summoned his remaining staff and advised them to leave. One of them grabbed a broomstick and, finding a doctor's frock coat to fashion into a white flag, led the staff out of the building.[14]

Soldiers had now breached the palace walls and were spilling inside. After a while, Pinochet received a report from inside the palace: 'Allende committed suicide and is dead now.'

Within days, amid a clampdown by the new government, the unions lifted their strike. Food began to reappear in the shops. The bureaucracy was then purged and filled with military men the new government could trust.

However, inflation remained stubbornly high, and the economy did not rebound. The government cut spending ruthlessly, as only authoritarian governments can do, hoping to slash inflation and encourage business people to resume investing. Beyond that the junta had little vision for the future. General Pinochet had never found economics interesting, let alone comprehensible, and many of his colleagues wanted to reverse course and relieve everyone's misery with a populist burst of government spending. But aside from such ad hoc solutions, the generals were at a loss for ideas.

Other Chileans weren't, though. During the purge, a former naval officer, Roberto Kelly, had been handed the Ministry for Government Planning. Even before Allende's 1970 election victory, in all of the Americas only communist Cuba had a proportionately larger public sector than Chile's, so Kelly inherited a lumbering behemoth. Belonging to a group of conservative intellectuals closely associated with the *El Mercurio* newspaper, he aimed to reverse this, and set about staffing his ministry with like-minded individuals.

Meanwhile, other departments came under the control of intellectuals from this same network, all of them infused with an evangelical
fervour to cut the state back and liberate the market. Men like Juan
Carlos Méndez (the budget director) and Jorge Cauas (at the finance
ministry) were united by the shared experience of an American education in the neoliberal creed. And because many of them had done
their postgraduate economics degrees at the University of Chicago,
they were known locally as the Chicago Boys. They were, the *Wall
Street Journal* reported at the time, 'champing to be unleashed'.[15]

Working together, the Chicago Boys devised a programme to
renew the Chilean economy, one which slashed public spending,
limited government powers, repressed wages and unions and tightened the money supply. But they needed some sign from on high
to give their mission authority and so break the resistance of the
doubters. In March 1975 they invited Milton Friedman, their teacher
from their Chicago days and soon to be a Nobel laureate, to visit
the country. Friedman flew down to Chile and, in a series of public
lectures, lauded his disciples. During his trip he delivered one speech
at Pinochet's headquarters which may have helped change the course
of history. By then, the junta had dissolved itself and Pinochet was
running the country on his own, which meant that if he could be
converted to the Chicago Boys' gospel, like a medieval king he would
ensure the baptism of his nation, fiery though it might well be.

Friedman – engaging, brash, articulate – did not disappoint his
disciples. Standing before the Chilean dictator, he asked rhetorically
if a step-by-step reform process would restore Chile's economy to
health. 'No,' he said, gradualism made little sense, because 'the
patient might die before the treatment takes effect'. He then added
ominously that it was time for Chile to consider something radical.
Thus he gave birth to the epithet that would be deployed over and
over, in countries around the world, for decades to come: shock
treatment – the rapid, sharp reduction of the state, reorganisation
of the economy, and if need be, redrafting of the country's legal
foundation.[16]

Thus anointed, the Chicago Boys launched their crusade. As flying torture-brigades travelled the country hunting down socialists, the finance minister announced that Chile would begin a programme of shock therapy of the sort Friedman recommended, with drastic cuts in government spending and tight monetary policy. It was a rebirth that would see Chile die for its socialist sins and wash itself in the blood of the free market.

Meanwhile, on the other side of the planet, a quieter, but even more profound conversion had just begun. For although in China, Deng Xiaoping toed the party line in public, as he had done in his UN speech, in private he was filled with doubt.

Having never really recovered from its nineteenth-century experience of Western imperialism, China had turned inwards after the 1949 Revolution. Following a brief experiment with Soviet-style central planning in the 1950s, the Chinese leader Mao Zedong had ended his friendship with Moscow, repudiated its economic system and decided to try a uniquely Chinese development model that substituted village economies for large-scale industrialisation. The Great Leap Forward would be a bold strategy to decentralise the economy by gathering the peasantry together into rural communes and installing 'backyard steel furnaces' in each of them.

It turned out that peasants, accustomed to managing their own affairs, didn't take well to communal farming. To meet their metal-production quotas, they were left to melt down all the steel they could find, including tools and pots that could have been put to better use on the farm. With its heavy reliance on Mao's guidance, almost as if it were divinely inspired, the Great Leap Forward depended heavily on faith in the leader's wisdom; some of its experiments tried simply because Mao thought they'd be a good idea, even though he knew little about metallurgy and spent little time consulting those who did when he came up with the idea of the backyard furnaces. Further, despite his farming background, he did little better with his plans for agriculture. For instance, he instructed that seeds be sown densely in the belief that seeds of the same class wouldn't compete with one another – an idea which, like Biblical literalism, owed more to rigid scriptural faith than scientific research (and ended up wasting good seed). Like many a high priest who, convinced of his miraculous powers, believes the truth of his doctrine trumps the messy enterprise of how things actually get made, Mao resembled a true believer who substitutes prayer or positive thinking for cancer treatment and medicines. Similarly, his Great Leap Forward presumed that theological consistency would win the favour of the economic gods. Defying such faith, the economy contracted and millions starved. In consequence, as Mao's aura tarnished, more pragmatic members of the Chinese leadership took over the direction of the economy.

However, no sooner was the economy back on track in the mid-1960s than Mao began worrying that perhaps this new stability was itself a problem. After some fifteen years of rising incomes, the fervour of the revolution seemed to be giving way to the mundane efficiency of administration, while rebels were becoming a bit too comfortable in their new roles as bureaucrats. To solidify the control of the central party over its increasingly complacent provincial barons, and to also reassert his own place in the hierarchy, Mao decided to launch a Cultural Revolution. He determined to purge China of its bourgeois contaminations. Just as religious fundamentalists decry 'book-learning' that draws people away from sacred scriptures or Romantics insist on the pristine innocence of childhood, the Cultural Revolution aimed to eradicate the vice that came with education and social standing, assuming that only common folk had the moral purity to renew China. Mao sent radical students and workers – the so-called Red Guards – fanning out across the country to flush out suspected reactionaries and cleanse the nation in an inferno that would expiate its sins. Professors and civil servants were sent to work on farms, where teams of Red Guards beat them into becoming good Maoists, as peasants and teenagers went to town to take their place.

Not surprisingly, this crusade proved no more effective than the Great Leap Forward in rejuvenating the economy. Although some would contend that the Cultural Revolution laid the pre-condition for future growth by finally ending China's fissiparous tendencies and bringing provincial barons firmly under central control, the cost in human lives, and in the destruction of much of China's historical heritage, was high. Whether this reflected a peculiarity in Chinese communism or simply that there are sacrifices involved in all religious crusades is a matter for some debate. To his critics, Mao Zedong stands as possibly the greatest mass murderer of all time. To his defenders, the loss of human lives must be set against China's massive population, and then set against the crusades to build a new society that took place elsewhere. Estimates of the death toll in the Cultural Revolution vary greatly, but if one goes with the high-end figure of three million put forth by Jung Chang and Jon Halliday,[17] then adds in the tens of millions who died in the Great Leap Forward, in proportionate terms (about 3 per cent to 4 per cent of China's then population), China's baptism into its new model puts it in a league with Britain's nineteenth-century free-market crusade or Russia's communist rebirth.

One can debate which of those crusades ultimately yielded a superior society, and whether the ends justified the means. The only thing that participants in the debate might agree on is that the cost in human lives of building the economies of the modern world was frequently high. But if in its relative scale Mao's experiments rank alongside other crusades, what may most distinguish his vision of conversion from the earlier cases mentioned is that rather than race forward into a brave new world, he sought to restore a lost one. Its particular twist aside, Mao's vision of a society purged of its vices stemmed from an apparently ancient longing humans have in troubled times to want to restore what they see as an age of innocence, requiring an assault on the wickedness in their midst. Mao was a sort of communist jihadi, turning a personal quest for self-improvement into a violent mission of social renewal. His version of communism, which had repudiated both the market and Soviet central planning to adopt a peasant-focused model, was not without its achievements. China's economy performed better than the other Asian behemoth, India, while such innovations as the spread of 'barefoot doctors' throughout the countryside brought dramatic gains in health.

However, the economy was extremely volatile, surging some years then falling back in others as per the changing whims of the leadership. Most importantly, at the time Deng delivered his 1973 UN speech, the economy was more or less standing still.[18]

And by then this was becoming a problem. Yes, this was a country which, after all, rejected the pursuit of wealth for its own sake and wanted to build a new kind of society – and indeed, for better or worse, was doing so. But China's problem was that the country wasn't alone in her neighbourhood. Of the handful of countries that had eschewed ISI in the decades following the Second World War, four stood out for their success – and all four of the 'little dragons' were in East Asia. Although Hong Kong had exploited its strategic position and developed using a relatively free-market regime, Singapore, South Korea and Taiwan had all looked back to Friedrich List rather than Adam Smith and used variants of the infant-industry model Japan had so successfully pioneered.[19] What resulted were economies that were leap-frogging their way towards First World status, doubling in size every seven or eight years while the share of manufactured goods in their exports rose dramatically.

All four had a relationship with the Middle Kingdom that could be described as, at best, ambivalent. South Korea had historically tense relations with China, and it stared with hostility across the northern border to China's ally, North Korea. Hong Kong was a corner of China the communists didn't yet control – Britain's lease not being due to expire until 1997 – and its dynamic capitalist hub thumbed its nose at Beijing. Singapore was an enclave of Chinese settlers who had opted to throw in their lot with the West. And worst of all, Taiwan was the renegade province to which the Nationalists had retreated when the communists chased them out of Beijing in 1949 – and from which they said they would one day return to retake the mainland.

Despite the fact that Taiwan had a sixtieth of China's population, the pledge didn't seem all that far-fetched. What the 'Made in China' label is today, the 'Made in Taiwan' label was back then and the island, thanks to its relative dynamism, produced an equivalent of one-seventh of its mainland rival's output.[20] Such a dynamic economy enabled the Nationalist government in Taipei to build a modern military which, given the relative backwardness of China's immense but poorly equipped People's Liberation Army, made Beijing's own pledge to retake Taiwan look increasingly hollow.[21]

Deng Xiaoping faced a seemingly impossible task. Chinese communism was faltering at home, yet abroad it, and Mao in particular, still inspired millions of young rebels, in dense jungles and on Western university campuses. Did he really want to take on that icon? Besides, there was something seductively beatific about purity amid hardship. 'I had rather be a doorkeeper in the house of my God, than to dwell in the tents of wickedness,' went the biblical scripture. Mao's repeated catharses filled the ancient longing of many a dreamer of a better world – to be poor but virtuous, unpopular yet true to oneself. The Cultural Revolutionaries, said Deng, presumed that 'poor communism was preferable to rich capitalism'. He now wanted to add some nuance to this. 'There was no such thing as poor communism. According to Marxism, communist society is based on material abundance. Only when there is material abundance can the principle of the communist society – that is "from each according to his ability, to each according to his needs" – be applied.'[22] Man can't live on bread alone. But he still needs bread, and in their determination to achieve moral purity, Beijing's communist leaders risked losing the Mandate of Heaven that Chinese regimes had sought since antiquity. Money was currently the god of East Asia and if China was to stay in the race with its capitalist neighbours, it needed to find a way to lift its economy.

Yet Deng had to tread warily because officially, in the mid-1970s, the Cultural Revolution was still on and Mao regarded his comrade with suspicion. The two men had perhaps too much history, going all the way back to 1935 when Mao's guerrilla army, on the defensive against the ruling Nationalist forces and staring at oblivion, set out on the Long March to Central China. But even though Deng had thereby earned his communist stripes, Mao had always looked askance at him. He seemed too fond of the good life – of card playing, creature comforts, and luxurious surroundings, and Mao had never taken kindly to Deng's criticisms of the Great Leap Forward, when he'd called on Mao to retreat to a more ceremonial role in the party. For such sins, Deng had already felt the weight of Mao's Cultural Revolution when he'd been cast out of Beijing and sent to work in a tractor factory far from the capital, in Jiangxi. Left to care for his ailing wife and ageing stepmother, chopping his own wood, breaking his own coal, and nursing his beloved son who'd been beaten into a cripple by Red Guards, it was an experience he was keen not to repeat.

With influential friends, Deng had been rehabilitated in 1973, after which he rose discreetly up the communist hierarchy. By 1976, at which time the Chicago Boys were in control of the Chilean economy, Mao was dying. It was clear another power struggle between radicals and reformists was about to erupt. On his death-bed, Mao threw his weight behind the radicals, who intended to oust Deng and his ilk as soon as the old man died. But if he wasn't a firebrand with a following like Mao's wife and radical leader, Jiang Qing, Deng was a politician who'd have made Machiavelli proud. Careful to have used his time in office to build a network of supporters, he ensured he had backers in high places once the final conflict began.

Once a prophet dies, his followers are at liberty to fight over who holds his true word, knowing that any ghosts can only watch in impotent silence. When, on 9 September 1976, China awoke to the news that Mao was no more, the showdown erupted into full view. The reformists in the party pounced so quickly, the radicals barely had time to prepare their speaking notes. Within weeks, four of their prominent leaders – the so-called Gang of Four, which included Jiang Qing – had been rounded up and sequestered, whereupon a massive media campaign turned public sentiment decisively against them. Meanwhile, behind the scenes, Deng was working his way back to the centre of Chinese power. Over the winter, documents emanating from the party centre revealed subtle changes of tone. Downplaying the Cultural Revolution, the new message placed stress on order, discipline and economic modernisation. Within one revolution, another was about to hatch.

By then, Chile's shock therapy was well advanced. The Chicago Boys induced a recession that shook down the economy and production plummeted, falling by a tenth in 1975 alone,[23] throwing hundreds of thousands of Chileans out of work. Real wages fell, poverty worsened and inequality widened. Yet the Chicago Boys were undeterred. If they could torture Chile's body but save its capitalist soul, the economy could be born again. Torture there was: Chile killed, maimed, tortured or simply 'disappeared' some 35,000 radicals[24] in the quest to rid society of the elements that would stand in the way of the country's rebirth.

'For the moment all discipline seems painful rather than pleasant,' wrote Saint Paul to the early Christians, 'but later it yields the peaceful fruit of righteousness.' Or, as Milton Friedman said, 'There's no such thing as a free lunch,' using the popular phrase as the title for a book he published soon afterwards. His neoliberal ethic spurned the received wisdom of the still-dominant Keynesian church, whose Epicureanism presumed that lunches could in fact be obtained for free: you paid with credit and the extra energy you got from a full stomach would then enable you to work it off. But the neoliberals believed that to claim the sweet prize of victory, you had to first go through the agonies of purging yourself. It was like fasting before communion or delirium in a sweat lodge, and its demand for stoicism appealed intuitively to individuals who, seeing thrift as a virtue and sacrifice as investment, shared that same kind of ethic.

Such sentiment was beginning to surface in Western countries, where some exiles from the Keynesian church had always rejected its easy path to heaven. Now, they swapped tales of Chile's experiment like missionaries who bring back news of conversions among the heathens. Mere weeks before Friedman's visit to Chile, the former Education Secretary Margaret Thatcher was elected leader of Britain's Tories. She seemed a most unlikely and discordant selection for the time; the same year that would see *Fawlty Towers* premiere on British television sets and the Sex Pistols make their shocking debut – the one a send-up of the peeling-plaster resignation of 1970s Britain, the other a vicious mockery of everything about it. Having reluctantly come around to its role as the steward of this genteel, post-imperial decline, the Conservative Party had joined the Church of England by incorporating Keynesianism into its own doctrine, seeing the welfare state as a sort of *noblesse oblige*, and looking merely to preserve some aspects of tradition in the era of state economic management.

So that kind of party seemed an unlikely home for someone like Mrs Thatcher. The product of an austere Methodist upbringing, her family came from the Wesleyan branch of the Church and repudiated socialism as an evil scourge. Having grown up listening to her preacher-father's sermons, she had inherited a fierce belief in liberty and individualism, and a conviction that people were to take responsibility for themselves and their families. 'I wonder,' she remarked, 'whether the state services would have done as much for the man who fell among the thieves as the Good Samaritan.' Although she'd become an Anglican to tick Tory boxes, she would always sit uncomfortably in the church's pews. Its bishops felt Christian compassion required the welfare state. She, however, was sure the welfare state weakened individual resolve and family life. 'Economics,' she said, 'is the method; the object is to change the soul.' A John the Baptist-like figure who stood outside the church, both Keynesian and Anglican, she railed against its decadence and called for true believers to join her in the desert. With a keen eye trained on Chile, she regarded General Pinochet and his economic experiment with admiration. As her inner circle began meeting regularly to discuss the new trends in economic thought, Milton Friedman quickly rose to the top of their reading lists.[25]

Shortly after her election as party leader, and just days before Chile began its shock therapy, Mrs Thatcher received a visitor in her small Commons office. Although she hadn't yet met him, she'd heard of Ronald Reagan and been impressed by the way he'd run California during his time as governor. Now touring Europe as part of his campaign for the US presidency, Reagan hit it off so well with Thatcher that their meeting ran twice its scheduled time.[26] As they parted, they promised to keep in touch.

Not only did inspiration for neoliberal evangelists come from places like Chile but also much of the impetus behind the conversion to a new doctrine. For the heartlands of empire were about to find the tail wagging the great imperial dog. What went on in their peripheries, and in particular in their hinterlands in the Middle East and central Asia respectively, would affect their economies back home, helping to plunge the old statist churches – Keynesianism in the West, communism in the East – into crises of faith.

CHAPTER 16

THE RETURN OF THE PROPHET

Although the trend would not become apparent until decades later, from the early 1960s the average rate of economic growth in Western economies had begun to decrease. Underlying this change appears to have been that labour productivity, the driver of growth, had begun to slow.[1] Since growth in developing countries remained even slower at the time, the gap between rich and poor countries continued widening. But even this had begun, ever so subtly, to change. For deep in the bedrock of the world economy, an important shift was underway. Unknown to anyone then, the centre of gravity in global capitalism was going to continue its long-standing tendency to radiate outwards, into new places: from its medieval origins in the maritime republics of Italy, to northern Europe then to Britain, then to the United States, and now to the global south; new economies were constantly rising, taking pride of place over long-established ones. Although the journey there would be rocky and difficult, beginning with a sharp and painful decline, the Third World was going to rise again.

So it was perhaps fitting that poor countries would provide inspiration for the neoliberal revolution about to sweep the world. Until now, the doctrines that shaped Third World economies had originated in Western centres, then fanned outwards to the world: Marxism was systematised in the British Museum and exported from Russia; Keynesianism was crafted in Cambridge and carried to the former colonies by the graduates who staffed the new states; neoliberalism was elaborated in centres like Chicago then carried to developing countries. But now, developing countries would be in the vanguard of change, and it was they who would help change the orientation of the world's economies.

The fall of the Shah of Iran reaffirmed the Middle East's tendency to act as America's Achilles heel, further compounding the economic headaches that had originated there. But for at least a few days at the beginning of 1979, President Carter got a break from his woes when the Chinese leader, Deng Xiaoping, paid him a visit. If the capitalist mecca was looking a bit threadbare that winter, it still shone bright enough to attract this communist pilgrim, out to study rival faiths. Mindful of this, at the welcoming ceremony on the White House lawn, Carter lauded China's decision to 'move boldly toward modernization'. In his reply to Carter's speech, however, Deng opted to dwell on his diplomacy's international dimension. 'Sino-U.S. relations have arrived at a fresh beginning,' he said, 'and the world situation is at a new turning point.' Later that evening, at a state banquet in the White House, he toasted the end of the two countries' thirty-year estrangement.[2]

For Deng, the visit was yet another feather in a cap already laden with unlikely honours. He'd begun the decade a frail old man, shivering in the exile Mao's Cultural Revolution had sent him into. He now finished it at the apex of power – formally a vice premier and head of the Military Affairs Commission, but informally the power behind the inscrutable Chinese throne. After Mao died in 1976 and the Gang of Four had been overthrown, the assumption of power by the reformers gave way to a period of consolidation. By 1978, Deng and his colleagues had reached the point where they could begin putting their economic reform programme into action, transforming China as profoundly as the Cultural Revolution had tried to do. Armies of Red Guards were now to be replaced by waves of investors. Instead of communist self-criticism sessions and 'struggle meetings', China would hold business seminars. What better way to signal China's new direction than with a visit to that heartland of capitalism, the United States?

Yet, whatever President Carter might have wanted to think, Deng hadn't come to take lessons from Washington. Instead, he dropped a clue to his motives when he seemed most excited by a visit to Atlanta's Coca-Cola plant. As soon as he returned to Beijing, he put the finishing touches on a proposal for presentation to a meeting of the Communist Party. The Four Cardinal Principles, as he called them, would reaffirm the party's absolute hold on political power. Not only would this tactic satisfy hardliners who suspected he wanted to water down communism, but it would also give the government the firm grip it needed to lead the nation through the years of dramatic change he foresaw coming with the economy's renewal. They would start modestly at first: the reintroduction of contracts in farming, a reduction of investment for heavy industry, some loosening of the rules on trade. But as each change passed successfully and opposition failed to coalesce, the next stage of reform would grow more ambitious.[3] Rather than a Chilean-style baptism by fire, this was going to be a slow initiation by a seeker, starting out in the back pews of the church.

After Deng returned to China, the pressures on Carter kept building. On 5 May 1979, the morning bulletin reported that Margaret Thatcher had won the British election. As Carter was sitting down for breakfast in the President's Dining Room, she was appearing before a crowd of journalists outside 10 Downing Street. Addressing them briefly, she quoted from the prayer of St Francis of Assisi, saying 'where there is error, may we bring truth; where there is doubt, may we bring faith' before declaring 'there is now work to be done'.[4]

Carter's opponents in the Republican Party had been watching the British election closely. Most interested of all were the economic conservatives, who'd been biding their time since Goldwater's defeat fifteen years before. Their most prominent spokesman, Ronald Reagan, who back in 1964 had delivered the nomination speech at the Republican Convention, saying Goldwater would 'stop the advance of socialism in the United States',[5] was now preparing his own run at the presidency. An actor who had originally made his name in a movie series starring opposite a chimpanzee, Reagan had used that speech to launch his political career. From there he had gone on to run for Governor of California in the 1966 election, campaigning on a pledge to send 'welfare bums' back to work. After two terms there, in 1976 he tried but failed to win the party's presidential nomination. Since then, when he'd first met Margaret Thatcher, their relationship had seasoned into a deep friendship. His supporters therefore regarded her own campaign as something of a bellwether. Although Reagan's sunny demeanour and seemingly boundless optimism was to many Americans a welcome counterpoint to Jimmy Carter's sullen hectoring, many in his party remained unconvinced that the country would vote for a candidate whose economic doctrine was so far to the right. Being tough on crime and hard on communists always went down well with Republican audiences; but ever since the war they had, like Britain's Conservatives before Thatcher, held to Keynesian doctrine in their economics. But they also reckoned that if Margaret Thatcher could get a mandate out of Britain, where the Keynesian consensus had been born and became more firmly entrenched than in the United States, Americans might be willing to take a punt on Ronald Reagan and his small-government, free-marketeering.[6]

They had good reason to feel energised, just as President Carter had good reason to feel worried. Margaret Thatcher had succeeded in making inroads into the very constituency supposed to be the left's backbone, the working class. The erosion of the Labour Party's bedrock was most noticeable among skilled manual workers,[7] those with good and relatively stable jobs, homes in the suburbs and children at university. Now, the Democratic Party's working-class base was starting to look similarly wobbly.

It was galling, in a way. The parties of the left that had built the Keynesian welfare state were confronting an unfair irony: it had apparently sowed the seeds of its own destruction. As incomes rose and workers moved to the suburbs, they joined the middle class, whose ranks were further increased by the expansion of the professions and the growth of middle management in modern firms. This new stratum in time became as large as the traditional working class, whose clubs and tight-knit neighbourhoods and social networks were starting to fray as the class fragmented and people moved further from their workplaces.

In the worker's self-identity, the shop floor was beginning to compete with the shopping centre, where they were buyers with increasing power. Given the post-war boom in home ownership and consumer credit, even working-class well-being was increasingly affected not merely by earnings, but by the cost of living and interest rates. Home ownership also altered the relationship of many workers to the state. Workers who lived in state-owned council houses still tended to regard the government as a benevolent patron and vote Labour, whereas those who owned their own homes tended to drift towards the Conservatives.[8] The Tories, it was reasoned, could be counted on to keep mortgage rates down and to preserve property values. In an age when the safety net had lessened the fear of unemployment, inflation was the new bogey. When, on top of that, the economy sank into recession and the Keynesian church couldn't deliver jobs in sufficient numbers, their ability to withstand a right-wing onslaught was further weakened. Britain's Conservatives played on rising unemployment and a wave of strikes to campaign in the 1979 election on a slogan of 'Labour isn't working'. Ronald Reagan made a similar pitch by saying, 'A recession is when your neighbor loses his job. A depression is when you lose yours. And recovery is when Jimmy Carter loses his.'

Conservative evangelising thus aimed straight at the heart of the Keynesian church, targeting its working-class choir section. Parties of the left found it difficult to respond, because they were handicapped by the two-class mindset that had structured the politics of Western societies since the Industrial Age. Made famous in a 1951 book by Maurice Duverger,[9] the two-class theory maintained that over time the politics of industrial societies would always polarise along class lines, with right-wing parties like Britain's Conservatives or the US Republicans speaking for business, and left-wing parties like Labour and the Democrats for the workers. To connect with its core constituency, therefore, a left-wing party had to tap into work- ers' concerns over unemployment, wages, workplace conditions, benefits and union rights. However, the welfare state had allayed many of these concerns. As a result, the usual litany of a left-wing campaign was starting to sound like archaic prayers in an ancient language. Thatcher had proved that a conservative campaign could connect with the more prosperous part of the working class by relating to them not as workers but as consumers, and by addressing their ambitions of upward mobility. That raised the possibility there might be millions of 'Reagan Democrats' in America who might also be willing to convert.

By the time Thatcher was taking the measurements at 10 Downing Street, Ayatollah Khomeini, the leader of Iran's Islamic revolu- tionaries, was back in Tehran. Having quickly grabbed the reins of the haphazard revolution, which had thrown together a motley opposition of socialists and religious fundamentalists, he crushed its radicals and proclaimed an Islamic Republic governed by sharia law. In place of the old monarchy, he would create a democracy. But at its apex would sit a council of religious scholars empowered to discipline and rein in the elected government, ensuring its actions accorded with religious orthodoxy. In a curious twist, therefore, he produced a constitution that would bear more than a passing resem- blance to the ideal neoliberal state, in which an independent central bank could tame politicians – save that in Iran Muslim scholars rather than economic ones would be the enforcers of orthodoxy.

Handsome, austere, remote; Khomeini's aloof and inscrutable personality only strengthened his authority. Fiercely opposed to modernity, he rejected the promises of worldly salvation offered by all economic doctrines, insisting that paradise remained God's domain. Yet paradoxically he had cemented his rise by mastering the tools and techniques of modernity. Where the Iranian state had failed to meet the needs of its urban slum-dwellers, his Islamist networks had moved in, raising alms in the bazaars and their global network, then distributing them to their supporters.[10] In effect, he had turned modernity against itself, using its tools to build a support base among its losers. God, it was said, had returned.

President Carter's deep religious faith led him to try to understand his enemies. Khomeini's made him despise his. Carter demurred for months on the deposed Shah's request to come to America for medical treatment, anxious not to annoy the Iranians. However, to such fumbling attempts to find a way to cooperate with Iran, Khomeini responded with disdain. When towards the end of 1979 Carter finally decided to let the Shah land in the United States – and even then only briefly – the Ayatollah fulminated at the 'Great Satan'. He then gave his blessing to radical students, who stormed the US Embassy in Tehran and captured its staff. As American hostages were paraded blindfolded before cheering crowds, Carter could do little more than stew.

Whatever stern rhetoric he could muster failed to convince many Americans. By the end of 1979 he was losing the home-front war as well, the economy's persistent stagflation resisting all his attempts to dislodge it. As if abandoning a sinking ship, his 'inflation czar', Alfred Kahn, threw up his hands in exasperation, declaring publicly that he had no idea why the president hadn't fired him. 'Actually, I do know,' he added. 'Nobody would be foolish enough to take this job.'

Any schadenfreude the Soviets might have felt at Western discomfiture during the persistent recession of the 1970s was offset by its own economic woes. And any delight the Kremlin might have taken in America's problems with Iran was eclipsed by their concerns over their own position. They had been on good terms with the Shah and Khomeini disliked the godless Russians as much as he did the Americans.[11] To make matters worse, Moscow had a further worry: Tehran's provocations might draw the Americans into an all-out conflict with Iran. The last thing the Soviets wanted was US troops on their southern flank – not when there was already enough going on to the east of Iran.

In Afghanistan, Islamist rebels were harrying a regime friendly to Moscow. What concerned the Soviet leadership was not only the prospect of their taking control in Kabul, but also the impact of a Muslim uprising at home. Although the Russians dominated the Soviet Union, it was a multinational empire and they comprised barely half the population. Worse, the Russian birth rate was declining whereas the populations of the Muslim southern republics, like Tajikistan, Uzbekistan and Turkmenistan, were rising. The risk that Muslims might one day turn against the officially atheist state could not be downplayed, especially now that Iran offered a successful model of Islamic revolt. Indeed, Moscow was already getting reports that Muslim rebels were crossing into the Soviet central Asian republics from Afghanistan.[12]

Also, if for reasons different from its rivals, Russia was struggling to keep its economy growing. The rates of industrial expansion that had so impressed the world back in the 1930s had long since given way to a slowing economy that, by the end of the 1970s, was practically stagnating. The basic problem was that Soviet central planning had been effective at what could be called extensive industrialisation: building factories and increasing their output, while bringing new resources into production. Once Stalin had taken control of everything, planners had been able to set production targets and allocate plant and farm managers the resources needed to meet them, then measure their performance against those targets. But while this system was able to increase quantities of output, it was much less effective at changing the output's *quality*.

This is where the market economy still had a crucial edge. When it came to buying a pair of shoes, for instance, consumers didn't care how many the country produced. They just cared that their own pair was comfortable, durable, attractive and reasonably priced. In a market economy, shoes that didn't meet their expectations got left on the shelf. The price then dropped as the retailer tried to clear the shelves. At that point the designer, as sales of that shoe declined, either had to go back to the drawing board or specialise in low-cost shoes. That's how the market assessed performance and signalled the need for product improvements. Soviet plant managers, in contrast, anxious that time spent on development would make them under-shoot their assigned targets, hesitated to develop new products or technologies.[13] Similarly, because they were allocated their inputs and so didn't have to worry about cutting costs, they had no incentive to use resources efficiently.[14] Soviet consumers got the shoes they got, whether they liked them or not; all while the country ravaged its natural resources.

It wasn't that the Soviets hadn't tried to manage a Chinese-style transition to a more flexible and responsive economy. On the contrary, nearly two decades before Deng's American tour, they'd experimented with reform. But the first tentative efforts to introduce market-based pricing, to manage the transition from extensive to intensive development, provoked unrest among people accustomed to a cradle-to-grave nanny state, and their leaders fell back on old ways.[15] Buying peace, they compromised their model's long-term viability. For, amid the resulting economic sluggishness, the cost of maintaining the Soviet military and subsidising the country's allies in Eastern Europe and the Third World made its empire and overseas ventures an increasingly costly burden.

Now, it had Afghanistan to worry about as well. While another foreign campaign was the last thing Moscow needed, her southern neighbour – the wild country cousin too independent to tame, too close to disown – posed a problem it couldn't ignore. For its part, nestled in among the Soviet Union, Iran and Pakistan, Afghanistan didn't have particularly warm relations with any of its neighbours. However, its dealings with Pakistan were especially fraught. Afghanistan's dominant ethnic group, the Pashtuns, straddled the border. Since that border had been imposed by the British during the colonial period, many Afghans refused to recognise it.[16] Thus, they had long sparred with Pakistan over a region that neither government fully controlled.

Pakistan had been a US client since the 1950s, shortly after it became independent from Britain. In response, Afghanistan had then reluctantly invited in the Soviets as a counterweight. And ever

since Moscow had been slipping agents into the country and building a network of sympathetic officials, particularly in the military.
Whether with Moscow's connivance, or for their own reasons, this
clique had overthrown the king in 1973, only to find they'd bitten
off more than they could chew. Radical modernisers who admired
Libya's Muammar Gaddafi, they had shallow roots in the country's
traditional governance structures, which were still dominated by
landholding and religious elites. Moscow found itself getting drawn
into the country's affairs, and in 1978 a coup installed a more
strongly pro-Soviet leader in Kabul. Noor Taraki was hardly the
most imposing of Moscow's friends, being something of a bon vivant
with decidedly un-Islamic tastes. But at least he was loyal to the KGB
(equivalent to the CIA).

Almost at once, though, an Islamist opposition, emboldened by
the spectre of atheistic communism, began to coalesce. Taraki only
worsened matters by rejecting Afghanistan's thousands of religious
teachers. As rebel groups began organising, fighting spread throughout the country. It became clear to Moscow that it could not rely
on the Afghan army to put down the rebellion. For his part, Taraki
began all but begging the Russians to invade, since his own country
was turning on him.[17]

Over the summer of 1979, the Russians began flying troops into
Afghanistan. Then in the autumn, Taraki was murdered, and a new
faction took power in Kabul with the aim of expelling the Russians.
In early December, the politburo met in the Kremlin to decide what
to do.[18] Although the situation in Tehran had heightened the risk
of an American intervention, it also created an opportunity. With
Washington – indeed, the world – distracted by events in Iran, the
Russian leadership had a cover for an invasion of its own.

Late on Christmas Eve, Russian aeroplanes began landing at
Kabul airport. Within hours, airborne units had seized airbases
throughout the country. By the time night fell on Christmas Day,
the 360th Motorised Infantry Division had begun crossing specially
constructed pontoon bridges and rolling into Afghanistan. Through
the icy Hindu Kush mountains, sending up clouds of frozen exhaust

and steam from its engines, the huge convoy rolled on until it reached Kabul on 27 December.

Any hopes that events in Iran would obscure the invasion soon proved misplaced. Washington was outraged. President Carter announced that the Americans would boycott the upcoming Olympic Games in Moscow and embargo grain shipments to the Soviet Union. Ronald Reagan, now campaigning for the Republican presidential nomination, was unimpressed. Deriding the president's grain embargo, he noted that it wasn't cows and chickens that had invaded Afghanistan.[19]

Carter was about to suffer an even more grievous blow than Reagan's snickering. As the Russians had guessed, the White House had been exploring military options in Iran. Overruling an outright invasion, Carter opted for a top-secret rescue plan. US commandos were to be airlifted from the naval fleet in the Persian Gulf, the helicopters flying below Iranian radar to escape detection. In Tehran they would stage a daring assault on the embassy. American aircraft would provide cover as more helicopters flew in to evacuate the hostages.

On 24 April, the president gave the go-ahead to launch the operation, then stayed up through the night, awaiting news. When word arrived that some of the aircraft had run into operational problems in the Iranian desert, Carter reluctantly gave the troops permission to abort the mission and return to the Gulf. Unfortunately, when the helicopters started their engines, they kicked up a cloud of sand that obscured their vision, and two of them collided. The ensuing explosion and fire killed eight American servicemen, whose remains had to be abandoned amid the evacuation. Carter dejectedly left it to his press secretary to relay the news. He awoke the next morning to face condemnation on all sides.

By July, when the Republicans were ready to hold their convention in Detroit, Reagan was neck and neck in the polls with Carter. Surveys revealed that the native optimism of ordinary Americans was fading. The inflation rate was approaching 20 per cent, the hostages continued to languish in Tehran, and the Russians were firmly ensconced in Kabul where the American ambassador had been murdered. Reagan declared it was time to renew the nation, and return to the simple faith of its forefathers. Standing before the assembled delegates in the brand-new Joe Louis Arena, he pledged to cut taxes and scale back the public sector, saying 'government is never more dangerous than when our desire to have it help us blinds us to its great power to harm us'.[20]

Reagan and Carter then hit the campaign trail at the height of summer. Like a mosquito buzzing tirelessly in the night or the refreshing breeze that refuses to blow while tempers wilt, the hot, dry summer of 1980 seemed only to aggravate America's irritable mood. The grasslands of the Great Plains dried up. Cattle died of thirst, evoking in older minds memories of the Depression. Eastern cities sweltered in heat waves and rationed their water. The once-green lawns of Washington turned dusty and brown.[21] As summer turned to autumn and the election drew near, pollsters found it impossible to predict a winner. Although Americans were deeply disappointed with Carter, Reagan, more right-wing than most of them, was proposing a conversion as big as Roosevelt's New Deal had been – but in reverse. Opinion surveys suggested that he elicited only tepid enthusiasm among his compatriots, who considered him old and inattentive – a perception fed by rumours that he had occasionally napped through California cabinet-meetings.[22]

Nevertheless, the true believers felt that fate would soon anoint them. Still basking in the fact that Margaret Thatcher had been elected in the UK, they felt a conservative train had begun rolling across the West, and the United States would be the next to board it. While Reagan toured the country, giving folksy speeches that called for a return to simpler times and old-fashioned values, his advisers – many of them supply-siders he had tipped to fill Treasury posts if he won, and who were united by their commitment to roll back the state[23] – were busy drawing up plans for America. When he closed the debate with Carter before a national television audience, Reagan left Americans with a question many of them were now pondering:

'Are you better off now than you were four years ago?' To Carter's view that Americans had to adapt to a new reality of slower growth, shared sacrifice and a more modest role in the world, Reagan insisted his miracle workers could raise the economy, and the country, back from its statist grave.

'What's his beef,' Ronald Reagan asked in February 1981 as he was rushed to hospital, moments after an attempt on his life. Barely two months into his presidential term, the shooting seemed to portend a difficult presidency.

But Reagan knew that if America was to be born again, it had to get rid of statism. His first battle came in the summer of 1981. PATCO, the national union of air traffic controllers, announced it would launch a nationwide strike, one that would shut down the American air transport system at the height of summer holiday travel, threatening to further set back the economy. Although the strike was illegal, PATCO had a strong card to play. The government could not find 17,000 air traffic controllers overnight to replace the strikers. Besides, the union enjoyed broad support and had, to top it all off, backed Reagan's nomination.

Reagan had his own song sheet. When he huddled with his advisers to consider their options, he quoted from one of his heroes, Calvin Coolidge, saying, 'There is no right to strike against the public safety by anybody, anywhere, any time.'[24] When most of the controllers took to the picket lines, Reagan fired them. The government then rushed to staff the system with military controllers. If anybody doubted their new president's resolve he set them straight then and there. His administration then forged ahead with the programme he had promised during the election campaign – tax cuts, spending cuts, deregulation and a war on inflation.

Reagan had inherited the tight monetary policy that Carter had adopted near the end of his presidency. Back in 1979, when inflation appeared to be running completely out of control, Carter had appointed a new chairman of the Federal Reserve, Paul Volcker. The dollar's value had begun declining so fast that Americans were switching their savings to gold and other hard assets, creating a speculative fever that only worsened inflation. So in October 1979 Volcker announced, at an unusual 'Saturday Night Special' press conference, that he would be sharply tightening the money supply. Raising interest rates, he now made it more expensive to borrow. This led consumers to spend less, thereby inducing a recession. The policy was still in place when Reagan took office in January 1981, and he saw no reason to alter course. As painful as it was, Reagan and his team saw it as a sort of economic purgatory. Convinced the exercise was trimming fat and waste, his policy team believed that in the end it would produce a leaner, fitter economy. So with Reagan's blessing, Volcker continued raising interest rates. By the summer of 1981 they had reached 20 per cent.

Margaret Thatcher was then nearly two years into her term of office, during which time she had taken Milton Friedman's advice and instituted an equally tight monetary policy to beat the UK's high inflation. Meanwhile, having come to office promising an entrepreneurial revolution, her government set about cutting taxes, selling state firms and deregulating the economy. But while the sharply reduced money supply wrestled record-high inflation back to earth, the cost was high. Onerous interest rates choked demand, driving the economy into a tailspin. Manufacturing capacity fell by a fifth and the unemployment rolls kept swelling. By 1981, close to 3 million Britons were looking for work.[25]

Thus, the two Western advertisements for a free-market revolution were recession-bound economies whose governments regarded joblessness as tough love. If things continued this way, the new doctrine was going to struggle to win converts. Despite Margaret Thatcher's famous claim that there was no alternative to grinning and bearing it, other countries seemed to suggest otherwise. Japan's economy, under extensive state guidance, kept booming throughout the Western recession. Then in the 1981 French presidential election, the socialist François Mitterrand came to power on a platform to tackle the recession in a way exactly contrary to what Reagan and Thatcher were doing: a big Keynesian stimulus package.

Beaten back in its British birthplace and under siege in America, Keynesianism was about to stage a rearguard attack. Everyone watched the French experiment with keen eyes, for it would reveal if the Keynesian model could still do its magic. As if they realised the importance of their victory, Mitterrand's supporters filled France's streets with giddy revelry on election night and celebrated in numbers not seen since the liberation of Paris from the Nazis. Riding this wave, Mitterrand called snap legislative elections, delivering his Socialists a huge parliamentary majority. He set about confronting his country's recession not with a neoliberal retreat by the state, but by a very aggressive advance: expanding public works, building social housing, creating government jobs for the unemployed, nationalising private firms, strengthening the unions and workers' rights, shortening the working week, imposing price controls, raising the minimum wage and boosting unemployment and welfare benefits. If the common foe in all the Western economic campaigns was the stagflation then gripping the advanced economies, the weapons of choice could hardly have been more different. The world now watched to see which of the competing doctrines would work.

If these were lonely times for Margaret Thatcher and Ronald Reagan, at least they still had one another. When foreign governments suggested they might close their skies to US planes in sympathy with the PATCO strikers, the British government announced that American aeroplanes would always be welcome in Britain.

The prospects for the future looked no more promising in Moscow. As the politburo looked south to Kabul they beheld a conflict that was sapping resources as surely as Vietnam had done to America.

In the cold Afghan winter, Russian soldiers huddled in their tents around wood stoves, trying to keep warm while the howling wind whipped around them. Their gloves had not arrived. Nor had proper bedding. The food was awful: they could go days without an adequate meal, and fruit or vegetables were a rare luxury. So was washing. Facilities were poor, making winter bathing a harrowing ordeal. The troops took it in turns to go on sentry duty, never sure when a bullet fired from an unseen location might come. For months, their location might not change, and they would man the same hill, only to return to the same tent, hour upon hour, day after day, month after month. Between the boredom and the horror, many found escape in drugs or alcohol, exchanging weapons for money, saying they had lost their arms in battle. Helicopter pilots dreaded going on missions, fearing the shoulder-launched missiles now being sent by the Americans to the mujahideen and used with devastating effect. These holy warriors, about whom they heard tales of savagery, were fighting for their homeland. The soldiers of the Red Army were just far from home and the comforts of warm families and familiar cooking. Within years, thousands of them would fly home in coffins. Many thousands more would return, maimed and disfigured, to families horrified by what greeted them at the airport or military base, shattering their hopes of joyful reunions.[26]

Vladimir Lenin's promise to build a brave new world and spread the revolution globally was dying a slow death in the frigid Afghan desert.

CHAPTER 17

THERE IS NO ALTERNATIVE

In 1630, while sailing across the Atlantic to his new life in the Massachusetts Bay Colony, the Puritan John Winthrop told his shipmates that the new society they were going to build would stand before the world as a model of Christian charity. 'We shall be as a city upon a hill,' he said, quoting from the Gospel of Saint Matthew, 'the eyes of all people are upon us.'

By the time the sermon had travelled across three centuries and landed in the speeches of Ronald Reagan, it had mutated into a rallying cry for a holy crusade. In the Cold War then raging between capitalism and communism, Reagan played Richard the Lionheart to Mikhail Gorbachev's Saladin, regarding him as a great man who tragically served a false god. And the rules of a holy war had been clear since antiquity: there could be but one victor, forcible conversions were done to save the souls of the conquered, and soldiers who betrayed their principles in battle were forgiven their crimes, for the cause was just.

Reagan's election had given Augusto Pinochet cause to smile, just as in London there was now a prime minister willing to look more tolerantly on the Chilean dictator's repression of socialism. It wasn't that Reagan and Margaret Thatcher were unaware of Pinochet's human rights abuses. It was that his evil was considered easier to accommodate than Allende's socialism. 'Let us pray for the salvation of those who live in that totalitarian darkness,' Reagan said of the communist heresy. 'Pray they will discover the joy of knowing God. But until they do, let us be aware that while they preach the supremacy of the state, declare its omnipotence over individual man, and predict its eventual domination of all peoples on the earth, they are the focus of evil in the modern world.'[1] Pinochet's crushing of Chilean socialism, which Reagan's advisers believed had preserved the liberty needed for a free market and an eventual return to democracy,[2] was seen as a necessary means to a greater end. No sooner had he taken office than Reagan shelved what one of his advisers called the Carter administration's 'theology'[3] about the Chilean junta's human rights abuses, and began improving Washington's ties to Santiago.

Reagan's economic doctrine similarly reflected his Manichean politics. Harry Dexter White's Keynesian ecumenism, which had made room for socialist central planning if the planner's heart was good, had now given way to upholding the universal laws of the neoclassical revival. In this fundamentalist theology, there was the market, and there were distortions – venal sins that led people away from the path of righteousness and prosperity. Augusto Pinochet, determined that his people not slide back into what he called their 'evil ways',[4] was busily purging them of their sins when Thatcher and Reagan came to office. All the same, his shock therapy would have tested the faith of the most resolute believer, rapidly accelerating the economic decline that had begun under the overthrown Allende regime. But the Chicago Boys stood by Pinochet, telling him to keep the faith and stay the course. And sure enough, around the time Reagan swore his oath of office, the Chicago School's promises seemed to start coming true. Chile's economy bottomed, then re-emerged from the grave. Inflation, meanwhile, remained low.[5] The great neoclassical sage Milton Friedman proclaimed it 'a miracle'.[6]

Emboldened by this success, the neoliberals were ready to launch what would be a great crusade. At the start of the decade, they had triumphed in just a few lands: Chile, Britain and the United States added to some earlier, less prominent conversions to the neoliberal faith, like New Zealand. That was about to change dramatically. Over the next decade neoliberalism would sweep across the planet. Not only would the Keynesian church crumble in many places where, like Britain, it had been the de facto state religion, but Marxism too would suffer one retreat after another – most significantly, in the very heartland of its first revolution, Russia. The world would witness mass conversions on a scale the missionaries of earlier eras could only have dreamed of.

Chile having been the first nation to deliver itself into the neoliberal fold, it was perhaps to be expected that neighbouring countries might be the next to convert, or that neoliberalism would spread across the developing world before it made further advances in the West. But such a future was far from evident at the start of the decade. To begin with, most First World audiences were still too horrified by the tales of torture, disappearance and murder to feel comfortable with Friedman's assessment that Chile's miracle testified to the superiority of the neoliberal god. As for Chile's neighbours, they were not necessarily inspired by events in Santiago. What would instead transform not only Latin America but much of the Third World was something different.

Back in the 1970s, when Gulf-state petrodollars had flowed through Western banks and then out to the Third World, governments imagined they had found a pot of gold they could raid to transform their economies. They didn't sell the family jewellery, but they did borrow against it, driving their debts to record levels. Why wouldn't they have? In its purest form, Keynesian doctrine justified such borrowing, saying that the resultant acceleration in economic growth would easily generate the revenue needed to pay back the loans. And in fact everything had worked fine until the Iranian Revolution prompted the second oil shock. But once stagflation returned in 1979 and Ronald Reagan endorsed Paul Volcker's tight monetary policies, the apparently happy arrangement of debt-fuelled growth ended abruptly.

Third World governments owed those debts in US dollars, the

standard currency of international banking. As a result, when interest rates soared in the United States, they were hit by something like a triple punch. First, rising interest rates drove up their payments, so they had to obtain more dollars to pay their debts. That is to say, they had to export more stuff. Second, rising interest rates also drove up foreign demand for the American dollar, since anyone with money to invest could get better returns by changing local currency into US dollars and lodging it in an offshore account. That's just what the Third World's rich started doing. Since their own currency therefore diminished in value relative to the US dollar, Third World governments had to export even more to get back the same amount of dollars as before. But third, and worst of all, this was no time to be in the export business. Once the oil shock sent First World economies into recession, and once Britain and the United States then deepened their own economic contractions with tight monetary policies, the obvious sources of demand for Third World exports dried up. It wasn't rocket science why: when they had to choose between keeping the heat on and buying more coffee, it was obvious which way Western buyers would go.

So Third World governments were forced to send more money out just as they found it harder to bring more money in. It didn't help that much of the money they'd borrowed in the 1970s had been used to fund current expenditure, like civil service pay increases or food subsidies. Countries that had been careless in their spending habits ended up like someone who toasts a new job offer by throwing a big party, only to get a call at the height of the revelry saying that the job has gone to someone else. Like many a preacher whose words are misquoted, Keynesians could argue that their teaching had been distorted – that they never said all state spending was in itself good, that it was only appropriate when used for the purposes of stimulus. But because the public had always conflated state spending with the Keynesian catechism – and because, in fairness, many left-wing politicians had done much the same thing – it got blamed for the apparent failures of public largesse. And once the church lost its flock, and thus its power base, Keynesianism would be vulnerable to the neoliberal assault in the seminar rooms as well, and ever more university economics departments would replace Keynesians with neoliberals whenever there were openings.

In any event, even Latin American countries that had acted prudently with borrowed money in good times, building the road networks to carry goods to market or hydroelectric dams to power new factories, often found that in the new recession, all the new plant and infrastructure lay idle. But they still had to pay the bills. Come 1982, some governments started missing their debt payments. They then faced a grim choice: either walk away from the debts, which would result in being frozen out of global credit markets for years to come, or get help to tide them over. However, the major private international banks, their fingers already burned since it was their loans not being paid off, were hardly in a mood to throw good money after bad. So Third World governments wanting bailouts had no choice but to turn to the major international lending agencies, the International Monetary Fund and the World Bank.

As if lying in wait, these agencies were ready with a new free-market catechism. Forged in discussions among the IMF, World Bank and US Treasury Department, all of which had headquarters in close proximity to one another in the US capital (the United States being the biggest shareholder, with the biggest vote, on each of the two multi-laterals' boards), the programme of action they drafted became known as the 'Washington Consensus'. Shaped by neoliberal doctrine, it would be preached and upheld by all US presidents over the next generation. This proselytism began in the earliest days of the Reagan presidency. Soon after taking office, he named a new president of the World Bank, who would take it in a new direction, shifting it away from providing loans for development projects (like those dams that now lay idle) to providing bridge financing for governments unable to meet their debt payments. But there was now to be a catch to its assistance. Governments would be told that if they wanted to obtain loans, they had to implement free-market programmes. Referred to as 'structural adjustment', these collective baptisms were usually resisted by Third World governments, but justified by their Washington architects as being imposed in the interests of their recipients – though unquestionably they helped draw these countries more closely into the Western economic orbit.[7]

Cutting government spending, privatising state firms, reducing trade barriers, deregulating economies and removing price controls caused no shortage of human suffering. Wages fell, public jobs were eliminated and food costs soared. Firms went out of business as cheap imports flooded the market, local manufacturers finding themselves overwhelmed by the cheaper goods coming from more advanced countries (which in some cases even took advantage of the new openness of Third World countries to dump excess stocks of goods, as the EU did with its agricultural surpluses).[8] But, neoliberal evangelists insisted, this hardship would expiate the past sins of Third World citizens and lead them back to economic righteousness – towards the eventual goal of being whole once more, and getting back onto the path to the promised land (which, in the descriptions often given by neoliberal visionaries, had begun to look remarkably like America itself).

It didn't help matters that in developing countries the Keynesian priesthood had often compromised its authority. Even the citizens of the forcibly converted countries could see that their own Keynesian high priests, whose catechism had apparently failed, now looked increasingly like washed-up illusionists, reduced to redistributing the fruits of future labours to the present with borrowed money, then blaming their failures on the vices of foreigners – accusing them, for instance, of underpaying for what they imported, overcharging for what they exported, and demanding usurious rates on the money they loaned out. And so, as one Third World government after another was forced to recite the neoliberal litany, the free-market revolution fanned across the developing world.

Third World countries could forget all the talk of the New International Economic Order they had floated during the oil decade, when they'd felt their star rising. The cartels they'd once imagined they could use to drive up the value of their exports seldom turned out to be as effective as OPEC, on which they'd modelled them. Unless one of a cartel's members controlled so much of a commodity that it could, like Saudi Arabia, swing the market, it proved very difficult to coordinate action among member states. The temptation to take a free ride on other countries' cutbacks, to cash in on higher prices by not sticking to one's reduced quota, was often beyond the discipline of any one country: Saudi Arabia could and sometimes did punish OPEC cheaters by flooding the market with oil and driving them out of production, but it was an unusually dominant player. Besides, most commodities turned out to have higher demand elasticities than oil. In 1980, if the cost of your heating bill went up, you still had to pay it. But if the cost of your cup of coffee went up, unless perhaps you were a sleep-deprived undergraduate with an exam the next day, you waved off that next cup.

As for the bold plan for more favourable trading terms and development assistance that had been proposed back in 1974 at the United Nations, when Deng Xiaoping delivered his 'I'm back' speech, Reagan wasted no time dispatching with it. In late 1981, he attended a development summit in Cancún. The original plan for the meeting had been to address the NIEO (New International Economic Order) proposals to increase aid, improve trade and allow Third World countries more say at the IMF and World Bank. But that agenda got torn up the moment Reagan was elected. In Cancún he now brought them a new commandment. In his opening remarks to the conference, he said that steering more resources to the developing world wouldn't do any good. 'History demonstrates that time and again, in place after place, economic growth and human progress make their greatest strides in countries that encourage economic freedom,' he said, claiming that it was independent farmers, and not an activist government, that had made early America great. He maintained that steering resources to the developing world, whether by inflating the prices paid for their exports or providing them with more development assistance, wouldn't encourage this kind of entrepreneurial spirit in poor nations. The state's role was therefore not to manage development, but to free entrepreneurs to pursue riches. 'The critical test,' he told his audience, 'is whether government is genuinely working to liberate individuals by creating incentives to work, save, invest, and succeed.'⁹

As one observer to the meeting put it, whatever the NIEO's virtues might have been, Reagan 'killed it with a smile'.¹⁰ Keynesianism, both globally and in domestic policy, was to be taken off the agenda. In its place, the free market would return. It would, furthermore, be restored with the passion of a believer who has reclaimed a desecrated temple.

The year 1982 would see the American recession reach its nadir. The economy contracted by 3 per cent, interest rates peaked and the stock market was worth four-fifths what it had been at the time Reagan took office. However, one day in August, when the neoliberal star seemed to be at its lowest ebb, the stock market suddenly staged a rally. In just one day it surged 5 per cent. As if they'd suddenly spotted light on the horizon, traders raced to buy shares while they were still cheap.

As it happened, just days later, satisfied he'd finally wrestled inflation back to manageable levels, the Federal Reserve chairman, Paul Volcker, cut interest rates for the first time in nearly three years. The market rally gained steam. Slowly but surely, Americans began sharing Reagan's optimism. They started to go back to the shopping centres, and by the following year the economy was growing once more.

Meanwhile, the British economy had also re-emerged from its funk. It was admittedly littered with debris after its monetarist storm – millions out of work and discontent so widespread that riots broke out in the summer of 1981. However, Margaret Thatcher's government didn't regard joblessness as being primarily its problem to solve. Her god would help those who helped themselves. In keeping with neoliberal doctrine, her government presumed that firms that had gone to the wall during the recession were unfit to begin with, and had thus been wasting good workers. Thrown out of work, they now provided an abundant resource, which new, dynamic entrepreneurs could employ at low cost to get their firms off the ground. All they had to do was find those employers. Mrs Thatcher's employment secretary, Norman Tebbit, who was then drafting legislation to restrict the powers of trade unions, remarked, 'I grew up in the thirties with an unemployed father. He didn't riot. He got on his bike and looked for work, and he kept looking till he found it.'

The last dyke in the Keynesian resistance to the neoliberal tide then burst in France in 1983, when François Mitterrand abandoned his attempt to reflate the economy with an ambitious stimulus pro-gramme. After its 1981 election, his socialist government had tried to restore growth by showering the economy with money: hiring the unemployed, giving pay rises, shortening the working week, and strengthening the bargaining power of unions. It did wonders – for German industry. Mitterrand found out the hard way how much Europe, and France, had changed since Keynes had written *The General Theory*. In 1936, economies had been relatively closed. Governments controlled foreign exchange and determined how much money could leave the country. But since the war, when France had joined Germany to form the European Economic Community, Europe increasingly operated like one economic space. So while the French government was doling out money and jacking up wages, German firms were able to contain their labour costs and produce goods more cheaply than their French counterparts, which the French eagerly snapped up with their new income. For France, the Keynesian episode – the last major experiment in the West with the Keynesian model – was a failure. The French budget deficit soared, aggravating inflation, yet the economy barely budged. In 1983, Mitterrand suddenly reversed course and sold off state companies, eased the regulations on the labour market, weakened the unions and opened France to foreign trade.

On the backs of their good fortune, Margaret Thatcher and Ronald Reagan campaigned for re-election. Both won landslides, in 1983 and 1984 respectively. Their opponents bickered and retreated into a nostalgic call for a return to the managerial state. Reagan and Thatcher gleefully picked up the support of middle-class homeowners who didn't want to return to the high-spending, high-inflation ways that would only have bumped up their mortgage payments. In the wake of their victories, as ever more politicians across the Western world concluded that the British and American neoliberal experiments had won the showdown with Keynesianism, more governments began implementing neoliberal policies. After conservative electoral victories (as in Germany and Canada), and when a socialist government followed the French pattern and did the deed (as in Scandinavia), governments across the West moved steadily rightwards in their economic policy.

Keynesian scholars would later protest that much of what had been passed off as Keynesianism had in reality been anything but. In particular, the continuation of deficit financing even after the economy was out of recession, which became standard in Western countries, was an obvious departure from Keynes's original thought. It may well be that most governments which called themselves Keynesian were no more Keynesian than Stalin was Marxist or a Spanish Inquisitor Christian. But just as most people judge a religion not by its foundational texts but by the actions of its followers, ordinary people evaluated economic creeds with a similar test. On its way up, an economic school's ascent was cemented when its followers could point to the doctrine's supposed achievements and cry a worldly equivalent of 'Our god is a great god!' even if the doctrine wasn't itself entirely responsible for the good fortune. And it would be the same if the economy was not working, when a doctrine's apostles would always say that their advice wasn't actually taken or that what happened wasn't their true intention. But by then a public that had judged them wanting would have already abandoned their temple for a new church.

In a Manichaean struggle, the first glimmers of victory appear when your opponent shows hints of losing faith in his god. In the showdown between the free-market West and the socialist East, the first blink came on the Russian side. And funnily enough it happened among the sort of people that in Cancún Reagan had said made America great: farmers.

Mikhail Gorbachev knew farming well. Born in a simple brick cottage in southern Russia, as a teenager he'd driven combine harvesters and tractors on a collective farm.[11] But from his humble origins Gorbachev had risen quickly through the ranks of the Communist Party. In 1980, at the age of forty-nine – a relative baby in the country's gerontocracy – he was made a full member of the politburo.

However, Gorbachev retained his interest in farming. As a child, he had lived through Stalin's famines. Later, he had been able to observe from near the productivity of the small market gardens that peasants kept on their home plots, working on them after they had put in a day on the collective or state farm. After joining the politburo, he took the agriculture portfolio. Much as Deng had done with his visit to the Coca-Cola plant, Gorbachev then toured Canadian farms in the early 1980s, searching for ideas on how to revitalise the Soviet farm economy. Accustomed to Soviet leaders who were stiff and formal, his Canadian hosts were struck by how relaxed he was. Chatty and inquisitive throughout his tour, at one point he stopped to ask a rancher in Alberta the secret of his success. 'I made no bones about giving him the answers,' the man told journalists, going on to relate how he advised Gorbachev to privatise the farms. 'He went along with that. He indicated it was a difficult thing for them to do but he could see the rationale behind it.'[12]

To the Soviet old guard, Gorbachev's willingness to dabble in markets was next to apostasy. And yet the young reformer had no desire to create a capitalist society. On the contrary, he wanted to revitalise the communist economy. However, he had come to the conclusion that to do that, the economy first needed restructuring – in Russian, perestroika. He believed that if plant and farm managers got more autonomy to deal directly with their customers, rather than only with a planning agency, they would get the incentives the Alberta rancher had said would improve their efficiency. He also reckoned that Russia could tolerate a few privately owned businesses if they helped the rest of the state-owned economy function better.

In effect, Gorbachev wanted to do something similar to what the Chinese were trying, with some success – but with one crucial difference. While China was still an agrarian society, the Soviet Union had developed a large industrial complex, and with that a much larger planning complex. Gorbachev was certain that any attempts to reform the economy would be stifled by this hidebound bureaucracy – the *nomenklatura* comprised of state and Communist Party officials, and which was heavily invested in the existing model. Simultaneous with economic reform, therefore, he judged it necessary to reform the country's politics to weaken the old guard. So, whereas China's government had solidified its political control in order to implement economic reform, Gorbachev believed Russia would need to couple its economic reforms with a policy of free speech and political 'openness' – in Russian, *glasnost*.

In 1985, after a few years of politburo dithering, he rose to become General Secretary of the Communist Party, the country's supreme post. By then the Soviet economy had nearly ground to a halt. At once Gorbachev began laying the groundwork for his economic renewal. But he also turned his attention to matters further afield. That's because he believed if the Soviet Union was to restore its health, it also had to disentangle itself from foreign misadventures.

To cement its foreign alliances, the Soviet Union operated something called the Council for Mutual Economic Assistance. Referred to sometimes as the communist European Economic Commission, in fact it was not a free trade zone like the EEC but instead extended central planning to the international sphere. Its ten members – Russia, its six buffer states in Eastern Europe, along with Vietnam, Cuba and Mongolia – would agree on certain goods they would exchange on barter terms: Russia might give Czechoslovakia oil, for example, and in return get cars. However, after the oil shocks raised the price of oil, the cheap terms on Russian oil amounted to a large subsidy. To Gorbachev, the price tag of world socialism had thus risen too high. Given the cost of subsidising inefficient economies in its East European allies and Cuba, not to mention the burden of supporting its network of friends in Africa and Asia to whom it gave military assistance, Moscow was spending money Gorbachev felt should be kept at home, where it could be invested in the economy.

Finally, there was Afghanistan. Within a year of taking office, Gorbachev told the Soviet Communist Party that Russia's military campaign in Afghanistan had become a bleeding wound. Not only lives were being lost, but the war was sucking millions of dollars each day from an economy that had little to spare.[13] The cause had been noble, he said, but the Soviet Union could not solve its own problems until it stopped trying to solve those of others. The country, he insisted, had to find a way to extricate itself from the Afghan mire.

For Ronald Reagan, there were no halfway houses on the journey to the economic Eden. As Friedrich Hayek had written, there was capitalism, there was communism, and there was the well-intentioned backsliding that led the former inevitably to the latter's perdition. So when in 1987 Gorbachev tabled his reform package before the Supreme Soviet – nominally the country's parliament, but in practice a rubber-stamp for decisions taken by the politburo – Reagan unsurprisingly declared that it didn't go far enough. He flew to West Berlin and, standing before the Brandenburg Gate, which separated the Western sector from the communist East, said, 'General Secretary Gorbachev, if you seek peace, if you seek prosperity for the Soviet Union and Eastern Europe, if you seek liberalization: Come here to this gate! Mr Gorbachev, open this gate! Mr Gorbachev, tear down this wall!' Reagan and his successors in the White House would not rest until communism was gone. Even at the start of 1989, as columns of Soviet tanks rumbled along the Salang Pass and through the tunnel Soviet engineers had built to link Russia with Afghanistan, leaving behind the country they had invaded ten years before, the Americans stepped up their aid to the Afghan rebels. Because although the Soviets had retreated they'd left behind a communist government. Complete victory was not yet won.

Curiously, though, Gorbachev seemed not to mind Reagan's advice about the Berlin Wall. In October of 1989, he flew to the other side of the Wall, landing in East Berlin. As he descended to the tarmac at the airport, he was met by the East German leader, Erich Honecker, greeting him with a kiss. The next day, the image was splashed across newspapers around the world. 'Kiss of death' read the headlines. They weren't far off the mark. Gorbachev was in fact on a tour to tell Eastern Europe's leaders that the Soviet Union would no longer prop them up and that, from now on, they would be on their own.

The six Soviet allies in Eastern Europe – East Germany, Poland, Hungary, Czechoslovakia, Romania and Bulgaria – had never enjoyed much popularity in those countries. Imposed by the Russians after 1945 when they'd liberated the countries from the Nazis, the ruling communists had little in the way of local support bases, being instead propped up by Moscow and backed by Russian tanks – which had, several times over the previous four decades, quelled East European uprisings. Once it became clear that governments were going to have to face their fate alone, their peoples took matters into their own hands.

Poland, where an opposition movement had been bubbling ever since the first Polish pope's first return visit to his homeland a decade earlier, was ready to erupt. In the summer of 1989, when the government sought a popular mandate in its first free elections since the war, it was trounced by the pro-market (and religious, in an officially atheist country) opposition. In the same month, in Hungary, the body of Imre Nagy, the leader of a short-lived reformist government in the 1950s that had been crushed by Soviet tanks, was returned to Budapest for a reburial that metamorphosed into a huge anti-government protest.[14] Soon afterwards, the Hungarian government lifted restrictions on its western borders and allowed its citizens, whose travel to the capitalist West had been previously impeded, to move freely. At once thousands, then hundreds of thousands of East Germans, separated by a wall from the lures of the West, entered Czechoslovakia; from there, now able to move about at will, they continued on down to Hungary, across to Austria and finally up to West Germany, where they enjoyed automatic rights of citizenship.

Mikhail Gorbachev had blown the roof off the East German state, and now its foundation was seeping out from under it. In a church in Leipzig, a small band of faithful launched candlelit vigils. From there, anti-government protests spread first in ripples, then in waves, across the land. The country's communists grew desperate. They dumped Honecker and opened the Brandenburg Gate, allowing their people to travel into West Berlin. Then, on the night of 9 November, in a spontaneous outpouring, crowds of East Berliners stormed the gates and forced open the Wall, later clambering on top of it and using sledgehammers, bare hands, or whatever they could fashion as tools, to tear it down.

A week later, a peaceful student demonstration gathered in Prague, the capital of Czechoslovakia. Seeing the collapse of their allies around them, Prague's ruling communists decided that giving any ground would only encourage the protesters, so they sent riot police into the city. When the students offered them flowers, they were beaten unconscious. An outraged public then filled the streets to express their common cause with the students. For the next ten days, mass demonstrations shut down the country's cities and spontaneous political meetings replaced performances in the nation's theatres. Workers' unions, supposedly controlled by the communist party, joined the strike, bringing the economy to a standstill. The ruling party tried to clamp down on the media to prevent the story getting out to those parts of the country not yet affected. But then the media too joined the rebellion. The government fell, and the opposition movement that had crystallised in the theatres of Czechoslovakia assumed control of the country.

Under similar pressure, the Bulgarian government had fragmented, though the communists were able to reconstitute themselves and retain some place in government. That left only Romania, the last bastion of East European communism. Nobody expected the iron rule of Nicolae Ceaușescu to end any time soon. He had effectively liquidated his opponents and run the country like a personal kingdom, complete with palaces worthy of a sun king. But trouble had been brewing in Timişoara, in western Romania. In December the city erupted in rebellion when the government tried to silence a prominent dissident pastor. When the army went in, workers put down their tools and went on strike. The army clamped down brutally. More people filled the streets, emboldening their compatriots elsewhere in the country. As Christmas approached the country was in open revolt. The security forces split, the army siding with the rebels, the secret police with Ceauşescu. The dictator tried to flee but was intercepted by rebel soldiers. On Christmas Day 1989, a grainy video broadcast to the world showed him and his wife in a makeshift courtroom, on trial behind some folding tables in a bare room of an army barracks. That evening, a firing squad shot them both dead.

By then Yugoslavia was splitting up and descending into civil war. Communism, which started in Russia in 1917 and then rolled outwards, had now been rolled back to its Russian frontier. Everywhere else in Europe it was fast becoming a distant memory. And in Russia, two years into its experiment with *perestroika* and *glasnost*, things were not going to Gorbachev's plan.

With Keynesianism in retreat across the West and communism embattled in its heartland, the flame of state-led economic policy now passed to East Asia. There, the Japanese model of a nurturing government, inspired by nineteenth-century institutionalism and successfully exported after the war to other East Asian countries, was still ticking over healthily. Critics of neoliberalism now looked to such 'developmental states' to support their besieged claim that there was not one sole path to economic salvation.

Six days after Ceauşescu's death, Japan's soaring stock market in fact closed at a new record high. Retreating after trading hours to their sake bars and long dinners, Tokyo's traders boisterously toasted the prosperity that had taken their country from being a war-ravaged nation four decades before to what some were now predicting would become the world's largest economy. However, Japan's economic supremacy, trumpeted in many a popular book at the time, and which had provided a refuge for many Keynesians in the 1980s, was about to give them another test. For as those Japanese traders collapsed into their beds that night, drunk and dishevelled from the partying that bonded Japanese 'salarymen' to one another, few could have realised they had just reached the summit.

When the market opened on the next trading day, it fell. As the year gathered pace, so did the descent. Soon, the property market caught the contagion. Having scaled dizzying heights as the Japanese bubble had inflated in the 1980s – by the end of the decade it was said that the emperor's garden was worth more than all the state of California – wealth began vanishing. The government tried to intervene to keep prices from falling too far, but it was too late.

Nevertheless, even as the Japanese financial sector imploded, in the rest of East Asia, in those countries like Japan that had eschewed the free market to use the state to spearhead capitalist development, growth continued as always. The demand from Japan that had carried the rest of the region aloft was now being picked up by the accelerating Chinese economy (which still had a very large state sector). So while most of the developing world was swimming in the neoliberal tide, East and South East Asia's booming economies, from South Korea to Thailand, felt no need to abandon their state-led models. All the same, even they, lured by neoliberals, both in Washington and at home, agreed to try one little part of the neoliberal catechism.

The Asian model had depended on a close and attentive management of financial markets. Governments had restricted foreign currency transactions in order to keep investment at home, while controlling the allocation of foreign exchange so as to steer money to the firms and industries they wished to nurture. Now, persuaded that lifting the restraints on currency exchanges would bring investment flooding in, they removed their controls on capital markets. The initial response vindicated the new doctrine's exponents. Money did indeed pour in. Since East Asian economies were growing faster than those of the West, hedge-fund managers in New York and London ploughed money into the newly opened markets so as to ride the wave. The sudden boost in demand for East Asian assets sent them surging. As their prices rose, firms could book the capital gains as increased profits. Increased profits meant higher dividends and wages, which in turn accelerated economic growth.

There, said the prophets of the new age: whereas in Japan the government had meddled with asset prices until they became so distorted that the market crashed, in East Asia the government's retreat from the markets started a boom. What better evidence did you need that the only viable capitalism was one that withdrew the government from the economy?

The Berlin Wall did not fall only in Europe. It tumbled right across the world. Once Soviet clients were left to fend for themselves, they looked as vulnerable as schoolyard bullies whose gang has disappeared. And once Soviet clients disappeared, the United States lost the need for many of its own.

Vietnam quickly reformed its economy along Chinese lines, allowing private enterprise to take hold. Following in its wake were reform processes in communist Laos and Cambodia. In Mozambique, the socialist government quickly abandoned its war on its Western-backed counter-revolutionaries and sued for peace. US and Soviet backing for the players in the Angolan civil war evaporated. South Africa, seeing that it was no longer required as a battlefront in the war against world communism, realised its loyalty was no longer needed; the Americans had no further use for its racist regime, and so a palace coup installed a reformist faction in Pretoria. No sooner were they in office than they freed the black opposition leader, Nelson Mandela, and commenced negotiations to end white-minority rule.

Cut off from the Soviet aid that had kept him in power, the leader of Ethiopia fled the country. It then broke up, its Eritrean province declaring independence. With Ethiopia out of the communist camp, the United States no longer felt the need for a regional counterweight, and so withdrew its aid to neighbouring Somalia. As that country's government crumbled, local warlords, some with Islamist leanings, took control. Next door in Sudan, an economic crisis enabled a shadowy Islamist clique to seize power. The last decade of the twentieth century thus opened with a spate of violence across the developing world as regimes fell, states fragmented and peoples struggled to define the new contours of their politics – a period of chronic warfare that, for the historically minded, bore no small resemblance to the birth of the nation state in the Wars of Religion, some four centuries before.

And in Chile, where it had all begun nearly twenty years before, Augusto Pinochet calmly stepped aside to make way for the country's first civilian president since the 1973 coup. Humiliated in a referendum on extending his presidency the year before, he had to step down. But not before he appointed himself commander-in-chief of the armed forces, a position he would use to prevent prosecutions of the military for human-rights abuses. As far as he was concerned, the book on the struggle between socialism and the free market was now closed. Now a moral tale, it would teach future generations about the lives of those who, by their sacrifices, saved them all from socialist damnation.

By this time, China's reform was well advanced, and its leaders had even reached the point of dabbling in the Chicago catechism.[15] Even though the Chinese Communist Party still controlled the government, with each passing year private players took over more and more of the market. That left only Russia as the last great bastion of communist state planning.

Yet by the end of the decade, it was clear that Mikhail Gorbachev's reform mission had gone adrift. Loosening controls on the economy did not allow entrepreneurship to flourish. As state agencies ceased to implement orders, the economy simply collapsed. When orders went unfilled, the supply chain managed from Moscow dried up. As for *glasnost*, as if a lid on a pressure cooker had been removed, free speech unleashed long-repressed anger. Many non-Russian republics, encouraged by Eastern Europe's revolts, started clamouring for independence. Ethnic tensions, in a country with over a hundred different nationalities, were rising.

Throughout the first half of 1991 the situation worsened. Hardliners in the communist leadership were now impatient to take control from Gorbachev, who was wavering between reformers and those who wanted to scrap his experiment and restore the old model. When in the early summer the ardent decentraliser Boris Yeltsin was elected as President of the Russian Federation, the largest and most powerful of the Soviet Union's fifteen republics, the old guard decided things had gone too far.

On 19 August, Moscow's residents awoke to the news that Gorbachev, while at his holiday dacha, had been taken ill and would be unable to perform his official duties. His vice president was to assume immediate control. No doubt to prevent his health deteriorating any further, soldiers then surrounded his dacha.

As the announcement was being read, Red Army tanks rolled into Moscow. Some politburo members then issued a statement saying that in light of the country's chaos, a state of emergency had been declared, which meant the recently granted press freedom would be revoked. Muscovites, who rather liked the taste of freedom *glasnost* had brought them, flooded the streets and berated the soldiers. Just as newspaper offices were being ringed with troops, a rumour came from the White House, the Russian Federation president's offices. Boris Yeltsin had cut short his vacation and rushed back to Moscow in a bulletproof vest, and decreed the emergency government unconstitutional. Armies of volunteers then fanned out from the White House to spread the message and appeal to the soldiers to join their side. Yeltsin's efforts to reach Gorbachev, however, were frustrated. 'He's resting,' somebody on the other end of the phone kept answering.

Protesters gathered around the White House and formed a human chain to keep the soldiers back. Then, as the crowd roared its approval, a few tanks turned their gun barrels outward to signify they were joining the rebellion. In the early hours of 21 August, word came that a KGB paratroop division was advancing on Moscow, reportedly in response to orders from Yeltsin. On hearing the news, the soldiers already in Moscow began to retreat. One after another the coup plotters were arrested. As dinner time approached, Gorbachev landed in Moscow, freed from house arrest by troops answering Yeltsin's call to resist the coup.[16]

Gorbachev was now in a gilded cage, a bird whose wings had been clipped, home only because his one-time protégé, Yeltsin, had flown him there. His powers were now merely formal. Seizing the moment of weakness at the centre, the republics of the Soviet Union declared their independence one after another, Russia itself joining the fray. Like the conversations that ignore the guest of honour at a retirement party, Gorbachev was left to read about it in the newspapers.

On 24 December 1991, Russia assumed the Soviet Union's seat on the United Nations Security Council. The next evening, in a televised speech scarcely anybody watched, Gorbachev declared the Soviet Union dissolved. The revolution that had started some seventy-four years before, in ten days that shook the world and eventually led to a Cold War between West and East over the soul of humanity, ended with a dull speech in a television studio just before the engineers locked up for the night and the colour bars appeared on the screen.

The Soviet Union, champion of socialism, fell to its capitalist foe not on any battlefield, but in the shopping centres. The Soviet model, designed to raise output, give jobs to all and distribute resources more equally, did just that. But as incomes rose and Russians became consumers, they couldn't find enough of the goods they wanted. The Soviet Union's famously long waiting lists for cars, queues at shops and clunky shoes meant that it lost the race against the Western market. Having set out to be a paradise for workers it failed to become a Mecca for shoppers.[17]

Embodying collective hopes and dreams, giving its believers a cause and identity greater than themselves that they could devote their lives to, demanding their sacrifice for the success of the group, communism had functioned like so many a church. But its promises of worldly salvation had long since worn thin. Gone were the heady days of the 1930s when many progressive intellectuals regarded the Soviet Union as a beacon of a better future. Stalin's show trials, purges and famines, the repression of dissent, the realisation of Rosa Luxemburg's fear that Lenin's dictatorship of the proletariat might become permanent; such things turned most Western radicals away from its model. By the time the Soviet Union collapsed, it had scarcely any fans left.

And yet for as long as the Soviet Union existed, it stood as witness to the falsity of the neoliberal claim, made famous by Margaret Thatcher, that there was no alternative to the free market. That mere fact kept alive the search for alternatives. So when the Soviet Union fell, it took with it the hopes of millions of radical thinkers. Left adrift, communist parties disbanded, socialist magazines mothballed their presses and radical intellectuals exchanged their jeans for pinstriped suits. Parties of the left, which had clung to their Keynesian faith, were now ready to make their confession.

Christian millenarians long believed that when the day came that all of humanity had converted to their creed, the earth would be ready for Christ's return. At that point history, which was merely the long record of our journey back to the Garden of Eden from which we'd been expelled long ago, would finally come to an end. Christian missionaries never succeeded in converting all of humanity to these ideas. But here, suddenly, was another doctrine, which, under their noses, was getting ever closer to pulling off a very similar feat. Neoliberalism had become the state religion across most of the planet, and the holdouts were diminishing by the year. Nevertheless, before the neoliberal church could claim its ultimate triumph over humanity, it needed to resolve one remaining theological flaw in its doctrine. At its heart, there remained a tension between its libertarian economics and the conservative Christianity of those who had first exported the faith, the scions of Reagan and Thatcher and William Buckley. Committed to economic freedom, it still kept a place for collective restraints on individual behaviour via its adherence to traditional morality. To truly reach its apogee as a belief system, to take precedence over all others and overcome even loyalties to the nation or to shared causes like socialism, neoliberal doctrine needed to annihilate the very principle of collective identity. In its stead, it had to make the liberated individuals who were free to pursue their own satisfaction the supreme ends of humanity. It would take a new generation of apostles to do that.

CHAPTER 18

THE NEW AGE

Within economics departments, the fall of Russian communism seemed to vindicate those who had argued it contravened the laws of human nature and was therefore doomed to eventual collapse. Strains of neoclassical thought that stressed the sanctity of unregulated markets, and which had begun circulating in the seminar rooms since the early 1970s, began to work their way into general discourse.

In particular, the rational-expectations thesis maintained that individuals were so rational in their decision-making that they factored the future impacts of present policies into all their investment and spending choices. So, for instance, when a government announced a Keynesian policy to stimulate a moribund economy with a burst of deficit spending, people would anticipate that when it came time for the government to repay its debts, it would raise taxes. In the meantime, the extra government borrowing would drive up interest rates, as increased demand for credit chased a fixed supply. That meant taxes and borrowing costs were going to rise down the road. So, rather than spend government stimulus money, everyone would put it under the mattress to prepare for future tax and interest charges. Such 'Ricardian equivalence', said this pure strain of neoclassical thought, would always neutralise any government attempt to manage the economy. Accordingly, any efforts by the state to influence markets would backfire. In this theology, no government could do a better job of guaranteeing economic health than liberated human activity did spontaneously.

This thinking restored the centrality of the individual to all social relations. Such a variety of neoclassical economics found its political voice in the writing of the libertarian philosopher Robert Nozick, much beloved among neoliberals, who said, 'There are only individual people, different individual people, with their own individual lives.'[1] It also seemed to dovetail with another one of the innovations in 1970s microeconomics, the efficient markets hypothesis. Pioneered by Eugene Fama,[2] the EMH argued that market prices fully reflected all publicly available information. Assuming information was freely available, prices therefore had to be right. It followed from this that the Soviet model of setting prices to reflect planning priorities or perceived human needs – say, keeping down food prices – or for that matter, the East Asian model's control of prices to encourage the growth of strategic industries, was condemned to failure. The upshot was that any attempt by any government to lead the way towards a brighter future would not work. The laws of economic nature dictated that humans and markets be left to their own devices, and any attempts to alter that went against our nature.

In a similar vein, public-choice theory, whose early antecedents went back to the 1950s[3] and 1960s,[4] but essentially amounted to a revival of Jeremy Bentham's ideas,[5] entered public discourse. The assumption of public choice was that humans acted like economic animals in all they did, not just in their economic transactions. The rules of the market equally applied to every other aspect of people's lives. Their utility-maximising behaviour did not stop at the door to their homes, churches or charities. In everything they did, from raising children to loving one another, they were out to maximise their welfare. In the logic of public-choice theory, this didn't necessarily make them selfish; some proponents maintained they could still be altruistic, but even then, went the reasoning, they'd set out to maximise their altruistic behaviour for the satisfaction it gave them.[6] In practice, though, once public-choice entered the public realm, it became associated with a conservative agenda to further roll back the power of the state. Its proponents reasoned that individuals working in the public sector, out to maximise their gain, would always look for ways to use public power and resources to further their personal ends. The only effective solution was to limit what the government could do to its core functions or, where there was a function that only government could perform – like running a prison or policing the streets – using market-incentives to govern public management: contracting government services to private providers where possible, using private-sector budgeting principles to manage government departments, or offering incentives to reward individual performance.

Such academic theories entered the public domain by way of neoliberalism, the distillation and popularisation of free-market economics. But neoliberal doctrine now faced a new challenge. Originally a hybrid of neoclassical thought, Austrian economics, libertarian philosophy and conservative Christianity, neoliberalism had from its early days been shot through with tensions. Because all its components were united by a hatred of communism, the Cold War had held them together. Now that common foe was vanquished, it wasn't clear what the doctrine's future would be. In Western democracies, the baby-boomers were becoming the largest cohort of the voting public. While they liked the tax-cutting individualism of neoliberal politics, they had less of an appetite for its father-knows-best morality. This was especially true of those who had availed themselves of the huge expansion in higher education that followed the war in order to enter the professional class. Having come of age on university campuses that were seething with radicalism in the 1960s and 1970s, the issues that mattered most to them differed from those that concerned their working-class elders. Socially pro-gressive, their leftist politics were much less class-conscious than those of the union meeting hall.[7]

The new strands of neoclassical thought flowing from the univer-sities seemed to offer an opportunity to resolve these tensions. While, for instance, Austrian theory celebrated free individuals, it also gave pride of place to irrational drives and multi-generational thinking. Friedrich Hayek had thus opposed inheritance taxes because he said

individuals were motivated to maximise not only their utility, but
that of their gene pool – a nebulous way of thinking that, even if
correct, muddled the pure individualism of the neoclassical model.
But rational expectations, efficient markets and public choice all
suggested a doctrine focused on the here and now, with the individual and his urges the sole basis of society. It did not require a moral
framework, as the conservatives and Austrians – and classical political economists themselves – had taken for granted. The free market
itself would provide the moral compass.

What was required to bring this doctrine to a mass public was a new
generation of intellectuals and political entrepreneurs who could find
a way to satisfy the 'Me Generation'. The children of the sixties that
had come off Western university campuses had raised the pursuit of
pleasure to the status of a sacred duty. Their trajectory was embodied in the personal narrative of a former hippie like Jerry Rubin.
Having started the 1970s as a campus radical, celebrating the pursuit
of pleasure as revolutionary and echoing Timothy Leary's famous
commandment by calling on his followers to 'Turn on! Drop out! Get
high!',[8] Rubin had finished the decade a multimillionaire corporate
executive. Nevertheless, despite this migration into the bourgeoisie
he had once derided, Rubin refused to adopt bourgeois morality.
On the contrary, he maintained he was still a rebel, replacing his
'Never trust anyone over thirty' battle cry with the more pinstriped
'Wealth creation is the real American revolution'. It might have
sounded a bit rich to younger, more cynical minds to hear, without
irony, baby-boomers declare that they pursued their own pleasure
solely to create a better world; but Rubin was, after all, the product
of a generation that had launched a revolution in Paris in 1968 to
protest a university not allowing male students to overnight in their
girlfriends' dormitories, thinking that was reason enough to call
themselves Trotskyists.

It hardly mattered if cynics found it all a bit earnest. The baby-
boomers were a massive crop of voters, rich for the picking. If a way
could be found to strip neoliberal doctrine of its moralistic aspects,

purifying it of all but its most libertarian elements, a bumper harvest of electoral support lay ahead. Better yet, if this transformation could be done on the left, it could ensure the absolute triumph of neoliberalism in its heartland. And since the left was struggling to redefine itself in the 1990s, toying with new forms of Marxism and neo-Keynesian thought, a new generation of prophets could offer a message with tremendous appeal to a public that, raised amid the great prosperity of the post-war period, no longer felt the need for a paternal state and wanted to be left to do their own thing.

As the former communist bloc was opened to Western investment and China continued deepening its ties to the world, talk of the new global age grew. Just as the protests to topple East European communism got underway, Francis Fukuyama published an essay that proclaimed the 'end of history', which he said had been attained in the 'unabashed victory of economic and political liberalism' across the globe. The creation of this 'universal and homogeneous state', in which all humanity lived by the same creed, ended the process of evolution towards an end point. Events would still occur, but there would be no progression beyond capitalist liberal democracy. History, in effect, had reached its destination. The secular millennium had been proclaimed.[9] Neoliberal globalisation was thus portrayed not as a policy choice from a menu of several options, but as the unfolding of natural will. In that vein, just as the laws of economics were said to be immutable, globalisation was held to represent the irresistible march of progress. Bill Clinton, one of the first baby-boomers to attain high political office, said:

Globalization is not something we can hold off or turn off. It is the economic equivalent of a force of nature, like wind or water. We can harness wind to fill a sail. We can use water to generate energy. We can work hard to protect people and property from storms and floods. But there is no point in denying the existence of wind or water, or trying to make them go away. The same is true for globalization. We can work to maximize its benefits and minimize its risks, but we cannot ignore it, and it is not going away.[10]

The millennium was about to dawn, and it was about to do so in a way no Christian evangelist or radical prophet had ever imagined possible.

Russia would be one of the first terrains on which this new vision would make its mark. Historians still debate whether a different reform process from what Mikhail Gorbachev had enacted might have renewed Russian communism. We'll never know, because Russian reform went awry. Rather than weaken the Soviet-era bureaucracy, the *nomenklatura*, as Gorbachev had intended it to do, *perestroika* actually strengthened it. Once central controls were lifted, managers were free to operate as independent agents. In an apparent vindication of the neoliberal vision, they then followed their own plans, not those of the government.[11]

So in the autumn of 1991, when Russia's new president, Boris Yeltsin, took the reins of his newly-independent country, he barely had time to toast its freedom before he had to confront the morning's hangover: the economy was collapsing. Gorbachev's partial reforms had lifted price controls but done little to invigorate industry. Inflation, hitherto unknown to Russian consumers weaned on decades of communist price control, bolted like a freed captive. As had happened in 1920s Germany, life savings and pensions evaporated. Farmers, waiting for higher prices, hoarded their grain. Amid the frantic uncertainty of what would come next, the large bureaucracy that had once compelled them to deliver goods to market ceased functioning.[12] The shops were bare, and it was not clear there would be enough bread for Moscow to make it through the approaching winter.

With no plan or vision of his own, Yeltsin turned to Yegor Gaidar, a beefy young economist who looked more like an academic recluse than a revolutionary. Appointing him finance minister, Yeltsin instructed him to do something, and do it fast. In the febrile atmosphere amid the state's near-collapse, Gaidar decided that the only option was to apply the lessons of Chile's neoliberal revolution. Russia had to realign an economy 'distorted' by decades of humans meddling with the laws of economic nature. It, therefore, had to implement shock therapy. The country would not only create a market economy, he decided, it would do it in a matter of months. And for guidance, Gaidar went to the source of free-market thinking. He invited a team of experts from Harvard University, led by Jeffrey Sachs, to fly to Moscow and advise his government on how to implement a crash course of liberalisation.

Despite his relative youth – Sachs was a thirty-something whizz-kid – he was already an old hand at this game, having recently advised the Polish government on its reform. The 'Harvard Boys' would trumpet that it was now they and not the 'Chicago Boys' who were bringing the new gospel to distant lands.[13] However, to anyone other than economists, the supposed disagreements between the two schools appeared like an arcane theological dispute between indistinguishable positions. For the Harvard commandments were much the same as preached by the Chicago Boys in Chile. However, given how all-encompassing the state's role had become in the Russian economy, the shock of the adjustment would be even greater. In rapid succession, price controls were to be lifted, planning would end and the country's entire economic structure – its factories, farms, property, shops and supermarkets, and everything that the Bolsheviks had nationalised in the 1920s and the planning ministry had built up since – would be put on the auction-block for sale to private investors.

Chile had undergone a baptism by fire, but compared with what Russia would experience, it now looked like an afternoon christening in a village church. Prices soared even more. Pensioners and others on fixed incomes sank into poverty. Soldiers on their bases went unpaid. Many either sold their weapons or used them to start lives of crime. Economic output nearly halved in the 1990s and unemployment, unheard of in the Soviet Union, now shot up to 12 per cent as firms ceased operations.[14] Criminal networks, partnering with former senior bureaucrats and some dubious entrepreneurs, wormed their way into the privatisation process.[15] As the *nomenklatura* completed the privatisation of its economic power, most of

Russia's endowment ended up in a small number of hands. Nutrition worsened as food became unaffordable for many. The once-vaunted health system deteriorated sharply. The death toll from hunger, illness and suicide shot up, and in just four years the average life expectancy of a Russian male plummeted from 63.8 years to 57.7 years. Never before, in peacetime, had a developed society experienced such an increase in mortality.[16] In the scale of human suffering, Russia's conversion to a new creed ended up rivalling many of the great religious crusades of the past.

But, Gaidar and his Harvard advisers did create a market economy of sorts. With a small and powerful capitalist oligarchy now able to manipulate the country's politics, they also ensured that the ghost of central planning could never be exhumed in Russia. Everyone who still owned an introductory textbook to the Soviet Union could now throw it in the bin. For their part, while they might at times later look back on communism with nostalgia, Russians would no longer have the option of returning there.

Nor was Russia the only major country to enter the free-market's 'win' column in 1991. As Yegor Gaidar was drafting his plans in Moscow, far to the south, in New Delhi, India's new finance minister was delivering startling news to his prime minister. Manmohan Singh, who had just taken office in a new government and had been given the task of assessing the country's books, revealed that India's state-led economy, which had been slowing for years, had now reached a critical point. The government was so stretched that its foreign reserves could barely cover two weeks' worth of imports. As a result, the country, already on the brink of bankruptcy, was going to miss its upcoming debt payments. That left it two options: default on its debt, or go to the IMF. Singh, an ascetic and soft-spoken Sikh, made it clear to his prime minister what that meant: India would be forced to abandon its model and implement a neoliberal programme of structural adjustment.

Since its independence in 1947, India had served as a test case for government-led economic development. While the former British colony's economy was privately owned, modern India's founders had been sufficiently enamoured of Soviet central-planning they had created a large bureaucracy to guide the young country's development. High tariffs and a complicated system of import quotas sheltered Indian firms from foreign competition, while foreign exchange could be obtained only through a rationing system. Since a firm's success depended all too often on good relations with the government, Indian managers tended to invest lots of time and energy building relations with and lobbying politicians.[17] Government contracts drove much of the economy, and the machinery that allocated them could be lubricated with kickbacks to the ruling party. By investing in politics rather than business, rich Indians and powerful politicians created a 'permit licence raj'[18]. Although the Indian economy hadn't done badly since independence, nor had it done particularly well. The world's second most populous country remained rural, backward and desperately poor. Famine had been eliminated, but most Indians still spent their lives in the villages they had been born in, at the mercy of powerful landlords, often shackled by debt, and with little hope of exit for them or their children.

Neoliberal evangelists said the problem was clear: too much government involvement in the economy. More agnostic economists noted the incongruity of the big-government-means-poor-economy claim, though, pointing to the fact that some of the East Asian 'tigers' – notably South Korea, Taiwan and Singapore – which were still among the world's fastest-growing economies, had if anything more expansive state sectors than India did. They argued that the problem was not big government but *bad* government. As one economist put it, India's planning constituted no more evidence against government economic management 'than a leaky pipe constitutes a general case against water engineering'.[19] But such counsels to moderation didn't get an audience. Singh knew that if he went to the IMF, whose neoliberal priests enjoyed the patronage of the United States, he would get no hearing for a middle course. Meanwhile the Russians, who in earlier days had provided a counterweight to Western pressure, were no longer around to bail anyone out. Telling his prime minister they had no choice but to face 'harsh realities', Singh returned to his office and placed a call to Washington.

After conducting its own examination of India's books, the IMF delivered its instruction. The country had to slash its spending, end subsidies on food and fertiliser, open the economy to more private investment, reduce the state sector, lift trade restrictions and protections on local industry against imports, ease rules on foreign investment, and relax controls on the financial sector. It was the end of an era. In a later speech to the Indian Parliament, where nearly a half-century before Jawaharlal Nehru had proclaimed the country's 'tryst with destiny', Singh quoted Victor Hugo in defence of his programme. 'No power on earth,' he said, 'can stop an idea whose time has come.'[20]

The irony was that Hugo had been speaking of socialism. Singh had just buried it.

With such conquests, neoliberal doctrine achieved a degree of hegemony that had eluded even the Keynesian church, which had never managed to penetrate the communist bloc. Twenty years after neoliberal prophets had won their first converts in Latin America, they were now ready to return home to wage war on Keynesian economics in the homeland that had once rejected them – the West itself. For, despite the rapidity and strength of its advance through the 1980s and early 1990s, neoliberalism enjoyed support across the planet that was a mile wide but an inch deep. Even in Britain and the United States, where the doctrine had secured its first toeholds, opposition remained strong. Among US Democrats and in Britain's Labour Party, the Keynesians retained a hold. More broadly, despite claims on the right that the fall of communism revealed the inevitable superiority of the free market, the future shape of the ex-communist world remained a work in progress. Many observers believed Russian and East European capitalism might end up looking more like Scandinavian social democracy than free-market liberalism. East Asia's state-led 'tigers' were still thriving, suggesting that reports of the managerial state's death were greatly exaggerated. China too, despite privatising more of its economy, was still doing so under strong public guidance. And even in Western Europe, the emerging union appeared to offer a different model, more reminiscent of the nineteenth-century Bismarckian structure of a strong state, with free trade inside its borders, but barriers and subsidies for exports outside. Meanwhile the great architects of the neoliberal revolution had passed their sell by dates. Fire-and-brimstone evangelists who'd railed against statist sin and damnation could now be edged aside for a gentler sort of preacher who sang of the sweetness of neoliberal salvation. The church was ripe for renewal.

It was a hot summer night in 1992 and in Madison Square Garden, the raucous home of the New York Rangers ice hockey team, the delegates to the Democratic National Convention were about to welcome their new presidential nominee, William Jefferson Clinton. The United States was just coming off its twelfth year of Republican government and the Democrats had suffered badly through the previous two elections. Although they still harked back to the New Deal days of Franklin D. Roosevelt, the country had changed a lot since then. Economic modernisation had created a large middle class, which, fearing inflation more than unemployment, had warmed to the neoliberal agenda of both Ronald Reagan and his successor George H.W. Bush. In relative terms, the working class that had once provided so many votes for the Democrats had shrunk. It had then been further beaten back by the economic and political changes of the Reagan years, which slashed membership in the unions that had previously done so much organising for the Democratic Party.

Meanwhile, Bush had started 1992 looking electorally unassailable. Fresh off trouncing Saddam in the Gulf War – when American cruise missiles had pulverised and scattered Iraqi armed forces – he'd begun the year with a job approval rating near 90 per cent. In consequence, many high-profile Democrats, deciding that running for president would be a lost cause that year, chose to sit out the race. The nomination fell into the lap of Bill Clinton, a little-known former governor from Arkansas, a Deep South state among the poorest in the country and which had an image among late-night comedians as a rural backwater filled with banjo-picking hillbillies.

Clinton, though, had something going for him. There had been a short recession the year before and although the economy had resumed growing, employment, as is typical after a recession, still lagged. So with many Americans not yet feeling the recovery, Bush's approval ratings began sinking, until by the summer the two men were neck and neck in the polls. Clinton also had an ace up his sleeve. Saying yes to lower taxes and reduced state spending but no to restrictions on abortion or sexual choice, he retained the economic agenda of neoliberalism but stripped out its social conservatism. Tough on crime and welfare, he produced a new form of neoliberalism that would appeal to the former rebels of his own baby-boomer generation. It was like leaving a barn dance for a nightclub which used the same caterer: no change in the menu, but a totally new style. With a high-powered and independent wife who had famously extolled the baby-boomers' pursuit of 'immediate, ecstatic and penetrating modes of living',[21] and his own reputation for immediate and ecstatic penetrations among Arkansas showgirls, Clinton seemed the very embodiment of Jerry Rubin's ideal new man: liberated, open-minded, out to prosper and enjoy life without the encumberance of moral codes.

All the same, the party mandarins watched nervously as he took the podium that night. Those who had followed his career knew he was capable of stirring oratory, but also long-winded speeches that struggled to find the exit. Clinton, speaking in the softened southern cadences that conveyed a slightly rakish down-home charm, began by declaring the fulfilment of the neoliberal dream. Earlier that spring, Francis Fukuyama had elaborated his argument about the end of history in a book with the same title, in which he had written: 'The end of history would mean the end of wars and bloody revolutions. Agreeing on ends, men would have no large causes for which to fight. They would satisfy their needs through economic activity.'[22] Echoing that triumphalism, Clinton started: 'Free enterprise has triumphed all around the world,' going on to chide Democrats who clung to FDR's New Deal legacy by saying, 'it is time for us to realize that there is not a government program for every problem.' He then gave them a litany of mantras to define his new form of liberalism: 'The old way won't work ... Big bureaucracies have failed ... we need a new approach to government ... A government that is leaner, not meaner; that expands opportunity, not bureaucracy; that understands that jobs must come from growth in a vibrant and vital system of free enterprise,' before finally adding that if he became President, he would 'end welfare as we know it'.

The leftists in the audience sat on their hands. However, Clinton was less anxious to please the old guardians of the party than he was to connect with a new audience. His advisers, who would pin the commandment 'It's the economy, stupid' on the walls of their offices to distil a campaign message that would focus on pocket-book issues, had done their focus-group research carefully. They were certain that, in Broadway parlance, this would play in Peoria.

'Fat Pope, skinny Pope' goes an old Italian saying. Used to describe the tendency of the Catholic Church to follow a pope who makes a big splash with one who quietly consolidates the changes announced by his predecessor, it also serves as a nice summary of the 'high neoliberalism' that Clinton offered his country. Pinochet's repression of communists, Thatcher's diatribes and Reagan's military build-up had all hastened the end of socialism. With the job done, it was now time to consolidate the free-market revolution. That meant smoothing some of the rougher and less appealing edges of the free-market catechism, while purging it of its inconsistencies and contradictions. What resulted was a doctrine that mirrored the neoclassical thought becoming increasingly dominant in economics departments: individualistic, utility seeking, keen to roll back government and deregulate markets, and with a faith that entrepreneurship and not social crusades would solve the problems of injustice.

The vision Clinton gave his audience that night in New York was, in effect, a restoration of the classical economic gospel. He argued that it was important to build a better society, but the way to do this was not through sacrifice in the service of others. On the contrary, the way to raise up deprived communities was by pursuing profit in them, and creating jobs for poor people. Seeing poverty as less threat than opportunity, he advised corporate investors to 'treat neglected parts of America as untapped markets and invest in them just as they invest in foreign countries in the developing world'.[23] Equally, despite the well-documented links between economic growth and environmental decline,[24] Clinton maintained that America could, effectively, shop its way to a cleaner, greener future. Insisting that 'environmental preservation will make people richer',[25] he said that prosperity would lead to technological innovation, which would in turn save the environment. The vision he offered, in effect, was of a neoliberal *deus ex machina*: look after yourself, and the neoliberal economy will look after everyone else. The invisible hand postulated by Adam Smith and turned into an article of faith by the marginal revolution now found its purest expression.

The faith of Clinton's campaign managers in the marketability of their message was vindicated in the 1992 election. It *did* play well in Peoria, and Americans made Clinton the 42nd President of the United States. Soon after taking office, he signalled he really was a 'New Democrat' when he signed the North American Free Trade Agreement (NAFTA) that President Bush had recently negotiated with Mexico and Canada. The unions, worried that free trade with Mexico would encourage firms to set up on the other side of the border to lower wage costs, had opposed the agreement. Clinton said it would raise growth and thereby create jobs. And he also said he would boost public investment to kick-start employment, though soon after taking office the Keynesians on his team were shunted aside in favour of 'deficit hawks', chief among them Robert Rubin, a banker who would later become his Treasury Secretary. He emphasised to Clinton one cardinal rule – keep Wall Street happy. Rubin and Fed Chairman Alan Greenspan would set the tone of the Clinton years as the president's most trusted economic advisers. Clinton indicated to his staff that under his watch the government would play a modest role by saying 'we're all Eisenhower Republicans'.[26]

Subsequently, after the Republicans took control of Congress in the 1994 elections, Clinton worked with them to reduce the welfare budget, limiting its coverage and directing recipients back onto the job market. Then, for every dollar he cut in welfare spending, he put $1.10 into building prisons, with the convenient result that he could claim to have reduced black welfare dependence and unemployment (without mentioning that, in effect, he'd done it by locking up unemployed black men).[27] He cut taxes, eliminated the deficit and deregulated the financial industry. He helped make it easier for low-income people to get mortgages by pressing the federal mortgage-issuance agencies to ease their eligibility requirements. Despite speaking eloquently of the need to assist Third World development; he cut foreign aid while in trade negotiations with poor countries his administration drove hard bargains.

With such actions, both large and small, Clinton helped undo the legacy of the man who until then had been the patron-saint of the Democratic Party, Franklin D. Roosevelt. 'F.D.R.'s mission was to save capitalism from its own excesses,' Clinton once said, echoing Ronald Reagan. 'Our mission has been to save government from its own excesses.'[28] Perhaps the most lasting reversal of this earlier legacy came in Clinton's repeal of the Glass–Steagall Act. Back in the depths of the 1930s Great Depression, FDR had signed the Act to prevent there ever being another stock-market crash. The Act had separated investment and commercial banking, thereby stopping retail banks from taking their depositors' money and putting them into riskier but potentially more lucrative stock-market investments. When in 1999 Clinton repealed the Act, the banks' traders rushed to the stock exchange. When the head of the Commodity Futures Trading Commission warned that they were making risky investments with their depositors' money, Clinton's Deputy Treasury Secretary, Lawrence Summers, pushed her out of the administration.[29]

By then, the stock market was surging and everyone wanted in on the action. Traditionally, rich Americans had invested in shares and ordinary Americans had put their money into savings accounts at their local banks. But now, in a swelling tide, small investors withdrew their money from bank accounts and sank them into mutual funds. The number of shareholders quadrupled during Clinton's presidency, and the assets they put into stock-market mutual funds increased twenty-four times over.[30]

Although Clinton would credit America's new golden age to the New Democrat creed he had brought America, in fact, the American economy was then benefiting from a couple of favourable tailwinds. With Saddam bottled up in Iraq and American, British and French aircraft patrolling the skies to ensure he didn't try to relaunch any moves on Kuwait, the oil kept flowing freely out of the Persian Gulf. Energy prices fell to historic lows in the 1990s. So too did other prices. Back during the 1992 election, the independent candidate Ross Perot had warned that if NAFTA went ahead, it would create a 'vast sucking sound' as manufacturers packed up and left for Mexico, taking the jobs with them. The 'out-sourcing' boom that had begun back in the Reagan years, as manufacturers took advantage of increasingly open trade and cheaper transportation costs, picked up speed in the 1990s, and jobs did leave. However, many of them went not to Mexico but to China, which grew more open to business. Although American workers, especially unskilled workers, lost out, middle-class consumers – which, after all, was the constituency on which Clinton was building his New Democratic coalition – were able to buy lots of cheap products. Cheap products, in turn, meant low inflation. Low inflation meant consumers could spend their incomes on other things, and spend they did. It also meant lower interest rates, which made it cheaper to borrow. Americans were able to buy more stuff for the same amount of credit, since their interest charges dropped, and they were also able to put money to work in the stock market.

With more money to spend in shopping centres, bars, restaurants and hotels, therefore, Americans drove an expansion in the service sector. At least for the time being, the jobs lost to China were replaced. Because store workers and fast-food counter attendants earned less than factory workers, average wages fell, so for most of the 1990s real earnings continued the long stagnation that had begun at the start of the 1980s. At the same time, the increased profits that resulted from the outsourcing boom and wage-repression drove up CEO compensation, with the result that inequality kept worsening. With firm managers able to avoid confronting unions by threatening to move offshore, organised labour was further weakened and its membership rolls continued thinning. Beneath the surface of the 1990s boom, Clinton's faith that the pursuit of profit would enrich everyone lacked solid evidence to support it.

Nevertheless, little of this was apparent yet in the headline figures. Faith in the new message of salvation was, if anything, growing. Since loans were cheaper, people could run up debts and live grandly. That's because, if they had bought into the stock market and housing booms, when they opened their bank statements each month, they found themselves richer than they had been the previous month. True, it left the fortunes of ordinary people hostage to a constantly rising stock market, and old hands warned this was a dangerous gamble; the billionaire investor Warren Buffett famously said, 'you only find out who is swimming naked when the tide goes out'.[31] Yet Buffett, who was then pushing seventy, seemed increasingly out of touch with the energetic new faith. At a time when the Internet was taking off and twenty-something web entrepreneurs were becoming overnight billionaires, his old-fashioned buy-and-hold fund was underperforming. As inflation and interest rates ignored the old economic laws, staying low amid rising growth, and as the American economy seemed to defy the laws of gravity, commentators on the increasingly ubiquitous business television channels, egged on by the administration,[32] declared that the 1990s had ushered in a 'new paradigm' in which the old laws of economics had been superseded. This cornucopia of riches, they told their viewers, was never going to end: the Dow Jones Index, which had been hovering around 4,000 at mid-decade, doubled over the next four years. The pundits of the new age saw no end in sight. Books with titles like *Dow 36,000* told how the new creed had delivered Americans a prosperity no previous faith had ever imagined.

Inspired by this apparent triumph of high neoliberalism, socialist parties elsewhere began reworking their old orthodoxies. Tony Blair took over and then rebranded the British Labour Party as 'New Labour' and promised his would be a 'Cool Britannia'. Surrounded by like-minded individuals who saw the party's political future in the middle rather than the working class – one of them mimicking Richard Nixon's earlier confession of economic faith by declaring 'we are all Thatcherites now'[33] – Blair led the erstwhile socialist party out of its two-decade political journey in the wilderness and back into power in the 1997 election. Although he did not share Clinton's fixation on small government, instead raising taxes to expand public services, he did lead the party's repeal of the clause supporting nationalisation, and did not reverse Margaret Thatcher's earlier limitations on union power. He thereby made it clear that free markets were here to stay. Moreover, he did share Clinton's faith that free trade and globalisation were necessarily forces for good, and echoed his American colleague's approach to crime by declaring himself 'tough on crime, tough on the causes of crime'. He also, as Clinton had done, dispensed with Thatcherite moralism and took a liberal approach to social issues, most notably on gay rights. Above all, during his time in office he aligned government with neoliberal principles: granting the central bank independence, making government more of a partner than a guide to business, delivering public services with market efficiency.

Similarly, in Germany, Gerhard Schroeder led the Social Democratic Party into the neoliberal temple under the mantle of a 'third way' and watched with equanimity as the party's old working-class left stormed out to create their own party. Schroeder would later go on to engineer a painful restructuring of the German economy: cuts in taxes and public services, a rollback of pensions and unemployment benefits, and a new unemployment regime which mirrored Clinton's welfare reform in pushing recipients to find jobs. Elsewhere, left-leaning governments were quietly proceeding with neoliberal policies, helping further consolidate the triumph of the new doctrine. With the Soviet experiment buried, with China freeing its markets, with the Third World having been converted to the free-market gospel in the earlier wave of structural adjustment, and with Western socialist parties turning neoliberal, the 1990s would be the decade that seemed to finally vindicate Margaret Thatcher's 'TINA' commandment – There Is No Alternative.

About the only holdouts in which the state maintained a strong presence in the economy – other than North Korea, whose reaction to the collapse of global communism seemed to be to freeze itself in red amber – were the East Asian tigers. Nevertheless, they were a thorn in the side of neoliberal evangelists. Their continued strong economic performance, leading the world in most growth indicators, apparently showed the falsity of the neoliberal claim of being the one true gospel. They thus provided hope and succour to the few remaining dissidents at the margins of economics departments, who clung doggedly to their Keynesian and statist faiths. Nevertheless, the missionaries of the new paradigm were about to seize the East Asian pulpit as well.

One effect of America's widening inequality was that the rich had more money to invest. Meanwhile, given the deregulation of the financial industry, they were able to move more of their money into the 'shadow' financial sector, where fund-managers could ignore government rules and seek out more lucrative, if riskier, opportunities. The managers of hedge funds, private investment firms that pooled the capital of rich investors, were always looking for new investment opportunities to juice their returns. The spread of the Internet in the 1990s and the continued advance of globalisation, in particular the outsourcing boom, were creating new opportunities for foreign investment in 'emerging markets' – the 1990s buzzwords for the Third World.

For a long time, the biggest rewards, in those fast-moving East Asian countries, had lain beyond the reach of Western investors; governments there had maintained a tight control over investment and foreign exchange markets and limited what outsiders could buy. However, early in the decade, the IMF had successfully prodded East

Asia's governments to try at least a taste of the neoliberal wine by lifting currency controls and thereby opening their markets to foreigners. They pointed to other countries that had taken their advice, like Mexico and Turkey, and which had experienced investment surges as a result. Besides, East Asian governments were told, such a move would enable them to sell their bonds on Western exchanges, where they could take advantage of low interest rates, while leaving the local savings pool to their private business sector. In the new, ultra-epicurean language of high neoliberalism, it was a 'win-win'.

Once the controls were lifted, money rushed in, just as the IMF had predicted would happen. The East Asian boom sped up even more. This sip of the neoliberal chalice left a sweet taste in everyone's mouth, and was brandished as yet another testament to the truth of the free-market gospel.[34] But there was one small problem. As all this new money chased stocks, bonds and real estate, the value of East Asian assets surged. Consumers in these countries enjoyed this 'wealth effect', which sent them flocking to Seoul's and Bangkok's shopping centres and thus accelerated their growth. But demand for East Asian assets, and particularly property, drove up prices. This encouraged developers to erect buildings, even if there was no need for them and they stood empty upon completion, simply because they could flip them to the next investor eager to get in on the boom. Worst of all, since foreigners coming into these markets had to change their money into local currency before they could go shopping for property or stocks, demand for cash drove up its value. With the Korean won and Thai baht growing dearer by the day, it also became more expensive for foreigners to buy the goods coming out of the countries' factories or off the countries' farms.[35]

Early in 1997, investors in Thailand could see a storm was gathering. In Bangkok, construction cranes filled the skyline and shoppers, many of them poor villagers who had come to the city to take construction jobs, filled the shopping centres. However, the export revenues underpinning the economy weren't keeping up, since the overvalued currencies were making them too expensive, all while the high cost of property drove up business costs. Sooner or later, everyone was going to realise that this was a gambler's game, and pull out. Sure enough, as soon as investors began detecting signs of a slowdown in the real economy, they took advantage of their new freedom to move their cash around the planet. Quietly, they began selling their Asian assets and depositing the proceeds into American, British and Swiss accounts, keeping their money safe until the storm passed. Once they offloaded their Thai investments, the bhat came under pressure as they rushed to change them. The government tried to preserve its value by selling off its dollar reserves and buying the currency. But that just encouraged more selling, and in the summer the baht crashed. Hedge-fund managers then panicked, and stampeded for the exits.

Keen to make up their losses, fund managers began selling their other East Asian assets. As a result, the panic radiated outwards from Thailand. In 1998, as contagion gripped the region, the foreign exchange markets were flooded with East Asian currencies. Their plunging value then drove inflation sharply upwards. The shopping centres emptied, the construction workers went home and the economies sank. At the same time, with everyone now selling assets, property values plummeted. Banks with property on their books found their asset portfolios sharply reduced and faced insolvency. Equally, as foreign investors tried to unload the bonds they had bought from both governments and private firms, their value fell too, which meant the effective rate of interest went up. Governments and private companies that had borrowed cheaply on the New York and London bond exchanges now had to pay much higher interest charges, which further worsened their financial position.

East Asian economies were fulfilling the ancient rule – that what goes up must eventually come back down. Economies growing at 9 per cent or 10 per cent came to a halt and unemployment rose just as the cost of living went up. By the summer of 1998, the shock waves from the East Asian epicentre were rolling outwards. The private investment funds that had burned their fingers in East Asia and needed to make up losses now started dumping *all* their emerging-market holdings. On the way out, they didn't bother treating each country on its merits any more than they had on the way in: if it was emerging, it was now submerging, and they wanted no more to do with it. Stock markets from Brazil to Moscow began plummeting. Come the autumn, the panic even reached the New York stock market: major funds that had lost money reported their losses, and investors began selling off shares there as well.

With governments everywhere running to the International Monetary Fund for assistance, the scale of the demand exceeded the IMF's resources. Meanwhile, few countries were in a position to help swell its coffers. The European economy, still hampered by the bill Germany had to pay for reuniting East and West Germany after the 1989 fall of the Berlin Wall, was not strong. Russia, which had only just resurfaced from its punishing post-communist collapse, had now fallen back. President Boris Yeltsin, who had dismissed his government as the stock market collapsed and interest rates approached 150 per cent, had been reduced to phoning Bill Clinton and begging him to use his leverage at the IMF to rescue his country. Thus, only the United States could now stave off a possible global recession, one which might conceivably expose neoliberalism as a false creed. Similar to the position that had temporarily resulted from the Second World War, when the United States had last stood as the sole superpower on top of the world, it now found itself in a position of being able to determine the future course of the planet's economies.

In the autumn of 1998, Bill Clinton persuaded Congress to lend the IMF enough money to enable it to rescue all these countries. But, he promised, America would get its pound of flesh. His deputy Treasury secretary, Lawrence Summers, would go through all the rescue packages the IMF put together line by line and ensure the neoliberal vision prevailed. Faced with the sort of massive capital flight then roiling through emerging markets, one obvious temptation for any government was to impose capital controls, limiting how much money could be taken from the country. But Summers would have none of it. He would only approve IMF assistance to countries that left their capital markets open. Unusually, the Clinton administration also used the exceptionally weak bargaining position of besieged governments to wade into areas not normally in the IMF purview. Whereas the Fund normally looked only at a government's finances in determining what should be cut, Summers looked at their entire policy framework, requiring them not only to balance their books but to open their markets to US exports.[36]

Such micromanagement, and the punitive demands that worsened social conditions in recipient countries, created alarm not only in their capitals but even within Washington. In a celebrated and, for the White House, embarrassing intervention, the chief economist at the World Bank, the future Nobel laureate (and former Clinton adviser) Joseph Stiglitz slammed US policy, saying its harsh conditions were exacerbating the Asian crisis. This was beyond the pale for Summers. Having helped to save the neoliberal temple from a major crisis, he wasn't now going to tolerate such heresy. Known in Washington as a fiercely intelligent workaholic who could barely contain his disdain for those he considered his intellectual inferiors, Summers used his leverage over the World Bank to have Stiglitz fired.[37]

One country that paid the price, forgoing IMF assistance so that it could impose currency controls, was Malaysia. In its overall performance during and after the crisis, it did no worse, and possibly even better, than its neighbours who drank from the IMF's chalice.[38] Had the application of neoliberal policy been a scientific experiment, therefore, the results would have been inconclusive. But as a theological exercise, the rescue plan concocted by the Clinton administration was a resounding triumph. Clinton wasn't asking those who had placed faith in him that summer night in 1992, when Democrats had taken a gamble and selected a neoliberal to be their presidential candidate, to be judged by what he was doing in poor countries. His creed would be judged by the fruits it yielded at home. And there, like a faith healer who commands lame people to walk away from their wheelchairs, he had apparently raised a mighty economy.

Following a moment of hesitation amid the Asian crisis, the American economy now roared even louder. The late 1990s boom would take the United States to unprecedented heights of prosperity. But, like many an apparent miracle, the drama onstage obscured the prosaic tricks going on behind the conjuror's veil. Having insisted that governments the IMF helped couldn't close their capital accounts, the Clinton administration had ensured the taps stayed open. And so, in their stampede for the exits, investors continued to leave the Third World, an effect intensified after their economies sank into the recessions that Joseph Stiglitz and other dissidents blamed the IMF for making worse.[39] Developing countries had gone from attracting an inflow of about $90 billion a year before the crisis to now shipping over $200 billion a year into the safe haven of the United States.[40] In effect, therefore, the American economy was getting a transfusion from the Third World equivalent to nearly 2 per cent of GDP. It was like plying someone who has high blood pressure with free coffee. The economy took off, the per capita growth rate surpassing 3 per cent at the end of the decade.

Asian money was generally used to buy US bonds. They were considered safe, and safety was what shaken investors wanted more than anything else. Increased demand for bonds thus drove up their prices. Since rising bond prices meant declining yields, interest rates fell. This effect had been further intensified by the Federal Reserve Board's response to the falling stock market in 1998, when it had cut interest rates. Meanwhile, the rush into US securities had heightened demand for the dollar, augmenting its value. A more expensive dollar meant that US consumers could buy more foreign goods with the same amount of money, adding to the dampening effect on global prices caused by Third World recessions. Thus, not only did Americans get virtually free money, what they could buy with it got cheaper.

Ordinarily, during a boom the Federal Reserve raised interest rates to prevent the economy overheating. But now, given that prices remained tame, it stood pat, leaving interest rates where they were. With interest rates low, investors bought shares, which drove up their value. Since Americans could now borrow for next to zero but invest in stocks that were rising annually by double digits, they lived on credit and rode the boom. Mutual funds swelled with cash, and the stock market rose yet further.

One February morning in 2000, while they were driving to work, Americans heard that the country had just recorded its 106th month of consecutive growth, a new record. Later that day, President Clinton was beaming when he strode up to the podium in the East Room of the White House for a press conference. By now, Third World cities were burning amid riots, as the austerity demanded by IMF rescue packages hit ordinary citizens. But these images were far from the minds of the White House press corps as Clinton addressed them, sounding like a revivalist preacher testifying to his god's blessings. 'We're in the midst of the longest and strongest economic expansion in our history,' he told the reporters, going through a laundry-list of what that meant: '21 million new jobs, unemployment at 4 percent, and solid income growth across all income groups.' At these rates of growth, he added, the American government would be out of debt in thirteen years. It would be the first time that had happened since 1835, when Andrew Jackson was in the White House and people moved around in stagecoaches. Within weeks, the Dow Jones stock-market index crossed the 10,000 mark for the first time in history. By the summer, it had already leapt past the 11,000 mark.

And the people cried Amen. Even for a steamy southern town like Washington, that summer was hot. The terraces of the bars and cafes along the Potomac river burst with patrons. At happy hour, they spent generously on new friends and watched the business channels on the televisions where pundits, asked when the stock market would stop setting new highs, would confidently reply, 'Never'. This, they said, was the 'Goldilocks economy', a perfect mix of high growth, full employment and low inflation. Georgetown's restaurants, packed early, stayed full until late. On weekends, the city's shopping centres thronged with people queuing for the latest gadgets – high-definition televisions, home theatre systems, mobile phones. They walked past bookshops whose windows brimmed with titles on how to play the market and get rich. The bestseller that summer was a book that

celebrated the 'rational exuberance' of small investors who, ignoring 'the outdated model that Wall Street has used to assess whether
stocks are overvalued' were rushing into the market by signing up
on the new Internet trading platforms. College dropouts registered
websites and then flipped them for huge profits, retiring to lives of
untold riches.

The Clinton administration had said that neoliberal faith and the
miracles of technology would solve everything and the historic boom
stood as evidence. The information age, the president assured his
people, had so revolutionised labour productivity that the economy
could now grow more or less endlessly, making everyone rich, while
keeping inflation and interest rates low. 'You *can* have it all' might
have been the epicurean motto of those years, and there seemed to
be no downside at all.

Not in America, at any rate. At least, not yet.

CHAPTER 19

MAGIC AND THE MILLENNIUM

At the beginning of the Reformation, Martin Luther dispensed with priestly authority, saying everyone had to find their own way to God. Although Luther made his peace with the secular authorities, others went the other way, taking his principle to its logical extreme. Stressing the equality of souls before God, the Anabaptists – so named because they said the saved had to be re-baptised in the new true faith – aimed to recapture a purified Christianity. With a goal of recreating the communism of the early Christian communities, some of them believed the apocalyptic prophecies at the end of the Bible were about to be fulfilled in their own time. A few went so far as to dig in, waiting for the Second Coming of Christ.

In 1533, a north German town named Münster joined the Lutheran fold. Since the surrounding region remained Catholic, Anabaptists were being persecuted, so many fled to take refuge in Münster. One group of them, led by a radical preacher, rejected the pacifism common to Anabaptists and said it was the duty of the oppressed to fight evil. He told them that Christ was about to return to the city, which had to prepare itself by abandoning its wicked ways. As he whipped his followers into frenzies of expectation with passionate sermons, crowds of people came to the city, preparing themselves for the millennium. Eventually they overwhelmed the local population, and in 1534 they took control of the city. They

seized all private property, tore down churches and restored polyg-
amy. Then they requisitioned all the food they could find and put
it in common stores. Expecting the rapture at any moment, they
didn't bother to keep working in their shops or on their farms, and
the economy ground to a halt.[1]

By then, troops led by the local bishop had surrounded the city
and begun a siege. As the supply of food from the surrounding countryside dwindled, conditions inside the city worsened. When their
leader was killed in a military sortie against the bishop's forces, it
might have seemed the game was up. However, two of the leader's
closest associates hatched a plan to bolster the people's faith (while
also improving their own lot). One of them, claiming to be descended
from the biblical David, said that eight days before his murder, their
fallen leader had appeared to him in a vision – his body sliced open,
an armed man standing next to him saying not to fear, he would be
appointed the successor. His associate, who was given to feverish
bursts of madness during which he had visions, then confirmed that
the 'King' had told him of this conversation at the time it happened.

Having invested their lives in this new faith, Münster's militants
were no doubt prepared to receive this prophecy, verified as it was by
an eyewitness. Had they been in a more sceptical mood, they would
have seen how flimsy the claim was. But this was a time for faith,
not doubt, and instead they cried, 'Oh, Father, give, give,' and began
dancing in celebration, the men drawing their swords for battle, the
women letting their hair down and baring themselves to the waist
as they sought to return to the innocent nudity of Eden.[2]

To further bolster their faith, the self-declared prophet announced
that a heavenly trumpet would blast three times to announce the
moment when the city's faithful should assemble. At that point, they
would pass freely through the surrounding armies and head to Zion.
When the moment came, it was the prophet himself who blew the
trumpet.[3] By then, the crowd, delirious with hunger and desperate
for salvation, were ready for the millennium. When they left the
city, though, they were cut to pieces by the bishop's soldiers and the
Münster dream died.

Such has been the tale of many a millennial frenzy throughout history. The setting, characters and beliefs change, but the plot remains the same. In the face of immovable reality, faith can lead people to seemingly superhuman tasks – and in the process reinforcing their faith, which is further bolstered by an apparent miracle here or confirmed prophecy there. Inevitably reality intrudes and as the end draws nearer, the religious expressions grow more outrageous, the faux miracles more desperate, until everything dissolves.

As the planet approached a real millennium at the end of the twentieth century, a similar drama was about to unfold in the United States.

How wondrous things seemed in 1999. That year, the gap between the rich countries of the West and the poor countries of the developing world reached its widest point in history. The handful of countries at the heart of the former European empires then consumed four-fifths of global output.[4] On average, workers in the West earned fifty times what their counterparts in the poorest countries did.[5] A new theory in economics departments, called endogenous growth theory, credited the West's technological superiority for this, and suggested that the gap would remain permanent. In his speeches on the roaring US economy, now growing at a pace last seen during the Reagan years, President Clinton lionised the Internet revolution for having inaugurated an age of endless growth. He announced that the federal government would now be running budget surpluses 'as far as the eye can see', then started his Christmas wish list. 'Save Social Security first,' he told Congress, urging it to strengthen the pension system before it went on to dish out other goodies.[6]

His eyes filled with the wonders of the new age, Clinton joined many tech visionaries in imagining all the new shores they'd discover – winning the war on cancer, starting a revolution against 'all deadly diseases', children who were now going to live into the twenty-second century, an environment that was cleaned up once and for all. He was just getting started. Because if the American economy really had found the elixir of youth, the secret formula that would enable it to renew itself endlessly into the future, that future would know no bounds. The euphoria of his homilies, the same euphoria that thrummed in the stock market every morning as the indexes hit new highs, bespoke the miracle underway.

For this new economy had apparently healed America of a terminal disease. Although it wasn't clear why, evidence had been accumulating that until the 1990s productivity growth had been slowing in the West and had been doing so for decades.[7] Moreover, the baby-boomers who had provided the abundant labour supply of the post-Second World War boom were ageing, and hadn't replaced their ranks with anywhere near the same relish for procreation their parents had shown. That meant the supply of extra workers to drive expanded output was not there as it had been after the war. Meanwhile the 'low-hanging fruit' of earlier productivity surges had all been picked. For example, the expansion of primary education in the Industrial Age had led to phenomenal increases in output, but with the population now educated, the returns on schooling diminished with each added year. Giving everyone college degrees was expensive, but did little for output if the graduates were doing jobs that had previously been done, almost as well, by high-school graduates.[8] As a result of this confluence of factors, underlying growth in the economy had been trending downwards across the West since the 1960s, and the United States had been no exception. In the 1960s, the country's per capita output had grown at an annual average rate of over 3 per cent per year; by the end of the 1980s that annual average had fallen below 1 per cent.[9]

But then, rather suddenly, productivity turned back upwards in the 1990s. Some economists were sceptical that anything significant or durable was going on: labour productivity was notoriously difficult to measure and more cautious scholars, for whom one or two swallows didn't make a summer, wanted to see a long-term change before they believed the prophet. But some researchers, with enthusiastic backing from the Clinton administration, began subscribing to the 'new paradigm' theory that was becoming ubiquitous on the business television channels. This new school of thought suggested the information revolution was reshaping the economy as profoundly as the telegraph, electricity and internal combustion engine had once done, thereby raising labour productivity to new levels. As a result, they said, the economy would grow at much faster rates than the historical norm and generate far higher incomes without raising the spectre of inflation.[10] Complementing the purported effect of new technology, it was argued, was the globalisation of trade and investment, which would create ultra-competitive markets and prompt further investments in productivity-raising education. 'What you earn depends upon what you learn,' Clinton said, a new commandment to replace the old belief that everyone was entitled to a job.[11] A few brave souls went so far as to suggest that with the economy operating with hyper-efficiency, the business cycle had become a thing of the past and the happy days need never end.[12]

This raised the possibility that the ancient and universal rules of economics were being changed through technology and neoliberalism. As miracles went, it would be hard to beat. Except that we'd heard this sort of thing before. In truth, minus the bloodshed, the late 1990s boom and the suspension of the old rules could have been drawn from the Münster tale: faith against facts, greased with the odd faked miracle or two. Behind the conjuror's veil, something quite different explained the soaring markets, rising incomes and tame inflation of the late 1990s – something a good deal less poetic than President Clinton's speeches.

Imagine you hadn't been born into what Warren Buffett called the lucky sperm club. And instead you were one of humanity's majority, born in a poor country – living in somewhere not far from America like Spanish Town or Kingston in Jamaica in the 1990s.

Suppose also that you were born into a typical working-class family – your mother a cook, or a housekeeper, your father a migrant labourer abroad. You were good at school and worked hard, spending your afternoons in the small public library to find an oasis of calm from the endless cacophony of the inner city while you pursued your dreams – getting to university, getting a good job, raising your family out of the ghetto. So the day the letter came from the university offering you a place was one of the happiest of your life.

But afterwards when you read through the admission package, you noticed the tuition fees had soared since the year before, far beyond what your family could afford. When you visited the university to ask why, you were told they had to raise their fees because the government had reduced its subsidy. However, they said you could get a loan, and directed you to the bank on the campus. You headed straight there, got an information pack, then discovered you needed a guarantor for the loan. If your parents owned their house, or had salaried jobs, you would qualify. But they had neither. You were on your own.

You knew then what it was to have seen the promised land, only to have it disappear. But you were determined not to lose hope. You told yourself that if you got a job, you could put aside money each month to save up for tuition money. You went to see your Member of Parliament, but he said that government cuts left few jobs for high-school graduates. With the economy in a funk, about the only companies then hiring people without degrees were security firms, so he sent you to one of his constituents.

You got a job manning the gate outside an office building. The hours were long – about seventy hours a week with double shifts. If you lived on rice and the occasional tin of corned beef, stayed at home in the cramped hot room you shared with your younger brother and never went out, you estimated you might be able to set aside $60 to $70 a month. After a couple of years, you might be able to cover your first year of tuition – after which you hoped your academic performance might win you some kind of scholarship for the rest of your degree. 'I will do this,' you said.

The work was hard. You left home before dawn after a quick breakfast of corn-meal porridge and tea, walked half a mile to the bus stop and another half a mile at the other end, hardly proud of your uniform but determined to maintain your dignity, and worked all day guarding the gate to the office building. Staff and especially visitors ignored and sometimes even abused you – you were, after all, just a guard, whose high-school education meant nothing to them. But you kept telling yourself that one day you'd be working in one of the air-conditioned offices inside. And as time went by your pool of savings grew. You started pulling out the university calendar you had kept by your bed, and started imagining your future once more.

Then one day you came home to find your younger sister in tears. You got her to confide in you. It turned out she had been raped some time ago and recently had found out she had contracted HIV as a result. She was afraid your mother would put her on the street. You told her you'd keep her secret. Taking her to a clinic, you sent her in to see the doctor, who explained that the only treatment for her condition was a hugely expensive combination of drugs. There was a much cheaper generic option, he added, but it wasn't available in Jamaica because the American government had blocked imports of the drugs to protect the patents of its own producers. So you promised your sister you would do everything in your power to care for her.

That night you retrieved all your savings but it was only enough to buy a few months of medication. After that, only a miracle could save her. But you couldn't bring yourself to break the promise you had made her and you would stay a security guard. And, once your money ran out, barring that life-saving miracle, your sister would be dead while you were still young.

Your little television set, with its cable box – the one thing in Jamaica that didn't seem expensive – set to the American network. And you watched the news, and as you did so you saw the US President boasting that thanks to good government policies and the miracles of technology, Americans were living in the most prosperous time in history, and that one day they would cure all diseases.

What might you have said? What might you have done?

In reality, Clinton's boasting that technology and 'the smallest government in 35 years' was behind the boom was a bit like an ancient priest, able to read stars and predict weather, performing a rite to make it seem like he was a rain-maker. The boom was only ever going to be temporary, and it was apparent to those looking at the

data that it was already in its late stages. Nor did it have anything
to do with the Internet. Yes, the new invention was changing our
lives radically. Even as Clinton spoke, people around the world were
following the gossip about his alleged affair with an intern on the
new blogs and news feeds (many of them steered there by the porn
websites that were multiplying with equal rapidity[13]). But the short-
lived productivity boost in America didn't last long, and by the end
of the decade the long downward trend resumed. The brief reversal
may, in fact, have had less to do with the technology of the future
than the management practices of the past.[14] Mobile phones allowed
our employers to monitor us like we were in a panopticon and keep
us working on the bus ride home.[15] The truth is that nobody could
provide really compelling evidence that the Internet had in any way
boosted productivity, confirming the famous quip of one Nobel
laureate that 'You can see the computer age everywhere but in the
productivity statistics.'[16]

No, there was something much simpler going on. It was that for a
brief time at the end of the century, things in the First World got so
good because things in the Third World got very bad. The American
toasting his swelling share-statement had to thank not the neoliberal
priests of the new age, but the Jamaican dreamer confronting a life
of shattered hopes.

Across much of the developing world, as the recessions caused
by the Asian crisis and aggravated by IMF austerity took hold,
conditions deteriorated. In Indonesia in 1998, after the IMF ended
subsidies, food prices rose by 80 per cent, leading to riots.[17] Protesters
clogged the streets of Jakarta for months, engaged in running battles
with the police, and ultimately toppled the government. That year, 80
million Indonesians, some 40 per cent of the population, fell below
the poverty line.[18] In Russia, it was nearly half who did so (even in
the Soviet period dismissed as 'dismal' by neoliberal missionaries in
the country, the poverty rate had remained in the low single digits).[19]
Anger at IMF programmes led to national strikes in Bangladesh,
Peru, the Dominican Republic, El Salvador, Colombia, Ecuador,
Burkina Faso, Pakistan and Romania. Anti-austerity protests turned

violent in Haiti, Chile and Côte d'Ivoire. Public-sector workers shut down the government in Brazil, Honduras, Jamaica, Guyana and Zimbabwe, while there were transportation lockdowns in Argentina, Ecuador and Nicaragua. In China, Argentina, Mexico and South Africa, slowing or contracting economies, rising unemployment and widening incomes drove up crime rates.[20] The rich in the Third World grew poorer and the poor grew desperate. As angry mobs went looking for scapegoats, ethnic riots erupted[21] and thousands of Chinese had to flee Indonesia.[22]

It was thus hardly surprising that, amid the economic haemor-rhage and consequent instability, anyone with a nest egg to protect joined the exodus into US dollars. Like an hourglass turned upside down, what resulted was a brief but sharp transfer of money from one part of the world to the other. Prior to the Asian crisis, the developing world, led by East Asia, had started to reverse the centuries-long divergence between itself and the West. As the Third World's economic growth rates began to pick up and eventually over-take those of the West, capital poured in, while Western investors kept their money at home. Between the start of the decade and 1997, the ratio of per capita GDP in the West to per capita GDP in low and middle-income countries had narrowed from about 27:1 to 23:1,[23] reflecting the dramatic gains that had been made particularly in East Asia. However, once the Asian-crisis bailouts deepened the reces-sions and prised the money gates open, that progress was reversed. At the peak of the American boom, as Bill Clinton was telling his compatriots that the American government would be eternally flush with cash, that ratio of per-capita incomes between rich and poor countries had bounced back up to nearly 26:1.

In effect, the American economy was sucking in hundreds of billions of dollars, enabling Americans to enjoy one last great party. Prior to the Asian crisis, the world economy had been growing by about $600 billion a year, with a rising share of that annual incre-ment coming from the Third World.[24] The Asian crisis interrupted this growth, inducing a short global recession in 1997. However, when in the following year the world economy got back on its feet, there was a striking change in the distribution of its fruits. Amid capital flight, the economies of the Third World continued con- tracting and incomes continued falling. The result was that the rich countries of the West, briefly interrupting the long-term trend of Third World development, captured all the added income produced by the growing world economy – the United States alone raking in three quarters of the new growth.[25] The vast sucking sound Ross Perot had predicted back during the 1992 election campaign, when he'd warned against the free-trade agreement Bill Clinton was about to sign with Mexico, was real enough. But it wasn't American jobs going south of the Rio Grande that made it; it was the torrent of Third World money coming into New York. Americans were literally feasting as millions across the Third World starved. In fact, they were feasting *because* the Third World starved. Rather than a new paradigm, what drove the US boom was the oldest imperial effect of all: a fillip from the periphery.

But there was one crucial difference. Earlier episodes in which the periphery had helped drive the expansion of the imperial motherland, like Britain in the eighteenth and nineteenth centuries, had occurred when the empire was ascendant, and dynamic. Britain was then developing, and would have done so regardless of the colonial reve- nues it got, their effect being mainly to add a gear or two to growth. This time, though, the trend was moving the other way, and it was doing so for the reason all empires reach their peak: the gap between the heartland and its periphery had grown too large to sustain (and was certainly far larger than it had been in the nineteenth century). Whatever technological innovations America might yet come up with, the simple fact was that existing technologies, applied in Third World countries where they hadn't yet been adopted, would lead to huge gains. Even allowing for the lower productivity of labour there, its cost was so much cheaper that firms were inevitably going to find a way to go south. The Asian crisis, and its management by the Clinton administration, could at best temporarily arrest this movement. But by the end of the 1990s, even this lease on life was running out.

*

'Since the end of the cold war,' wrote Joseph Stiglitz in a fierce critique of the Washington consensus behind the IMF's treatment of East Asia, 'tremendous power has flowed to the people entrusted to bring the gospel of the market to the far corners of the globe.'[26] President Clinton, however, was unrepentant, insisting the pain and misery being suffered in Third World countries was the 'tough medicine' they needed to put their errant economies on the path to economic salvation.[27] His was an ancient moral injunction, echoing the guidance given back in the Middle Ages by the Inquisitor Bernard Gui (he who was dramatised in Umberto Eco's *The Name of the Rose*), who had instructed his deputies not to regret the suffering they caused their victims since 'it redounds to their good and to the salvation of their souls when those who are infected and implicated in error are detected so that they can be corrected and converted from error to the way of truth.' The only difference was that Gui had promised salvation in the next world, Clinton in this one – that is, for those who made it through the tribulations alive.

Mind you, Clinton chose not to mention that prior to the Asian crisis the same countries now being rescued had been among the planet's fastest-growing economies, nor that many economists were moving towards Stiglitz's position that the crisis had been caused by a too-rapid opening of the region's capital markets[28] – which is to say, by one of the key tenets of the neoliberal catechism. Clinton had the pulpit now, and his deputies recited the litany along with him. At the height of the crisis, Lawrence Summers, his deputy Treasury secretary, gave a speech in which he declared the Asian countries were beset with 'crony capitalism' and that the Clinton administration was helping them to finally break up the oligarchies saddling growth. Responding to critics who said the IMF and Treasury Department were acting like the imperialists of old by ignoring the will of hundreds of millions of people and undermining fragile Third World democracies, Summers recited the neoliberal catechism that democracy had always to be 'balanced' against policies that the experts at the IMF and Treasury had approved. He then added there could be no justification for bailing out 'investors who should have known better'.[29]

Summers may have had his tongue in his cheek as he said this. Because at around the same time he was giving his speech in Milwaukee, the New York Federal Reserve Board was putting together a bailout for a hedge fund hit by the Asian crisis. Since its creation in 1994, Long Term Capital Management had been delivering stellar returns to a handful of ultra-rich investors by placing so-called 'short' bets – when you bet an asset will fall in value, so you borrow it off someone who owns it, sell it, then buy it back at the lower price to return to the previous owner, pocketing the difference. With two Nobel laureates on an investment panel comprised of Wall Street nobility, LTCM had devised a complex model to anticipate movements in assets, satisfying itself it had perfected the science of investing. But oddly, it failed to anticipate a crisis, something you needed only a pocket economic history or a long memory to know was always a risk. Summers himself had once told the economist who devised the model that its basic premise was flat-out wrong, calling it 'the most remarkable error in the history of economic theory'[30] and summarising his stance on the rationality of markets by saying, 'There are idiots, look around.'[31] Which is to say, the investors who lost their shirts in LTCM most certainly 'should have known better'.

But because everyone who was anyone on Wall Street had bought into LTCM, there was a widespread fear that the losses could multiply. One man's crony, it seemed, was another's 'systemic risk'. It turned out there was a place for activist government after all. Just not in poor countries.

Journalists, seemingly too dazzled by the apparent miracles of the neoliberal priesthood, seldom bothered to probe such inconsistencies. On the contrary, this was an age of faith, not doubt, and rarely were the experts held in higher regard. In a bit of hagiography that typified the heady period, and describing the role they played in the Asian crisis, *Time* magazine characterised Summers, Treasury Secretary Robert Rubin and Federal Bank chairman Alan Greenspan – who had already been christened the 'Maestro' by a fawning acolyte[32] – as 'The Committee to Save the World'. Lauding

Greenspan in particular for the 'sweetness of his soul' and his 'shaman-like power over global markets', the article said:

> ... politicians such as Malaysian Prime Minister Mahathir Mohamad complain that Rubin, Greenspan and Summers – and their henchmen at the International Monetary Fund – have turned nations like Malaysia and Russia into leper colonies by isolating them from global capital and making life hellish in order to protect U.S. growth. The three admit they've made hard choices – and they'll even cop to some mistakes – but they still believe that a strong U.S. economy is the last, best hope for the world.[33]

No heretic, forced to recant error, will thank his Inquisitor, and probably not many Third World leaders sent Bill Clinton thank-you cards that year. But that is the price one pays for saving souls, and Robert Rubin celebrated Clinton's heroic disregard for the opinion polls, telling *Time*: 'I really don't know what would have happened with this global climate if we hadn't had a President who had within him the framework to do what was best for the global economy.'[34]

Hoovering money out of poor countries did bring about the strong American economy that Summers said would be the planet's salvation, but it wasn't the only thing behind the boom. There was also a good deal of financial wizardry, like what LTCM was doing. But like any bit of magic, this act depended on some artful sleight of hand.

With the growth of labour-productivity in decline, the engine powering the economy was slowing, pulling overall rates of economic growth down with it. However, any mechanic knows that you can add a bit of kick to the motor by opening its air flow or adding lead to its petrol. But that violates legal regulations. Similarly, there were some standards in the US economy which, if good for overall safety, restrained its dynamism somewhat. The experts had long warned that if the government ever lifted those standards, the car would risk crashing. Fortunately, the new neoliberal priesthood offered a different take on the old expertise – and with that, a new morality to replace the prudence of the past.

There had always been a basic rule in economics, that risk and return vary in equal proportions. You can, for instance, make far more money at the racetrack than from your savings account, but you also stand to lose everything. Mindful of this, governments had imposed rules on what banks could do with people's money, precluding them engaging in the equivalent of heading to the racetrack. Investors seeking yield were thus forced to go outside the regulated banking system, where the government wouldn't vouch for their money in the way they did for retail savers, who were given deposit insurance. But that was now changing.

One of neoliberalism's acknowledged downsides was that the rich were getting richer faster than everyone else. That meant they had more to invest. But given the underlying trends, the returns on conventional investments were also diminishing. So, particularly in the 1990s, private investment firms and hedge funds like LTCM became popular among the rich.[35] Attracting a small number of very rich investors who were willing to forgo the security of deposit insurance in return for escaping the scrutiny of regulators, these investment clubs could dabble in risky but potentially lucrative ventures.

They tried various things. Some went looking for higher yields in riskier developing markets, which explains why the United States was so eager to open East Asia for investment earlier in the decade. Others preferred to stay at home, taking over firms with large cash piles, then raiding them for dividends. Another option was to look for companies whose shares were cheap because they were losing money, whereupon they would 'restructure' them: sell off assets or break up the unions so as to drive down wages, and thereby boost profits. None of these methods necessarily did much good for long-term growth, since they often ran down existing capital or simply shipped it offshore. But perhaps the most controversial method of all was to forgo investing in firms altogether and to buy the innovative securities being devised by the newly deregulated financial sector.

Most of these, like the short-selling done by LTCM, amounted to rather elaborate forms of gambling.

In the short term LTCM's bailout put the car back on the road. Previously, the rationale for allowing private financial firms to evade public scrutiny was that the price of that freedom was the loss of security. By rescuing LTCM, the Federal Reserve sent a message that if a financial firm was 'too big to fail' – especially if it had insinuated its way into the regulated banks by selling them shares, as LTCM had done (and as the deregulation pursued by the Clinton administration now allowed them to do) – the government would bail them out if things went wrong. In effect, the government had set a floor beneath which it wouldn't allow asset values to fall.

Intensifying this effect was the 'Greenspan Put'. Back in 1987 when Alan Greenspan had been made chairman of the Federal Reserve Board, just two months into his term he'd confronted a stock-market crash on a scale hardly seen since the Great Depression. In just one day, stocks had lost a fifth of their value. Greenspan had then cut interest rates and issued a press release declaring the Federal Reserve's 'readiness to serve as a source of liquidity to support the economic and financial system'.[36] Investors quickly likened this to a 'put option', a contract that gave a security's owner the right to sell it at a fixed price in the event the market-price fell below that. The message to investors, which they carried with them ever after, was clear: if the market crashed, they would get rescued. It was like a plenary indulgence to a feudal king, telling him that no matter what sins he committed on his crusade to the Holy Land, he would never go to hell.

The downside of indulgences, though, is that someone still has to play the role of the martyr, taking humanity's sins onto the cross to give it a fresh start. That task, needless to say, fell to the taxpayer. The reason speculative ventures paid high returns is that they remained risky. Just as conservative moralists will say the more pleasurable the vice, the more painful its consequence, so too a basic principle of economics is that the greater a market-move's potential returns, the greater its potential losses. But if the government says it will cover all losses, who's going to bother with the old-fashioned virtue? Sooner or later, the people were going to have to climb up on the cross.

Initially the bailout of LTCM encouraged investors to seek one high-yield bubble after another. When one burst, they'd await the rescue, then go on to the next. In the early years after LTCM, these rescues took the form of interest-rate cuts. By cutting interest rates, central bankers could discourage savers from putting their money into ordinary accounts and encourage them to come back into the market, while making borrowing cheaper and thereby releasing new funds into the economy. Moreover, the now enshrined efficient markets hypothesis provided a moral justification for bubbles, saying that the prices in a soaring market could not possibly be wrong: if a bubble was inflating, investors would know it, and would factor that into the price, adding a risk premium.

Bubbles had been inflating throughout the 1990s, when the opening of Third World markets created new opportunities for Western investors. Even before the Asian crisis, earlier in the decade there had been bubbles and crashes that served as trial runs for what would later follow in Asia, the most significant one for America being the 1994 Mexican peso crisis. Late in the decade, another bubble in the United States began to inflate: the dot-com bubble.

The Internet was still relatively new then. Reading the papers without having to go to a newsagent or buying a book without having to leave your house were such bold ideas that people began to fantasise about the glories that might result. The dot-com boom began with some sensible inventions, like Amazon or the new search engines, which would make it possible to find what you were looking for without needing to browse thousands of websites. But before long, it started to get a bit loopy. Investors rushed in to buy just about anything with a domain name. Young entrepreneurs with little more than a vague idea for a product would register a domain name, then flip it to investors. Or they'd sell shares on the stock market for companies that were often little more than some binary code on a computer server. So wild did this ride become that some share-valuations rose by 1,000 per cent a week. Few of these companies actually made any money. Some made nothing at all. If their founders were clever, they'd get out as quickly as they'd gone in, retire as twenty-something millionaires and leave someone else with the risk. Telecommunications companies went heavily into debt building the broadband networks they believed would power the new companies, while dot-com offices became infamous for being lavishly appointed workspaces where university dropouts spent their days playing Nerf ball before hitting the bars. Soon, the whole nation caught the fever. Day-trading became the new craze. Ordinary people quit their jobs and spent their days on computer terminals in the new cybercafes playing the stock market, buying and selling stocks several times a day just to catch the updraughts.

As bewildering as the mania was to market observers, true believers like Alan Greenspan seemed genuinely convinced this could go on for ever. Their simple faith in the neoliberal gospel insisted that markets couldn't possibly be wrong. A decade after the LTCM bailout, testifying before Congress in the wake of another bubble's explosion, an ashen-faced Greenspan confessed, 'I still don't understand why it happened.' Here was someone who had studied at the feet of Ayn Rand, the priestess of self-interest who had taught Greenspan that markets were 'an expression of the deepest truths about human nature and that, as a result, they will ultimately be correct'.[37] In light of that, his admission he must have been mistaken in his belief that self-interest would always prevent investors taking excessive risks with their money was tantamount to a Christian saying Jesus was, actually, just another bloke. Soon afterwards, like someone who says that something must be literally true because the Bible says it, Greenspan would retreat into the besieged bastion of his faith by claiming that whatever might have gone wrong couldn't possibly have been his fault, since before his death the great neoliberal sage Milton Friedman had given him his blessing.[38]

But Greenspan and his ilk could not plead ignorance – other than perhaps the wilful variety of the sort found on bumper stickers trumpeting: 'God said it, I believe it, that settles it.' There were plenty of voices warning that this was bound to end badly. In March 2000 the Yale economist Robert Shiller published a book called *Irrational Exuberance* in which he said that the market had shot way ahead of itself and would sooner or later have to revert to its historical mean. Warren Buffett avoided dot-com stocks altogether, pointing to basic maths: throughout America's history, only a few firms had risen in any given year to become major corporations, but now investors were betting that dozens or even hundreds were going to do so, bidding the share values of some companies so high they rivalled Ford and General Motors, regardless of whether they actually made a penny.

However, such voices of caution were drowned out in the din of excitement and easily dismissed as yesterday's lost souls. Buffett, after all, was an old man from Nebraska who dined at Wendy's and just couldn't understand the sheer novelty of the information age. As for Shiller's historic means, that was the past. The new economy had changed the game, and a new breed of celebrity economists, people like Abby Joseph Cohen and Ralph Acampora, were urging investors to snap up tech stocks. There could be no greater proof they were right than that they were making people rich – one market bull touting Cohen for having 'the hottest hand of anybody in the game'.[39] Buffett's investment fund, stuck with old bricks-and-mortar companies, was underperforming Cohen's stock-picks by a mile.

Besides, nobody wanted to call time on this high-stakes gambling for the simple reason that it had licked the problem of slowing growth. The 'wealth effect' – when people spend more because the rising value of their assets makes them feel richer – made up for the diminishing returns caused by slowing productivity. Sure, inequality was getting worse, but with a rising tide lifting all boats, who was going to complain? On paper, Americans who'd bought in to the bubble felt richer, so they could boost the limits on their credit cards and go shopping. That in turn gave a jolt to the rest of the economy. One big question was left hanging: what happens when everyone decides to pay their debts and tries to convert their paper wealth back into cash? Everyone was rushing in, but hardly anyone, apart from the odd entrepreneur who flipped a dot-com invention quickly, was getting out. They were piling up debts while awaiting a stock-market slowdown. It had become a sort of pyramid scheme in which everyone bought shares because they were rising, and shares rose because everyone was buying them.

It resembled a bartender dealing with a stroppy customer. He's been buying drinks all night and providing lots of laughter, so you let him run up a tab. But after he crosses that drink threshold, the one where his mood goes from jovial to aggressive, you realise that the longer you postpone cutting him off, the worse it will end. So instead you watch the clock, keep serving him drinks, and just hope your shift ends before he loses the plot.

In April 2000, a few weeks after Shiller's *Irrational Exuberance* appeared in bookshops, and as the New York Stock Exchange hovered near record highs, President Bill Clinton convened a conference on the new economy at the White House. Standing before some of the most prominent apostles of the new economy – stock analyst Abby Joseph Cohen, Treasury Secretary Lawrence Summers, Federal Reserve Chairman Alan Greenspan – Clinton proclaimed the achievements of the high-growth, low-inflation American paradise they'd delivered. 'From small businesses to factory floors to villages half a world away, the information revolution is changing the way people work, learn, live, relate to each other in the rest of the world,' he told them. 'The performance of the new economy has been powered by technology, driven by ideas, rooted in innovation and enterprise,' he said, going on to wave aside those who said America was chasing a bubble. He assured them that the new economy had 'challenged our very understanding of economics'. Floating the idea that 'speed-limits' – rates of growth that would trigger inflation – might no longer exist, he pointed out that: 'Information technology today represents only 10 percent of American jobs, but is responsible for about 30 percent of our economic growth. It accounts now for about half of business investment' (that, incidentally, was precisely the problem, as Robert Shiller had pointed out). He then invited

Abby Joseph Cohen to open the first panel discussion: 'Is the New Economy Rewriting the Rules on Productivity and the Business Cycle?'[40]

A week later the New York Stock Exchange went into free fall. Overnight, plummeting technology stocks wiped $2 trillion off the paper wealth of American investors. Within months, the market had tumbled so far that savers, stuck with heavy debts and greatly diminished portfolios, curtailed their spending. Bill Clinton's vice president, Al Gore, left to begin his election campaign to succeed his boss as president amid a recession, ended up being the bartender who inherits the unruly patron.

The deep Third World recession that followed the Asian crisis had, as all recessions eventually do, run its course by then. As the new millennium dawned, growth resumed in the poor countries. That in turn caused the wave of violence and instability to attenuate again. Life began to return to normal. As it did so, Third World oligarchs who had parked their reserves in Western securities started bringing them back home and putting them to work in their own markets. As they sold off their Treasury bills, their yields began rising, which meant that interest rates on US government debt began rising. Interest rates throughout the rest of the economy followed them upwards. As if it were a last desperate attempt to keep the boom going, the Clinton administration cited its belief in eternal budget surpluses – which later turned out to be as real as the tooth-fairy – as an excuse to start buying back government bonds.[41] Lawrence Summers, having been elevated to Treasury secretary, announced that buying back debt was 'a welcome continuation of the virtuous cycle that Americans have recently enjoyed – reduced public borrowing, lower interest rates, more rapid economic growth, leading to higher budget surpluses, further reductions in debt, further reductions in interest rates, and still more rapid economic growth.'[42]

However, it was like paddling a canoe upriver. Capital had begun flowing to the Third World for the simple reason that the returns there were so much higher.[43] The gap between First and Third World incomes had grown so vast, the low labour costs in developing countries became irresistible to firm managers. Companies stood to improve their profits substantially by shifting labour-intensive assembly offshore. Moreover, the higher population growth rates of the poor countries ensured there would be lots of cheap labour for the foreseeable future. In contrast, workers in the rich countries were not only comparatively expensive, they were also in relative terms getting harder to find.

With the Third World subsidy gone, productivity-growth slowing and with labour supplies expanding more slowly, the underlying trend in the Western economy continued to contract. To try to charge it back up, all that remained were conjuror's tricks.

Throughout the Asian crisis, President Clinton was battling an attempt by Congressional Republicans to impeach and remove him from office for lying under oath over his affair with an intern. Yet oddly, even though it was only the second time in American history that a president was subjected to a Senate trial, the stock markets barely registered a shiver. When asked how investors could be so blasé about it all, one of them joked it wasn't as if someone really important, like Alan Greenspan, was being impeached. Further underscoring the point, one day during the drama the governor of the Brazilian central bank did resign, whereupon the New York Stock Exchange sold off sharply.

But in fact this equanimity testified to the triumph of neoliberalism, whose constitution had been quietly but successfully transposed onto America's democracy. Yes, the people had elected their president and Congress. But now, like a caliph or a pope – or Iran's supreme leader – the central banker, surrounded by a council of experts who had devoted their lives to mastering the state religion, oversaw the elected politicians and imposed limits on what they could do. Democracy's 'Yes we can' had morphed into the new regime's 'No you can't'. That meant that markets could now function with the assurance that whatever happened, doctrinal conformity would be maintained throughout. Whether or not the president was toppled, the money gods would continue smiling on America.

Nevertheless, politicians hadn't become irrelevant, far from it. Like Iran's president and parliamentary representatives, they provided the new regime with democratic legitimacy, and still enjoyed substantial room to affect policy – provided they stayed within the confines imposed by the priesthood. Clinton himself was a very articulate evangelist for the new church. The left in the Western world might never have converted to the neoliberal faith had it not been for the sermons of politicians like him. During the Asian crisis he reassured his compatriots that poor countries were suffering for their sins, from which America was helping to save them, whereas Americans themselves were growing rich due to their own genius. Such a 'victor's theology' was not new, of course, having been essentially lifted from the Victorian era's narrative about the white man's burden. However, this new and improved packaging reached a new segment of the political market that didn't want to think of itself as conservative, let alone Victorian.

Very importantly, Clinton used the federal government's leverage over mortgage provision to enable more people than ever to get mortgages. Amid worsening inequality and the cutbacks his government was implementing, giving poor Americans a slice of this small part of the American dream became a way to sprinkle a dash of old-time progressive politics amid the neoliberalism. Although people who wanted a mortgage approached their own bank, two large corporations known colloquially as Fannie Mae and Freddie Mac acted as clearing houses for most of the mortgages in America. Because they were overseen by the federal government, Clinton was able to prod them to offer more mortgages to people who previously did not qualify for loans. The lenders reduced deposit requirements, loosened eligibility rules on income and collateral and provided interest-only loans and variable-rate mortgages. That way a borrower could forgo fixing at a rate that reflected his or her credit risk and pay instead a little above the current Federal Reserve rate on short-term loans. As millions who previously couldn't afford to buy homes now entered the market, the so-called 'sub-prime' mortgage came into existence.[44] It didn't take much imagination to realise this was just another way of tinkering with the car's safety features. But with the wind now blowing through everyone's hair as they took to the open highway, who would object?

Given that the Federal Reserve had slashed interest rates in the wake of the dot-com crash, someone with no job or savings could walk into a bank and borrow money to buy a house they could not normally afford by taking an adjustable-rate, interest-only loan. From the borrower's point of view, this seemed like free money, in the same way margin loans had appeared like free money. For as long as the property rose in value, you could always sell it later, pay off the loan, and pocket the difference, trading up to a bigger house. Of course, it was all premised on one key assumption: that house prices would continue rising. At first, with so many new buyers coming into the market, the extra demand did in fact drive up prices. And as prices rose, more people bought houses, sometimes adding a second one as an investment. After all, if the house kept rising in price, it didn't matter if it lay empty. And as people bought houses, developers built them, hiring construction workers who then had more money to spend – and so bought yet more houses.

Even after Clinton left office, politicians of all stripes would maintain these policies – not only because they were vote-getters, but because the resulting housing-boom enjoyed the pontifical seal. Signs of trouble were starting to show up, and that old killjoy Robert Shiller resurfaced with a price index that suggested house prices – which by 2004 were rising by nearly 1 per cent each month, far beyond the historic norm – were becoming grossly overvalued. So it fell to the *primus inter pares* of the world's central bankers, Alan Greenspan, to provide the authoritative opinion. That autumn he made a much-anticipated speech on housing. Beginning by referring euphemistically to the growing number of Americans with sub-prime loans as clients with 'previously unrecognized borrowing capacities', Greenspan ruled that the number of those who were overextended had 'not meaningfully increased'. Then he rendered his final verdict. 'The household sector seems to be in reasonably good financial shape with only modest evidence of an increased level of household financial strain … a significant decline in consumer incomes or house prices could quickly alter the outlook; nonetheless, both scenarios appear unlikely.'[45]

Although expressed in technical language, the meaning was clear to all the faithful: Go do ye the same, for the new age has begun. This wasn't another bubble, the banks could keep on lending, the good times could keep on rolling, and the neoliberal miracles performed by the 'Maestro' and his apostolic brotherhood seemed never to cease.

CHAPTER 20

'HONEY, I SHRUNK
THE ECONOMY!'

The Western world was in a position similar to the one that had faced
Münster's end-timers, six centuries before: ringed on all sides by an
irresistible force. What goes up must come down, and after two centuries in which the net flow of capital had gone from the periphery
of the world economy to its Western core, helping to fuel economic
growth there, the direction had now gone into reverse. From the
turn of the century, the influx of money into emerging markets had
been steadily rising and speculative bubbles became the last tool
rich countries could use to prevent themselves being overtaken by
poor ones as magnets for capital. This set them on a path to destiny.
Generations of promises made by politicians to their flocks – cradle-
to-grave health care, long and comfortable retirements, expanding
public services and constantly rising living standards – had all been
premised on long-term growth rates of 2–3 per cent per year. A rate
half or less than that, which was where it was now headed, was going
to starve the citadel.

It's not that we all faced a bleak future of declining incomes. On
the contrary, slower growth was still growth, and technological
advance continued unabated. But, as Münster's self-styled prophet
had done, the apostles of the money god had promised their followers heaven on Earth. Theirs was not a prosaic god that looked for

ways to make the most of this life; theirs was a triumphalist faith that promised a whole new, different life. As the inevitable day of reckoning drew ever closer, the Münster drama repeated itself: false prophecies, trick miracles, the chiliastic fervour of a people partying as if they are about to die, all against a backdrop of the relentless encroachment of a fate delayed – and the longer the delay was, the worse the final collapse was going to be.

If you lived in or visited London in the late 1990s, you will remember the Millennium Dome. Now a hall for pop concerts, it stands as a testament to a lost age of utopian visions. Intended as a symbol of the new 'cool Britannia' that New Labour ushered in, it was to showcase the British-made technology that would supposedly change the world, from the 'millennium' washing machine to the world's first 'intelligent' submarine. Touring it shortly before its opening, Prime Minister Tony Blair called it 'an international symbol of the millennium' and said only 'those who despise anything modern, those who are made uneasy by success' would be able to find fault with it.[1] To celebrate the dawning of this new age, two weeks later, at midnight on New Year's Eve, London rang in the millennium with a fireworks display so lavish that the smoke along the Thames thickened almost to the point where some in the crowd could barely see the pyrotechnics running along both banks.

It was said of Tony Blair that he was Bill Clinton minus the 'bimbo eruptions'. Although 'Blairism' was arguably more rooted in traditional leftist thought than Clinton's neoliberalism, focusing as it did on the rights and responsibilities of communities and individuals and willing to expand rather than contract government to improve public services, similar millennial motifs to those in Clinton's speeches recurred in Blair's. Like his American counterpart, he substituted free markets for statism, and extended market logic into the operations of government itself. In a 2002 speech extolling Britain's entry into 'the new markets that globalisation and technology are creating' he announced a change to Britain's system of unemployment relief, saying that 'instead of the old benefit mentality' that Margaret

Thatcher had once said sapped individual initiative, claimants would henceforth be 'treated as customers and potential employees – given high-quality advice and support by professional advisers in a business-like environment'. So too would employers be treated as customers. The government's job was no longer to guarantee full employment with public jobs, but to plug a gap in an otherwise free market.[2]

Such a spirit of entrepreneurship pervaded British society. Typical of that time was the move by many building societies to abandon their normal strategy of simply using members' savings to provide mortgage loans. One of these high-fliers was a Newcastle building society called Northern Rock. A mutual with roots in the mid-nineteenth-century movement to help workers obtain their own homes by pooling their savings and lending to one another, in the 1990s Northern Rock decided to abandon its stodgy old model and to list itself on the London Stock Exchange. Its members now became shareholders, their share values leaping as the bank rose quickly on the LSE, joining its blue-ribbon FTSE 100 index. Aggressively expanding its operations, it no longer looked to members' small deposits to expand its lending, but moved into the global league by obtaining large loans from multinational investment banks, which charged comparatively low rates of interest. This enabled the bank to widen its clientele, as new borrowers ran in to take advantage of the cheap credit. More clients meant more revenue, bigger profits, higher share prices and better bonuses for bank staff.

However, over the summer of 2007, something changed. Investment banks started to get jittery about Northern Rock's portfolio. Having adopted a business model that relied on credit for liquidity, Northern Rock depended on open credit lines; however, now its lenders weren't returning its calls as promptly as they used to. As a result, Northern Rock was finding it increasingly difficult to get credit on favourable terms. By September, there wasn't enough new money flowing into its coffers to pay all the regular expenses it had, so it approached the Bank of England for a loan to tide it over. As soon as the news broke, many of its clients, worried that Northern

Rock might have to commandeer their savings, decided to play it safe and withdraw their funds. Queues quickly formed outside its branches, and when other depositors heard the news, they rushed to join in. Before long Britain had its first run on a bank since the Great Depression. The authorities tried to reassure savers that everything was under control, the chairman of the House of Commons Select Committee saying, 'The banking system in the United Kingdom is strong.' But it did little good. As panic erupted, police were deployed at several branches to maintain order,[3] and in Cheltenham angry clients barricaded the branch manager in her office.

The warning signs that problems would develop in the housing market had been multiplying for a while. But the prophets kept swatting them down and the faithful, fully invested in their promises, were as determined to believe their leaders as Münster's last holdouts had been. Earlier that spring, Jim Cramer, a one-time hedge-fund manager who had become an American celebrity with a television programme in which he called out his top stock-picks, was asked on a panel discussion to assess the state of the US economy. 'Fantastic', he said, going on to detail his vision of an American future of rising profits and falling inflation. Cramer, a charismatic televangelist for the new economy, exuded the boundless optimism of a revivalist preacher. There had never been, Cramer told his audience, a better time to buy shares.

Inflation had fallen slightly that winter. But pressure had been building over the previous couple of years, with surging house prices creating a 'wealth effect'. Homeowners whose valuations had been rising by the month were going to their banks, getting new lines of credit and hitting the shopping centres. It was like the dot-com days all over again. 'Use your home as your ATM,' was the buzz-phrase among financial advisers and, with the galloping US economy driving demand for Japanese video games and German cars, the boom spread far and wide. Meanwhile, since the deregulation of American finance freed New York's banks and hedge funds to chase new opportunities, foreign banks rushed in to take loans. Raising capital in New York, they were then able to stoke similar housing-booms abroad. British house prices rose, Ireland's economy was mushrooming amid a wave of new construction, and Spanish developers were hiring anyone they could find to meet the rapidly expanding demand for new houses. Most dramatically, in the case of remote little Iceland, pretty well everyone in the country docked their fishing boats and took up banking, packaging mortgage securities for foreign buyers, then lending them back out to foreign borrowers. So dynamic was the country's newest industry that the value of the loans created ultimately amounted to three times the country's annual output.

Driving this construction boom were the complex new financial instruments, which investment banks had been concocting ever since the 1990s deregulation. The derivatives, credit-default swaps and collateralised debt obligations (CDOs) the investment banks were putting together for mortgage-providers like Northern Rock were so complex, and the mathematical models used to assess their risk so bewildering, that even the bank CEOs didn't always understand them. But if their design – by physics PhDs applying advanced mathematics – seemed ultra-modern, they served an ancient function. Like a temple-priest using a sacred language or a witchdoctor mouthing incomprehensible spells, they sold a fairground trick to buyers who trusted in their authority. Equally, their basic purpose was straightforward: to expand the availability of mortgages by linking house-buyers to investors in search of new investment opportunities. The slowing growth and widening inequality of the neoliberal age made it easier for investment banks to enter housing markets and for poor people to buy houses, and enabled governments of the new left to kill two birds with one stone. First, by giving rich investors new opportunities to boost profits, they revved the economy up a notch or two while also pleasing wealthy donors, who had become very important to both Bill Clinton's and Tony Blair's political (and eventually, personal as well) fortunes, seeing that they were among the key donors to their political campaigns. Second, by making it possible for people who were previously considered too poor to

qualify for mortgages to now buy homes, they enabled their traditional support bases to feel that, despite stagnant real incomes and
widening inequality, the neoliberal economy wasn't bypassing the
less well off.

Previously, if Americans wanted to buy a house, they had to
approach their local bank or building society, which assessed their
credit-worthiness. If it deemed them a good risk, it drew upon its
own funds to provide them with a mortgage. The interest rate the
client paid reflected their manager's assessment of the risk they might
at some point default on their loan, as well as the rate the bank had to
offer its savers to raise enough funding for the loan. The bank looked
at their clients' income, their previous credit history and their assets,
asking them to put some of their own money down so as to both
create a margin against a possible fall in the house's price, but also
to make them put skin in the game. However, that sort of prudence
meant that millions of people with insecure or low-paying jobs and
no savings – which is to say, poor people – couldn't get mortgages.

With its epicurean faith in 'enlightened self-interest' the high
neoliberalism of the Clinton administration declared such prudence
old fashioned. This was now the time to go forward into the new
economy, and who better to lead the way than investment banks?
With their investors seeking higher returns, they loved risky investments. When such bets worked out, they paid a much higher rate of
return. And where better to find high returns than in the high-risk
business of loans to the poor? Having booked their profits from
the Asian and dot-com bubbles, the investment banks were now
looking for the next frontier, and the lure of the high-risk mortgage
market was irresistible. For their part, commercial banks wanted
to put some of their depositors' money into the investment banks,
since that would boost their profits and thus increase their year end
bonuses (which were becoming a bigger share of CEO compensation). That's why the American banking sector had lobbied so
aggressively to repeal the Depression-era Glass–Steagall Act, which
had created a firewall between investment and commercial banks
to prevent another crash ever occurring. Ever since taking over the

Federal Reserve, Alan Greenspan had used his chairmanship to ease the application of Glass–Steagall's provisions, and in Bill Clinton he found a disciple, the president signing the repeal of Glass–Steagall in 1999. Wall Street had greeted the repeal like manna from heaven, the president of Citigroup (which along with many other banks had spent lavishly lobbying politicians for the legislation's removal) subsequently adorning his office with 'a hunk of wood – at least 4 feet wide – etched with his portrait and the words "The Shatterer of Glass–Steagall"'.[4]

With the dot-com boom then on its last legs, Glass–Steagall became the latest safety feature to be removed from the American economy, enabling it to maintain its cruising speed even as its fuel-supply dwindled. Once the wall separating investment from commercial banks was knocked down, managers no longer needed to use their bank's own resources to give their clients mortgages. Instead, mortgages could be re-sold to investment banks as 'asset-backed securities' at which point the local banks would use their clients' mortgage payments to pay the investment banks dividends on those securities. But investment banks only dealt in large trans-actions involving millions and millions of dollars, so they weren't going to get into the business of managing mortgages. Instead, the retail banks pooled together thousands of their clients' mortgages, sliced and diced the total sum into individual securities, then resold them to investment banks, which invested in the securities the same way they invested in shares or bonds.

And then, things started to get really interesting. Banks were now able to attract new clients by offering mortgages to borrowers who previously couldn't get them at affordable rates. By mixing these sub-prime mortgages with high-quality ones, they averaged out the risk: even if some clients defaulted on their loans, went the reasoning, there would be enough income from the safer borrowers to ensure the whole pool remained solvent. Pooling risk enabled lenders to lower the interest rates on sub-prime loans, making cheap credit available to millions of poor people. There was no better testament to high neoliberalism's main article of faith, the doctrine of unintended consequences, which held that the individual out to maximise his interest would end up inadvertently benefiting others. In the new Beatitudes enunciated by Bill Clinton, blessed were the poor for therein lay a rich business opportunity. The way to eliminate poverty was for the rich to chase profits, for as the investment banks swelled their revenue streams, poor people got houses.

Now, your grandmother or your old Uncle Steve who survived the Great Depression and knew a thing or two about risky investments would have told you that one bad apple spoils the barrel. If any of those mortgages stopped getting paid, any bank's income stream would have fallen below the level it needed to meet its obligations to its investors, and everyone would have a problem. But that's where the mathematical models came in. Even if they were too complicated for even the CEOs to understand, in truth, the CEOs weren't that interested in the science behind them. Like a medieval prince who doesn't care to hear his Jesuit confessor's elaborate casuistry about what makes a sin permissible, but just wants to know *if* it's permissible, the CEOs simply wanted to know if the securities were safe. If the answer was yes, they bought them. And since the magicians who'd devised them said the maths didn't lie, they had to be safe. And a crowd desperate to cling to the promises their oracles had made, cried Amen.

Nevertheless, for all their purported science, the models ultimately rested on what was nothing more than a leap of faith: that home prices would continue rising indefinitely. It was not just the models' architects who needed to believe that. Everyone from the CEO down to the smallest depositor, who wanted to be assured that her life savings were in good hands, had to keep faith that the magicians knew what they were doing. It was, in fact, an awfully big leap of faith, given that entire economies had come to hang on it. Sustaining it therefore required the priesthood to reassure the faithful continually. It did just that. Not only had Alan Greenspan issued his authoritative ruling in 2004, saying there was no reason to expect house prices to fall in any serious way, but legions of prominent economists advised the banks and reassured the public of the same thing. So there followed a self-fulfilling prophecy. With all that new house-buying, prices rose, and as prices rose, more people bought houses. The West was shopping its way to the promised land. There can be miracles, when you believe.

This euphoria in the housing markets then radiated outwards, enabling the economies of the West to enjoy one last great party before the eventual end of the millennial dream. That's because it wasn't just home buyers who were now able to get cheap credit. In some cases, it was entire countries.

Throughout the US boom in the 1990s, the economy of the European Union had been comparatively restrained due to the hangover caused by the cost of German reunification. However, with the advent of the new European currency at the turn of the century, the continent appeared to have turned the corner. Overseen by an independent central bank with a mandate to keep inflation low, the euro began a long rise in value vis-à-vis the US dollar, to the point that by 2007 American rap videos keen to showcase ostentation began substituting euros for dollars in the money their characters splashed around.

As confidence in the euro rose, so too did confidence in European government bonds. Since all member states of the Eurozone shared the same central bank, investors calculated that in a pinch, the EU and its institutions would backstop any government borrowing. This created a curious anomaly. Governments in southern Europe whose profligate ways relative to the Germans or Dutch had long ensured that lenders demanded higher interest rates on the loans they gave them, now got to issue bonds denominated in euros, with the full confidence of the central bank backing them. That meant, for instance, that the Greeks got to continue spending like Greeks, all while paying for it like Germans. Needless to say, they and other countries that previously had been forced by high interest rates to limit their spending, went on shopping sprees. Given the jobs, pay rises and benefits the government started handing out, Greeks could have been forgiven for thinking that in joining the single currency they passed through the gates of an earthly heaven.

Obviously this was bound to end badly. However, nobody cared to do much about it for the time being because everyone was in on the ride. When the Greek government lavished money on the population, they used it to buy German cars. German manufacturers were thus riding the credit boom while German banks, which were making lots of those loans to the Greek government, were earning good and, they had reason to believe, safe money on the loans they were making. The outcome was yet another self-reinforcing cycle of debt-fuelled growth, in which mounting government debts didn't worry anyone overmuch since the rising government revenues needed to pay them back were easily generated on the back of a healthy economy.

Never did the European project look more promising. With long vacations, secure jobs (compared to the United States and Britain), abundant welfare provisions and generous government subsidies for research and public works, the EU seemed to offer a different model of globalisation and integration to the American, neoliberal one. In contrast to that vision, the EU seemed to stay in the European tradition of the institutional and historical schools by offering a nurturing state, principles of democratic accountability – Europeans got to vote in both national and Europe-wide elections, and governments retained their sovereignty – a foreign policy that seemingly pursued peace instead of war, and a combination of internal free trade with external protection for traditional, family-owned farms and businesses.

But in fact, this was about as much of an illusion as the US fiction that a rising tide would eternally lift all boats. Beneath the surface, once Germany adopted its neoliberal reform programme in 2002, the politics of the EU were bound to move in a similar direction. European policy was determined by a combination of central directive from Brussels and the influence of major capitals. As the largest and richest of the EU countries, Germany was going to exercise an outsized impact on the future direction of the Union. Given too that German prudence weighed heavily on the monetary policy of the central bank, European largesse was really just a function of prosperous times. If the money ever ceased to be so abundant, so might the generosity.

This risk was not peculiar to Europe, it hovered over all Western countries. But within countries, if people had a voice in their government, compromises could in principle be reached through the usual exercise of democratic politics, messy though the course might be. In Europe, because countries retained their sovereignty, there remained the possibility that if a fight for scarce spoils ever broke out, countries might turn on one another and revive some of the memories of 'recent history'. Now that they were tied to a German-dominated financial system, countries that had once been occupied by German soldiers would resent any effort by a future German government to compel them to start saving like Germans – just as Germans would resent any calls to underwrite what they considered to be the spendthrift behaviour of some other European governments.

The economy of much of the Western world began to resemble a raucous casino. Having created these new securities, the next profit-making opportunity for US investment banks was to market them abroad, to other banks in places like France and Germany that wanted to keep up with their rivals. Equally, there was now no reason commercial banks couldn't go shopping abroad for better deals on loans, as Northern Rock had done. So the bubble spread far and wide. That's how Iceland turned itself overnight into a global banking centre, while the Irish and Spanish economies exploded into a building-boom.

Everyone trusted the temple guards to stay awake, and assumed that the US government was keeping a close eye on its banks. That gave other governments the confidence to let their own banks transact business in New York. But this turned out to be an even bigger leap of faith, since the US government was more or less letting the banks do as they liked. Why constrain miracle workers who had revealed themselves to have divine powers? Not only had the US government and the Federal Reserve been lifting regulations, they had also been pressing their regulators to be more forgiving of the bankers and to trust in their innate goodness and wisdom. And in those increasingly rare cases where regulators still insisted on doing their job, the government could always summon the high priests to expose the regulators' heresy, using it as a pretext to defrock them. In one prominent example, when in 1999 the chairman of the US Commodity Futures Trading Commission, Brooksley Born, began warning publicly that the boom might end badly if the government didn't step in, the high priests came out in force. Alan Greenspan, Treasury Secretary Robert Rubin and Deputy Treasury Secretary Lawrence Summers denounced her before Congress, and Born, like a prophet who pays the price of speaking an uncomfortable truth, had to resign. As one observer later remarked, 'Alan Greenspan was the maestro, and both parties in Washington were united in a belief that the markets would take care of themselves.'[5]

More mundanely, many of the regulators simply found themselves out of their depth. Years of pay rises in the banking sector amid a push to make government leaner meant that the most expensive people were being recruited by the banks, leaving regulators to make do with second-best economists and the odd conscientious objector – who usually grew disillusioned at being repeatedly ignored or restrained. During the housing boom, for example, the billionaire Bernie Madoff ran a private investment fund that turned out to be a $50-billion pyramid scheme (whereby the scheme operator takes new deposits to pay the dividends on the 'assets' – which don't exist because all the money that comes in goes straight back out). A private citizen, Harry Markopolos, had done the maths and determined it was a fraudulent scheme, and repeatedly alerted regulators. Typical of the responses he got was that of one New York official, who 'never expressed even the slightest interest in asking me questions'.[6] Markopolos concluded the regulators simply lacked the ability to comprehend the evidence he kept putting before them. Or, as Lord Adair Turner, one-time chairman of the UK Financial Services Authority, said, it was a 'competition of high-skilled people versus high-skilled people, and the poachers are better paid than the gamekeepers'.[7]

With the regulators out of the way, it fell to private ratings agencies, like Standard & Poor's and Moody's, to look at bundles of mortgage-backed securities, then rate them for investors on their relative quality: a free-market solution to head off a potential free-market problem. The highest rating, AAA, meant that the agency found the security to be as close to risk-free as possible. Such a coveted rating made securities attractive investments, which in turn meant the banks selling them could ask better prices. However, far from looking at these new products with critical eyes, the ratings agencies gave almost everything placed before them a top rating. The reason was plain to see: the banks that were asking them to rate the products were the very people paying for the ratings. If a rating agency came down too hard on a product, the bank could always threaten to take its business elsewhere. It was as transparently dubious a validation as the Münster prophet's confirmation of his self-appointed king's revelation. But, as was the case then, there was too much now at stake for the faithful to begin questioning. Besides, the priests of finance assured everyone that the ratings were so good because, thanks to their genius, they had designed perfect products and created a nearly fail-safe economy.

Therefore the housing market had become something of a government-sanctioned pyramid scheme. People kept buying houses because real estate prices kept going up, and prices kept going up because people kept buying houses – including second homes purchased as investment properties. You didn't even need to find a tenant for an investment property since, for as long as it was rising in price, you could always sell it, pay off the loan and pocket the difference. The mortgage payments wouldn't set you back, either, because the growing availability of zero-deposit, interest-only loans meant you put in no capital and made only a small monthly payment. So builders kept putting up houses even as more and more of them lay empty. Ireland built entire villages with scarcely any inhabitants.[8] All it was going to take for the whole scheme to come crashing down was for the new supply of house buyers to dry up. If house prices stopped rising, people with debts to pay would begin selling their properties to bank their profits. But if everyone started selling together, the estate market would be overstocked and prices would fall. That would encourage yet more people to sell, on and on in a downward spiral.

The earliest signs that such trouble might be brewing came early in 2005. Prices on holiday homes in Ocean City, New Jersey, which had been rising by double-digits for years, suddenly fell. It wasn't a big drop, just 4 per cent.[9] But it was enough to prompt anyone looking to cash in on the boom to avoid that particular market.

However, throughout the following year the problem areas multiplied, even though in the country as a whole prices were still rising. By early 2007, when Jim Cramer was reassuring his flock that the economy was in better shape than ever, troubling reports were accumulating. The banks couldn't help but notice that a growing number of their clients were starting to miss their monthly payments. Earlier in the decade, they had attracted many of them with 'teaser' loans, which offered very low interest rates for an initial period, after which they'd adjust upwards. By mid-decade, a wave of such adjustments began hitting sub-prime borrowers particularly hard, which induced a wave of selling.[10] As they tried to offload their houses, prices fell: many of their neighbours were unfortunately trying to do the same thing while buyers, aware that prices were now falling, felt no particular need to make offers. They could tell, from the agent's excessive pressure or his clients' anxious glances, that they could bide their time. So prices fell further, and more borrowers missed payments – or simply walked away from their homes, leaving their keys in the banks' night deposit boxes.

Bankers soon began to dread this 'jingle mail'. Not only did it reduce their cash flow and create the risk that they wouldn't be able to meet their own payments to the holders of their mortgage-securities, but they were stuck with houses that had declined in value. When they prepared their quarterly financial statements, the total stock of their assets would decline, showing up on the books as losses. And once such losses became public knowledge, savers and investors began to think twice about giving them any more money.

Then banks and investment firms stopped lending the mortgage lenders money. Since abandoned houses generated no income the cash-flow of mortgage lenders started falling below what they needed to keep paying their investors. If this kept up, it would soon turn ugly. The last rampart before the city fell would come when the government stepped in and used taxpayers' money to rescue a struggling bank, thereby restoring public confidence in the financial system. The first of these rescues came in the autumn of 2007 when Gordon Brown, newly installed as prime minister, announced that the British government would bail out Northern Rock.

In the short term, his intervention worked like a charm. The queues outside Northern Rock branches evaporated, and business returned to normal. Brown's approval rating shot up. However, while few people in the industry foresaw it at the time, Northern Rock had merely been the canary in the mine.

The following spring, Jim Cramer was denouncing the doubters, his stridency testifying to their growing number. Rumours had begun circulating that the investment bank Bear Stearns, which had heavily invested in mortgage-backed securities, had run out of cash. But, emblematic of the neoliberal faith that while individuals and the odd firm can make a mistake, the market as a whole can never be wrong, Cramer told his viewers not to pull their money out of Bear Stearns. 'No! No! No!' he yelled at the camera, 'Bear Stearns is not in trouble!' In fact, Bear Stearns was very much in trouble. Four days later the market wiped more than 90 per cent off its stock price.

By the summer of 2008, as home prices fell and ever more financial firms reported losses, panic began spreading through financial markets. The Dow Jones stock index, which had peaked above 14,000 the year before and had been hovering around 13,000 when Cramer was busily reassuring the faithful, shed another 2,000 points in July. Things then seemed to stabilize, and the market took a breather as brokers left for their summer holidays, keeping their BlackBerrys by their beach chairs as they anxiously watched the newsfeeds and market quotes that these impressive new devices could now provide them. However, it turned out to be the calm before the storm. No sooner did the traders return from their summer holidays than the dam burst.

On the morning of 15 September, the world woke to the news that the night before, after a frantic weekend that climaxed with a virtual riot at its head office, Lehman Brothers had been forced to declare bankruptcy. A huge investment bank founded in 1850, and lately captained by a man who once boasted he would rip out his rivals' hearts and eat them, Lehman's collapse would shatter the faith that had sustained the boom.

Over the following weekend, the outgoing Bush administration made a high-stakes gamble. It was determined to draw a line under the government backstop laid down back in the 1998 bailout of LTCM, repeatedly reinforced by Greenspan Puts, and then again underscored by the rescue of Bear Stearns (which the Federal Reserve had helped orchestrate the previous spring). Aware that this pattern of repeatedly picking up the tab for the banks' ill-judged punts was only pushing them into ever riskier behaviour, the Bush administration decided to send everyone a message: there would be no more indulgences, and banks and borrowers who had sinned would have to suffer the consequences. The government told Lehman Brothers it was on its own.

The Bush administration, which was instinctively more stoical than the Clinton White House had been – Bush, for instance, having rejected Clinton's cake-and-eat-it brand of green politics, saying America could choose between a clean environment or a growing economy, but couldn't have both – was trying to restore a bit of old-time religion in the banks. But after a generation of life in an epicurean temple, where the voice of a god had repeatedly echoed, assuring them they were in good hands, the announcement hit like a realisation that the booming voice had merely been a temple-servant hiding behind the columns. As soon as news broke that Lehman Brothers wouldn't get a bailout, pandemonium broke out in financial markets. Their faith shattered, financial firms, told they were now responsible for their own salvation, raced to harness their treasure. They called in their loans to any other banks that might be overexposed to the mortgage market – by now, that was pretty much everyone – and stopped giving credit, unsure if anyone might not be hiding Lehman-style dirty secrets. In consequence, credit markets froze. Any banks that needed cash had no choice but to start selling the assets on their books. However, with everyone hoarding their cash, nobody was buying, and prices plunged. As soon as the markets re-opened the Monday after the announcement, the Dow Jones went down another 500 points.[11] In the space of a few hours, nearly $1 trillion of wealth evaporated. Pensioners suddenly faced the alarming possibility that, as had happened to Russians in the 1990s, their retirement income might simply disappear.

Ever since the deregulation of the previous decades had knocked down the national walls separating countries' banks from one another, the global financial sector had evolved into one huge, amorphous entity. On any given day, as banks lent and borrowed from one another, up to $4 trillion sloshed around the globe. If you'd strung that many dollar bills together, they'd have reached beyond Jupiter. Most of that lending was short-term credit, like fronting a freighter's captain the money he needed to fuel his ship's tanks or giving a plant manager a credit note that enabled him to pay for some urgent repairs or supplies. Because operating this way saved firm managers the hassle and expense of keeping cash on hand, the modern economy functioned almost entirely on credit. Once the banks stopped taking one another's calls, the world economy was like an engine racing at full speed whose oil tank had just drained. The engine block melted and the car seized up.

That's what then happened to the world economy. Once bankers lost faith in one another, money simply disappeared. Ships stayed in port, warehouses that couldn't restock emptied, workers were told to stay at home and money became scarce; everyone stashing their cash under metaphorical (and, occasionally, actual) mattresses. Like the impact of the sudden death of a cult leader whose followers had believed he was immortal, this jarring loss of faith brought the economy crashing down. As talk spread of the next Great Depression, or worse, a return to the Stone Age as commerce ground to a halt and everyone retreated to the hills, nobody knew what to believe or who to trust. The economy couldn't budge. For the money gods to have any power, we all had to believe in them and to trust the priesthood could still mediate for us. We had all lost that faith.

Almost all of us can remember – try as we might not to – at least one incident in our lives when we found ourselves in a crowd and the mood was infectious and things started to turn in a direction we knew we would later regret, but still we did the thing we said we would never do, and forever afterwards we would hope it never came up again and if it ever did we would just say: 'What was I thinking?' You know the kind of incident. Things happen.

Funnily enough, though, many economists seem never to have these experiences. Maybe they need to get out more, but they tend to take a much rosier view of crowds than those of us who've experienced Ibiza. They, in contrast, hark back to 1907, when Charles Darwin's cousin Francis Galton made a rather startling observation at a county fair. Among the fairground attractions was a competition to guess the weight of a prize ox. Contestants, some of whom were livestock experts, placed their guesses in a box, and the prize went to whoever got it right. Few did. But when Galton calculated the average of all the guesses, he discovered it was just a few pounds off the ox's actual weight. As the conservative philosopher Edmund Burke once put it, individual humans may be foolish, but the species together is wise.[12]

That was the sort of reasoning behind Eugene Fama's efficient markets hypothesis. This article of faith, so central to the neoclassical canon, reassured all the true-believers that as wild as market behaviour became in the years leading up to the financial crisis, it couldn't be wrong. As with Galton's ox, individuals could make bad guesses, but the crowd would be right.

But in fact, as your spring-break or pub-night recollections will remind you, crowds are often terrible at making judgements. In *Irrational Exuberance*, Robert Shiller had noted the effect of 'herding' behaviour on asset prices. Although the neoclassical model takes humans to be like discrete atoms, in fact humans are social animals who seldom want to be the only one to miss out on the action or to feel left behind. Look at Ibiza. Just as people tend to cheat less if they know others will notice – even if they will suffer no official sanction, like a reduced grade, for their cheating[13] – so too do people tend to want to do what everyone else is doing. As investors rush into a market and drive up prices, Shiller pointed out, rather than stay away from dearer assets, the tendency is for even more investors to rush in. The reason Warren Buffett had grown so rich following his own advice to be greedy when everyone else was scared and scared when everyone else was greedy, was that so few of us could bring ourselves to go against the crowd. Who wants to be the only person to stay home during the big party, or to go to a restaurant that is empty when the one around the corner is packed?

In theory, as prices rise, demand drops. But in reality, when it comes to spending decisions, both investors and shoppers frequently raise their demand in response to price rises. Behavioural psychologists who wanted to see if the articles of faith in economics actually withstood scientific examination began conducting laboratory experiments with real humans to see how they acted in markets. They made many intriguing discoveries that rendered the foundations of neoclassical doctrine shaky. For instance, they found it was possible to boost sales of a given product not by cutting but by *raising* the price, because buyers could be easily tricked into thinking they were getting a better product. Equally, by planting positive thoughts or images in a shopper's mind, sellers could lead shoppers to be more favourably disposed towards buying their goods, even when the feel-good images had nothing to do with the product itself. A marketer just had to 'frame' buyers' minds before they made a purchasing decision.

Faced with such evidence, not a few neoclassical scholars responded the way a religious fundamentalist does to overwhelming proof that God didn't actually create the Earth in six days – they looked away and simply reasserted their faith in the efficient markets hypothesis. They also fell back on an acid test Milton Friedman had given them way back in the 1950s. Friedman had then argued that economists didn't need to trouble themselves overly with whether a model's assumptions were correct, provided the model's predictions seemed to accord well with reality.[14] And given that prices had kept on rising all through the boom, it was obvious to the faithful that the prices had to be right, because rational people wouldn't pay them if they weren't. Consequently, in his own writing on speculative bubbles, Friedman had more or less ruled them out as a possibility in an economy whose markets were free and whose money was stable.[15]

The financial crisis, which the then recently appointed Federal Reserve chairman Ben Bernanke called the worst in global history,[16] exploded the neoliberal myth. Next to the reality, the model now resembled little more than a fairy tale. As faith in the high priests of economics dissolved, it was left to the government, for so long derided by the free-market doctrine, to rescue the markets. The tax-slashing Bush administration had to chuck its commitment to a market-based solution and, amid the bedlam that followed the fall of Lehman Brothers, reverse course. Within twenty-four hours, when the insurance giant AIG revealed it would be the next firm to go to the wall, the administration announced it would use its own funds to cover AIG's losses. It then rushed to Congress for its approval, since it was going to need a big increase in its budget. There followed a mad two weeks in which the government begged a Congress filled with fellow Republicans, a good number of whom clung to Austrian economics and its belief that crashes were a needed culling of the herd, to allow it to print another $700 billion in cash to build a rescue fund for any banks headed to the wall – which at the moment, appeared to be almost all of them. As the no votes to the measure were tallied live on television, the stock index in the corner of the television screens ran downward like the milliseconds on a stopwatch, then crashed when the final 'no' vote was announced. Pandemonium broke out in the Capitol and bankers screamed that the end was nigh, so the government pressed for a second vote. Under intense pressure, Congress then relented, and the government got the go-ahead.

With the world economy at a standstill, the only player left who could restore hope to the markets was the American government. It more or less told the world that with its power to tax its people – in effect, its power to compel Americans to give the government some free labour-time in the future – it would find a way to get the economy moving again. Like a levitation-trick in which a magician is raised by an unseen cord pulled by a backstage crew, the miracle of free markets and the new economy, which was supposed to produce growth out of nothing but ingenuity, had to be sustained by ordinary Americans, who would have to augment their future work-rate to pay off the government's debts. The pulley they'd have to operate would in time turn out to be mighty heavy.

Soon, the stories in the press began to resemble the otherworldly anecdotes of an apocalyptic tale. As 2009 began, a German billionaire threw himself under a train; a French aristocrat whose investment fund had gone bankrupt slit his wrists in his Manhattan office; an Austrian banker who feared the Russian mafia would come for its money disappeared[17] and an American broker faked his own death in a plane crash while trying to escape to Mexico. Entire countries were falling like dominoes. Iceland, which had ridden the boom on credit, became insolvent. The economy collapsed, and the government had to ration imports in order to ensure that enough food and medicine still came to the island. Within a couple of months, Ireland's unemployment rate doubled and angry protesters filled Dublin demanding the heads of the bankers and politicians who'd sold them their now-worthless snake oil. In America, busloads of angry demonstrators were spilling out in front of Wall Street bankers' Connecticut homes while poor Jim Cramer was hauled onto The Daily Show, Jon Stewart's faux-news programme, where he tried to eat a bit of humble pie. Admitting he could have done better, Cramer was subjected to an excruciating ordeal of watching old videos revealing things he once said which he had subsequently denied saying. An angry Stewart looked straight at him and, in a moment bereft of any of the comedy with which he usually regaled his audiences, and despite Cramer's pained smile, told him: '... this isn't a fucking game.'

Between bailing it out and letting it die, the government had a third option for dealing with Lehman Brothers. It could have done what the British government had done with Northern Rock: taken it over, cleaned out its Augean Stables, replaced the boss, then re-privatised it. But the Bush administration, with its fervent commitment to free markets, never wanted to get into the business of taking over private firms – the rot had spread so far and wide in the financial sector that it would have found itself forced to do the same with many other insolvent banks.

However, on the night of 11 November, America's ever-loquacious political pundits suddenly found themselves choked up and speechless when 'Obama Elected' flashed on the nation's television screens. Almost immediately, a street party began outside the White House while in the massive crowd that had gathered outside Barack Obama's campaign headquarters in Chicago, people hugged and cried and fell to their knees in prayer at the news that America had just elected its first black president.

Obama had captivated Americans, and especially young Americans, with a message of hope and change which promised to shed Bill Clinton's neoliberal legacy and restore a collective vision to the Democratic Party. Among his advisers were some economists who regarded the financial crisis as something of an opportunity to finally clean up America's overweight and politically powerful banking system. Seeing as they were stepping into the shoes of power just as the banks were at their most vulnerable, and would take the Bush administration's baton in implementing the bailouts, they enjoyed one of those rare moments of seemingly limitless power. Some in Obama's entourage took the view that the banks should be taken into government hands and broken up before being put back on the market.

However, when Obama named his Treasury secretary and chief economic adviser, the president-elect surprised many of his supporters by pulling up two people with impeccable Wall Street ties: Federal

Reserve Bank of New York president Tim Geithner and – possibly nodding to the principle that to catch a thief, you need a thief – the very man many Americans held largely responsible for the deregulation that had caused the crisis, Lawrence Summers.[18] Almost at once, Geithner and Summers announced the banks were 'too big to fail' and had to be bailed out, with their direction and ownership more or less intact.

So reassured were the bankers that business as usual had been restored by their old friends that one of the first things AIG did with its own bailout money, once the government's cash-injection shored up its share price, was to pay its executives fat bonuses. It didn't take a long memory to recall that this was the same Lawrence Summers who had, a decade before, condemned the supposed crony capitalism of the Third World.

By staving off an implosion of the financial system, politicians and central bankers averted what would have been the second Great Depression. The economies of the West contracted, but they did not collapse. Our leaders would thus congratulate themselves on having learned the lessons of the past, and managed to restore faith in money, no matter how shaky that faith might now be. However, time would reveal the cure to be so bitter, it wasn't obvious to everyone that it was better than the disease.

The 1929 crash had wiped out millionaires, and the Depression that followed was indiscriminate in the victims it took, shattering rich and poor alike. But one consequence of this broad-based pain was that there was an equally broad-based consensus that a new faith was needed. Even the fashions of the 1930s reflected this, as the ostentation of the 1920s gave way to styles of dress that yearned for modest elegance that was widely accessible. That kind of common culture made it possible for politicians to build the coalition needed to forge ahead with such profound social and political changes as the New Deal and the creation of the Keynesian welfare state.

This time around, in 2008, few billionaires were wiped out. Following a few weeks of panic in the autumn of that year, most watched as their portfolios resumed an upward rise, their fortunes quickly restored by the bailouts of the financial system. However, in the subsequent denouement of the crisis, as the recession lingered and governments were forced to deal with the challenge of lean times, societies polarised between those who'd emerged unscathed from the crash and those who were now being forced to bear the brunt of the pain. The fashion and style of the Kardashian age would declare wealth as a sign of moral virtue, celebrity culture occupying the place once filled in our imaginations by the cult of saints. But as this division between the winners and losers of the neoliberal age came into stark relief, the politics of Western societies split just as deeply. It seemed like half the people thought the temple looked just fine as it was, the others wanted to burn it to the ground. Social cohesion frayed, and as the high priests of economics withdrew to their cloisters, the West entered a new age of political uncertainty. Politicians, corporate elites, the media, anything that smacked of the 'establishment', 'immigrants' and above all the 'experts' all came in for fierce denunciation by populists looking for scapegoats for the failed harvests of the neoliberal age. With its mantras now failing millions, economics entered a crisis.

CHAPTER 21

LET THEM EAT DSGE MODELS

Despite the complexity of the financial instruments behind the crash of 2008, the plot of the crisis is simple and the tale ancient. To illustrate, let's recount it as a storyteller might.

Imagine you were a baker, or a blacksmith, in an isolated village. There was money there, but no inflation to speak of. So what you charged for your work didn't change in any given year. You could raise your income only by improving what you did or developing new products.

One day you sat down with pen and paper and worked out what you'd earn in your lifetime. Between setting up your shop and retirement, you thought you would work a total of perhaps 80,000 hours. That gave you a rough idea of what your lifetime income was going to be.

You'd never used the village bank, preferring to hide your savings under the floorboards. However, you knew that lots of villagers trusted the woman who managed it and left their money in her care. So with your estimate of lifetime earnings in hand, you went to call on her and proposed a deal. You told her that if she used her influence to persuade the carpenter – who you happened to know kept his savings in her bank – to build you a new home, you'd commit to setting aside a portion of your future earnings to pay him, and a smaller portion for her as a fee for mediating the deal.

She could see you were fit and strapping and were building up a clientele and she'd heard enough about you to know you were good for your word. She also thought that even if you were to drop dead before you fulfilled the terms of your contract, someone else would happily take over paying the carpenter in return for possession of your home. However, she said, there was one small snag in your otherwise sound plan. The carpenter, she explained, wasn't going to accept his payment in instalments over the next twenty or so years. He wanted all the money as soon as the job was done. However, she had a way to eliminate this snag and explained how her bank worked.

She made lots of deals like these and always ensured that everyone kept their end of the bargain. What she did was print IOUs – money – equivalent to the value of the labour-time you would give her over the next twenty years to pay back the loan. You would then use that money to pay the carpenter, and she'd collect your payments from now on, adding a surcharge for what she called her 'interest' in the deal. This struck you as a brilliant idea. You shook hands, and the next day she gave you the money. You paid the carpenter, and watched proudly as your new house went up. Every month thereafter, you gave the banker some of your earnings.

One day, a stranger wandered into your shop. He told you he had a magical box which could make money out of nothing. But the catch was that you could only open it once. The longer you left it closed, the more money it would make. Although this sounded too good to be true, you couldn't help imagining what your life would be like if it *were* true.

So the next day, you went to consult your priest, and were told that, yes, the box was real. Still you had doubts. So you went to see the village headman, who told you that, yes, what the visitor said was true – and indeed that the headman had invited the stranger to the village precisely because he was a brilliant man who had discovered a magic formula. The headman went on to tell you about all the wondrous ways this magical box was going to transform everyone's lives and make the village rich.

You were now pretty well sold on the idea and ready to buy.

But the box was expensive, more than you could afford at that moment. So you went back to your banker, and you proposed her another deal. If she agreed to lend you some more money to buy the box, you'd commit more of your future work to paying her back. She happily agreed, and printed you some more of her promissory notes.

You bought the box and put it under your floorboards. Time passed, and without even being opened it started working its magic. More and more people wanted to get hold of these boxes. But the visitor, who disappeared into the forest each day and returned with another box, could only produce one a day. So people knocked on your door, offering to buy your box. They competed for it by outbidding one another, and the box grew to be worth even more than you had paid for it. But you also knew the money accumulating inside the box was growing even faster, so you didn't want to sell it. But then you got a clever idea.

You went back to your banker, who by now was getting to know you pretty well, and you offered to commit yet more of your future work in return for yet more money. Because the box was worth more than before, you knew you'd never have to actually do that extra work for her because you could just pay her back by either selling the box, or opening it and using the money it had created. She agreed and gave you yet more IOUs.

On it went for some time, the box becoming ever-more valuable, and the money inside growing faster by the day. More people were buying the boxes, more people wanted them, and their price just kept going up and up. By now the stranger was a rich man and had built himself the biggest house in the village. But you didn't begrudge him this luxury since, after all, he had made you rich. On the contrary, each day you went to the village square to applaud as the headman gave rousing speeches saying how the box was ushering the village into a new golden age, and would make it possible for its inhabitants to do all kinds of exciting things. As the headman spoke, the priest, now dressed in much finer robes, sat behind and nodded in agreement.

Then one day, you noticed a neighbour's box for sale in his window. The price was lower than you expected. Not that this troubled you, since the price was still far higher than what you paid for your box. But it left you puzzled. The following day, you noticed the box was still for sale, but now for a lower price. Wondering what the visitor was now selling his boxes for, you went to look for him only to find his shop abandoned: since everyone in the village now had boxes – some people had even bought several – nobody was buying them any more.

You decided the time had come to sell your box. You put it in your shop window at a price just below your neighbour's – still a handsome profit over what you had originally paid for it. But nobody came knocking. The next day you lowered the price a bit more. Still nobody came knocking. In fact, some of your neighbours started putting their boxes up for sale as well. And you kept reducing the price until one day it fell below the amount of money you calculated was in the box – a smaller profit than before, but still a tidy one, and enough to pay your debt to the banker.

So having failed to sell the box, you decided to open it, pay the bank and pocket the difference. Reflecting briefly on the good times you had had, you felt wistful they were now finished and you'd have to go back to your old lifestyle. But the memories were great. And you opened the box. And it was empty.

And that is the children's tale of the 2008 financial crisis.

Any good illusionist will recognise both the ancient lineage and simple function of the instruments behind the property bubble. Like the magic box in our tale, or like the optical tricks, veils and smokescreens a magic act uses to distract your attention from what is going on behind the scenes, they were instruments which, by their impenetrability, prevented us from 'opening the box' and examining its contents to see if they were real. Few if any of us who rode the boom understood the magic behind it, and when we consulted the high priests for explanations, we were told that before we could even hope to apprehend what was going on, we had to understand the mystical language of economics, which it took years of study to master. Our leaders, meanwhile, were able to point to the roaring economy around us, and cite the evident genius of the high priests in leading us to it, to persuade us that what was inside our own box of instruments was indeed very, very real. Leave it to the experts, they said.

The ultimate reality the banks produced turned out to be more complicated than the empty box in the tale above. It is the children's version, after all. Real things did ultimately come out of the bubbles, such as dot-com survivors like Amazon or all those Irish houses (some of which may yet find owners). However, their aggregate value turned out to be much less than what we'd been led to believe in the boom days. Furthermore, since so much money got spent in the bubble-days in the form of cash advances or equity loans against those inflated wealth figures, we were, like the poor protagonist in our village tale, left with debt that will saddle us for years.

Some of the magicians behind the bubble, like Bernie Madoff, were like the village visitor in the children's tale: frauds and liars. Many, probably most, were only strands in a web of deceit their hubris inadvertently wove. The theoretical physicist who designed the model didn't understand how the banker turned it into money, and the banker didn't understand the model at all, but both could see that it was doing what it was meant to do. Moreover, the high priests of economics – living by Milton Friedman's golden rule that if the predictions a model makes turn out to be correct, so must be the model that made them – continued to give the instruments and the resulting boom their blessing.

That's not to say there weren't economists who didn't criticize what was going on, insisting that a dangerous speculative bubble was inflating. Robert Shiller was the most prominent, but long before him Hyman Minsky had built upon Keynes's work to develop a cyclical model of the economy that concluded that booms and busts were more or less inevitable. Minsky argued that the longer an economy remained stable and healthy, the more distant would memories of the last crisis become. Thus, as investors became more complacent, they'd take more risks. And as they took more risks, asset-values would rise, creating a 'wealth-effect' that inflated spending, strengthening the economy and persuading everyone that busts were a thing of the past. To get on the ride before asset-prices rose too high, investors would then, like the blacksmith in our tale, take on debt, which would further inflate the bubble. But when debts finally reached the point that borrowers had to start paying them back, they'd start selling assets. As selling exceeded demand, asset prices would plunge, and the bubble would burst.[1] Charles Kindleberger later refined Minsky's work into a model of manias, panics and crashes throughout history.[2]

Unfortunately, throughout the neoliberal age, the work of Minsky and Kindleberger got little attention from academic economists. Adair Turner, chairman of Britain's Financial Services Authority at the time of the 2008 crisis, would later remark that Minsky had been 'largely and dangerously ignored in his lifetime'.[3] As a result, it was only after the bubble burst that everyone started cracking the spines of their books, though even then their popularity was greater among investors and policy-makers – the people involved in the actual business of economics – than among academic economists.[4] Partly this was due to the fact that Minsky's and Kindleberger's scholarship contradicted orthodoxy, Kindleberger explicitly rejecting Friedman's presumption of market-rationality. Minsky drifted even further outside the canon and into the wilderness altogether, since he rejected not only the neoclassical model but the Samuelson synthesis, leaving no place for him in any of the post-war churches. Specifically, Minsky said that the Samuelson synthesis, which its adepts believed they could use to micromanage the economy scientifically so there need never be another recession, encouraged governments to run permanent deficits (which they justified as investments in future growth). Minsky, though, insisted a pure Keynesian model could only ever accommodate deficits during times of recession, and that their persistence after growth had resumed helped lay the foundations of the next bubble by prompting too-rapid economic growth.[5] While the model seemed to accord quite well with the lessons of history, it was not only heretical but, like Kindleberger's work, was not even written in the temple language in which economists held their debates. Eschewing the applied mathematics that had become the *sine qua non* of economic scholarship, Minsky's and Kindleberger's more traditional narrative approaches precluded them from serious consideration. You can't work at the Vatican if you don't speak Latin.

Once the crisis hit, the neoliberal temple emptied, leaving the priests alone at their altar. At the moment politicians most desperately needed advice on what to do next, the economics discipline broke out in squabbling, with many voices calling for a root-and-branch reform of the curriculum.[6] Left to their own devices as the world fell down around them, therefore, governments everywhere chucked their neoliberal catechism and pulled their old Keynesian bibles off the shelf. Flying by the seat of their pants, central bankers and politicians crafted ad hoc solutions under the immense pressure of the need to do something, anything, before the global financial system crumbled completely.[7] Cobbling together bailout programmes to keep the bank doors open, cutting interest rates and printing money to keep it flowing, making public statements to persuade everyone to believe in them again by saying they'd do whatever was needed to keep the economy going, and running up huge debts to engage in aggressive stimulus of the economy the way one applies electrical charges to a patient in cardiac arrest, our leaders managed to stave off an economic apocalypse. Even conservative governments normally averse to deficit spending splashed out the money, while in Europe the 'automatic stabilisers' of generous welfare states stepped in to do the job.

Taken all together, governments across the world pumped several trillion dollars into the world economy in the years following the crisis.[8] In the West, the economy's heart resumed beating – feebly at first, and when it finally rose off the operating table, it was admittedly much weaker than it had been before. But at least it was alive.

And for a brief time, the Keynesians, so marginalised during the high age of neoliberalism, found their church pews filled once more as the faithful, like the bankers who filled Wall Street's churches after the 1929 crash, sought comfort in the old faith.

Their conversions didn't last long, though.

Having won the US election in the middle of the crisis, Barack Obama had to begin coordinating immediately with the outgoing Bush administration. His team crafted an $800 billion stimulus package to extend unemployment benefits, create jobs, build roads and bridges, repair schools, increase government wages, develop green energy and cut taxes.

Orthodoxy flew out of the window as schism tore through the church once more. When it came time to give a verdict on the government's plan, economists split into two factions. Some two hundred of them joined three Nobel laureates and took out a newspaper advertisement saying the stimulus wouldn't work. Five other Nobel laureates led another two hundred in writing a letter to Congress saying it would. Only months before, a paper had circulated in seminar rooms extolling the broad consensus economists had reached in their deliberations about economic management. Befitting such confidence that economists had found the holy grail of economic management, the Nobel laureate Robert Lucas – who once noted approvingly that by the late twentieth century, the church had so effectively purged itself of Keynesianism that 'the audience start(ed) to whisper and giggle to one another' when a Keynesian thought popped up at a seminar – declared that he and his peers had now mastered the science of economic management: 'the central problem of depression-prevention', he announced to a conclave of his peers, 'has been solved'.[9]

That was then, when the College of Cardinals could give its ruling. Now, the princes of the church were throwing the palace furniture at each other. Lucas called the stimulus package 'schlock economics'. In response, another Nobel laureate, Paul Krugman, decried the 'Dark Age' of Lucas's Chicago School. It was once again left to ordinary Americans to decide which set of gurus they would believe – especially since their fallen high priest, their tarnished 'Maestro' Alan Greenspan – remained surprisingly muted. When asked what he thought of the stimulus proposal, the former Federal Reserve chairman (since succeeded by Ben Bernanke) said he 'had little to add'.[10]

However, if economists were mired in controversy and dispute, for a brief moment it appeared the rest of America had united around a shared purpose. Barack Obama arrived in Washington, a city that normally made an art of rancour, to a chorus of goodwill. As he visited the homes of Republican leaders and made social calls on conservative journalists, everyone seemed to revel in the warm buzz that came from the realisation that Americans, for all their faults and racist history, had buried one of the ugly ghosts of their past and elected a black president. Even though Republicans opposed the stimulus package, it was nevertheless sailing through Congress at the time the new president swore his oath of office. Within weeks of his moving into the Oval Office, the legislation arrived on his desk and he signed it into law. He then announced that along with the stimulus package, Congress had approved a $75-billion package to help distressed home owners keep their houses.

That's when the goodwill evaporated.[11] Early the next morning, one of the television business channels held a panel discussion on the new plan. At one point in the conversation the host turned to one of the network's journalists, Rick Santelli, who was reporting live from the Chicago Mercantile Exchange, to ask him his thoughts. She got an earful. Yelling into the camera above the din of the exchange, Santelli launched into a tirade against a government that he said was 'promoting bad behaviour'. 'How about this, President New Administration,' he said before suggesting sarcastically that Obama should use his campaign's much-vaunted tech savvy to put up a website where Americans could vote 'to see if we really want to subsidise the losers' mortgages' or instead 'reward people that can actually carry the water instead of drink the water'. The floor around him erupted in cheers. Turning to face the watching crowd, he yelled, 'How many of you people wanna pay for your neighbour's mortgage that has an extra bathroom and can't pay their bills?' He then turned back to the camera and shouted, 'We're thinking of having a Chicago Tea Party in July.'

The clip went viral. Within hours, websites with the name 'tea-party' had begun appearing. The next day, a Facebook page was up. A week later, forty American cities joined a coordinated protest at which demonstrators dressed up in Revolutionary-era outfits. All voiced the same message: rejection of the president's stimulus package, a demand for smaller government, and lower taxes.

Around this time, like the relapse of a disease that had been thought cured, the financial crisis revealed it still had some bite in it. During the housing bubble, it turned out that Goldman Sachs had been playing both sides of the casino, not only selling derivatives but also buying insurance against them – thereby profiting both on their way up and their way down. Early in 2010, Matt Taibbi published an article in *Rolling Stone* that decried the investment bank as a 'vampire squid wrapped around the face of humanity'.[12] It therefore hardly did wonders for the bank's PR when, almost simultaneously, it transpired it had also been helping the Greek government to hide its debts, enabling it to conceal the true scale of its spending from its creditors.

With less than a fiftieth of the EU economy, Greece's dodgy book-keeping might have been brushed off as yet another bit of naughtiness by a lovable but incorrigible relative, best dealt with by a stern talking-to and no more pudding (the pudding being, in this case, cheap credit). Unfortunately, though, the problems didn't end at the Greek border. When the euro had been created at the end of the 1990s, all countries intending to adopt it had to sign a 'stability and growth pact' whereby they agreed to keep their deficits and debts within prescribed limits. In practice, the enforcement mechanism of the SGP turned out to be something of a leaky sieve. Several governments had been flouting the limits for years. So when the recession hit and governments were forced to boost their deficits to cover lost tax revenues and to meet the increased spending (like unemployment relief) that resulted, their accounts got really stretched.

When the Greek government ran out of cash and had to admit, early in 2010, that it had been cooking the books and that the true value of its debt was higher than it had previously acknowledged, the news fell like a spark in a tinderbox. Investors who held Greek government bonds, anxious to play it safe after their brush with death in the 2008 crash, started dumping them to safeguard their money. It didn't stop there. As had happened in the Asian crisis, investors eager to make up their losses began targeting several other European countries they thought bore too much of a family resemblance to Greece in their liberal spending habits. Some of the high-fliers of the boom days, like Ireland, Portugal and Spain, watched as investors unloaded their bonds on the market. In the short term, the rush to sell hurt only the holders of the securities, since they were forced to sell them at less than face value and record the sales as losses in their accounts. But since falling bond prices translate into rising yields, interest rates on government debt rose sharply. The most vulnerable governments were going to have to pay sharply higher interest on any money borrowed. This would force them either to cut their spending drastically, or declare themselves insolvent. The rising panic only stoked the selling further and interest rates across almost all of Europe began soaring.

It played out gradually at first. Addressing problems as they arose, on a case-by-case basis, the EU and its member states managed one crisis after the next. However, it soon became apparent that the Union's cumbersome political structure of overlapping authorities, which seemed so democratic back in the good days, was struggling to offer the continent's economy any clear direction now that bad times had hit. Anxiety smouldered, then smoked, then eventually burst into flames. In late 2011, the pace of selling sped up, and a fully fledged panic broke out. At one point, Greek interest rates soared to nearly 30 per cent, while those in Portugal and Ireland rose into the double digits. At this rate, it was just a matter of time before governments ground to a halt.

Nor did the problems stop at the Treasury doors. In the same way banks all over the world had invested in the securities behind the US housing boom, so had the financial system bought a lot of European government paper back in the boom days. German and French banks in particular had invested in the comparatively speculative bonds of southern Europe. Now that these bonds were plummeting in value, huge losses were showing up on their books. Shareholders in the banks, anxious to get out quick, then started dumping their shares, and the second chapter of the global crisis was underway. Amid this lack of direction from the EU's governments, the president of the European Central Bank, Mario Draghi, declared in the summer of 2012 that, 'the European Central Bank will do whatever it takes to preserve the Euro,' underlining his resolve by then adding, 'And believe me, it will be enough.' The markets turned, bond yields falling back to manageable levels, and the worst of the crisis ended.

Now the really hard work began. Rather than allow governments to walk away from their debts, even when all parties secretly agreed they were probably unpayable (as was the case for Greece), a 'troika' of the European Commission, European Central Bank and International Monetary Fund came together to coordinate rescue packages for afflicted governments. As north European governments joined the fund in marshalling the resources needed to keep their southern counterparts solvent, relief was offered on condition that governments implement punishing austerity programmes. With strong influence by the German government – which was not only conservative but retained Germany's long-standing preoccupation with runaway spending, going back to its 1920s experience with hyperinflation – the new regime imposed stoicism on a continent that had long prized its Epicureanism, relative to the joyless Anglos. Whatever path the EU had once charted, it showed that its future would now be thoroughly neoliberal.

*

In the months that followed Rick Santelli's 'rant heard round the world', US Tea Partiers began organising into local groups, turning up at Republican primaries and demanding small-government candidates. Pushing the party further to the right, they succeeded in toppling centrist Republicans whose hands, they believed, had been sullied by too many handshakes with liberals, and replacing them with candidates they considered purer conservatives. In the following year's mid-term elections, they would go on to overwhelm President Obama's Democratic Party, helping Republicans recapture the House of Representatives, from which perch they began to frustrate any efforts at compromise. The ghost of Savonarola had come to cleanse the Republican soul of its years of sin and error.

By then, Britain's Conservative Party had narrowly defeated the Labour government in elections, campaigning on a platform to reduce the deficit and cut government spending. Amid the severity of the global recession, the new chancellor, George Osborne, continued the stimulus programme begun by his Labour predecessor, but then implemented his commitment to austerity – though it would be selective, cutting spending in some areas, like education and welfare, but maintaining or even increasing it in others, like pensions and health care. In Germany and Canada, after a similar burst of stimulus, conservative administrations put the restoration of lean government on the agenda. Germany would then use its leverage over the European Union to press European countries to do the same. This would open a deep rift in European politics.

Countries such as Greece and Italy would have liked to do as the United States had done and stimulate their way out of their recessions, but were forced to cut their spending to rein in deficits. Arguably their previous profligacy was unsustainable. Yet, had they been able to walk away from the debts accumulated by previous governments and then start living within their means – as they could have done had they kept their own currencies – they could have at least made a clean break. But because German taxpayers had bailed out their banks, they wanted their pound of flesh. That meant governments had to cut their budgets, at times savagely, not just to live within their means, but to keep making their debt payments. For their part, the high priests were undeterred. The IMF, which in the 1990s Asian crisis had operated like an arm of the US Treasury, now involved itself in European affairs and worked closely with the governments of Germany and the European Union to push the new doctrine. Across western Europe austerity ruled, but at the expense of economic recovery. The European economy barely budged, replicating the long and tenacious stagnation that had beset Japan ever since its 1989 crash. Greece was hardest bit, as deep cuts to government spending slashed a quarter off its output and drove the unemployment rate to 25 per cent – twice that among young people. If somewhat less deep, recessions were still brutal in Spain, Ireland and Portugal. When recoveries finally came, years later, they were tepid, with their gains concentrated in a comparatively small number of hands.

Almost everywhere, within months of its return, Keynesianism had been ejected again from the temple. The stage was set for the Chicago School to launch its counter-reformation. Amid the turmoil, the Queen opened a new building at the London School of Economics. Since it was, after all, a school of economics, she thought it a good place to ask what on earth was going on in their corridors. Describing the financial crisis as 'awful', she asked innocently, 'Why did nobody notice it?'[13] None other than Robert Lucas took it upon himself to provide the answer. In a guest column for the *Economist*, he insisted that, 'One thing we are not going to have, now or ever, is a set of models that forecasts sudden falls in the value of financial assets' – choosing to overlook the work of people like Robert Shiller and Hyman Minsky who had done just that. Leaning on a bit of reasoning that a logician would recognise as a syllogism – a rhetorical device in which the Sorbonne had trained its priests in the days of Adam Smith – he said this conclusion followed naturally from a premise he declared irrefutable: Eugene Fama's efficient markets hypothesis. (That Shiller, for one, rejected the EMH as false was no doubt the reason Lucas treated him the way one does a heretic: ignoring him, and simply reasserting the commandments.) In a manner reminiscent of medieval scholastics who reasoned from a divinely inspired premise to establish practical guidelines for living, he went on to make a statement that elicited a collective dropping of jaws. Defending his colleagues who had been criticised for producing models before the crisis that predicted continued rises in asset prices, he said their predictions hadn't failed because they'd been made 'conditional on a crisis not occurring'.[14]

The prophet who'd said the rains would never fail now added that his prediction had been conditional on there not being a drought.

To stave off financial collapse and help restart the economy, central banks everywhere had cut interest rates to nearly nothing – and in the odd case actually dropped them below zero, which meant savers had to *pay* their bank to hold on to their rainy-day fund. Needless to say, this encouraged people to spend their hoard and to invest their savings elsewhere – which is just what central banks had hoped they would do. Those with nest eggs began buying shares or property again. Not only did this arrest the stock-market slide, but it helped end the recession.

However, since you need to have a cash hoard before you can spend or invest it, this policy benefited most those who already had assets – which is to say, the richer members of society.[15] With their stock-market portfolios once more rising in value, the good times began rolling again for the fortunate few. And moreover, because the economy was in such a slump, prices remained low – which is to say, those with money could spend more freely than before. There emerged the incongruous spectacle of a thriving market for luxury goods while the soup kitchens filled with new clients.

That's because at the other end of the social scale, things didn't look so good. New jobs either remained scarce or, where they returned, as in the United States and UK, were comparatively poorly paid. Thus, real earnings for most people continued declining – and when rebounds did occur, as happened in the United States in 2015, they came much later in the business cycle than usual and to levels still below pre-crisis peaks, raising doubts about their long-term solidity.

Once austerity kicked in, life became especially challenging for young people. Jobs in manufacturing continued migrating to low-wage regions, restricting job opportunities for the unskilled working class. But even university graduates faced a frozen job market. Previously one of the most common routes for young people who'd been to university had been to take jobs in the public sector. But now governments had reduced openings. In countries like France, which protected the rights of workers, firms that couldn't cut costs by laying off staff did so by freezing new employment, or offering new recruits only temporary jobs. British firms began experimenting with 'zero-hours' contracts, which meant they would recruit workers, keep them on call, but pay them only for the hours they worked (with no guarantee of getting any work at all in any given week). While such 'labour market flexibility', so idealised by the neoliberal creed, suited some employees – like students who wanted to pick up work on the side – they helped further dampen wages.[16] Meanwhile, unions began negotiating 'differential' contracts – existing workers got to keep all their current pay and benefits, whereas new employees were given much less generous deals: new employees in the Spanish car industry, for instance, had to content themselves with temporary contracts and a sixth less than what their older peers were paid.[17] The 'We're all in it together' of an earlier age had mutated into 'We're in at different depths, get used to it.'

As a result, the age-old pattern of people earning their best money while young and then later living off their savings and turning to their children for help, was reversed. Everywhere, youth unemployment soared, reaching 50 per cent in countries like Greece and Spain. Young people began moving back in with their parents. With it developed a new literary genre produced by jobless young people living in their parents' basements. A few got lucky and, like Lena Dunham, wrote blogs that attracted large readerships among people in the same boat. More, though, showed up in the casualty figures of mental-health wings.[18]

Austerity wasn't just eliminating employment opportunities, though. With governments eager to retain the support of older voters, who turned out in greater numbers at election time, pensions, health care and other forms of government spending that benefited older people were most often roped off from the austerity scalpel. That meant governments cut elsewhere – even when, as was the case in the UK, overall government spending actually increased to accommodate privileged constituencies. Given that home owners have always been more likely to vote than renters[19] – a long-standing relationship going back to the principle that you take more interest in politics when you have investments to defend – and that 'Generation Rent' were increasingly being pushed off the 'property ladder', they were obviously an easy target for austerity. Tuition fee increases and cuts to social assistance for young people became the norm. The worse the austerity, the worse it got for young people. Athens filled with university dropouts who tried to scrape together a living by selling packs of tissues on street corners, and London squatters broke into some of the thousands of vacant properties that the global elite were then snapping up with the money central banks were throwing at them.

The high priests of finance and economics may have got the economy back 'under control' as Robert Lucas had declared in his encyclical, but to many ordinary people it was a control that excluded them. In contrast to the great wealth-transfer of the imperial age that had benefited almost everyone in the West, governments now seemed to turn their attention inwards to see who they could squeeze for more money. The British parliamentarian David Willetts published a book called *The Pinch* in which he said that baby-boomers were effectively stealing from the young. In Britain in the years that followed the crisis, real incomes for retirees rose by a tenth, while those of young people fell by the same amount.[20] As the baby-boomers settled into retirement, it seemed to some of austerity's younger victims that the same 1960s generation, which had a half-century before fought for the right to pursue their desires without restraint, would now defend that right to their deaths (even if that meant denying others that same right).

But if there was any truth in the allegation that old people were milking the young, inter-generational wealth transfer probably paled next to another type that affected people of all ages: the transfer from poor to rich. In theory, the aggressive use by central banks of interest-rate cuts and 'quantitative easing' – the purchase of government bonds by central banks to put money in the hands of investors who wanted to unload the bonds they owned – was meant not only to kick-start spending, but investment as well. Since most government bonds were owned by banks, giving the banks all this extra money was meant to prompt them to lend to firms, which could then expand their operations.

That was what the theory said. But the world had changed since the theory had been written down. To begin with, where banking regulations were tightened after the crisis, banks had to set aside more cash as 'buffers', an effect intensified by their own desire to 'self-insure': they had so burned their fingers in the financial crisis that they wanted to set aside a lot of the money central banks gave them. That way if another 'Lehman Brothers moment' ever hit, they'd have lots of cash to ride out the storm. In addition, given the long-term decline in the underlying rates of economic growth in Western economies, returns on investments in old-fashioned businesses were also declining. The big money was elsewhere. A lot of money went south, as banks aided the flow of investment to developing countries. Since growth rates were higher there, borrowers were able to pay higher interest rates, and so banks could make better returns. In a startling reversal of what had happened during the Asian crisis, this time Western central banks were helping to subsidise Third World development.[21]

Moreover, with money so cheap and the dangers of borrowing lowered – when you're paying next to zero interest, you can risk bigger losses on your punts – investors went looking for the next bubble. Whether it was London property, commodities, or the next dot-com wave – this time, the 'app' economy of start-ups like Facebook and Twitter – investors crowded into assets simply because other investors were doing it.

Housing became an especially popular magnet for capital. If lots of new houses had resulted, it would have increased the supply and enabled young people to climb onto the 'property ladder'. But that wasn't the case. Amid punishing recessions, house prices fell in some regions where there had previously been bubbles. But in places where policymakers were congratulating themselves for having avoided the recession, the outcome was that amid sluggish growth house prices soared. In London, New York, Vancouver and San Francisco, speculative money flooded into property, driving up the prices. This effect was further intensified by some of the services to have emerged out of the recession. Airbnb was accused of helping to withdraw properties from the rental market to convert them into pricey short-term lets – an ironic outcome since sharing services had originated as a way for people to stretch resources. The combined effect of these moves was to drive houses in many cities beyond the reach of first-time buyers. Although the 'wealth effect' led asset-owners to loosen their purse strings, helping recovery, underlying output rose more sluggishly since the cost of doing business was also rising. Entrepreneurs needed a place to set up shop, after all. Meanwhile, with all the demand for loans in relatively safe property, banks moved their lending away from more-risky new ventures to lend to people expanding their property portfolios.[22]

When you're sitting on property, buying a second home to let, or putting money into the next mobile app, your investment is creating few new jobs. In fact, it may even be killing them. A hundred years ago in America, the explosive new sector was car-making, and Ford Motor Company alone employed tens of thousands of workers and created over a million jobs indirectly in showrooms, garages and workshops. At the start of the twenty-first century, the explosive new sector was information technology, giving us the likes of Facebook and Twitter. In the decade after their creation they created barely 15,000 jobs between them. As for indirect employment, Facebook probably helped eliminate more jobs than that among journalists alone. Meanwhile, those who worked in the new media companies that Facebook had helped spin off were typically young university graduates who spent their days in cafes on their computers churning out content hoping they could get enough 'likes' to produce a trickle of advertising revenue. The result is that in the wake of the crash, those of us who owned assets got richer by the day while those looking for work found it harder than ever, and had less government support to assist them. The net effect of this 'bubblenomics' was that the rich got richer and the poor got poorer – something of a twenty-first century Enclosure movement. Hardly anybody sitting on a central bank board was happy with this state of affairs. But hardly anyone could come up with a better idea.

So yes, strictly speaking, the high priests had prevented a depression on the scale of the 1930s, and could thus still congratulate themselves on their wisdom. But how abundant was that wisdom? In the 1930s, five years after the US economy bottomed, it resumed growing at an average rate of 7 per cent per year. Five years after the shallower recession that followed the crash of 2008, it was doing so at 2 per cent per year. Like the steward in a biblical tale who buries his master's wealth to prevent it disappearing, the priesthood had claimed success by saying it had simply set out not to fail. To the bereft in the pews who'd been promised miracles just a few years before, it was a hollow boast indeed.

In 2011, the US Congressional Budget Office published a study revealing that over the previous thirty years – roughly since the dawn of the neoliberal age – the top 1 per cent of the country's population had doubled its share of the nation's income.[23] In the same year, the Swiss Federal Institute of Technology conducted a network analysis of the global corporate elite, which uncovered a small web made up of a few hundred tightly networked and extraordinarily wealthy individuals, dominated by bankers commanding vast pools of capital.[24]

On the Internet that summer, the phrase 'We are the ninety-nine per cent' began turning up. Within weeks protest camps began popping up outside stock exchanges and other centres of financial power. Inspired by the success of popular occupations of public squares in Tunisia and Egypt earlier that year, which had brought down governments, and also impressed by the spread of austerity protests across southern Europe in the spring, these young people said they would occupy their own cities' public squares and demand an economic system which better served their needs. Within weeks, there were Occupy protests in nearly 1,000 cities across the world.

Older journalists, particularly those who compared this wave of youth revolt with that of their own generation in the 1960s, regarded the Occupiers with bemusement, and sometimes outright scorn. The movement's anarchic and spontaneous nature meant that there was no clear coordinating body. Despite some significant voices, and in particular that of the radical Canadian magazine *Adbusters*, Occupy articulated no single goal or ideology. Rather, it united around a set of common themes: a reversal of the power of high finance, a crackdown on tax evasion, greater equality and more opportunity for those currently marginalised by the system.

Like a Gestalt drawing, which depending on your angle reveals either a fashionable young woman or a withered old lady, the same image may simply have revealed different tales to different observers. Occupy had roots in the 1990s anti-globalisation movement, which had brought together a multitude of different voices and given them unity in numbers while allowing them to also go their own way. They all agreed what they were against, namely neoliberalism in all its guises. They didn't feel as strongly that they needed to agree what they were for, not if they could first create a political environment in which they were able to express themselves. Even if they could be mobilised around specific causes, as they were for the 2008 election of Barack Obama, studies showed that young people tended not to vote but involved themselves in grassroots activism and community organisation.[25] They tended to forgo the top-down organisation strategies of conventional politics in favour of horizontal coordination over social media – in which they were so savvy and which the Arab Spring protesters, who also tended to be young, well-educated, unemployed and economically frustrated, had used to such devastating effect.

The occupations themselves would have short lives. Despite the

best efforts of the New York protesters in Zucotti Park (two blocks
north of Wall Street) to curry favour with the forces of law and order,
the police had just been given a pay rise and knew which side their
bread was buttered. Using force to clear out the camps, they moved
on one settlement after another. One of the last to hold out was in
London, which after being evicted from in front of the London Stock
Exchange was invited by the canon of St Paul's Cathedral to set up
in front of its steps.

St Paul's is in the heart of the City of London, where London's
financial district is centred. A square-mile city like the Vatican, it
also resembles the tiny papal enclave in being practically a sovereign
state – beyond the rule of Parliament, and with an administration
elected largely by the lords of finance.[26] Because it shared the square
in front of St Paul's with the cathedral, rumours soon circulated that
the City was pressuring the cathedral to evict the protesters. The
cathedral chapter agreed to begin proceedings and the canon resigned
in protest. Soon afterwards, the police took matters into their own
hands and moved in and shut down the camp early in 2012.

But while the public squares were emptied by police, Occupy didn't
so much disappear as change shape. Its participants returned to their
communities where they helped to organise new political parties,
or started influencing existing ones. New political groupings of the
radical left, which like Occupy brought together disparate factions
with common concerns, like Syriza in Greece or Podemos in Spain,
emerged to challenge the mainstream parties. In Britain they would
later penetrate the Labour Party and tilt it leftwards. In America
they helped to besiege the Clintonian wing of the Democratic Party
and spur the ascent of left-wing populists like Elizabeth Warren and
Bernie Sanders. Others turned to radical economic action to challenge the status quo, creating crypto-currencies like bitcoin to bypass
banks, or inventing new apps to nurture the sharing economy, which
enabled people to share cars, food, even handbags – a new form of
anti-consumerism amid the sluggish economy brought about some
innovative solutions.

Rather like the Sorbonne at the time of Adam Smith, the

priesthood had held the university, but lost its following outside the walls. Among the many who lost faith in the old religion, who eschewed the academy to take their debates into the salons and the streets, there was talk of revolution, then and now. More broadly, the politics of the West tended to mimic polarisation in the economy – splitting between the haves and have nots. The haves stuck with establishment parties, seeking at most piecemeal changes to a system that was serving them well. The have nots tended to go to the extremes, either a militant left or right. Very roughly, the first group appealed to young, educated people, who tended to blame the rich and the older generation for their woes. The second appealed more to older, working-class voters, who tended to blame foreigners for taking their jobs or driving down their wages. As far removed from one another as the politics of these factions were, they were united in their repudiation of the system as it existed, and their rejection of the priesthood of 'experts' who guided it. If their divisions were sometimes too great to prevent either faction taking power, together they could usually frustrate those in power, bogging politics in heightened conflict.

One legacy of the high neoliberalism of the late twentieth and early twenty-first centuries was that it precluded the search for a broad social vision to chart a way forward. After a generation of being steeped in a creed that said everyone needed only to pursue their own self-interest for the invisible hand to work its magic and create a just society – with an admixture of miraculous intervention by technology entrepreneurs thrown in to complete the job – too few were asking the question that Adam Smith would have taken for granted: what sacrifices or changes might I make to help create a better society? Politicians still occasionally paid lip service to grand visions, as when David Cameron expressed his dream of a 'Big Society' in which civic groups complemented government in delivering public services, but in practice, parties almost always prioritised their constituents' interests. The victims blamed the establishment and the establishment the victims. Whether the victims were depicted as 'lazy millennials' or 'angry white males', it was easy to de-legitimise their complaints. Amid such a dialogue of the deaf, it was inevitable that politics in Western societies would get angry. It was to become, in that regard, the worst of times.

CHAPTER 22

THE TWILIGHT OF THE MONEY GODS

'What were you thinking!?'

That may be what your grandchildren say when they first learn about the history of the housing bubble and the crash of 2008. Tell them not to be surprised. Tell them we all have a bit of Alice's White Queen in us, able to believe quite incredible things when it's convenient. We'll just add the housing bubble to the annals of mass hysteria; one of those occasions that recur throughout history when, whipped into a frenzy by our spiritual and political leaders, we made incredible things briefly seem real and thereby created self-fulfilling prophecies – our generation's Salem Witch Trials (but with carnage that wasn't confined to a village).

However, the economists of our grandchildren's generation might not be so forgiving of their forebears. They will say that scientists are supposed to withstand mass hysteria. At this, our generation's economists will reply they did not cause the crisis – that it was not they who deregulated the financial sector to allow gamblers to swoop in, not they who demanded higher and higher returns on their investments so they could sustain their spending, not they who took out all the debt to bail out the banks, and above all, not they who designed the models and invented the complex instruments that nearly brought the world economy crashing down around us. It was the politicians who changed the rules, the mathematicians and theoretical physicists working for the banks who came up with the crazy inventions, and the rest of us who demanded more and more money.

Yet while truthful, this defence will probably not get an easy ride from history's jury. That's because it's only truthful in the way it's truthful to say the Catholic Church didn't repress Galileo for saying the Earth orbited around the sun. It didn't, it shut him down for his Platonic atomism.[1] But so what? The Church's preference for Aristotelian physics, which happened to better chime with its doctrine of communion, turned out to be just as wrong: the Vatican had taken an authoritative position on science without being scientific, and then abused its power to get its way.

Throughout the boom, no small number of economists in influential positions helped to create a climate of conviction that made it possible for the magicians to peddle their wares – and, as the documentary film *Inside Job* would later reveal, some of those economists did so while running lucrative side businesses consulting for the banks behind the crisis (apparently vindicating Upton Sinclair's adage that it's difficult to get a man to believe something when his pay cheque depends on him believing the opposite[2]). Alan Greenspan was hardly alone in repeatedly using his pulpit to assure the faithful there was nothing to fear. When, for instance, the IMF chief economist Raghuram Rajan presented a paper to the Federal Reserve's annual conference in 2005 warning that the new speculative instruments posed tremendous risks, Lawrence Summers ridiculed him as a Luddite who simply disliked technological change. At that, the chorus present cried Amen. Rajan later described the experience of speaking to the neoliberal high priesthood, which included not just celebrity economists like Summers but a 'who's who of central bankers' that, 'I felt like an early Christian who had wandered into a convention of half-starved lions.'[3]

Like any church, economics arguably does its best work when it is in opposition, speaking truth to power and challenging received wisdom, as John Maynard Keynes did in the darkness of the Depression and Milton Friedman did amid the complacency of the 1950s and 1960s. Once it is established and working in unison with the politicians, like

any church, it has interests to defend. At times, it may therefore feel
the need to turn a blind eye to the abuses in its corridors. History will
thus perhaps date the beginning of our current crisis to 4 January
2003, the day that Robert Lucas delivered his presidential address to
the American Economics Association, when he celebrated his church's
triumph. Reminding his colleagues that macroeconomics had been
born in the Depression precisely to try to prevent another such disaster
ever recurring, he declared that he and his colleagues had reached their
own end of history: 'macroeconomics in this original sense has succeeded' he instructed the conclave. 'Its central problem of depression
prevention has been solved.'[4]

We should have read the warning signs. If history teaches anything,
it's that whenever economists feel certain they've found the holy grail
of endless peace and prosperity, the end of the present regime is nigh.
Irving Fisher advised people to go out and buy shares on the eve of the
1929 crash, Keynesian economists in the 1960s said there would never
be another recession because they had perfected the tools of demand
management, and the neoliberal evangelists assured us similarly of
their ability to deliver eternal stability. No sooner do we persuade
ourselves that the priesthood has finally broken the old curse than it
comes back to haunt us all: pride always goes before a fall.

Hubris, never a particularly good thing, may be especially dangerous in economics because its scholars can acquire Daedalus-like
powers to change the way the world works. Any scientist will tell
you she can't alter the laws of nature. At best, having observed and
developed an understanding of them, she can try to manipulate them
to human advantage. But economists don't just observe the laws of
nature, they help *make* them. If the government, guided by its priesthood, changes the incentive-structure of society to align with the
assumption that people behave selfishly, then lo and behold people will
start to do just that. They are rewarded for doing so and penalised for
doing otherwise. If you are educated to believe greed is good, then you
will be more likely to live accordingly. We therefore need to be certain
we trust the prophet and not merely the prophecy; and to be reassured
moreover that the prophet has our interests at heart.

The hubris in economics came not from a moral failing among economists, but from a false conviction: the belief that theirs was a science. It neither is nor can be one, and has always operated more like a church. You just have to look at its history to realise that.

The American Economics Association, to which Lucas gave his address, had been created in 1885, just when economics was starting to define itself as a distinct discipline. At its first meeting, the association's founders proposed a platform which declared: 'the conflict of labor and capital has brought to the front a vast number of social problems whose solution is impossible without the united efforts of Church, state, and science.'[5] It would be a long path from that beginning to the market evangelism of Lucas and his peers.

Yet even at that time, such social activism provoked controversy. One of the AEA's founders, Henry Carter Adams, subsequently delivered an address at Cornell University in which he defended free speech for radicals and accused industrialists of manipulating xenophobia to distract workers from their mistreatment. Unknown to him, the New York lumber king and Cornell benefactor Henry Sage was in the audience. As soon as the lecture was done, Sage stormed into the university president's office and insisted: 'This man must go; he is sapping the foundations of our society.' When Adams's tenure was subsequently blocked, he agreed to moderate his views. Accordingly, the final draft of the AEA platform expunged the reference to 'laissez-faire' as being 'unsafe in politics and unsound in morals'.[6] Thereafter, this free-market orthodoxy was enforced by the economists themselves. As Bernard A. Weisberger and Marshall I. Steinbaum wrote in their history of the association, 'ambitious professionals had determined how the balance of interests lay with respect to the prestige and influence of their own discipline, especially if they could forge a workable ideological consensus among the credentialed.'[7]

So was set a pattern that has persisted to this day. Powerful political interests helped to shape the canon of economics, which was then enforced by its scholarly community. And it's not just rich industrialists who constitute powerful interests – although they do, as the generous patronage that benefactors offer many economics and business schools attests. At critical junctures in the history of the discipline, as we have seen, electorates have helped tip the balance in debates among its followers. Having said that, the establishment of orthodoxy is not merely a matter of horse-trading, and AEA meetings are not political conventions. What is in dispute are finely argued scholarly positions in recondite debates. Thus the appeal to a 'popular, inexpert audience to resolve an academic dispute'[8] is not a democratic exercise. Rather, the public serves as final arbiter of the articles of faith produced by a given doctrine.

Once a principle is established as orthodox, its observance is thus enforced in much the same way that a religious doctrine maintains its integrity: by repressing or simply eschewing heresies. In *Purity and Danger*, the anthropologist Mary Douglas observed the way taboos functioned to help humans impose order on a seemingly disordered, chaotic world. The premises of conventional economics haven't functioned all that differently. The 'whispers and giggles' which Robert Lucas said once greeted Keynesian statements at economics conferences served to remind practitioners of the taboos of economics: a gentle nudge to a young academic that such shibboleths might not sound so good before a tenure committee. This preoccupation with order and coherence may be less a function of the method than of its practitioners. Studies of personality traits common to various disciplines have discovered that economics, like engineering, tends to attract people with an unusually strong preference for order, and a distaste for ambiguity.[9]

The irony, therefore, is that in its determination to make itself a science that can reach hard and fast conclusions, economics has had to dispense with scientific method at times. We'd never arbitrate disputes in theoretical physics or evolutionary biology the way it's done in economics – or at least, when we last tried, in Stalin's Russia or in Galileo's time, it came off rather badly. If we're honest we'll admit that bending economic doctrine to fit the will of a New York industrialist (or an electorate, for that matter) isn't that different from the Soviet geneticist T. D. Lysenko declaring that 'progressive biological science is indebted to the geniuses of mankind, Lenin and Stalin'[10] – a smart career move, perhaps, but dodgy science.

Nevertheless, if the method of economics resembles medieval scholasticism more than economists might like to admit, they will maintain that what sets them apart from the monks is that they must still test their hypotheses against the evidence. Well, yes, but this statement is actually more problematic than many mainstream economists may realise. Physicists resolve their debates by looking at the data, upon which they by and large agree. The data used by economists, however, is the bone of a great deal more contention. When, for example, Robert Lucas insisted that Eugene Fama's efficient markets hypothesis had time and again been 'thoroughly challenged by a flood of criticism which has served mainly to confirm the accuracy of the hypothesis',[11] he did so with as much conviction and supporting evidence as Robert Shiller had mustered in rejecting the hypothesis. When it comes to deciding whether the efficient markets hypothesis is spot on or dead wrong, it more or less comes down to a coin-toss. Almost literally, at times. For instance, when it had to decide who would win the 2013 Nobel Prize in Economics, the Swedish Central Bank was torn between Shiller's claim that markets frequently got the price wrong and Fama's insistence that markets always got the price right, so it opted to split the difference and gave both men the medal – a bit of Solomonic wisdom that would have elicited howls of laughter had it been a science prize (just imagine the sort of headline that might have followed: 'Evolutionary Biologist and Intelligent Design Creationist Share Prestigious Science Prize'). In economic theory, very often, you believe what you want to believe – and as with any act of faith, your choice of heads or tails will as likely reflect sentimental predisposition as scientific assessment.

It's no mystery why the data used by economists and other social scientists so rarely throws up incontestable answers: it is *human* data. Unlike us, subatomic particles don't lie on opinion surveys or change their minds about things.[12] Mindful of that difference, at his own presidential address to the American Economics Association nearly a half-century ago, another Nobel laureate, Wassily Leontief, struck a more modest tone than Lucas. He reminded his audience that the data used by economists differed greatly from that used by physicists or biologists. For the latter, he cautioned, 'the magnitude of most parameters is practically constant',[13] whereas the observations in economics were constantly changing. Data sets had to be regularly updated to remain useful. Some data was just simply bad. Collecting and analysing the data requires civil servants with a high degree of skill and a good deal of time, which Third World countries may not have in abundance. So, for example, in one year alone Ghana's government – which probably has one of the better data-gathering capacities in Africa – recalculated its economic output by 60 per cent.[14] Testing your hypothesis before and after that kind of revision would lead to entirely different results.

Leontief had wanted economists to spend more time getting to know their data and less time in mathematical modelling. However, as he ruefully admitted, the trend was already going the other way. Today, the economist who wanders into a village to get a sense of what the data reveals is a rare creature. Once the model is ready to be tested, number crunching ends up being done largely at computers plugged into large databases. It's not a method that fully satisfies a sceptic. For, just as you can find a quotation in the Bible that will justify almost any behaviour, from torture to pacifism, you can find human data to support almost any statement you want to make about the way the world works. That's why ideas in economics, unlike physics, can go in and out of fashion. Keynesianism buried much of neoclassical theory, but the Great Awakening brought it back stronger than ever. Like the Emperor Constantine's conversion or Martin Luther's Reformation, once you can win converts and gain powerful patrons, you can enshrine orthodoxy. Lose your flock, however, and you lose the pulpit.

Trying to make economics into a science was an exercise bound to end badly because by its very nature the success of an economic doctrine depends on our faith in it and our confidence in the priesthood. Even so, since economic faith forms only part of our belief-system, economics can only ever complement, and not wholly replace, our wider belief systems. That's because at heart we are not 'homo economicus'. Being the complex creatures we are, at times we behave like economic animals and at others we have different, contrary drives.

The Irish have been known to describe their notionally Catholic land as one where a thin Christian veneer was painted over an ancient paganism. The same might be said of our own adherence to today's neoliberal orthodoxy. Despite outward observance of a well-entrenched doctrine, we haven't fully transformed into the economic animal we are meant to be. Like the Christian who attends church but doesn't always keep the commandments, we behave as economic theory predicts only when it suits us. Or we go through the motions of observance without any real conviction, eager to seize the first opportunity that comes along to quit the church. Rational utility-maximisation has its limits for us. If contemporary research is anything to go by, we still remain reasonably altruistic and selfless.[15] Maximising our gain is not always our principal motive for action,[16] nor is it clear that the endless accumulation of wealth always makes us happier.[17] And when we do make decisions, especially those having to do with matters of principle, we seem not to engage in the sort of calculus that orthodox economic models take as a given.[18] The truth is, in much of our daily life we just don't fit the model all that well.

For decades, neoliberal evangelists replied to such objections by saying it was incumbent on us all to adapt to the model, which was held to be immutable – one recalls Bill Clinton's depiction of neoliberal globalisation, for instance, as a 'force of nature'. And yet, in the wake of the 2008 financial crisis and the consequent recession, there has been a turn against globalisation across much of the West. More broadly, there has been a wide repudiation of the 'experts'. Although the experts were virtually unanimous in rejecting both Brexit for the UK referendum and Donald Trump in the 2016 US election, the voting public ignored them in large numbers.

It would be tempting for anyone who belongs to the 'expert' class, and to the priesthood of economics, to dismiss such behaviour as one of those hopeless and quixotic clashes between faith and facts, in which the facts are bound to win in the end. In truth, the clash was between two rival faiths – in effect, two distinct moral tales. So enamoured had the so-called experts become with their scientific authority that they blinded themselves to the fact that their own narrative of scientific progress was, at the end of the day, embedded in a moral tale. It happened to be a narrative that had a happy ending for those who told it, for it perpetuated their own relatively comfortable position as the reward of life in a meritocratic society that blessed people for their skills and flexibility. And that narrative made no room for heroism among the losers of this order, whose resentments were derided as being a reflection of their boorish and retrograde character – which is to say, their fundamental vice. The best this moral tale could offer everyone else was incremental adaptation to an order whose caste system had become calcified. For an audience yearning for a happy ending, this was bound to be a tale of woe.

The failure of the grand narrative of economics is not, however, a reason for students of economics to dispense with narratives. Narratives will remain an inescapable part of the human sciences for the simple reason that they are inescapable for humans. It's funny that so few economists get this, because businesses do. As the Nobel laureates George Akerlof and Robert Shiller write in *Phishing for Phools*, marketers use them all the time, weaving stories in the hopes we'll place ourselves in them and be persuaded to buy what they are selling.[19] Akerlof and Shiller contend that the idea that free markets work and that government is the problem is itself 'a phish for phools', a kind of story that is actually misleading people into adjusting their behaviour in order to fit the plot. They believe storytelling is a 'new variable' for economics, since 'the mental frames that underlie people's decisions' are shaped by the stories they tell themselves. In a similar vein, when anticipating future demand, businesses often opt for anthropological over statistical methods, geared towards collecting stories rather than just points of data.[20] And if this sounds 'unscientific' it's worth recalling, as the mathematician Paul Lockhart writes in his book *Measurement*, that mathematical models are themselves narratives, whose attraction lies in their beauty, yet which still convey an imaginary world and not the 'complicated disaster' that is 'physical reality' (where 'nothing is at all what it appears to be'). Lockhart notes that 'a mathematical argument [is] otherwise known as a *proof*. A proof is simply a story. The characters are the elements of the problem, and the plot is up to you.'[21]

No, the goal must not be to dispense with our narratives, but to leave their construction and selection to the experts – which is to say, to the storytellers in all of us. Most of us, faced with the question of why we believe what we believe, will ultimately fall back on the insights we have gleaned from experience, then organise them into a coherent plot by reference to those tales that inspire or guide us. Ultimately, therefore, the narrative of our own life story shapes our intellectual journey. Economic models are then dropped into that plot when they explain the reality we have encountered. We all, in sum, begin with a tale. Reflecting on that, and on the way we want that tale to finish, can give us an appreciation of the virtue of humility about what we can actually know about a world that is, in the end, filled with billions of other storytellers.

Economists arguably do their best work when they take the stories we have given them, and advise us on how we can help them to come true. Such agnosticism demands a humility that was lacking in economic orthodoxy in recent years. Nevertheless, economists don't have to abandon their traditions if they are to overcome the failings of a narrative that has been rejected. Rather they can look within their own history to find a method that avoids the evangelical certainty of orthodoxy.

It was in the early years of the neoclassical revival that Wassily Leontief used his presidential address to the American Economics Association to counsel against the dangers of self-satisfaction. He noted that although economics was starting to ride 'the crest of intellectual respectability ... an uneasy feeling about the present state of our discipline has been growing in some of us who have watched its unprecedented development over the last three decades.' Saying that pure theory was making economics more remote from day-to-day reality, he said the problem lay in 'the palpable inadequacy of the scientific means' of using mathematical approaches to address mundane concerns. So much time went into model construction that the assumptions on which the models were based became an afterthought. 'But,' he warned – a warning that the sub-prime boom's fascination with mathematical models, and the bust's subsequent revelation of their flaws, now reveals to have been prophetic – 'it is precisely the empirical validity of these assumptions on which the usefulness of the entire exercise depends.'

Leontief thought that economics departments were increasingly hiring and promoting young economists who wanted to build pure models with little empirical relevance. Even when they did empirical analysis, Leontief said economists seldom took any interest in the meaning or value of their data. He thus called for economists to explore their assumptions and data by conducting social, demographic and anthropological work, and said economics needed to work more closely with other disciplines. And, without naming him, he implicitly repudiated Friedman's positivist doctrine, adding that 'uncritical enthusiasm for mathematical formulation tends often to conceal the ephemeral substantive content of the argument behind the formidable front of algebraic signs.'[22] Alas, Leontief admitted, few of his colleagues seemed to share his fear that the discipline was moving in the wrong direction.

Leontief's call for humility some forty years ago stands as a reminder that the same religions that can speak up for human freedom and dignity when in opposition, can become obsessed with their rightness and the need to purge others of their wickedness once they attain power. When the Church retains its distance from power, and a modest expectation about what it can achieve, it can stir our minds to envision new possibilities and even new worlds. Once economists apply this kind of sceptical scientific method to a human realm in which ultimate reality may never be fully discernible for the simple reason that it is fluid and constantly being re-defined, they will probably find themselves retreating from dogmatism in their claims.

Paradoxically, therefore, as economics becomes more truly

scientific, it will become less of a science. Acknowledging these limitations will free it to serve us once more.

Of course, the facts can sometimes come back to haunt us. The happy ending can be throttled when it turns out that the slain villain was not really dead after all. In that respect, the great challenge for economists will be to construct narratives that can deal with the facts their science does uncover, and which confound our preferred moral tale.

If there's one thing economics appears to have got right, it's that when severe imbalances emerge in a system, somehow it finds its way back to balance. Whether the free market does it on its own, or people organise collectively to demand political change, or indeed a combination of both, the seesaw always seems to level off again. Every empire in history had its time, and so will ours – a moment which, it appears, happens to be the very one in which we are living. As we struggle to make the adjustment to a future of slower growth, the planetary divergence wrought by two centuries of Western dominance has come to an end. As capital goes south and labour comes north, convergence has begun, with average economic growth rates in the developing world outpacing those in the West for the first time in centuries. This has thrust us into a painful transition. Although its underlying features had been coming into view a generation ago, politicians and policymakers had managed to repeatedly push back its start until the crash of 2008 made it impossible. Now we in the West are going through what citizens of the developing world underwent a generation ago. Amid government austerity and harsh choices, we are increasingly being left to face the cold winds of the market on our own. And so, for the first time in memory, we are slowly waking up to the realisation that we can't have it all. Politicians may still tell us otherwise, claiming to have secret plans or bold platforms that will raise our growth rates or bring money flooding back into the country. On occasion, they may even succeed in recreating the bubble conditions of the past and thereby juicing growth for a year or two here and there. However, as was the case with earlier bubbles, they will do this with more of the sleight of hand that merely redistributes growth from the future to the present – as was done in the dotcom and housing bubbles, with the result that subsequent growth ends up being even lower after the bubble bursts – or redistributes it from one group in society to another, as we have been doing since the crash.

Ultimately, we will have to face up to an epochal choice. If we can no longer have it all, and must discard some of the family jewellery, what will we take with us? To which of the legacies of our imperial past will we cling: that of Adam Smith, or that of Thomas Thistlewood? They were always inseparable. There would have been no Adam Smiths, no Enlightenment or scientific revolution – or at least, not quite as we knew them – had it not been for the Thomas Thistlewoods, sitting up at night on their verandahs, reading the new literature and telling themselves they were helping to build the new world. Do we cling to the extraction of riches from the planet and its inhabitants at all costs so as to maintain our material state, the legacy of Thomas Thistlewood (and if we are to cling to the fruit of his legacy, let us be honest and render thanks to those like him who did the dirty deeds for us)? Or do we instead cling to the intellectual and spiritual legacy of the West, taking the doctrines of liberty enunciated by the likes of Smith to the furthest reaches of the planet, where it still can have purchase?

Abba Eban used to say that humans always act wisely, but only after first exhausting all other options. Maybe we're running through the options right now, of which denial appears pretty attractive. It's been too tempting to continue blaming our existential woes on others, too tempting to resist the seemingly obvious analogies between contemporary immigration from the Third World and the barbarian invasions that brought down Rome. The historian Niall Ferguson has written of Islamist terrorism in Europe:

> Let us be clear about what is happening. Like the Roman Empire in the early fifth century, Europe has allowed its defenses to crumble. As its wealth has grown, so its military prowess has shrunk, along with its self-belief. It has grown decadent in its shopping malls and sports stadiums. At the same time, it has opened its gates to

outsiders who have coveted its wealth without renouncing their ancestral faith.[23]

However, Ferguson's narrative has a fatal flaw: to ring true, it must edit out the stories of the 'barbarians'. In his history of Rome's fall,[24] Peter Heather argues, contra the likes of Ferguson, that empires create their own barbarians. As he has put it in what he calls 'Newton's Third Law of Empires': 'the exercise of imperial power generates an opposite and equal reaction among those affected by it, until they so reorganize themselves as to blunt the imperial edge.'[25] Yes, those who sneak in through the vectors of communication created by immigration to blow up our loved ones are savages who enjoy watching people burn to death. But then our own prosperity was built in no small part by our Thomas Thistlewoods, who enjoyed equally horrific forms of sadism while doing the work of squeezing out the surpluses that helped our economic ascent. Like any religion, economics could, when necessary, sacrifice lives in the pursuit of heaven. Political economy abetted mass starvation, communism delivered millions to their graves in man-made famines and neoliberalism justified ignoring and even imposing widespread suffering in the Third World in the name of economic progress. But unusually among religious doctrines, economics only ever sacrificed the lives of *others*. Unlike most religions, it had no doctrine of martyrdom or a culture of asceticism, it didn't call for its practitioners to make their own sacrifices for the good of the community, instead just giving them a justification for the suffering they were imposing or tolerating among others.

At the end of the day we are left facing a fact of life. As satisfying as it might feel to build walls or send immigrants back where they came from, we'll quickly find that we can't do it and our leaders will back-pedal on their promises – or in the cases where they stick to their plans, time will expose the high price-tag of their promises. As population growth slows in the West, as the population ages and the share of the population that is working declines, we can either continue importing our labour and outsourcing our production, or we can learn to live with a declining standard of living. We can't likely have it both ways. If there's to be a happy ending to this tale, it will have to come from an entirely new narrative.

Adam Smith and his peers wrestled, uncomfortably but honestly, with the issues of slavery and imperial exploitation. Their later descendants, sadly, largely ignored them. Instead, we developed an economics that presumed a free market in which individuals are liberated to pursue their self-interested goals will necessarily lead to just outcomes. That doctrine could only function in an economy that imported capital and outsourced injustice. That was the job of the Thomas Thistlewoods, of the conquistadors, of the early settlers who seized land and riches in overseas colonies, of contemporary industrialists who exploit the loose labour laws or environmental and safety regulations of poor countries to deliver us cheaper goods and thereby keep raising our living standards. Some ends may have justified some means, but the means were usually hidden from us, enabling us to concentrate on building and celebrating a great civilisation.

Now, however, the direction of capital has been reversed, and the injustice has started to come home.[26] With the flow of resources no longer sufficient to meet all demand, the pursuit of self-interest has led to a tribalisation in our politics – a politics of fear over hope, and of false hope over truth. Politicians slice and dice the electorate to favour their own constituents and thus retain their support base, but this ancient method of governance almost always ends badly. If you squeeze revenue from taxpayers in order to steer resources exclusively to a favoured in-group, you can create an imbalance between what everyone else pays their government and what they expect to get in return. Students of politics since at least the time of Ibn Khaldun[27] have known that once people perceive they are not getting a fair return on their taxes, and that public resources are used to benefit private interests rather than the collective good, they find ways to withdraw from the tax net. That way lies a path of erosion in public services that can become self-reinforcing, since reducing services while keeping taxes constant can encourage even more evasion. Ultimately, the nation state as we have known it could cease to function.

However, the outline of a more just economics can be found in
Adam Smith's own work. The crude politics of blaming others, and
of trying to find someone else to stiff with the bill of justice, is now
producing diminishing returns. And while populists on the left say
that all we need to do is tax the 1 per cent to fund continued redistribution, they might be uncomfortable to discover how close to home
that will hit. Canadian schoolteachers and London home owners – in
fact, almost everyone likely to be reading this passage – are or will
soon be in the global 1 per cent.[28] On current form, they will continue
to be so, their ranks supplemented by the rising elite of the developing
world, both groups drawing closer together as they pull further away
from the rest of their home societies.[29] Meanwhile, taxing what's been
hidden by the ultra-rich in offshore bank accounts, while symbolically
helpful in rebuilding a sense of social cohesion, will in itself barely
pay the interest on the current debts of Western countries.[30] It will
do nothing to cover the future costs of promises already made, to say
nothing of any other promises governments might choose to make to
their voters in upcoming elections.

The simple fact is that the person who has to make the change to
create a more sustainable economics for all is now the person in the
mirror. But in a way, that's good news. It means we have not only a
challenge but the power to rise to it. Moreover, the challenge is not
one that economics has never faced before. Adam Smith, let's recall,
embedded the market in a system of ethics. And on paper, the future
has never looked brighter. Our potential is far beyond anything Smith
could have envisioned. With enough wealth to satisfy all the immediate
needs of everyone on the planet, with future growth likely to be slower
but not necessarily to end, with technological improvements yielding
fewer productivity gains but still making possible dramatic improvements in our lives, with major diseases on the verge of eradication as
existing cures spread across the planet, we are facing possibilities our
ancestors could only reach in worlds they dreamed up.

Nevertheless, we have reached a critical impasse – critical in the
medical sense that we're at a fork in the road. We can try to cling
to the faith of our recent forebears and let things continue on their

current course. That would possibly mean an increasingly powerful global oligarchy could use its mastery of technology to oppress us and free themselves of all social responsibility, while aggravating a political fragmentation that could badly undermine political stability and even cause more fragile regimes to collapse. It's always worth remembering that there's never anything inevitable about a civilisation's endurance. Once it fails to serve its people's needs, they revert to looking out for themselves. Sure, Rome built glorious monuments, but ordinary people needed to build houses, so they cannibalised what then became ruins in order to do it.

Alternately, we could look with fresh eyes at the faith of our ancestors and ask if it is still working for us. A new wave of religious conversion, this time away from the economic doctrines that so dominated the planet as no creed ever did before, may be upon us. Thousands of belief-systems have risen and fallen throughout history, to often disappear for ever. Our age may be ringing the death knell of economics. Or, better yet, it may instead be driving the rebirth of economics into a new avatar. Indeed, the promised land may yet be within reach. And, curiously, we may even find the road map there among the very same people currently accused by some populists of leading us to decay.

In London, south of the Thames and a couple miles from Westminster Palace, there is a bustling and noisy community called Brixton. The spiritual heart of Britain's Jamaican community since the 1950s, when the first banana boats disgorged the masses of Caribbean labourers Britain needed to rebuild its post-war economy, Brixton was for decades a West Indian community. Today, it has become a crossroads of the world, with a polyglot and crowded street culture clustered around its iconic old market.

Brixton thus finds itself at the frontier of the new global economy. If there is to be a clash of civilisations, it will first manifest itself in many communities like this across the developed world. In the community's streets, staunch Christians from Africa walk past Algerian butchers displaying pamphlets warning Muslims against Christian proselytes.

Here, too, the white working class, decimated by the globalisation that shipped to other lands jobs they would have once taken, apply for benefits to public servants from the immigrant communities that have made Brixton their own. In the past Brixton's mosque was a centre of radical Islam. Unveiled women don't feel comfortable walking alone into some of the Muslim cafes, and racial tensions are always beneath the surface, Brixton having been the setting for both riots against a police force seen as racist and acts of terrorism perpetrated by white supremacists. On the crowded pavement outside the Underground station where you must walk gingerly to avoid a collision, Nation of Islam missionaries in suits and bow ties compete for space with bellowing evangelical preachers.

Nevertheless, if in Brixton you might always feel yourself to be just on the edge, especially late at night as the clubs and bars expel their drunken patrons and drug peddlers begin cruising the pavements seeking out prospective buyers, most of its residents would not choose to live anywhere else. If indeed the front lines of the clash of civilisations run through these streets, it says a lot about the potential future of the conflict. Yes, Islamists who despise the West use the legitimate vectors of communication opened by emigration from the global south to infiltrate terrorists into the West; and yes, young Brixtonians who experience a profound sense of alienation from the dominant culture and frustration at the lack of economic opportunity will occasionally gravitate to radical Islam as a solution. Yet, for all that, Brixton has not been a rich seam for jihadists in foreign wars. The mosque maintains active social programmes to get young people off the streets and away from the gangs, and its children play football with friends from other religious backgrounds in the sprawling Brockwell Park, many of them dreaming of one day playing for England.

Walk into that mosque, or any one of its many churches, and you'll find them packed with a wide variety of people from all over the world. Unlike what you experience in English village churches, where on a Sunday you might find a dozen mostly elderly people singing a quiet hymn to the accompaniment of the church organ (supplemented by the odd young family, hoping to secure a place in an over-subscribed parochial school), in Brixton's churches, you'll come across raucous choirs, loud praise and dancing. Enough of a bond gets formed among people here that they learn to live with their differences when they go back into the street. At the community's popular recreation centre, young Arabs and Somalis play sport and work out with Nigerians and Colombians.

Many of them may proudly claim their ancestral label, fly the old country's flag during the World Cup and bristle at the aspects of British culture they find most stifling. But they often also like their full English breakfast and sticky-toffee pudding and almost all of them, upon flying to their ancestral or home countries, speak proudly with their Brixton accents, cheer for the England football team, and chide their compatriots for being too illiberal on many of the issues on which, back in Britain, they might occasionally appear to be a tad conservative. Ambassadors for the best of what the West has to offer, but not apologists for the ways it has sometimes failed to adhere to its own principles, they are also a bridge along which the budding entrepreneurs of the global age are moving. Young Britons of Indian or Nigerian ancestry sometimes fly back to ancestral homelands to set up the joint ventures that will enable them to marry British know-how to a Third World work ethic. In the process, they are melding their hybrid heritage into the new culture that can define the global age. The 'barbarians' who threaten our civilisation are, if anything, the resource that will help renew it, creating and sustaining the vectors of communication along which a more just globalisation could flow.

Precisely because it is a work in progress, it's hard to say what the new civilisation will look like. Perhaps, like Brixton, we in the West will draw more sustenance from the spiritual and cultural endowment of the people we once colonised, all while we, and they, further the material transformation of the developing world. The result might be a more balanced world for all. Meanwhile in economics, the big issues will increasingly become ones of ethics, and less of technocratic management. The bigger, deeper questions will revert to the church halls, pubs, cafes and seminar rooms. How do we create a society that works for everyone, and not just well-connected elites? What is the correct balance between the natural environment and economic growth? How, if at all, might unbridled wealth maximisation limit our humanity? None of these are questions in which technical competence matter more than the voices of ordinary people – least of all the people in the streets, mosques and temples of communities like Brixton, who spend a lot of time pondering just these questions in the context of their own lives. Who knows? Maybe the high priests of economics will even go back to their origins as servants to moral philosophy and ethics.

Thirty years ago, the 'largely and dangerously' ignored Hyman Minsky wrote:

> ... if economics is too important to be left to the economists, it is certainly too important to be left to economist-courtiers. Economic issues must become a serious public matter and the subject of debate if new directions are to be undertaken. Meaningful reforms cannot be put over by an advisory and administrative elite that is itself the architect of the existing situation.[31]

If we made the mistake of ignoring Minsky's advice before, now is as good a time as any to take it. In Brixton's cafes, in its places of worship, in the impromptu seminars and discussion groups in its council estates and pubs and public squares, in the arguments and debates that occur in its bus queues, in the jostling between street preachers and those they are trying to convert, these issues come up every day, blending both material and spiritual considerations in the pursuit of a more just society. Brixtonians might look to the experts to advise them on how to get what they want. But if they ever did, they no longer look to them to tell them what to want.

The money gods have fallen. Thus, economists are once again free to begin doing the one thing they have always been good at – finding practical solutions to the problems that the public square has asked them to solve. Leaving it to others to identify the promised land, they will simply try to work out how to find the water in the desert.

Ours is, in that respect, the best of times.

NOTES

Chapter 1: I Believe I Can Fly

1 Geoffrey Ingham, *The Nature of Money* (Cambridge: Polity Press, 2004).

2 David Graeber, *Debt: The First 5,000 Years* (New York: Melville House, 2011).

3 Branko Milanovic, *The Haves and the Have-Nots* (New York: Basic Books, 2011).

4 Robert Nelson, *Economics as Religion* (University Park: Pennsylvania State University Press, 2001), p.17.

5 The Nobel Laureate Joseph Stiglitz, in particular, frequently uses the term in critiques of neoliberalism.

6 Avner Offer and Gabriel Söderberg, *The Nobel Factor* (Princeton: Princeton University Press, 2016).

7 Lionel Robbins, *An Essay on the Nature and Significance of Economic Science* (London: Macmillan, 2007), p.110.

8 J. Doyne Farmer, 'Hypotheses non Fingo: Problems with the Scientific Method in Economics', *Journal of Economic Methodology* 20, 4 (2013), pp.377–385.

9 Long Wang, Deepak Malhotra and J. Keith Murnighan, 'Economics Education and Greed', *Academy of Management Learning and Education* 10, 4 (2011), pp.643–660.

10 In *The Structure of Scientific Revolutions* (Chicago: University of Chicago Press, 1962), the philosopher of science Thomas Kuhn argued that scientific communities create their own orthodoxies, or what he called paradigms, in this manner, by reaching agreement within communities of scholarship. What distinguishes economics in this respect is that the community is not limited to the scholars of the discipline, but to interests in society and political constituencies.

11 In nominal terms. When adjusted to reflect changes in the value of

money – namely, that a shilling today buys much less than a shilling did a hundred years ago – the increase becomes more modest. But even then, to use the Maddison database as reference, per capita incomes in Britain have risen an estimated twenty-five times since 1500, reflecting a level of abundance unimaginable then.

12 The title of a book by Tyler Cowen. While economists debate whether the effect will be permanent, none dispute that the average rate of economic growth in Western countries has slowed markedly since the 2008 crash.

Chapter 2: God of Gold

1 The economic historian Eric Jones calls it a 'miracle' that Europe came to rule the world. See *The European Miracle* (Cambridge: Cambridge University Press, 2013).

2 As William McNeill wrote in *The Rise of the West* (Chicago: University of Chicago Press, 1989), 'the riposte to this setback carried European explorers, merchants, missionaries and soldiers all round the globe and made the oceans of the world the highroad of Western overseas expansion. The success of this second, oceanic phase of European expansion dwarfed the scale of the first Baltic and Mediterranean ventures and inaugurated a new era in world as well as in European history.' (p.147)

3 Charles Tilly, 'War Making and State Making as Organized Crime', in *Bringing the State Back In*, edited by Peter Evans, et al. (Cambridge: Cambridge University Press, 1985).

4 Jared Diamond, *Guns, Germs and Steel* (London: Vintage, 1998).

5 Walter Rodney, *How Europe Underdeveloped Africa* (London: Bogle-L'Ouverture, 1972).

6 At one time, some historians maintained that slavery was an inefficient economy that had to go before capitalism could thrive, and this accounted for abolition. However, more recent scholarship has established that not only did slavery play a central role in the rise of capitalism, but that it was in fine economic health at the time of abolition. See, for example, Walter Johnson, *River of Dark Dreams* (Cambridge: Harvard Belknap, 2013), Seymour Drescher, *Econocide: British Slavery in the Era of Abolition* (Pittsburgh: University of Pittsburgh Press, 1977) and Robin Blackburn, *The American Crucible* (London: Verso, 2013).

7 Barbara L. Solow and Stanley L. Engerman, eds., introduction to *British Capitalism and Caribbean Slavery: The Legacy of Eric Williams* (Cambridge: Cambridge University Press, 1987); see also Joseph Inikori, 'Slavery and the Development of Industrial Capitalism in England', in Solow and Engerman.

8 Hugh Thomas, *The Slave Trade* (New York: Touchstone, 1997), p.449.

9 Barbara L. Solow, 'Capitalism and Slavery in the Exceedingly Long Run',

in Barbara L. Solow and Stanley L. Engerman, eds., *British Capitalism and Caribbean Slavery: The Legacy of Eric Williams* (Cambridge: Cambridge University Press, 1987).

10 Hugh Thomas, *The Slave Trade* (New York: Touchstone, 1997), p.450.

11 The means by which Europeans formalised their claims to lands varied, from simple declarations the land was theirs to actually negotiating purchase. But when the latter occurred, aboriginal sellers were often negotiating from positions of weakness or under duress, and sometimes had an understanding of the transaction that differed from the Europeans (for instance, assuming that allowing another the right to settle and farmland did not remove one's rights to hunt on it). See Jean-Pierre Morin, 'Concepts of Extinguishment in the Upper Canada Land Surrender Treaties, 1764–1862', *Aboriginal Policy Research* 7 (2013), pp.15–40.

12 Data from the Maddison Project database on historical growth rates: www. ggdc.net/maddison/maddison-project/home.htm

13 Ben Anderson, *Imagined Communities* (London: Verso, 1983).

14 Karen Armstrong, *A History of God* (London: Vintage, 1999), p.10.

15 Richard Dawkins, *The Selfish Gene* (Oxford: Oxford University Press, 1989).

16 Don Cupitt, *After God* (London: Weidenfeld and Nicolson, 1997).

17 Karl Jaspers, *The Origin and Goal of History* (London: Routledge & Kegan Paul, 1953), trans. Michael Bullock.

18 John Man, *The Gutenberg Revolution* (London: Bantam, 2010), pp.14–16.

19 Ricardo Duchesne, 'Asia First?', *The Journal of the Historical Society*, 6, 1 (March 2006), p.83.

20 Ben Anderson, *Imagined Communities* (London: Verso, 1983); see also Bertrand Russell, *A History of Western Philosophy* (London: Unwin Paperbacks, 1946), p.19.

Chapter 3: Prophets for a Material Age

1 An account of Adam Smith's time in Paris can be found in Ian Simpson Ross, *The Life of Adam Smith* (Oxford: Clarendon Press, 1995), p.209.

2 Robert L. Heilbroner, *The Worldly Philosophers* (New York: Touchstone, 1995), p.45.

3 Robert L. Heilbroner.

4 From a speech he gave at Harvard University in 1998, quoted in Matt DiLallo, 'Why Warren Buffett Hates Gold', *The Motley Fool*, 13 September 2014, www.fool.com/investing/general/2014/09/13/why-warren-buffett-hates-gold. aspx.

5 As Landreth and Collander wrote, so large did Quesnay loom over the other physiocrats that their own writings 'were mainly designed to convince others of the merit of Quesnay's economics'. See Harry Landreth and David

C. Collander, *History of Economic Thought*, fourth edition (Boston and Toronto: Houghton Mifflin, 2001), p.59.

6 The physiocrats demonstrated quite an interest in China, about which they obtained abundant information due to the active presence in China of the Jesuit order, which researched Chinese society extensively and published its findings in Paris. See Derk Boddie, 'Chinese Ideas in the West', www.learn.columbia.edu/nanxuntu/html/state/ideas.pdf.

7 On the development of the modern state see Gianfranco Poggi, *The Development of the Modern State* (Stanford, Calif.: Stanford University Press, 1978); Perry Anderson, *Lineages of the Absolutist State* (London: Verson, 1974); Charles Tilly, *The Formation of National States in Western Europe* (Princeton: Princeton University Press, 1975); William H. McNeill, *The Pursuit of Power* (Chicago: University of Chicago Press, 1982). On the nexus between warfare and commerce, see Frederic C. Lane, 'Economic Consequences of Organized Violence', *Journal of Economic History*, 18, 4 (December 1958): pp.401–417; Douglass C. North and Robert Paul Thomas, *The Rise of the Western World* (Cambridge: Cambridge University Press, 1973), chapter 2; Charles Tilly, 'War Making and State Making as Organized Crime', in *Bringing the State Back In*, edited by Peter Evans, et al. (Cambridge: Cambridge University Press, 1985).

8 Although the invisible hand is often referenced by admirers of Smith, in fact he used the term only once in his volume, in a discussion on international trade. Nonetheless, it does appropriately convey his reasoning throughout all of *The Wealth of Nations*.

9 Robert H. Nelson argues that all economic theory takes such a moral foundation for granted, and fails to appreciate the import to its model of this. See the introduction to his *Economics as Religion* (University Park: Pennsylvania State University Press, 2001).

10 Spencer J. Pack and Robert W. Dimand, 'Slavery, Adam Smith's Economic Vision and the Invisible Hand', *History of Economic Ideas* 4, 1–2 (1996), pp.253–69.

11 *The Wealth of Nations*, Book IV.

12 Unusually for a Jamaican planter, Thistlewood kept extensive diaries in which he recorded, in minute and sometimes excruciating detail, the passage of his days, including which slaves he slept with or raped and what beatings he meted out. A reconstruction of his life from these diaries can be found in Trevor Burnard, *Master, Tyranny and Desire* (Chapel Hill: University of North Carolina Press, 2004).

13 Trevor Burnard, pp.110, 113.

Chapter 4: The Early Conversions

1   On the class conflict behind the Enclosure Movement, see Maurice Dobb, *Studies in the Development of Capitalism* (London: Routledge, 1946); Rodney Hilton, *Bond Men Made Free* (London: Routledge,1977); Robert Brenner, 'The Origins of Capitalist Development: A Critique of Neo-Smithian Marxism', *New Left Review* (1977). For a critical commentary see Stephan R. Epstein, 'Rodney Hilton, Marxism and the transition from feudalism to capitalism', *Past and Present*, 195 (Suppl. 2, 2007), pp.248–69.

2   Gregory Clark and Anthony Clark, 'Common Rights in Land in England, 1475–1839', *Journal of Economic History*, 61, 4 (2001), pp.1009–36.

3   Stephan R. Epstein stresses the role of this institutional change in enabling the changing class relations of the society to be channelled productively. See 'Rodney Hilton, Marxism and the transition from feudalism to capitalism', *Past and Present* 195 (Suppl. 2, 2007), pp.248–69.

4   Rick Szostak, *Transportation in the Industrial Revolution* (Montreal and Kingston: McGill-Queen's University Press, 1991), chapter 1.

5   *A History of the County of Lancaster* Volume 4 (London: Victoria County History, 1911), pp.37–8.

6   Boyd Hilton, *Corn, Cash, Commerce: The Economic Policies of the Tory Governments 1815–1830* (Oxford: Oxford University Press, 1977).

7   Owen Chadwick, *The Victorian Church, Part One: 1829–1859* (Eugene, Oregon: Wipf and Stock, 1987), chapter 1.

8   See John Foster, *Class Struggle and the Industrial Revolution* (London: Methuen, 1974) and R. H. Tawney, *Religion and the Rise of Capitalism*.

9   Malthus in his 'Principles of Political Economy', quoted in Geoffrey M. Hodgson, 'Malthus, Thomas Robert', *Biographical Dictionary of British Economists*, edited by Donald Rutherford (Bristol: Thoemmes Continuum, 2004).

10 Harold Perkin, *The Origins of Modern English Society 1780–1880* (London: Routledge & Kegan Paul, 1969), chapter 7.

11 Norman McCord, *The Anti-Corn Law League* (London and New York: Routledge, 1958), p.23.

12 Cheryl Schonhardt-Bailey, 'Specific Factors, Capital Markets, Portfolio Diversification and Free Trade: Domestic Determinants of the Repeal of the Corn Laws', *World Politics* 43, 4 (1991), pp.545–69.

13 Paul Bairoch and Gary Goertz, 'Factors of Urbanisation in the Nineteenth Century Developed Countries: A Descriptive and Econometric Analysis', *Urban Studies*, 23 (1986), p.288.

14 William Acton, *Prostitution* (London: J. Churchill, 1857). Acton is seen today as a product of his time, reflecting as he did the Victorian views of female sexuality. Nevertheless, the impact his work had on contemporary

political discourse testifies to the way his work was considered authoritative in its time. See Ivan Crozier, 'William Acton and the history of sexuality: the medical and professional context', *Journal of Victorian Culture* 5, 1 (2000), pp.1–27.

15 After the repeal of the Corn Laws, the nominal price of grain fell only modestly. However, given that repeal coincided with grain shortages due to bad harvests, prices that remained protected would probably have surged. Some scholars estimate that the effective price cut may therefore have been as high as 30 per cent. See Susan Fairlie, 'The Corn Laws and British Wheat Production, 1829–76', *Economic History Review* 22, 1 (1969), p.106.

16 Scott C. James and David A. Lake, 'The Second Face of Hegemony: Britain's Repeal of the Corn Laws and the American Walker Tariff of 1846', *International Organization* 43, 1 (Winter 1989), pp.1–29.

17 Rick Szostak.

18 Stephen Broadberry, et al., 'British economic growth: 1270–1870'. Working paper, Department of Economics, University of Warwick. CAGE Online Working Paper Series 2010, 35.

19 www.vam.ac.uk/content/articles/g/great-exhibition-queen-victorias-journal

20 Andrew Lambert, 'Economic Power, Technological Advantage, and Imperial Strength: Britain as a Unique Global Power, 1860–1890', *International Journal of Naval History*, 5, 2 (August 2006).

Chapter 5: Filling the Pews

1 J. R. Lucas, 'Wilberforce and Huxley: A Legendary Encounter', *Historical Journal* 22, 2 (1979), pp.313–30.

2 See his *Through Nature to God* (Boston and New York: Houghton Mifflin, 1899).

3 See Steve Miller, 'Public Understanding of Science at a Crossroads', *Public Understanding of Science* 10 (2001), p.116.

4 On the development of the welfare state see Peter Flora and Jens Alber, 'Modernization, Democratization and the Development of Welfare States in Western Europe', in *The Development of Welfare States in Europe and America*, edited by P. Flora and A. J. Heidenheimer (New Brunswick, NJ: Transaction Books, 1984); and Ian Gough, *The Political Economy of the Welfare State* (London: Macmillan, 1979).

5 Owen Chadwick, *The Victorian Church, Part One: 1829–1859* (Eugene, Oregon: Wipf and Stock, 1987), chapter 1; John Foster, *Class Struggle and the Industrial Revolution* (London: Methuen, 1974); R. H. Tawney, *Religion and the Rise of Capitalism*; John F. Glaser, 'English Nonconformity and the Decline of Liberalism', *American Historical Review*, 63, 2 (January 1958), pp.352–63.

6 Christophe Jaffrelot, *The Hindu Nationalist Movement in India* (New York: Columbia University Press, 1998).

7 Ironically, a starring role among British abolitionists was played by William Wilberforce, father to the anti-Darwinist Samuel. In his son's time, the Church would become quite conservative in its response to rebellion in the colonies, supporting repressive measures that crossed into illegality, as happened in Jamaica's Morant Bay Rebellion in 1865.

8 Charles Forsdick, 'Haiti and France: Settling the Debts of the Past', in *Power and Politics in Haiti*, edited by Kate Quinn and Paul Sutton (New York: Palgrave Macmillan, 2013).

9 Angus Maddison, *Chinese Economic Performance in the Long Run*, second edition (Geneva: OECD Development Centre, 2007), p.13.

10 Barry Buzan and George Lawson, 'The global transformation: the nineteenth century and the making of modern international relations', *International Studies Quarterly*, 57, 3 (2013), p.624, citing David Christian, *Maps of Time* (Berkeley: University of California Press, 2005).

11 In *The Social Origins of Dictatorship and Democracy* (Boston: Beacon Press, 1966), Barrington Moore uses this to account for the de-radicalisation, relative to its European counterparts, of the American working class: the US could postpone creating a welfare state by giving people land.

12 See Lloyd Reynolds, 'The Spread of Economic Growth in the Third World', *Journal of Economic Literature* 21 (1983): pp.941–980 and *Economic Growth in the Third World, 1850–1980* (New Haven: Yale University Press, 1985).

13 Patrick O'Brien, 'European Economic Development: The Contribution of the Periphery', *Economic History Review* 2nd series 35, 1 (1982), pp.1–18; Harold Perkin, *Origins of Modern English Society* (London and New York: Ark Paperbacks, 1969), pp.9–10.

14 Paul Bairoch, 'International Industrialization Levels from 1750 to 1980', *Journal of European Economic History* 11, 2 (Autumn 1982), p.275.

15 Paul Bairoch and Gary Goertz, 'Factors of Urbanisation in the Nineteenth Century Developed Countries: A Descriptive and Econometric Analysis', *Urban Studies* 23 (1986), pp.286, 288; US Bureau of the Census: www.census.gov/population/www/documentation/twps0027/tab08.txt

16 Mark Metzler, 'The Cosmopolitanism of National Economics: Friedrich List in a Japanese Mirror' in A. G. Hopkins, ed., *Global History* (New York: Palgrave Macmillan, 2006).

17 Friedrich List, *The National System of Political Economy* (New York: Augustus M. Kelly, 1966).

18 D. Gibson, *Wealth, Power, and the Crisis of Laissez Faire Capitalism* (New York: Palgrave Macmillan, 2011), p.28.

19 Dorothy Ross, 'The Development of the Social Sciences', *Discipline and History: Political Science in the United States*, edited by James Farr and Raymond Seidelman (Ann Arbor: University of Michigan Press, 1993).

20 Mark Metzler, 'The Cosmopolitanism of National Economics: Friedrich List in a Japanese Mirror', *Global History*, edited by A. G. Hopkins (Palgrave Macmillan, 2006), p.115.

21 Nicholas V. Riasanovsky, *A History of Russia*, third edition (New York: Oxford University Press, 1977), pp.471–2.

22 Guy P. Palmade, *French Capitalism in the Nineteenth Century*, trans. Graeme M. Holmes (New York: Barnes and Noble, 1972), p.173; Tom Kemp, *Economic Forces in French History* (London: Dennis Dobson, 1971), pp.165–7.

23 W. O. Henderson, 'Friedrich List and the French Protectionists', *Journal of Institutional and Theoretical Economics*, 138, 2 (June 1982), pp.262–75.

24 Max Roser, 'Life Expectancy' (2016), ourworldindata.org/life-expectancy/.

25 Max Roser.

26 Abbott Payson Usher, 'The Growth of English Shipping, 1572–1922', *Quarterly Journal of Economics* 42, 3 (1928), p.469.

27 Data are from the Maddison Project database on historical growth rates, www.ggdc.net/maddison/maddison-project/home.htm

28 Heather Cox Richardson, *West from Appomattox: The Reconstruction of America After the Civil War* (Yale: Yale University Press, 2008), p.131.

Chapter 6: Horsemen of the Apocalypse

1 Terry Pinkard, *Hegel: A Biography* (Cambridge: Cambridge University Press, 2000), p.228.

2 Georg Wilhelm Hegel, *Lectures on the Philosophy of World History*, edited by H. B. Nisbet and Duncan Forbes (Cambridge: Cambridge University Press, 1975), p.63.

3 Francis Wheen, *Karl Marx* (London: Fourth Estate, 1999), p.75.

4 Francis Wheen, p.115.

5 The concept of eternal recurrence would be later elaborated by Friedrich Nietzsche, but Walter Kaufmann suggests he got the idea from Heinrich Heine, who had studied under Hegel in Berlin. See Kaufman, *Nietzsche* (Cleveland and New York: Meridian, 1950), p.376.

6 David McLellan, *The Thought of Karl Marx* (London: Macmillan, 1971), p.52.

7 Sylvia Nasar, *Grand Pursuit* (London: Fourth Estate, 2011), p.34.

8 Francis Wheen, p.74.

9 Francis Wheen, p.8.

10 David McLellan, p.64.

11 The phrase is contained in his afterword to the second German edition of *Capital* (1873), but Marx had reached his position on the misplaced energy of future speculations decades before, in his critique of utopian socialism (*The German Ideology*, 1846) and in his 1850 address to the Communist League.

12 *Capital*, volume 3.

13 *Capital*, volume 1, section 8.

14 *The German Ideology*.

15 Francis Wheen, p.38.

16 The subsequent volumes would be produced after his death from notes assembled by Engels, with an anticipated fourth volume being edited and put out by Karl Kautsky early the next century.

17 David McLellan.

18 Scott Reynolds Nelson, 'The Real Great Depression (Panic of 1873)'.

19 William Stanley Jevons, *The Coal Question*, p.326, archive.org/stream/coalquestionanioojevogoog/coalquestionanioojevogoog_djvu.txt

Chapter 7: The Neoclassical Schism

1 See the introduction to his *Contribution to the Critique of Hegel's Philosophy of Right* (1844).

2 See, for instance, Frederick B. Pike, 'Latin America', *The Oxford Illustrated History of Christianity*, edited by John McManners (Oxford: Oxford University Press, 1990).

3 Stephen Strauss, 'Public Ignorant about Science, U.S. and British Surveys Suggest', *Globe and Mail* (Toronto), 18 January 1989, p.A9.

4 Anthony Randazzo and Jonathan Haidt, 'The Moral Narratives of Economists', *Econ Journal Watch* 12, 1 (January 2015), pp.49–59.

5 Letter to Arnold Ruge, September 1843, published in *Franco-German Annals*, 1844.

6 Theodore Levitt, 'Alfred Marshall: Victorian Relevance for Modern Economics', *Quarterly Journal of Economics* 90, 3 (August 1976), p.436.

7 Marshall's attachment to his dictum only strengthened over time: originally contained in the text of *Principles of Economics*, by the eighth and final edition in 1920 he had moved it to the frontispiece, declaring in his preface that 'economic evolution is gradual'. See *Principles of Economics* (London: Macmillan, 1959).

8 Marshall, *Principles of Economics*; see Geoffrey M. Hodgson, 'The Mecca of Alfred Marshall', *Economic Journal* 103, 417 (March 1993), pp.406–15.

9 From *Memorials of Alfred Marshall*, edited by A. C. Pigou (New York: A. M. Kelley, 1966), pp.427–28.

10 Philip Mirowski, 'Physics and the "marginalist revolution"', *Cambridge Journal of Economics* 8 (1984), p.364.

11 The term was coined by Thorstein Veblen in his essay 'The Preconceptions of Economic Science', *Quarterly Journal of Economics* 14, 2 (February 1900), pp.240–69.

12 See chapter 22.

13 See, for example, Kenneth F. Kiple, *Plague, Pox and Pestilence* (London: Weidenfeld and Nicolson, 1998).

14 See, for example, Solomon M. Hsiang, et al., 'Quantifying the Influence of Climate on Human Conflict', *Science* 341 (2013).

15 See, for instance, Douglas E. Booth, *The Environmental Consequences of Growth* (London and New York: Routledge, 1998).

16 John Rapley, *Understanding Development*, third edition (Boulder and London: Lynne Rienner, 2007); see also Emilio Padilla and Alfredo Serrano, 'Inequality in CO_2 Emissions across Countries and its Relationship with Income Inequality: A Distributive Approach', *Energy Policy* 34 (2006), pp.1762–72.

17 Ayn Rand, *The Virtue of Selfishness* (New York: New American Library, 1964).

18 In the *Principles*, he wrote, 'Experience seems to show that the more ignorant and phlegmatic of races and of individuals, especially if they live in a southern clime, will stay at their work a shorter time, and will exert themselves less while at it, if the rate of pay rises so as to give them their accustomed enjoyments in return for less work than before. But those whose mental horizon is wider, and who have more firmness and elasticity of character, will work the harder and the longer the higher the rate of pay which is open to them; unless indeed they prefer to divert their activities to higher aims than work for material gain.' Marshall, quoted in Levitt, p.436.

19 Milton Friedman, 'The Methodology of Positive Economics', *Essays in Positive Economics* (Chicago: University of Chicago Press, 1953).

20 Mark Blaug, *The Methodology of Economics*, second edition (Cambridge: Cambridge University Press, 1992), p.241.

21 Steven B. Smith, 'Beware the Tyranny Trap', *National Interest*, 14 August 2016.

Chapter 8: The Golden Age

1 Friedrich Nietzsche, *The Anti-Christ*, trans. R. J. Hollingdale (London: Penguin, 1968), p.116.

2 Cormac O'Grada, *The Great Irish Famine* (Cambridge: Cambridge University Press, 1995), pp.36–8.

3 Cormac O'Grada, p.44.

4 George L. Bernstein, 'Liberals, the Irish Famine and the Role of the State', *Irish Historical Studies* 29, 116 (1995), pp.513–26.

5 Although Davis focuses particularly on the Indian famine of 1876–8, he also includes famines outside the empire, such as Brazil and China, arguing however that their financial and commercial dependence on Britain at the time made them susceptible to British imperial policy.

6 Figures on death tolls for the Crusades and Wars of Religion are taken from Steven Pinker, *The Better Angels of Our Nature* (London: Penguin, 2011), pp.169–172.

7 Hillaire Belloc, *The Modern Traveller* (London: Edward Arnold, 1898).

8 Susan Strasser, *Waste and Want: A Social History of Trash* (New York: Metropolitan, 1999).

9 Max Roser, 'Life Expectancy', (2015), ourworldindata.org/data/population-growth-vital-statistics/life-expectancy/

10 Late nineteenth-century Boston stands as a good illustration. The top 1 per cent of the population held two-thirds of the wealth and 10 per cent had 95 per cent, while a high white-collar professional earned 60 times the income of a skilled craftsman and some 200 times that of an unskilled craftsman. Yet despite having a Gini coefficient (.946) that by contemporary standards is astonishing, Boston was typical of American cities at that time. See Steven Herscovici, 'The Distribution of Wealth in Nineteenth Century Boston', *Explorations in Economic History* 30 (1993), pp.321–35.

11 Adam Hochschild, *King Leopold's Ghost* (New York: Macmillan, 1951).

12 Amiya K. Bagchi, 'The Great Depression and the Third World with special reference to India', *Social Science Information* 18, 2 (1979), pp.197–218.

13 Paul Sharp, 'The Long American Grain Invasion of Britain: Market integration and the wheat trade between North America and Britain from the Eighteenth Century' (Copenhagen: Department of Economics Discussion Paper, University of Copenhagen 08-20, 2008).

14 As Greeley noted, he did not originate the phrase but borrowed it from John Babsone Lane Soule, who had earlier used it in a newspaper article. However, the opinion was one that Greeley had been espousing for decades.

15 Data from the Maddison Project database on historical growth rates, www.ggdc.net/maddison/maddison-project/home.htm. Cf. Sally Hills, Ryland Thomas and Nicholas Dimsdale, 'The UK recession in context – what do three centuries of data tell us?' (Bank of England, 2010).

16 E. P. Hennock, 'Social Policy under the Empire: Myths and Evidence', *German History*, 16, 1 (1998), pp.58–74.

Chapter 9: Into the Valley of the Shadow of Death

1 Peter Cain, 'Political Economy in Edwardian England', in *The Edwardian Age: Conflict and Stability, 1900–1914*, edited by Alan O'Day (London: Macmillan, 1978).

2 Peter Cain, p.41.

3 Andrew S. Thompson, 'Tariff Reform: An Imperial Strategy, 1903–1913', *The Historical Journal*, 40, 4 (1997), pp.1033–54.

4 Harry Landreth and David C. Collander, *History of Economic Thought*, fourth edition (Boston and Toronto: Houghton Mifflin, 2001), p.338.

5 Roger E. Backhouse, 'History of economics, economics and economic history in Britain, 1824–2000', *European Journal of the History of Economic Thought*, 11:1 (Spring 2004), pp.107–27.

6 Roger E. Backhouse, p.114.

7 Hobson, quoted in Harry Landreth and David C. Collander, p.361.

8 Harry Landreth and David C. Collander, p.363.

9 Massimo d'Azeglio.

10 George Feifer, 'No Finland Station', in *More What If?*, edited by Robert Cowley (New York: Putnam, 2001), pp.230–31.

11 Richard Cavendish, 'The Russian Socialist Movement Divided on November 16, 1903', *History Today*, 11 November 2005.

12 Ariadna Tyrkova, *From Liberty to Brest-Litovsk* (1918): reprinted at spartacus-educational.com/RUStyrkova.htm.

13 J. P. Nettl, *Rosa Luxemburg* (New York: Schocken, 1969), pp.17–18.

14 See chapter 8 of Luxemburg, *The Russian Revolution* (1918).

15 From the manifesto of the German Social Democratic Party, 25 July 1914, quoted in www.rosaluxemburgblog.wordpress.com/2012/08/02/on-this-day-2-3-aug-1914/

16 J. P. Nettl, p.371.

17 Helen Scott, 'Rosa Luxemburg: In the Storms of the Struggle', *International Socialist* Review 81 (January 2012), isreview.org/issue/81/rosa-luxemburg-storm-struggle.

18 From Rosa Luxemburg, 'The Russian Revolution', in *The Rosa Luxemburg Reader*, edited by Peter Hudis and Kevin B. Anderson (New York: Monthly Review Press, 2004), p.306.

19 From one eyewitness's testimony, in Nettl, p.486.

20 J.P. Nettl, p.489.

21 J.P. Nettl, p.489.

22 Dadabhai Naoroji, *Poverty and Un-British Rule in India* (London: Swan Sonnenschein and Co., 1901), p.v.

23 Rosa Luxemburg, *The Accumulation of Capital* (1913).

24 V. I. Lenin, *Imperialism: Highest Stage of Capitalism* (1917).

25 John A. Hobson, *Imperialism: A Study* (1902).

26 Andrew Mango, *Ataturk*, (New York: Overlook, 2002), p.198.

27 Andrew Mango, pp.32–3.

28 Andrew Mango, p.434.

29 Andrew Mango, p.435.

30 Richard Toye, *Churchill's Empire* (New York: St. Martin's Griffin, 2011), p.121.

31 See 'The Fiscal Problem' in *Official Papers of Alfred Marshall: A Supplement*, edited by Peter D. Groenewegen (Cambridge: Cambridge University Press, 2009).

32 Address to the American Society of Newspaper Editors, Washington D.C., 25 January 1925.

33 Alexander Jung, 'Germany in the Era of Hyperinflation,' *Spiegel Online*, 14 August 2009, www.spiegel.de/international/germany/millions-billions-trillions-germany-in-the-era-of-hyperinflation-a-641758.html

34 Alexander Jung.

35 Robert Sobel, *The Big Board* (New York: Free Press, 1965), p.271.

36 Gordon Thomas and Max Morgan-Witts, *The Day the Bubble Burst* (New York: Doubleday, 1979), p.313.

37 Gordon Thomas and Max Morgan-Witts, p.395.

Chapter 10: The People in Darkness

1 *New York Herald Tribune*, 24 January 1930.

2 Richard Davenport-Hines, *Universal Man: The Seven Lives of John Maynard Keynes* (London: William Collins, 2015).

3 J. M. Keynes, *The Economic Consequences of the Peace* (1919), chapter 7.

4 R. F. Harrod, *The Life of John Maynard Keynes* (London: Macmillan, 1951), p.446.

5 T. E. Gregory, 'Britain and the Gold Standard', *Foreign Affairs*, January 1933.

6 J. M. Keynes, 'The Pure Theory of Money: A Reply to Dr. Hayek', *Economica* 34 (1931), p.394.

7 F. A. von Hayek, 'A Rejoinder to Mr. Keynes', *Economica* 34 (1931), pp.398–403.

8 Bertrand Russell, *Autobiography, 1872–1914* (Boston: Little Brown, 1951), pp.94–95.

9 Bertrand Russell, *The Practice and Theory of Bolshevism* (section on Lenin, Trotsky and Gorky), skepticva.org/Russell/bolshevism. html#VIII

10 Bertrand Russell, *The Practice and Theory of Bolshevism* (Preface).

11 S. G. Wheatcroft, R. W. Davies and J. M. Cooper, 'Soviet Industrialization Reconsidered: Some Preliminary Conclusions about Economic Development between 1926 and 1941', *Economic History Review*, second series, 39, 2 (1986), pp.264–94.

12 See her 'Open Letter from a Keynesian to a Marxist' reprinted in *Jacobin Magazine*, 17 July 2011, www.jacobinmag.com/2011/07/joan-robinsons-open-letter-from-a-keynesian-to-a-marxist-2/

13 Geoff Harcourt and Prue Kerr, eds., *Joan Robinson: Critical Assessments of Leading Economists* (London: Routledge, 2002), p.49.

14 Volker Ullrich, *Hitler: Ascent 1889–1939*, trans. Jefferson Chase (London: Bodley Head, 2016).

15 Richard F. Hamilton, *Who Voted for Hitler?* (Princeton: Princeton University Press, 1982).

16 James D. Shand, 'The Reichsautobahn: Symbol for the Third Reich', *Journal of Contemporary History* 19, 2 (April 1984), p.191.

17 Data from the Maddison Project database on historical growth rates, www.ggdc.net/maddison/maddison-project/home.htm; see also Carmen

M. Reinhart and Kenneth S. Rogoff, 'Recovery from Financial Crises: Evidence from 100 Episodes', *American Economic Review – Papers and Proceedings*, May 2014.

18 Herbert Hoover, radio address at Fortress Monroe, Virginia, 18 October 1931.

Chapter 11: The Keynesian Revelation

1 Lucretius, *De Rerum Natura*, trans. C. H. Sisson (London: Carcanet New Press, 1976), book IV, p.132.

2 Tomasz Zaleskiewicz, 'Beyond risk seeking and risk aversion: Personality and the dual nature of economic risk taking', *European Journal of Personality*, 15 (2001), S105–22.

3 Harry Landreth and David C. Collander, *History of Economic Thought*, fourth edition (Boston and Toronto: Houghton Mifflin, 2001), p.439.

4 R. F. Harrod, *The Life of John Maynard Keynes* (London: Macmillan, 1951), p.451.

5 Robert Skidelsky, *John Maynard Keynes 1883–1946* (London: Penguin, 2003), p.147.

6 J. M. Keynes, *General Theory*, chapter 24, part III.

7 *General Theory*, chapter 24, part III.

8 *General Theory*, chapter 24, part I.

9 Harry Landreth and David C. Collander, p.440.

10 R. F. Harrod, p.642.

11 Paul A. Samuelson, '"Revolutions" in Economics', *Method and Appraisal in Economics*, edited by Spiro Latsis (Cambridge: Cambridge University Press, 1976), p.208.

12 *General Theory*, chapter 10, section 6.

13 Mark Blaug, *Economic Theory in Retrospect*, third edition (Cambridge: Cambridge University Press, 1978), pp.684–6.

14 *General Theory*, chapter 10.

15 For instance, his dismissal of Friedrich Hayek's critique of his work rested in no small part on his claim that Hayek simply couldn't get the maths. See Keynes, 'The Pure Theory of Money: A Reply to Dr. Hayek', *Economica* 34 (1931), pp.387–97.

16 Walter Eucken, quoted in Viktor J. Vanberg, *The Freiburg School: Walter Eucken and Ordoliberalism* (Freiburg: University of Freiburg Discussion papers on Constitutional Economics 04/11, 2011).

17 Pierre Birnbaum, *The Heights of Power* (Chicago: University of Chicago Press, 1982); see also chapters 5, 7 and 8 of Andrew Shonfield, *Modern Capitalism* (Oxford: Oxford University Press, 1965).

18 Franklin D. Roosevelt, Address Accepting the Presidential Nomination at the Democratic National Convention in Chicago (2 July 1932), www.presidency.ucsb.edu/ws/?pid=75174

19 James D. Horan, *The Desperate Years* (New York: Bonanza Books, 1967), p.61.

20 James D. Horan, p.96.

21 Franklin D. Roosevelt, Inaugural Address (4 March, 1933), www.presidency. ucsb.edu/ws/?pid=14473

22 R. F. Harrod, p.447.

23 R. F. Harrod, p.448.

24 Charles H. Hession, *John Maynard Keynes* (New York: Macmillan, 1984), p.275.

25 William E. Leuchtenburg, *Franklin D. Roosevelt and the New Deal: 1932–1940* (London: Harper Perennial, 2009).

26 Something similar to this idea would comprise part of Milton Friedman's critique of Keynesianism, in the form of the permanent income hypothesis. See *A Theory of the Consumption Function* (National Bureau of Economic Research, 1957), econpapers.repec.org/bookchap/nbrnberbk/frie57-1.htm

27 Congressional Budget Office, *The 2013 Long-Term Budget Outlook*, p.10, Figure 1-1, cbo.gov/sites/default/files/cbofiles/attachments/44521-LTBO2013_0. pdf

28 The woman in question is variously Labour MP Bessie Braddock or the Conservative Lady Astor (who was Britain's first-ever female MP, and was known for her caustic wit). Richard Langworth claims one of Churchill's bodyguards confirmed the version involving Braddock, www.independent. co.uk/news/uk/home-news/my-dear-you-are-ugly-but-tomorrow-i-shall-be-sober-and-you-will-still-be-ugly-winston-churchill-tops-8878622.html

29 Whether or not Hayek actually approved of Churchill's presentation of his ideas, however, is open to question. See Jeremy Shearmur, 'Hayek, *The Road to Serfdom*, and the British Conservatives', *Journal of the History of Economic Thought* 28, 3 (2006), pp.309–14.

30 Harold Perkin, *The Origins of Modern English Society 1780–1880* (London: Routledge and Kegan Paul, 1969), chapter 5.

31 Angus Maddison calculates that during the Industrial Revolution, from the late eighteenth century to the mid-nineteenth century, Britain's real GDP per capita rose by about 40 per cent. Charles H. Feinstein calculates that in this period, the real standard of living of the average worker rose by only about 10–15 per cent, though. See 'Pessimism Perpetuated: Real Wages and the Standard of Living in Britain during and after the Industrial Revolution', *Journal of Economic History* 58, 3 (September 1998), pp.625–58, and especially p.650.

32 Peter Laslett, *The World We Have Lost*, third edition (New York: Scribner, 1984), p.247.

33 Peter Laslett, p.246.

34 Peter Laslett, p.247.

35 David Kynaston, *Austerity Britain, 1945–51* (London: Bloomsbury, 2007).

36 Brian Thompson, 'Forties Pain, Fifties Gain,' *Guardian* (London: 20 May 2007), www.theguardian.com/books/2007/may/20/historybooks.features

37 Christian L. Glossner and David Gregosz, *The Formation and Implementation of the Social Market Economy by Alfred Müller-Armack and Ludwig Erhard* (Berlin: Konrad-Adenauer-Stiftung, 2011).

38 Chalmers Johnson, *MITI and the Japanese Miracle* (Stanford: Stanford University Press, 1982). See also Penelope Francks, *Japanese Economic Development* (London and New York: Routledge, 1992).

39 Andreas Bergh, 'The Rise, Fall and Revival of the Swedish Welfare State: What are the Policy Lessons from Sweden?' (Stockholm: Research Institute of Industrial Economics, IFN Working Paper No. 873, 2011).

40 See, for example, Andrew Shonfield, *Modern Capitalism* (London: Oxford University Press, 1965), especially chapter 4. The optimism of Keynesian economists is captured in a quotation from Michael Stewart, who once wrote, 'The days of uncontrollable mass unemployment in advanced industrial countries are over.' Quoted in Derek W. Urwin, *Western Europe Since 1945*, fourth edition (London: Longman, 1989), p.152.

41 See Peter Flora and Jens Alber, 'Modernization, Democratization and the Development of Welfare States in Western Europe', in *The Development of Welfare States in Europe and America*, edited by P. Flora and A. J. Heidenheimer (New Brunswick, NJ: Transaction Books, 1984) and Ian Gough, *The Political Economy of the Welfare State* (London: Macmillan, 1979).

42 *The Wealth of Nations*, book I, chapter 4.

43 Glyn Davies, *A History of Money*, third edition (Cardiff: University of Wales Press, 2002), p.26.

44 John Calvin, *Institutes of the Christian Religion*, quoted in *Protestantism*, edited by J. Leslie Dunstan (New York: George Braziller, 1962), p.62.

45 See Theodore Levitt, 'Alfred Marshall: Victorian Relevance for Modern Economics', *Quarterly Journal of Economics* 90, 3 (August 1976), pp.425–43.

46 *The Treatise on Money*.

47 Robert H. Nelson, *Economics as Religion* (University Park: Pennsylvania State University Press, 2001), p.17.

48 Robert H. Nelson, p.51.

Chapter 12: The New Jerusalem

1 Richard J. Evans, *The Third Reich at War* (London: Penguin, 2008), pp.321–22.

2 James M. Boughton, *Why White, not Keynes? Inventing the Postwar International Monetary System* (Washington, DC: International Monetary Fund Working Paper 02/52, 2002), p.12.

3 Cary Fraser, 'Understanding American Policy Towards the Decolonization

of European Empires, 1945–6', *Diplomacy and Statecraft* 32, 1 (1992), pp.105–25.

4 Benn Steil, *The Battle of Bretton Woods* (Princeton: Princeton University Press, 2013).

5 James M. Boughton, 'American in the Shadows: Harry Dexter White and the Design of the International Monetary Fund' (Washington, DC: International Monetary Fund Working paper 06/6, 2006), papers.ssrn.com/sol3/papers.cfm?abstract_id=888151

6 Benn Steil.

7 Robert Skidelsky, 'Keynes, Globalisation and the Bretton Woods Institutions in the Light of Changing Ideas about Markets', *World Development* 6, 1 (January–March 2005), p.22.

8 Although Keynes would have preferred for international accounts to be settled with a multi-lateral currency regime, his 'support for the new Bretton Woods institutions was clear and vocal, as he clearly saw in them the seeds of the new order'. Unfortunately, says Nadia F. Piffaretti, those seeds 'never grew into an international monetary system', though Keynes died before he would have had the chance to make this discovery, let alone do something about it. See 'Reshaping the international monetary architecture: lessons from the Keynes Plan', *Banks and Bank Systems* 4, 1 (2009), pp.45–54.

9 Roy Harrod described White as 'an ardent admirer of Keynes's economic work' although he was more than just a parrot: as early as 1932 he had been advocating the use of counter-cyclical policies to combat the Depression. See James M. Boughton, 'Why White, not Keynes? Inventing the Postwar International Monetary System', pp.5–6.

10 David McCullough, *Truman* (New York: Simon & Schuster, 1992), p.436.

11 Paul Kennedy, *The Rise and Fall of the Great Powers* (London: Unwin Hyman, 1988), p.358.

12 Ian Jack, 'Noble Words', *Guardian*, 1 May 2007, www.theguardian.com/world/2007/may/01/jawaharlal-nehru-tryst-with-dignity-speech-introduction

13 'Delhi rejoices and Mr Gandhi fasts', *Guardian*, 15 August 1947, www.theguardian.com/theguardian/1947/aug/15/greatspeeches1

14 Cary Fraser, 'Understanding American Policy Towards the Decolonization of European Empires, 1945–6', *Diplomacy and Statecraft* 32, 1 (1992), pp.105–25.

15 See Amrita Narlikar, *The World Trade Organization: A Very Short Introduction* (Oxford: Oxford University Press, 2005).

16 Peter Heather, *The Fall of the Roman Empire* (London: Macmillan, 2005), p.31.

17 Daniel Thorner, *The Agrarian Prospect in India*, second edition (Bombay: Allied Publishers, 1976).

18 Even in the late twentieth century, travellers to remote villages in India could report meeting people who had no experience of the Indian state.

19 John Rapley, *Understanding Development*, third edition (Boulder and London: Lynne Rienner, 2017), chapter 3.

20 R. Prebisch, *The Economic Development of Latin America and Its Principal Problems* (New York: United Nations, 1950), and H. W. Singer, 'The Distribution of Gains Between Investing and Borrowing Countries', *American Economic Review* 2 (1950). See also Ragnar Nurkse, 'Balanced and Unbalanced Growth', in *Equilibrium and Growth in the World Economy*, edited by Gottfried Haberler and Robert M. Stern (Cambridge, Mass.: Harvard University Press, 1961).

21 Theodore H. Cohn, *Global Political Economy*, sixth edition (London: Longman, 2012), p.308.

22 John Rapley, *Globalization and Inequality* (Boulder and London: Lynne Rienner, 2004), chapter 4.

23 John Rapley, 'Convergence: Myths and Reality', *Progress in Development Studies* 1, 4 (2001), pp.295–308.

24 *New York Times*, 4 January, 1971.

Chapter 13: The End of Eden

1 people.hofstra.edu/geotrans/eng/ch2en/conc2en/carprod_evolution.html

2 Fred Halliday, *Arabia without Sultans* (London: Penguin, 1974).

3 Daniel Yergin, *The Prize* (London: Simon & Schuster, 1991), pp.594–97.

4 Daniel Yergin, p.604.

5 Daniel Yergin, pp.606–07.

6 www.marxists.org/reference/archive/deng-xiaoping/1974/04/10.htm

7 Robert J. Gordon, 'Is U.S. Economic Growth Over? Faltering Innovation Confronts the Six Headwinds' (Cambridge, Mass.: National Bureau of Economic Research Working Paper 18315, 2012), www.nber.org/papers/w18315.pdf

8 Gerard de Villiers, with Bernard Touchias and Annick de Villiers, *The Imperial Shah*, trans. June P. Wilson and Walter B. Michaels (Boston: Little Brown, 1976); Ashraf Pahlavi, *Faces in a Mirror* (Englewood Cliffs, NJ: Prentice-Hall,1980).

9 Gerard de Villiers, with Bernard Touchias and Annick de Villiers, *The Imperial Shah*, trans. June P. Wilson and Walter B. Michaels (Boston: Little Brown, 1976).

10 Above passage drawn from Daniel Yergin, pp.678–82; see also Iran: Virtual Library: Chronology of Revolution; Excerpt His Destined Hour from William H. Forbis, *Fall of the Peacock Throne* (New York: Harper & Row, 1980).

Chapter 14: The Great Neoclassical Awakening

1 See his *Capitalism, Socialism and Democracy.*

2 F.A. Hayek, 'The Use of Knowledge in Society', *American Economic Review* 35, 4 (September 1945), pp.519–30.

3 Francis Spufford, *Red Plenty* (London: Faber & Faber, 2010), which cites the Russian-language paper.

4 Nicholas Wapshott, *Keynes Hayek: The clash that defined modern economics* (London: Norton, 2011), p.110.

5 F. A. von Hayek, 'Reflections on the Pure Theory of Money by Mr. J. M. Keynes', *Economica* 33 (1931), pp.270–95.

6 J.M. Keynes, 'The Pure Theory of Money: A Reply to Dr. Hayek', *Economica* 34 (1931), pp.387–97.

7 Nicholas Wapshott, p.70.

8 Nicholas Wapshott, p.110.

9 Nicholas Wapshott, p.109.

10 Nicholas Wapshott, p.73.

11 Nicholas Wapshott.

12 Todd D. Bucholz, *New Ideas from Dead Economists* (New York: Plume, 2007), p.201.

13 Dieter Plehwe, introduction to *The Road from Mont Pèlerin*, edited by Philip Mirowski and Dieter Plehwe (Cambridge, Mass.: Harvard University Press, 2009).

14 Milton Friedman, quoted in Henry Landreth and David C., Collander, *History of Economic Thought*, fourth edition (Boston: Houghton Mifflin, 2001), p.413.

15 Henry Landreth and David C., Collander, p.382.

16 Rob Van Horn and Philip Mirowski, 'The Rise of the Chicago School of Economics and the Birth of the Neoliberalism' in Philip Mirowski and Dieter Plehwe, pp.164–65.

17 Milton Friedman, 'The Role of Monetary Policy', *American Economic Review* 58 (1968), p.17.

18 Milton Friedman, 'The Role of Monetary Policy', pp.1–17.

19 Ben Fine, 'Economics Imperialism and the New Development Economics as Kuhnian Paradigm Shift?', *World Development* 30, 12 (2002), pp.2057–70.

20 See, for instance, Paul Krugman, 'Who Was Milton Friedman?', *New York Review of Books*, 15 February 2007, www.nybooks.com/articles/archives/2007/feb/15/who-was-milton-friedman/

21 www.4president.org/speeches/barrygoldwater1964announcement.htm

22 As one contemporary observation put it, Goldwater was the 'minority candidate of a minority party' and thus didn't even appeal to all Republicans, let alone independents and wayward Democrats. Americans still had a broadly favourable view of government programmes, and so his

depiction of government as the problem resonated with few. See Philip E. Converse, Aage R. Clausen and Warren E. Miller, 'Electoral Myth and Reality: The 1964 Election', *American Political Science Review* 59, 2 (June 1965), pp.321–36.

23 Eliza Filby, *God and Mrs Thatcher: The Battle for Britain's Soul* (London: Biteback, 2015), pp.129–130.

24 'Ayn Rand, R.I.P.', *The National Review*, 2 April 1982.

Chapter 15: Missionaries in Heathen Lands

1 The terms of global trade continued to go against developing countries at this time: see Enzo R. Grilli and Maw Cheng Yang, 'Primary Commodity Prices, Manufactured Goods Prices, and the Terms of Trade of Developing Countries: What the Long Run Shows', *World Bank Economic Review* 2, 1 (January 1988), 1–47. Having only recently won their independence, developing countries had not yet built the negotiating capacity to secure better trade agreements.

2 John Rapley, *Understanding Development*, third edition (Boulder and London: Lynne Rienner, 2007), chapter 3.

3 John Rapley, chapter 3.

4 John Rapley, chapter 3.

5 John Rapley, chapter 3.

6 See chapter 2 of John Rapley, *Globalization and Inequality* (Boulder and London: Lynne Rienner, 2004).

7 The estimate was made by the Philippines government's ombudsman; Reuters, 3 October 1995.

8 When Allende had taken office in 1970, per capita GDP growth was stagnant. In the first year of his economic programme, it shot up to 7 per cent, but all these gains were reversed by 1973, by which time the economy was contracting at the same 7 per cent rate: World Bank, *World Development Indicators* database.

9 Steve H. Hanke and Nicholas Krus, 'World Hyperinflations', *The Handbook of Major Events in Economic History*, edited by Randall Parker and Robert Whaples (London: Routledge Publishing, 2013).

10 Importantly, the US had received quiet assurances from the Soviet Union that it wasn't going to try to resist the financial blockade, and indeed would offer little assistance to the Allende regime in the event of a coup. See Ricardo Israel Z, *Politics and Ideology in Allende's Chile* (Tempe: Arizona State University Center for Latin American Studies, 1989), pp.179–80; Lois Hecht Oppenheimer, *Politics in Chile* (Boulder: Westview, 1993); Edy Kaufman, *Crisis in Allende's Chile: New Perspectives* (New York: Praeger, 1988).

11 Paul E. Sigismund, *The Overthrow of Allende and the Politics of Chile 1964–1976* (Pittsburgh: University of Pittsburgh Press, 1977).

12 Mary Helen Spooner, *Soldiers in a Narrow Land: The Pinochet Regime in Chile* (Berkeley: University of California Press, 1994), p.38.

13 Mary Helen Spooner.

14 Mary Helen Spooner.

15 Andre Gunder Frank, 'An Open Letter about Chile to Arnold Harberger and Milton Friedman', *Review of Radical Political Economics* 7, 2 (Summer 1975), pp.61–76.

16 Genaro Arriagada, *Pinochet: The Politics of Power*, trans. Nancy Morris with Vincent Ercolano and Kristn A. Whitney (Boston: Unwin Hyman, 1988), pp.19–20.

17 Jung Chang and Jon Halliday, *Mao: The Untold Story* (London: Jonathan Cape, 2005), p.569.

18 World Bank, *World Development Indicators* database.

19 See chapters 3 and 6 of John Rapley, *Understanding Development*, third edition (Boulder and London: Lynne Rienner, 2007).

20 International Monetary Fund, *World Economic Outlook* database.

21 On the international context of China's reform, see Gordon White, *Riding the Tiger: The Politics of Economic Reform in Post-Mao China* (Stanford, Calif.: Stanford University Press, 1993), chapter 1.

22 From an interview with Mike Wallace, 2 September 1986, www.china.usc.edu/deng-xiaoping-interview-mike-wallace-60-minutes-sept-2-1986.

23 World Bank, *World Development Indicators* database.

24 Figures come from Chile, National Commission on Political Imprisonment and Torture Report (2004) and Chile, National Commission for Truth and Reconciliation Report (1991).

25 W. Frazer, 'Milton Friedman and Thatcher's Monetarist Experience', *Journal of Economic Issues* 16, 2 (June 1982), pp.525–33; Dennis Kavanagh, *Thatcherism and British Politics: The End of Consensus?* (Oxford: Oxford University Press, 1987), p.114.

26 Geoffrey Smith, *Reagan and Thatcher* (London: Bodley Head, 1990).

Chapter 16: The Return of the Prophet

1 Robert J. Gordon, 'Is U.S. Productivity Growth Over? Faltering Innovation Confronts the Six Headwinds' (Cambridge, Mass.: National Bureau of Economic Research Working Paper 18315, 2012); see also Tyler Cowen, *The Great Stagnation* (New York: Dutton, 2011).

2 'Vice Premier Deng Visits the United States,' *Beijing Review* (9 February 1979), www.bjreview.com.cn/special/2011–01/14/content_325314.htm

3 Maurice Meisner, *The Deng Xiaoping Era* (New York: Hill and Wang, 1986).

4 Margaret Thatcher, Remarks on Becoming Prime Minister (Margaret Thatcher Foundation), www.margaretthatcher.org/document/104078

5 http://www.reagan.utexas.edu/archives/reference/timechoosing.html

6 Geoffrey Smith, *Reagan and Thatcher* (London: Bodley Head, 1990), p.22; see also Richard Harwood, 'Americans', in *The Pursuit of the Presidency*, edited by David Broder et al. (New York: Berkley Books, 1980).

7 Robert Garner and Richard Kelly, *British Political Parties Today* (Manchester: Manchester University Press, 1998).

8 Robert M. Worcester, 'The Polls: Britain at the Polls 1945–1983', *Public Opinion Quarterly* (1984).

9 Maurice Duverger *Political Parties* (London: Methuen, 1954).

10 Vanessa Martin, *Creating an Islamic State: Khomeini and the Making of a New Iran* (London: IB Tauris, 2000), p.73.

11 Zhores Medvedev, *Andropov* (New York: W.W. Norton, 1983).

12 Henry S. Bradsher, *Afghan Communism and Soviet Intervention* (Oxford: Oxford University Press, 1999).

13 John S. Reshetar Jr., *The Soviet Polity*, second edition (New York: Harper and Row, 1978), p.240.

14 See Robert V. Daniels, *The End of the Communist Revolution* (London: Routledge, 1993).

15 For a fictionalised account of this aborted transition, see Francis Spufford, *Red Plenty* (London: Faber and Faber, 2010), pp.283–301.

16 Peter Levi, *The Light Garden of the Angel King* (Newton Abbot: Readers Union, 1973).

17 Henry S. Bradsher, Jonathan Steele and Erik Abraham, *Andropov in Power* (Garden City: Anchor Press, 1984).

18 Henry S. Bradsher, Vladimir Solonyov and Elena Klapikova, *Yuri Andropov: A Secret Passage into the Kremlin*, trans. Guy Daniels (New York: Macmillan, 1983).

19 Hamilton Jordan, *Crisis: The Last Year of the Carter Presidency* (New York: Putnam, 1982).

20 Ronald Reagan, Address Accepting the Presidential Nomination at the Republican National Convention in Detroit, 17 July 1980, www.presidency. ucsb.edu/ws/?pid=25970

21 Richard Harwood, 'Labor Day 1980', in David Broder, et al., *The Pursuit of the Presidency 1980* (New York: Berkley Books, 1980).

22 John F. Stacks, *Watershed: The Campaign for the Presidency* (New York: Times Books, 1981).

23 For example, Norman Ture (Chicago MA 1947, PhD 1968), an ardent supply-sider, would become Undersecretary for Tax and Economic Affairs, while Beryl Sprinkel (Chicago MA 1948, PhD 1952), a strict monetarist, would become Undersecretary for Monetary Affairs. See Ronald Brownstein and Nina Easton, *Reagan's Ruling Class: Portraits of the President's Top 100 Officials* (Washington, DC: Presidential Accountability Group, 1982).

24 Brian Trumbore, 'In Honor of Ronald Reagan', www.buyandhold.com/bh/ en/education/history/2001/ronaldreagan.html.

25 Angela Monaghan, 'UK recession in 1980: what was it like', *Telegraph* (London), 23 January 2009, www.telegraph.co.uk/finance/recession/4323064/ UK-recession-in-1980-What-was-it-like.html

26 On the Russian war experience, see Artyom Borovik, *The Hidden War* (New York: Grove Press, 1990); see also Mohammad Youssaf and Mark Adkin, *Afghanistan: The Bear Trap* (Havertown, PA: Casemate, 2001).

Chapter 17: There Is No Alternative

1 Ronald Reagan, 'The "Evil Empire"', speech to the National Association of Evangelicals, 8 March 1983, in Douglas B. Harris and Lonce H. Bailey, *The Republican Party: Documents Decoded* (New York: ABC-Clio, 2014).

2 In particular, in a 1979 essay in *Commentary* magazine titled 'Dictatorships and Double Standards' Jean Kirkpatrick, who advised Reagan on foreign policy during his 1980 election campaign and subsequently was named his ambassador to the United Nations, argued that authoritarian states preserved a private space which allowed the possibility of a return to democracy whereas communist states tried to eliminate the private sphere altogether, and could thus not be reformed.

3 In the words of one of Reagan's advisers, from the introduction to Morris Morley and Chris McGillion, *Reagan and Pinochet* (Cambridge: Cambridge University Press, 2015).

4 So Pinochet said in a meeting with the American ambassador at large, Vernon Walters in 1982, www.fc95d419f4478b3b6e5f-3f71d-0fe2b653c4f00f32175760e96e7.r87.cf1.rackcdn. com/3A3FE1CCCE1046E4BC96D8A29918AA62.pdf

5 Genaro Arriegada, *Pinochet: The Politics of Power* (Boston: Unwin Hyman, 1988), p.42.

6 In his *Newsweek* column in January 1982.

7 See chapter 4 of John Rapley, *Understanding Development*, third edition (Boulder and London: Lynne Rienner, 2007).

8 John Rapley.

9 Ronald Reagan, 'Statement at the First Plenary Session of the International Meeting on Cooperation and Development' (Cancún, Mexico: 22 October 1981).

10 Michael Manley, quoted in Alvin Wint, *Corporate Management in Developing Countries* (Greenwood, 1995), p.48.

11 George J. Church, et al., 'Mikhail Sergeyevich Gorbachev: An Intimate Biography of the Private Man', *Time*, 4 January 1988.

12 Patrick Nagle, 'Gorbachev wowed Canadians with easy manner in 1983', *Montreal Gazette*, 12 March 1985, www.news.google.com/newspapers?nid= 1946&dat=19850312&id=HSAyAAAAIBAJ&sjid=4aUFAAAAIBAJ&pg=

5303,339956&hl=en

13 Mohammad Youssay and Mark Adkin, *Afghanistan: The Bear Trap* (Havertown, PA: Casemate, 2001).

14 Michael Calvocoressi, *World Politics since 1945*, sixth edition (London and New York: Longman, 1991), p.258.

15 Stephen N. S. Cheung, 'Deng Xiaoping's Great Transformation', *Contemporary Economic Policy* 16 (April 1998), pp.125–35.

16 Yevgenia Albats, 'Diary of the Coup', *Moscow Times*, 14 August 2001; Valeria Korchagina, 'The Coup that Changed Our World', Ibid.

17 As one scholar put it, 'The USSR became a society of rising expectations and rising frustrations.' Robert V. Daniels, *The End of the Communist Revolution* (London and New York: Routledge, 1993), p.68. Or as Jerry F. Hough put it, 'The exchange programs of the West were far more crucial in destroying communism than the military buildup of the early 1980s', *Democratization and Revolution in the USSR, 1985–1991* (Washington, DC: Brookings Institution, 1997), p.497.

Chapter 18: The New Age

1 Robert Nozick, *Anarchy, State and Utopia* (Oxford: Blackwell, 1974), p.33.

2 Eugene Fama, 'Efficient Capital Markets: A Review of Theory and Empirical Work', *Journal of Finance* 25, 2 (May 1970), pp.383–417.

3 See Gary Becker's *Economics of Discrimination* (Chicago: University of Chicago Press, 1957).

4 James M. Buchanan and Gordon Tullock, *The Calculus of Consent* (Ann Arbor: University of Michigan Press, 1965).

5 Christopher Hood, 'Doing Public Management the Individualist Way,' in *The Art of the State* (Oxford: Oxford University Press, 2000).

6 Gary S. Becker, 'The Economic Way of Looking at Behavior', *Journal of Political Economy* 101, 3 (June 1993), pp.385–409.

7 Ronald Inglehart, *The Silent Revolution* (Princeton, NJ: Princeton University Press, 1977).

8 From his book *Do It!* (New York: Simon & Schuster, 1970).

9 Francis Fukuyama, 'The End of History?', *The National Interest* (Summer 1989). Subsequently, Fukuyama elaborated the argument into a book, *The End of History and the Last Man* (New York: Free Press, 1992).

10 Remarks at Vietnam National University in Hanoi, Vietnam (17 November 2000), www.presidency.ucsb.edu/ws/?pid=1038.

11 Olga V. Kryshtanovskaya, 'Transformation of the Old Russian Nomenklatura into a New Russian Elite', *Russian Social Science Review* 37, 4 (1996), pp.3–17; Akos Rona-Tas, 'The First Shall Be Last? Entrepreneurship and Communist Cadres in the Transition from Socialism', *American Journal of*

Sociology 100 (1994), pp.40–69.

12 Jeffrey D. Sachs, 'Russia's Tumultuous Decade: An Insider Remembers', *Washington Monthly*, March 2000.

13 Jeffrey Sachs, interviewed for 'The Commanding Heights' documentary on PBS. Transcript available at www.pbs.org/wgbh/commandingheights/ shared/minitextlo/int_jeffreysachs.html#6.

14 Anders Aslund, 'Why Has Russia's Economic Transformation Been So Arduous?' (Washington, D.C.: the Annual World Bank Conference on Development Economics, 28–30 April 1999).

15 Mark Tomass, 'Mafianomics: How Did Mob Entrepreneurs Infiltrate and Dominate the Russian Economy?' *Journal of Economic Issues* 32, 2 (1998) pp.565–74; Federico Varese, 'Is Sicily the Future of Russia? Private Protection and the Rise of the Russian Mafia', *Archives Europeenes de Sociologie* 42, 10 (2001): pp.186–220.

16 F. C. Notzon et al., 'Causes of Declining Life Expectancy in Russia', *Journal of the American Medical Association* 279, 10 (11 March 1998), pp.793–800, www.ncbi.nlm.nih.gov/pubmed/9508159.

17 Stanley Kochanek, *Business and Politics in India* (Berkeley: University of California Press, 1974).

18 After the term coined in the late 1950s by C. Rajagopalacharia: Paul R. Brass, *The Politics of India since Independence*, second edition (Cambridge: Cambridge University Press, 1994), p.286.

19 John Toye, *Dilemmas of Development* (Oxford: Basil Blackwell, 1987), p.77.

20 From rediff.com, 14 May 2004, www.rediff.com/money/2004/may/14spec. htm?zcc=rl

21 From her college commencement address, 1969, www.wellesley.edu/events/ commencement/archives/1969commencement/studentspeech

22 Francis Fukuyama, *The End of History and the Last Man* (New York: Free Press, 1992), p.311.

23 'President Clinton's Poverty Tour,' *Seattle* Times (8 July 1999), seattletimes. nwsource.com/archive/?date=19990708&slug=2970489

24 See chapter 7 of John Rapley, *Understanding Development*, third edition (Boulder and London: Lynne Rienner, 2007).

25 Nathan Gardel, 'Power behind Politics', *New Politics Quarterly* 22, 4 (Fall 2005), www.digitalnpq.org/archive/2005_fall/11_clinton.html

26 Iwan Morgan, 'Jimmy Carter, Bill Clinton, and the New Democratic Economics', *Historical Journal* 47, 4 (December 2004), pp.1015–39.

27 Michelle Alexander, 'Why Hillary Clinton Doesn't Deserve the Black Vote', *The Nation* (10 February 2016).

28 Iwan Morgan, p.1039.

29 Transcript of 'The Warning', PBS Frontline, www.pbs.org/wgbh/pages/ frontline/warning/etc/script.html

30 Investment Company Institute data.

31 Berkshire Hathaway Annual Report 2002, www.berkshirehathaway.com/
    2001ar/2001letter.html

32 Another important influence among Clinton's economic team was Alice
    Rivlin, who believed the Internet was profoundly changing not just society,
    but the economy. See, for instance, Robert E. Litan and Alice M. Rivlin,
    'Projecting the Economic Impact of the Internet', *American Economic
    Review*, 91, 2, Papers and Proceedings of the Hundred Thirteenth Annual
    Meeting of the American Economic Association (May, 2001), pp.313–17.

33 Peter Mandelson.

34 See, for example, Stanley Fischer, *Capital Account Liberalization and the
    Role of the IMF* (International Monetary Fund, 1997).

35 Yung Chul Park and Chi-Young Song, 'The East Asian Financial Crisis: A
    Year Later', *IDS Bulletin*, 30, 1 (January 1999), pp.93–107.

36 For details see United States, General Accounting Office, *International
    Monetary Fund: Trade Policies of IMF Borrowers* (Washington, DC, 1999),
    www.gpo.gov/fdsys/pkg/GAOREPORTS-NSIAD-GGD-99-174/html/
    GAOREPORTS-NSIAD-GGD-99-174.htm

37 See Robert Wade, 'The Asian Debt-and-development Crisis of 1997-? Causes
    and Consequences', *World Development* 26, 8 (1998), pp.1535–53.

38 Joseph Stiglitz, 'Capital Market Liberalization, Economic Growth, and
    Instability', *World Development* 28, 6 (2000), pp.1075–86.

39 Joseph Stiglitz, 'What I Learned at the World Economic Crisis', *New Republic*,
    17 April 2000, www.yorku.ca/drache/talks/2000/pdf/stiglitz_worldban.pdf

40 From a speech by Ben Bernanke in 2005, see www.federalreserve.gov/
    boarddocs/speeches/2005/200503102/

Chapter 19: Magic and the Millennium

1 Norman Cohn, *The Pursuit of the Millennium*, revised and expanded
    (Oxford: Oxford University Press, 1970), chapter 13.

2 Friedrich Reck-Malleczewen, *A History of the Münster Anabaptists*, trans.
    and edited by George B. von der Lippe and Viktoria M. Reck-Melleckzewen
    (New York: Palgrave Macmillan, 2008), p.54.

3 Friedrich Reck-Malleczewen, p.102.

4 World Bank, World Development Indicators data.

5 Ha Joon Chang, *23 Things They Don't Tell You about Capitalism* (London:
    Penguin, 2010), p.24.

6 From his 1998 State of the Union address, www.presidency.ucsb.edu/
    ws/?pid=56280

7 For a summation of these arguments, see Tyler Cowen, *The Great
    Stagnation* (New York: Dutton, 2001). On the productivity slow-
    down, see Robert J. Gordon. 'Is US Economic Growth Over? Faltering
    Innovation Confronts the Six Headwinds' (Cambridge, Mass.: National

Bureau of Economic Research Working Paper 18315, 2012).

8   Ha Joon Chang, *23 Things They Don't Tell You about Capitalism*.

9   See World Bank, World Development Indicators.

10 For some examples of this optimism about the effect of information technology on the economy, see Dale W. Jorgenson, 'Information Technology and the U.S. Economy', *American Economic Review* 91, 1 (2001), pp.1–32; Dale W. Jorgenson and Kevin J. Stiroh, 'Productivity Growth: Current Recovery and Longer-Term Trends', *American Economic Review* 89, 2 (1999), pp.109–115; William Lehr and Frank R. Lichtenberg, 'Computer Use and Productivity Growth in US Federal Government Agencies, 1987–1992', *Journal of Industrial Economics* 46, 2 (1998), pp.257–79; Stephen D. Oliner and Daniel E. Sichel, 'The Resurgence of Growth in the Late 1990s: Is Information Technology the Story?', *Journal of Economic Perspectives* 14, 4 (Fall 2000), pp.3–22; Erik Brynjolfsson, Erik and Lorin M. Hitt, 'Beyond Computation: Information Technology, Organizational Transformation and Business Performance', *Journal of Economic Perspectives* 14, 4 (Fall 2000), pp.23–48; Robert E. Litan and Alice M. Rivlin, 'Projecting the Economic Impact of the Internet', *American Economic Review* 91, 2, Papers and Proceedings of the Hundred Thirteenth Annual Meeting of the American Economic Association (May, 2001), pp.313–17.

11 Flavio Romano, *Clinton and Blair: The Political Economy of the Third Way* (London: Routledge, 2006), p.8.

12 Steven Weber, 'The End of the Business Cycle?' *Foreign Affairs*, 76 (July–August 1997), pp.65–82.

13 BBC, 15 September 1998, news.bbc.co.uk/1/hi/events/clinton_under_fire/latest_news/171740.stm. 11 per cent of the readers of the Starr report came from such sites.

14 Lawrence F. Katz and Alan B. Krueger explore the impact on the labour market of greater insecurity by a working class that had become less organised in 'The high-pressure U.S. labor market of the 1990s / Comments and discussion', *Brookings Papers on Economic Activity* 1 (1999), pp.1–65.

15 For example, the use of global-positioning systems and on-board computers enabled managers of trucking firms to keep trucks on the road more of the time. Gone was the stereotype of the trucker who spent long afternoons flirting with waitresses in road-side diners. See Thomas N. Hubbard, 'Information, Decisions, and Productivity: On-Board Computers and Capacity Utilization in Trucking', *American Economic Review* 93, 4 (September 2003), pp.1328–53.

16 Robert M. Solow, 'We'd better watch out', *New York Times Book Review* (12 July 1987), p.36.

17 www.pbs.org/wgbh/pages/frontline/shows/crash/etc/cron.html

18 www.pbs.org/wgbh/pages/frontline/shows/crash/etc/cron.html

19 Joseph Stiglitz, 'What I Learned at the World Economic Crisis', *New Republic*, 17 April 2000, www.yorku.ca/drache/talks/2000/pdf/stiglitz_worldban.pdf

20 John Rapley, *Globalization and Inequality* (Boulder and London: Lynne Rienner, 2004), chapter 6.

21 Amy Chua, *World on Fire* (New York: Anchor Books, 2004).

22 Joshua Cooper Ramo, 'The Three Marketeers,' *Time* (15 Feb. 1999), content.time.com/time/world/article/0,8599,2054093,00.html

23 The figures for the West are for the high-income OECD countries, those for the Third World are for low- and middle-income countries. See World Bank, World Development Indicators.

24 World Bank, World Development Indicators.

25 From 1997–1998, the world economy grew by just over $1 trillion. However, the combined economies of low- and middle-income countries contracted during this time, yet the economies of the West (high-income OECD countries) grew by $1.36 trillion, while that of the United States alone grew by just over $1 trillion, a sharp departure from the long-term trend. World Bank, World Development Indicators.

26 Joseph Stiglitz.

27 Richard W. Stevenson, 'Clinton Conditionally Supports U.S. Role in Bailout', *New York Times*, 2 December 1997, www.nytimes.com/1997/12/02/business/clinton-conditionally-supports-us-role-in-bailout.html

28 See chapter 6 of John Rapley, *Understanding Development*, third edition (Boulder and London: Lynne Rienner, 2007).

29 Lawrence H. Summers, 'The Global Economic Situation and What It Means for the United States', Speech to the National Governors Association, Milwaukee, 4 August 1998, www.treasury.gov/press-center/press-releases/Pages/rr2626.aspx

30 Orrin H. Pilkey, Linda Pilkey-Jarvis, *Useless Arithmetic: Why Environmental Scientists Can't Predict the Future* (New York: Columbia University Press, 2007), p.41.

31 Paul Krugman, 'How Did Economists Get It So Wrong?' *New York Times* (6 September 2009), faculty.econ.ucdavis.edu/faculty/kdsalyer/LECTURES/Ecn200e/krugman_macro.pdf

32 Bob Woodward, *Maestro: Greenspan's Fed and the American Boom* (New York: Simon & Schuster, 2001).

33 Joshua Cooper Ramo.

34 Joshua Cooper Ramo.

35 Angel Ubide, 'Demystifying Hedge Funds', *Finance and Development* 43, 2 (International Monetary Fund, June 2006), www.imf.org/external/pubs/ft/fandd/2006/06/basics.htm

36 John Tamny, 'In 2008, Shades of October 1987', *Forbes*, 2 July 2008, www.forbes.com/2008/07/01/fed-bernanke-greenspan-oped-cx_jt_0702dollar.html

37 Joshua Cooper Ramo.

38 In an article in which he, rather curiously, blamed China for the housing crash, Alan Greenspan cited an article by Milton Friedman that had appeared in the *Wall Street Journal* in 2006 in which Friedman had written of Greenspan's

tenure as the Federal Reserve chairman that, 'There is no other period of comparable length in which the Federal Reserve System has performed so well.' See Alan Greenspan, 'The Fed Didn't Cause the Housing Bubble', *Wall Street Journal*, 11 March 2009, www.wsj.com/articles/SB123672965066989281

39 Jim Cramer, quoted in Sandra Sugawara, 'Abby Joseph Cohen's Words Move Markets', *Washington Post*, 29 March 2000, www.washingtonpost.com/wp-srv/digest/biz002.htm

40 William J. Clinton, 'Remarks at the First Session of the White House Conference on the New Economy', 5 April 2000, www.presidency.ucsb.edu/ws/index.php?pid=58330

41 Even at the time, prominent economists saw this as a political move rather than prudent fiscal management. See Caroline Baum, 'Time for the Awful Truth about Debt Reduction', in *Just What I Said* (New York: Bloomberg, 2005), pp.69–70.

42 Press Briefing by Secretary of the Treasury Lawrence Summers, 1 May 2000, www.presidency.ucsb.edu/ws/?pid=48064

43 Data from Institute of International Finance.

44 Steven A. Holmes, 'Fannie Mae Eases Credit To Aid Mortgage Lending', *New York Times*, 30 September 1999, www.nytimes.com/1999/09/30/business/fannie-mae-eases-credit-to-aid-mortgage-lending.html

45 Remarks by Chairman Alan Greenspan at America's Community Bankers Annual Convention, Washington, D.C., 19 October 2004, www.federalreserve.gov/boardDocs/speeches/2004/20041019/default.htm

Chapter 20: 'Honey, I Shrunk the Economy!'

1 Nicholas Watt, 'Blair goes to bask in dome's futurist glories', *Guardian*, 15 December 1999, www.theguardian.com/world/1999/dec/15/millennium.uk1

2 www.theguardian.com/society/2002/jun/10/socialexclusion.politics1

3 'Rush on Northern Rock Continues', *BBC News*, 15 September 2007, news.bbc.co.uk/2/hi/business/6996136.stm; 'Northern Rock: Businessman barricades in branch manager for refusing to give him £1 million savings', *Mail Online*, 15 September 2007, www.mailonsunday.co.uk/news/article-481852/Northern-Rock-Businessman-barricades-branch-manager-refusing-1-million-savings.html

4 From the *New York Times*, quoted in Report, p.55.

5 www.businessinsider.com/the-warning-brooksley-borns-battle-with-alan-greenspan-robert-rubin-and-larry-summers-2009-10?IR=T

6 Harry Markopolos in Congressional testimony. See 'Madoff Tipster Markopolos Cites SEC's 'Ineptitude', *Bloomberg*, 4 February 2009, www.bloomberg.com/apps/news?sid=axvJfch6PDjs&pid=newsarchive

7 Financial Crisis Inquiry Report (Washington, DC: Final Report of the National Commission on the Causes of the Financial and Economic Crisis in the United States, 2011), p.64.

8   See chapter 3 of Michael Lewis, *Boomerang* (New York: Penguin, 2012).

9   *Financial Crisis Inquiry Report* (Washington, DC: Final Report of the National Commission on the Causes of the Financial and Economic Crisis in the United States, 2011), p.215.

10 *Financial Crisis Inquiry Report*, Chapter 7.

11 *Financial Crisis Inquiry Report*, p.339.

12 'The individual is foolish; the multitude, for the moment is foolish, when they act without deliberation; but the species is wise, and, when time is given to it, as a species it always acts right.' From a speech to the House of Commons, 7 May 1782.

13 Mark K. Covey, et al., 'Self-Monitoring, Surveillance, and Incentive Effects on Cheating', *Journal of Social Psychology* 129, 5 (1989), pp.673–679.

14 Friedman, *The Methodology of Positive Economics* (Chicago: University of Chicago Press, 1953).

15 Charles P. Kindleberger and Robert Z. Aliber, *Manias, Panics, and Crashes: A History of Financial Crises*, fifth edition (Hoboken, NJ: Wiley, 2000), see especially p.40.

16 *Financial Crisis Inquiry Report*, p.354.

17 Nelson D. Schwartz and Julia Werdigier, 'Austria's "Woman on Wall St." and Madoff', *New York Times*, 6 January 2009, www.nytimes.com/2009/01/07/business/07medici.html?pagewanted=2&fta=y&_r=o

18 After his first stint in government in the Clinton administration, Summers built close ties to Wall Street banks and hedge funds. In 2008–2009, he argued strongly for a bailout that preserved the capital of these firms. After leaving Obama's administration, he went back to work for some of the same firms he had helped bail out. Louise Storey and Annie Lowrey, 'The Fed, Lawrence Summers, and Money', *New York Times*, 10 August 2013, www.nytimes.com/2013/08/11/business/economy/the-fed-lawrence-summers-and-money.html?pagewanted=all&_r=o

Chapter 21: Let Them Eat DSGE Models

1   Hyman P. Minsky, *John Maynard Keynes* (New York: McGraw-Hill, 2008).

2   Charles P. Kindleberger, *Manias, Panics, and Crashes*, third edition (New York: Wiley, 1996).

3   Adair Turner, 'Monetary Equilibrium in the Modern Economy', GLS Shackle Memorial Lecture, St Edmund's College, University of Cambridge, 25 February 2016.

4   Justin Lahart, 'In Time of Tumult, Obscure Economist Gains Currency', *Wall Street Journal*, 18 August 2007, www.wsj.com/articles/SB118736585456901047

5   Hyman P. Minsky.

6   Students at Harvard University walked out of Gregory Mankiw's economics course in protest at its conservative content while at the University

of Manchester students launched a campaign to redesign the curriculum (see *The Econocracy*, Manchester University Press, 2016). Meanwhile, George Soros endowed a think tank, called the Institute for New Economic Thinking (ineteconomics.org), to generate new approaches to old topics.

7 John Kay, 'A Realm Dismal in its Rituals of Rigour', *Financial Times* (London), 25 August 2011, www.ft.com/content/faba8834-cf09-11e0-86c5-00144feabdc0

8 Among the most significant were the American (US$800 billion) and Chinese ($600 billion) fiscal stimulus programmes. Relying as it did on 'automatic stabilisers', the European programme was much less significant in relative terms. An even bigger injection came from the monetary stimulus programmes the US Federal Reserve Board's bond-buying programme alone injecting $1 trillion a year to the economy (OECD Economic Outlook, Volume 1, 2013, p.55).

9 Paul Krugman, 'How Did Economists Get It so Wrong?', *New York Times*, 2 September 2009, www.nytimes.com/2009/09/06/magazine/06Economic-t.html?_r=0

10 Eamon Javers, 'Greenspan: Fix system before stimulus', *Politico*, 17 February 2009, www.politico.com/story/2009/02/greenspan-fix-system-before-stimulus-018968

11 Historians will debate for years to come what caused the bipartisan spirit that greeted Obama's inauguration to evaporate so quickly. Democrats blame Republican intransigence, typified by Senate Majority Leader Mitch McConnell's 2010 declaration that 'the single most important thing we want to obtain is for President Obama to be a one-term president'. Republicans, however, contend that Democrats sowed the seeds of ill-will much earlier, when Obama let House Democratic leader Nancy Pelosi pursue a partisan strategy of passing the stimulus bill without Republican support (see e.g. Ray Lahood, *Seeking Bipartisanship: My Life in Politics*, Cambria Press 2015). This will probably go down as one of those cases in which there is plenty of blame to go around for everyone.

12 Matt Taibbi, 'The Great American Bubble Machine', *Rolling Stone*, 5 April 2010, www.rollingstone.com/politics/news/the-great-american-bubble-machine-20100405

13 'The Queen asks why no one saw the credit crunch coming', *Telegraph* (London), 5 November 2008, www.telegraph.co.uk/news/uknews/theroyalfamily/3386353/The-Queen-asks-why-no-one-saw-the-credit-crunch-coming.html; 'The Queen gives her verdict on global credit crunch', *Daily Mail*, 6 November 2008, www.dailymail.co.uk/news/article-1083290/Its-awful--Why-did-coming--The-Queen-gives-verdict-global-credit-crunch.html

14 Robert Lucas, 'In defence of the dismal Science', *Economist* (London), 6 August 2009, www.economist.com/node/14165405

15 In his authoritative treatment of inequality, Thomas Piketty argued that there was a long-run tendency for returns on capital to exceed economic growth,

446

JOHN RAPLEY

widening the gap between rich and poor, and that policy interventions were
needed to mitigate this tendency. Piketty, *Capital in the Twenty-First Century*,
(Harvard: Harvard University Press, 2014). Ironically, the policy responses
to the 2008 crisis had just the opposite effect: by leaning more heavily on
monetary than fiscal stimulus, policies bolstered returns on capital.

16 United Kingdom Office for National Statistics, 'Contracts that do not
guarantee a minimum number of hours' (March 2016), www.ons.gov.uk/
employmentandlabourmarket/peopleinwork/earningsandworkinghours/
articles/contractsthatdonotguaranteeaminimumnumberofhours/march2016

17 www.ft.com/content/155f4564-42ec-11e3-8350-00144feabdco

18 See, for example, Amaia Bacigalupe, Santiago Esnaola, and Unai Martín,
'The impact of the Great Recession on mental health and its inequalities:
the case of a Southern European region, 1997–2013', *International Journal
for Equity in Health* 15, 17 (2016), www.ncbi.nlm.nih.gov/pmc/articles/
PMC4727262/

19 See, for instance, Matthew J. Holian, 'Homeownership, Dissatisfaction and
Voting', *Journal of Housing Economics* 20, 4 (December 2011), pp.267–75.

20 Sonia Sodha, 'Baby boomers v the rest: is age the great new divide?',
Guardian, 12 April 2015, www.theguardian.com/politics/2015/apr/12/baby-
boomers-v-the-rest-generation-gap-election-2015

21 See Elliott James, Kate McLoughlin and Ewan Rankin, 'Cross-border
Capital Flows since the Global Financial Crisis,' *Reserve Bank of Australia
Bulletin* (June 2014), p.69.

22 Adair Turner points out that real-estate purchases now account for about 60
per cent of bank lending in the developed economies. 'Monetary Equilibrium
in the Modern Economy', GLS Shackle Memorial Lecture, St Edmund's
College, University of Cambridge, 25 February 2016.

23 United States, Congressional Budget Office, *Trends in the Distribution of
Household Income between 1979 and 2007* (Washington, DC, 2011), www.
cbo.gov/publication/42729?index=12485

24 Stefania Vitali, James B. Glattfelder and Stefano Battiston, *The Network of
Global Corporate Control* (Zurich: Swiss Federal Institute of Technology,
2011), arxiv.org/pdf/1107.5728.pdf

25 This tendency appeared to have deep roots, going back at least to the
1990s. See Miranda Yates and James Youniss, eds., *Roots of Civic Identity:
International Perspectives on Community Service and Activism in Youth*
(Cambridge: Cambridge University Press, 1998) and Mark Strama,
'Overcoming Cynicism: Youth Participation and Electoral Politics', *National
Civic Review* 87,1 (Spring 1998), pp.71–77.

26 See George Monbiot, 'The medieval, unaccountable Corporation of London
is ripe for protest', *Guardian* (London), 31 October 2011.

Chapter 22: The Twilight of the Money Gods

1 Pietro Redondi, *Galileo Heretic*, trans. Raymond Rosenthal (London: Allen Lane, 1988).

2 As Sinclair himself put it, 'It is difficult to get a man to understand something, when his salary depends upon his not understanding it!' Upton Sinclair, *I, Candidate for Governor: And How I Got Licked* (Berkeley: University of California Press, 1994), p.109.

3 *Financial Crisis Inquiry Report* (Washington, DC: Final Report of the National Commission on the Causes of the Financial and Economic Crisis in the United States, 2011), p.17.

4 Robert E. Lucas, Jr., 'Macroeconomic Priorities', *American Economic Review*, 93, 1 (March 2003). Defenders of Lucas might still argue that strictly speaking his claim was justified, since in the wake of the Great Crash, a depression on the scale of that of the 1930s was averted: whereas after the 1929 crash US output collapsed by over a fourth, the 2008 crash was followed by a comparatively modest 3 per cent contraction. But apart from the complaint made by people like John Kay that this was taking criticism for what they didn't do – post-crash management having been characterised by ad hoc reactions by policymakers – an even stronger criticism is that the claim rests on semantics: defining 'depression' in such a way as to serve your hypothesis. When in the Great Depression the US economy resumed growing in 1933, it did so at high average annual rates and twelve years after the crash the economy was a quarter bigger than it was before. Today the US economy is growing at barely 2 per cent per year and on current form will perform proportionately scarcely any better when the dozen year mark is reached. Meanwhile the profound political reforms of the 1930s, which ensured that the economic gains would be widely distributed, have been absent in the United States today. Americans in the 1930s took their pain upfront and shared it widely; today they've spread the pain over time and concentrated the gains in a few hands.

5 Bernard A. Weisberger and Marshall I. Steinbaum, 'Economists of the World, Unite!', *Democracy: A Journal of Ideas*, 40 (Spring 2016), democracyjournal.org/magazine/40/economists-of-the-world-unite.

6 Bernard A. Weisberger and Marshall I. Steinbaum.

7 Bernard A. Weisberger and Marshall I. Steinbaum.

8 Bernard A. Weisberger and Marshall I. Steinbaum.

9 Diego Gambetta and Steffen Hertog, *Engineers of Jihad: The Curious Connection Between Violent Extremism and Education* (Princeton: Princeton University Press, 2016).

10 'The Situation in the Science of Biology', Address delivered by Academician Trofim Denisovich Lysenko at a session of the All-Union Lenin Academy of Agricultural Sciences, 31 July–7 August 1948, www.marxists.org/reference/archive/lysenko/works/1940s/report.htm

11 Robert Lucas, 'In defence of the dismal Science', *Economist* (London), 6 August 2009, www.economist.com/node/14165405

12 I'm indebted to Lindsay Stirton for this pithy analogy.

13 Wassily Leontief, 'Theoretical Assumptions and Nonobserved Facts', *American Economic Review* 61, 1 (March 1971), p.4.

14 Morten Jerven and Magnus Ebo Duncan, 'Revising GDP estimates in Sub-Saharan Africa: Lessons from Ghana', *African Statistical Journal* 15 (August 2012), pp.13–22.

15 See, for instance, Ernst Fehr and Urs Fischbacher, 'The Nature of Human Altrusim', *Nature* 425 (23 October 2003), pp.785–91; Keith Jensen, Amrisha Vaish and Marco F.H. Schmidt, 'The emergence of human prosociality: aligning with others through feelings, concerns, and norms', *Frontiers in Psychology*, 29 July 2014, journal.frontiersin.org/article/10.3389/fpsyg. 2014.00822/full and Robert Hepach, Amrisha Vaish, and Michael Tomasello, 'A New Look at Children's Prosocial Motivation', *Infancy* 18, 1 (2013), pp.67–90, www.researchgate.net/publication/257608480_A_New_Look_at_Children's_Prosocial_Motivation

16 The work of behavioural psychologists like Daniel Kahneman and Amos Tversky has found that humans are motivated by a complex of drives, few of which are susceptible to any kind of maximising formula.

17 Research in psychology appears to suggest that there is such a thing as over-earning (see Christopher K. Hsee, Jiao Zhang , Cindy F. Cai, and Shirley Zhang, 'Overearning', *Psychological Science*, 24, 6 (2013), pp.852–9). Most famously, Richard Easterlin uncovered the paradox that from the mid-twentieth century to its end, real per capita incomes in Western societies increased four times over, but there was no discernible increase in overall human happiness. See Richard A. Easterlin, 'Income and Happiness: Towards A Unified Theory', *Economic Journal* 111 (July 2001), pp.465–84 and Richard A. Easterlin, et al., 'The Happiness-Income Paradox Revisited', *Proceedings of the National Academy of Science of the United States* (2010), 107, 52: 22463-22468. Cf. Betsey Stevenson and Justin Wolfers, 'Subjective Well-Being and Income: Is There any Evidence of Satiation?', American Economic Review – Papers and Proceedings 103, 3 (May 2013), pp.598–604.

18 Studies of people who sheltered Jews during the Holocaust, putting their lives at great risk without anything in return – not even recognition, because many of them even insisted on anonymity afterwards – found that few of them could offer a rationale for what they did. Asked why they had done it, they'd usually reply to the effect of 'it was the only right thing to do'. See Kristen Renwick Munroe, *The Economic Approach to Politics* (New York: Harper Collins, 1991).

19 George Akerlof and Robert Shiller, *Phishing for Phools* (Princeton University Press, 2015).

20 Intel's Genevieve Bell, for instance, used this strategy effectively when she ran its Interaction and Experience Research for the company.

21 From the introduction to Paul Lockhart, *Measurement* (Cambridge, MA: Harvard Belknap, 2012).

22 All quotes from Wassily Leontief, 'Theoretical Assumptions and Nonobserved Facts', *American Economic Review* 61, 1 (March 1971), pp.1–7.

23 'Paris and the Fall of Rome', *Boston Globe*, 16 November 2015, www.bostonglobe. com/opinion/2015/11/16/paris-and-fall-rome/ErlRjkQMGXhvDarTIxXpdK/ story.html?s_campaign=8315

24 Peter Heather, The *Fall of the Roman Empire* (London: Macmillan, 2005).

25 Peter Heather, *Empires and Barbarians* (London: Macmillan, 2009).

26 For example, Thomas Frank argues that the Clinton presidency sliced and diced the electorate and opted to favour professionals over workers, with a model in which 'the ascendance of the first group requires that the second be lowered gradually into hell' – thereby carrying on in the tradition of which Thomas Thistlewood had been a foot-soldier. See: www.salon. com/2016/03/13/bill_clintons_odious_presidency_thomas_frank_on_the_ real_history_of_the_90s/

27 Ibn Khaldun noted the retreat of over-taxed farmers to remote lands where they could avoid supervision: Hazem Beblawi and Giacomo Luciani, Introduction to *The Rentier State* (London: Croom Helm, 1987), p.5.

28 Credit Suisse's annual *Global Wealth Report* calculates the assets required to place a person in the top 1 per cent of the global population. The value of pension funds alone places most public-service professionals in the West in the category.

29 Branko Milanovic, *The Haves and the Have-Nots* (New York: Basic Books, 2011).

30 The Tax Justice Network estimates that the planet's super-rich have by now stashed some $2 trillion, or roughly the equivalent of the American and Japanese economies combined, in offshore tax havens. By the TJN's own estimate, managing to tax a third of the income generated by this wealth would yield about $300 billion a year: a bit more if capital gains, inheritance and other taxes were added to the mix. However, the total aggregate national debt of the developed OECD countries now exceeds $40 trillion.

31 Hyman P. Minsky, *Stabilizing an Unstable Economy* (New Haven: Yale University Press, 1986), p.321.

ACKNOWLEDGEMENTS

I first conceived this book four years ago, when amid the crisis of economic theory in the wake of the Great Crash of 2008, I felt that economic thought had to go back to its basics, and probe its origins in political economy. Subsequently, my agent, Andrew Gordon at David Higham Associates, helped me to craft it into a workable format and find it a home. At Simon & Schuster, Iain MacGregor and Ian Marshall have been astute and skilled editors who persevered through the manuscript's evolution, until we finally reached this finished product.

There is a long list of people who have, in myriad ways, supported and assisted me on the journey, and without who I would have never managed to pull it off. Kei Miller, Lindsay Stirton, Bruna Piscopo, Jack Roberts, Drew Lapsley, Spyros Flogaitis, Wencke Meteling and Axel Jansen have all been both friend and colleague, nurturing and supporting me throughout.

As the manuscript took shape, I received expert guidance from specialists in various of the fields I explore, including Terry Barker, Verene Shepherd, Peter Nolan, Richard Whatmore, Colin Leys, Bruce Berman, Richard Spaulding, David Hornsby, Rodney Holder, Alex Mitchell, Tony Payne, Michael Woolcock and Grant Amyot. My one-time home, the South African Institute of International Affairs, hosted me during a brief residency as I wrote the first draft of the manuscript; while my college in Cambridge, St Edmunds, has provided me with an excellent place from which to ponder the universe. I especially want to thank our College Master, Matthew Bullock, who has been a strong supporter of this project.

My parents, Robert and Elizabeth Rapley, have been unfailing and steadfast guides on the whole journey. My children, Christian, Gabriel and Lauren, and their mother Marianne, have been patient and encouraging, and I hope they will all feel I have done them some credit.

All deserve my gratitude for the ways they have made my work possible. None deserve blame for any failings on my part to meet their standards. I will merely hope that in this book, I have managed to give all of them something in which they can find satisfaction, and perhaps even a bit of pride.

INDEX